☒ INSIGHT GUIDES

THE NILE

INSIGHT GUIDE
THE NILE

Editorial
Project Editor
Dorothy Stannard
Editorial Director
Brian Bell

Distribution

UK & Ireland
GeoCenter International Ltd
The Viables Centre, Harrow Way
Basingstoke, Hants RG22 4BJ
Fax: (44) 1256 817988

United States
Langenscheidt Publishers, Inc.
46–35 54th Road, Maspeth, NY 11378
Fax: (718) 784 0640

Canada
Thomas Allen & Son Ltd
390 Steelcase Road East
Markham, Ontario L3R 1G2
Fax: (1) 905 475 6747

Australia
Universal Press
1 Waterloo Road
Macquarie Park, NSW 2113
Fax: (61) 2 9888 9074

New Zealand
Hema Maps New Zealand Ltd (HNZ)
Unit D, 24 Ra ORA Drive
East Tamaki, Auckland
Fax: (64) 9 273 6479

Worldwide
**Apa Publications GmbH & Co.
Verlag KG (Singapore branch)**
38 Joo Koon Road, Singapore 628990
Tel: (65) 865 1600. Fax: (65) 861 6438

Printing

Insight Print Services (Pte) Ltd
38 Joo Koon Road, Singapore 628990
Tel: (65) 865 1600. Fax: (65) 861 6438

©2002 Apa Publications GmbH & Co.
Verlag KG (Singapore branch)
All Rights Reserved
First Edition 1991
Fourth Edition 2002

ABOUT THIS BOOK

This guidebook combines the interests and enthusiasms of two of the world's best-known information providers: Insight Guides, whose titles have set the standard for visual travel guides since 1970, and Discovery Channel, the world's premier source of nonfiction television programming.

The editors of Insight Guides provide both practical advice and general understanding about a destination's history, culture, institutions and people. Discovery Channel and its website, www.discovery.com, help millions of viewers explore their world from the comfort of their own home and encourage them to explore it firsthand.

Insight Guide: The Nile is structured to convey an understanding of the Nile Valley and its people as well as to guide readers through its sights and activities:

◆ The **History and Features** section, indicated by a yellow bar at the top of each page, covers the natural and cultural history of the destination in a series of informative essays.

◆ The main **Places** section, indicated by a blue bar, is a complete guide to all the sights and areas worth visiting. Places of special interest are coordinated by number with the maps.

◆ The **Travel Tips** listings section, with an orange bar, provides a handy point of reference for information on travel, hotels, shops, restaurants and more.

The contributors

This edition of the book was produced by **Dorothy Stannard**, a man-

aging editor in Insight Guides' London office. The new edition builds on the work of the first edition, supervised by **Andrew Eames**, a UK-based writer and editor.

Eames's aim was to produce an informative, entertaining and beautifully illustrated guide that would prove an indispensable companion on any journey down the Nile.

To this end, he employed a team of experts on Egypt, beginning with **Rowlinson Carter**, who wrote most of the highly readable history section of the book.

To tackle the all-important places section, Eames commissioned **Jill Kamil**, a Kenyan-born journalist and author who has lived most of her life in Egypt, to write on Upper Egypt and Memphis, Giza and Saqqarah, and **John Rodenbeck**, to cover

Cairo. Rodenbeck has lived in Cairo on and off since the 1960s, working as an academic, writer, actor and publisher. For nine years he headed the prestigious American University in Cairo.

Max Rodenbeck, John's son, wrote the section on the Nile Delta. A writer and journalist, he received worldwide praise for his book *Cairo the Victorious*, an exploration of the city's many extraordinary layers.

The chapter on wildlife was written by **Cassandra Vivian**, an American who spent many years working in Egypt, and The Nile in the Cinema was by the late **Dilys Powell**, for many years the film critic for Britain's *Sunday Times*.

This edition of the guide was revised by **Sylvie Franquet**, an Arabic scholar who worked in Cairo as a model, translator and tour operator before starting to write. As well as fully updating the book, Franquet added new chapters on Nubia and Lake Nasser, an area that has seen a huge growth in tourism in recent years, and expanded the text on Aswan; Aswan to Luxor; Luxor; Memphis, Giza and Saqqarah; Cairo and Alexandria, and added new features on modern-day smuggling and The Republic. She also updated the Travel Tips section, expanding the lists of recommended hotels and restaurants.

The photographs in the book do full justice to the beauty of the Nile. Many different photographers are credited in the back of the guide, but special mention should go to **Richard Nowitz**, **Tor Eigeland** and **Sarah Louise Ramsay**. The proof-reading and indexing were completed by Penny Phenix.

Map Legend

—··—	International Boundary
—·—	National Park/Reserve
————	Ferry Route
Ⓜ	Metro
✈ ✈	Airport: International/ Regional
🚌	Bus Station
❶	Tourist Information
✉	Post Office
✝ ✝	Church/Ruins
✝	Monastery
☾	Mosque
✡	Synagogue
🏰	Castle/Ruins
🏠	Mansion/Stately home
∴	Ancient/Archaeological Site
∩	Cave
⚱	Statue/Monument
★	Place of Interest

The main places of interest in the Places section are coordinated by number with a full-colour map (e.g. ❶), and a symbol at the top of every right-hand page tells you where to find the map.

![Insight Guide THE NILE]

CONTENTS

Maps

Introduction

History

Features

Sailing by in
Upper Egypt

Travel Tips

◆ **Full Travel Tips index
is on page 305**

Places

Information panels

THE WONDER OF THE NILE

The confluence of two great rivers brought the desert sands to life – thus providing the backdrop to Egypt's rich history

Egypt only exists thanks to a bit of geographical nonsense. The line of least resistance for water escaping from two African lakes 1,600 km (1,000 miles) apart, one of them actually straddling the equator, was not a quick dive into the Indian Ocean and Red Sea which lay close at hand. Instead, one went off as if looking to join the Congo River for its immense journey west to the Atlantic. The other went roughly south for hundreds of kilometres before that, too, proved to be a feint. Between them, the two rivers logged some 5,600 km (3,500 miles) of idle wandering before combining their forces for a 3,200-km (2,000-mile) mercy mission through what would otherwise have been one of the most barren places on earth.

Replenished by only one tributary and hardly ever by rainfall, a lesser river than the unified streams of the White and Blue Niles would have petered out in the insatiable sands of the desert long before it reached the Mediterranean. The Nile not only survived but at the hottest and driest time of every year conjured up a tidal wave of flood water.

The sheer volume of silt which the flood brought defied comprehension. In any one year it seemed sufficient to have stripped the lands from whence it came to skeletal bones, yet there was always more, year after year. Moreover, it was silt of great fertility, capable of turning a vast tract of desert into an agricultural paradise. In southern (Upper) Egypt, the miracle was confined to a narrow ribbon along the banks but, with only 160 km (100 miles) to go, the river seemed in several minds about where to empty into the Mediterranean and the result was what the Greeks recognised as the shape of their letter Delta, seven channels which merged during the floods into a coastal lake.

Wherever the silt was deposited, all a farmer had to do was wait for the water to subside, scratch seeds into the ground, let his livestock trample them in, and sit back to watch them grow. The feeding of the river people more or less took care of itself.

The pyramids and all that followed were built on the unique combination of effortless subsistence, efficient communications and transport. Prevailing winds blew couriers and cargo vessels up the Nile, the current brought them down. The engineers who constructed the pyramids did not have the wheel; as long as they stayed close to the river, they didn't need it. ❏

PRECEDING PAGES: lips of Ramesses II at Luxor Temple; the sail of a *felucca*; docking at Elephantine Island, Aswan; the Pyramids of Giza.
LEFT: a *felucca* sails through Upper Egypt.

David Roberts, R. A

Decisive Dates

EARLY DYNASTIC PERIOD, 3100–2649 BC
1st and 2nd Dynasties: Memphis founded as the capital of Egypt. Rulers buried in tombs at Saqqarah, where the first pyramids were later built.
OLD KINGDOM, 2649–2134 BC
2649–2575 3rd Dynasty. Zoser Complex, Saqqarah.
2575–2465 4th Dynasty. Centralised government; pyramids at Dahshur, Giza and Abu Rawash.
2455–2134 5th and 6th Dynasties. Pyramids and Sun-Temples at Abu Sir and Saqqarah.

FIRST INTERMEDIATE PERIOD, 2134–2040 BC
7th–10th Dynasties. Collapse of central government; country divided and governed by local rulers; famine and poverty.
MIDDLE KINGDOM, 2040–1640 BC
11th–13th Dynasties. Reunification by Theban rulers; powerful central government; expansion into Nubia (Sudan). Pyramids at Dahshur and Hawarah built by Amenemhet III (1842–1797). Pyramids at Al-Lisht, Mazghunah and South Saqqarah.
SECOND INTERMEDIATE PERIOD, 1640–1532 BC
14th–17th Dynasties. Country divided again. Asiatics ("Hyksos") rule in Delta.
NEW KINGDOM, 1550–1070 BC
1550–1307 18th Dynasty. Reunification under The-

ban kings; annexation of Nubia in south. Period of prosperity, with Thebes (Luxor) as main royal residence. Pharaohs include Akhenaton (1353–1335) and Tutankhamun (1333–1323).
1307–1196 19th Dynasty. Ramesses II (1290–1224) builds many monuments, erects colossi.
1196–1070 20th Dynasty. Invasions by Libyans and "Sea Peoples". Weak kings rule from the Delta.
THIRD INTERMEDIATE PERIOD, 1070–712 BC
21st–24th Dynasties. Capital of Tanis is displaced as Egypt is divided among several rulers.
LATE PERIOD, 712–332 BC
712–657: 25th Dynasty from Kush (Sudan) unites country. Assyrian invasions in 667 and 663.
664–525 26th Dynasty rules from Sais in Western Delta. First settlement of Greeks at Memphis.
525–405 27th Dynasty (Persian). Canal linking Nile with the Red Sea built under Darius I (521–486). Memphis and Heliopolis visited by Herodotus.
404–342 28th–30th Dynasties. Slow decline.
342–330 31st Dynasty (Persian).
PTOLEMAIC EMPIRE, 332–30 BC
332–30 Alexander the Great conquers Egypt. Ptolemy I rules as governor after Alexander's death in 323 BC, then after 304 BC as first king of dynasty that ends with Cleopatra VII and her children.
ROMAN PERIOD, 30 BC–AD 324
Rule from Rome. Fortress rebuilt at Babylon in AD 116 under Trajan (98–117). Spread of Christianity, despite persecution, from 251 onward.
BYZANTINE PERIOD, 324–642
Rule from Constantinople (Byzantium).
324–619 Christianity made state religion, 379. Coptic (Egyptian) Church separates from Catholic Church, 451. Last pagan temple in Egypt (Philae) converted into church, 527.
619–29 Third Persian occupation.
629–39 Re-establishment of Byzantine rule.
ARAB EMPIRE, 642–868
639–42 Arab conquest under Amr ibn al-As, who founds new capital, Al-Fustat, next to Babylon. Rule by governors on behalf of caliph.
642–58 The Rashidun ("Orthodox" or "Righteous") caliphs.
658–750 Umayyad caliphs rule from Damascus.
750–878 Abbasid caliphs rule from Baghdad. Al-Askar built. First Turkish governor appointed, 856.
TULUNID EMPIRE, 878–905
Ahmed ibn Tulun, Turkish governor, declares independence, founds Al-Qatai, builds great mosque which carries his name, 876–9.
ABBASID INTERIM, 905–935
Reassertion of power from Baghdad.

FATIMID EMPIRE, 969–1171
Cairo's first golden age. Some 30 monuments and a vast number of objects remain as evidence.
970–72 Al-Azhar mosque built.
996–1021 Reign of al-Hakim, "The Mad Caliph" Mosque of al-Hakim completed.
1168 Frankish invasion, Fustat destroyed.

AYYUBID EMPIRE, 1171–1250
Saladin (Salah ad-Din) and his successors conduct campaigns against Franks and other invaders.
1174 Crusader invasion repelled.
1187–92 Jerusalem retaken from crusaders.
1219–21 Frankish invasion by sea; occupation of Damietta and advance on Cairo culminates in Muslim victory at Mansura in the Delta.
1249 Frankish invasion under St Louis culminates in second Muslim victory at Mansura.

BAHRI MAMELUK EMPIRE, 1250–1382
Era of expansion and prosperity. Some 100 monuments remain as evidence.
1260–79 Reign of Baybars al-Bunduqdari. Extension of empire from Sudan to Anatolia, from the Euphrates to Cyrenaica.
1279–90 Reign of Qalawun.
1293–1340 Three reigns of An-Nasir Muhammed ibn Qalawun. Architectural splendour in Cairo.
1340–82 Reigns of sons, grandsons and great-grandsons of An-Nasir Muhammed. Pillage and destruction of Alexandria by Franks, 1365.

BURJI MAMELUK EMPIRE, 1382–1517
Continuation of massive building programmes (130 monuments survive) under the rule of 23 sultans.

OTTOMAN PERIOD, 1517–1914
Egypt province of the Ottoman Empire.
1517–1798 Ottoman rule through 106 governors.
1798–1805 French invasion and occupation.
1805–48 Muhammed Ali Pasha. Programme of modernisation thwarted by European intervention.
1848, 1849–54 Ibrahim Pasha.
1854–63 Said Pasha. Suez Canal concession granted. Cairo–Alexandria rail link, Nile steamship service, telegraph established.
1863–79 Ismail the Magnificent. Assertion of autonomy. Assembly of Delegates established (1866), principle of primogeniture accepted. Title of "Khedive" granted (1867). Suez Canal opened (1869).
1879–92 Khedive Tewfik. British Occupation in 1882.
1892–1914 Khedive Abbas II Hilmi. Monuments include Egyptian Museum and Rifai Mosque.

LEFT: mask of Tutankhamun (1333–1323 BC).
RIGHT: Ibrahim Pasha, Muhammed Ali's soldier-son.

POST-1914
1914–17 Sultan Husayn Kamil. British Protectorate declared, martial law instituted.
1917–22 Sultan Fu'ad. Revolution of 1919.
1922–36 King Fu'ad I. Constitutional monarchy established.
1936–52 King Farouk. During World War II Egypt is neutral, but reoccupied by Britain.
1952–53 July Revolution deposes Farouk in favour of his infant son, Ahmad Fu'ad, then declares Egypt a republic. Gamal Abd an-Nasir (Nasser) becomes leader.
1956 Nationalisation of Suez Canal.
1961 Introduction of Socialist Laws in July.

1967 The Six Day War against Israel.
1970 Anwar Sadat succeeds Nasser as president.
1973 The October War against Israel.
1974–77 Open Door Policy, political liberalisation.
1979 Camp David accords lead to peace treaty with Israel. Egypt boycotted by rest of Arab World.
1981 President Anwar Sadat assassinated. Hosni Mubarak becomes President.
1996–8 Escalation of Islamic terrorism, including the murder of 58 tourists in Luxor, in 1997.
1999 Mubarak endorsed for a fourth six-year term as president. He survives a third assassination attempt
2001 Mubarak expresses his support for the coalition against terrorism following the destruction of the World Trade Center in New York. ❑

THE SEARCH FOR THE SOURCE

Where did the Nile begin? Solving this great geographical puzzle
was a preoccupation of many of the great 19th-century explorers

A large, ginger-haired Scot was standing on a mountain in Ethiopia in 1770 when he suddenly tore off his shoes and went bounding down the slope. He was twice thrown headlong but, undaunted, charged on until he was knee-deep in a patch of swamp. "I stood in rapture… in that spot which had baffled the genius, industry and inquiry of both ancients and moderns, for the course of nearly three thousand years. Though a mere private Briton, I triumphed here in my own mind, over kings and their armies." James Bruce was exultant because he had discovered the source of the Nile, or so he thought.

Alas, says Alan Moorehead, whose two books on the Nile are fascinating reading for anyone interested in the subject, "he was on the wrong river… He was even on the wrong part of the wrong river." Moreover, he was mistaken in thinking that he was the first European to reach that particular spot.

Nevertheless, Bruce's expedition was a remarkable victory over considerable hurdles. Only the race to the moon in modern times has mirrored the kind of excitement which was generated by the search for the source of the Nile. The objective of exploration was clearly defined but infuriatingly elusive. It was not simply a matter of sailing or even walking up the river until it stopped. The ancient Egyptians as well as the Persians, Greeks, Romans, Arabs, and sundry Europeans had all tried that, but had run into impenetrable barriers.

Starting with a trickle

Before the aeroplane, the source could only be approached methodically from the other side, as it were, and even then it remained to be proved that a particular lake, spring or indeed Bruce's little swamp was what ultimately flowed past the pyramids. Explorers who started

from what they supposed to be the source were all too familiar with the sickening realisation that the river they were doggedly following was turning to go the wrong way. What they had pinned their hopes on as the Nile turned out to be the Congo, Niger or some other river. In the hundred years which followed Bruce's barefoot

charge down the mountain, the source of the Nile became, in the celebrated phrase of the historian Sir Harry Johnston, "the greatest geographical secret after the discovery of America."

Bruce's mistakes

The Nile divides near Khartoum in the Sudan into the White Nile and Blue Nile, and Bruce's fundamental mistake was in thinking that the latter was the main river, the former merely a tributary. In fact, at the confluence, the White has already flowed for some 3,200 km (2,000 miles), the Blue for only about 800 km (500 miles). The mistake was easily made because when the Blue floods it builds up such momen-

LEFT: 1587 map illustrating the confusion over the river's route.
RIGHT: Burton and Speke as portrayed in the film *Mountains of the Moon.*

tum over the 1,800 metres (6,000 ft) descent from the Ethiopian highlands that it causes its more sedate partner to dam back on itself. The effect is discernible because, although not quite blue and white, the waters are distinctly coloured. At normal times of the year, the two streams flow shoulder to shoulder before blending for the remaining 2,800 km (1,750 miles) to the Mediterranean.

Tall stories

The cruel reward for Bruce's heroic efforts was that many refused to believe him. They scoffed at the thought of tribesmen who wore rings in

their lips rather than ears and smeared themselves with the blood of cows, and at clouds of tiny flies striking terror into animals and humans alike. Bruce did not easily tolerate disbelief of his stories. He lost patience with a fellow diner at a country house weekend who said no one would or could eat raw meat. Storming off to the kitchen, he returned with a slab of uncooked beef, sprinkled it with salt and pepper "in the Ethiopian manner", and rammed it into the sceptic's face. "You will either eat that, sir, or fight me!" The startled guest looked up at the towering figure and tucked in. "Now, sir," Bruce thundered as the last morsel went down, "you will never again say it is impossible." Nevertheless, the arguments went on for long after his death, the result of an accident reminiscent of his charge down the mountain; he fell down the staircase of his mansion in Scotland, breaking his head.

In producing his five-volume *Travels to discover the Sources of the Nile, in the years 1768, 1769, 1770, 1772, and 1773,* Bruce had few references to work from. The richest source of material was Herodotus, as had been the case for more than 2,000 years, but on the source of the Nile even the "Father of History" was suspect.

Classical accounts

Visiting Egypt in about 460 BC, Herodotus had to rely on what contemporaries could tell him about the Nile, and he did not believe half their stories either. There were all sorts of theories, including the idea that the Nile flowed backwards from the sea, but the one he found least plausible was ironically closest to the truth, namely that "the Nile flows from melted snow". How could that be, he asked, since it flowed from places which were even hotter than Egypt? He thought it more likely that the sun sucked up water and deposited it on the catchment area. The least he could say was that the Nile entered Egypt "from parts beyond".

Other Greeks investigated, and the Roman Emperor Nero sent an expedition upriver, but the hardest information was in a map produced by the geographer and astronomer Ptolemy in AD 150. Based on the work of the Syrian geographer Marinus of Tyre, the map showed the Nile rising from two great lakes in Central Africa which were fed by what he called the Mountains of the Moon.

WHAT'S THE WEATHER LIKE?

James Bruce's audiences at home were curious about the weather in Africa. "I call it hot," he told them, "when a man sweats at rest and excessively on moderate motion. I call it very hot when a man with thin or little clothing sweats much, though at rest. I call it excessive hot when a man in his shirt, at rest, sweats excessively, when all motion is painful, and the knees feel feeble as if after a fever. I call it extreme hot when the strength fails, a disposition to faint comes on, a straitness is found round the temples, as if a small cord was drawn round the head, the voice impaired, the skin dry, and the head seems more than ordinary large and light. This, I apprehend, denotes death at hand…"

The intellectuals who accompanied Napoleon's army to Egypt in 1798 managed to get as far as the cataracts at Aswan; they might have gone further because there are navigable stretches above the cataracts. The hopeless difficulties begin where the Sobat tributary joins the river near the town of Malakal in what is now the Sudan – the dreaded Sudd.

"This region is neither land nor water," says Alan Moorehead of the Sudd. "Year by year the current keeps bringing down more floating vegetation, and packs it into solid chunks perhaps 20 ft thick and strong enough for an elephant to walk on. But then this debris breaks away in islands and forms again in another place, and this is repeated in a thousand indistinguishable patterns and goes on forever." The result is "a vast sea of papyrus ferns and rotting vegetation, and in that foetid heat there is a spawning tropical life that can hardly have altered very much since the beginning of the world; it is as primitive and as hostile to man as the Sargasso Sea."

The Blue Nile, it transpired, springs from the snows and monsoon rains which feed Lake Tana in the Ethiopian highlands. The river leaves the lake calmly and unobtrusively, gliding towards the Tisisat Falls 32 km (20 miles) away. There it explodes. Bucking and rearing at the narrow confines of the gorge below, the river begins a furious descent which over a million years has carved a gorge in places 1.5 km (1 mile) deep and 24 km (15 miles) wide. Tackling it by boat was, and is, out of the question. In a few places where the valley widens there may be the odd village, but they are cut off from one another by the impassable walls of the gorge. Even wild animals steer clear of the malarial torpor in the valley.

Eccentric explorers

The challenge of the Nile attracted some improbable characters. In 1812, Thomas Legh, a British Member of Parliament, went on holiday to Turkey with his friend, The Reverend Charles Smelt. An outbreak of plague drove them to Egypt and, once there, they felt they ought to look around. A slave whom they bought to help with chores as they explored the sites 160 km (100 miles) south of Philae proved

LEFT: the 18th-century Scottish explorer James Bruce.
RIGHT: the 19th-century Swiss explorer John Lewis Burckhardt, aka "Shaykh Ibrahim".

so efficient that they took him back to England. They also offered a passage to Donald Donald, a Scot they ran into, who had been taken prisoner by the Turks, enslaved, circumcised and converted to Islam. He declined the offer, saying he was quite content where and as he was.

Another outbreak of plague persuaded Legh and Smelt to postpone their departure and remain at Minia. They were consoled by girls, but bored by life in the Turkish garrison. "When the antiquities that may exist in the neighbourhood have been examined, and any local interest ceases to amuse, nothing perhaps can be more melancholy than the prospect of a long

residence in a Turkish town, where the absolute want of books, the frivolous conversation and the excessive ignorance of the natives, the daily smoking of tobacco and drinking of coffee, form the chief features of the torpid and listless existence to which a stranger is condemned."

The most puzzling acquaintance they made was a certain "Shaykh Ibrahim", not least because he spoke perfect English with an upper-crust accent. The mystery was not solved until they returned to England, and established that he was really John Lewis Burckhardt, Swiss by birth but a product of Cambridge University. With a view to becoming an explorer, Burckhardt had read Arabic and toughened himself up by trudging around the English countryside in bare feet, sleeping rough and living exclusively on vegetables and water.

Burckhardt managed to attach himself to an organisation calling itself the Association for Promoting the Discovery of the Interior Parts of Africa. After growing a heavy beard, he first assumed the identity of "an Indian Muhammedan merchant" and then changed to Shaykh Ibrahim ibn Abdullah, an authority on Islamic law. To prove that he had perfected Arabic, he

BURCKHARDT'S LEGACY

Burckhardt died in Egypt of dystentery when he was only 33. His letters and notes were published and, in lifting the lid on places like Shendy, stirred the anti-slavery sentiments.

ckhardt's health could not long withstand the 10 hours per day he forced himself to march. Nevertheless, he entered parts of the Sudan which few, if any, Europeans had seen. One of these was Shendy, known as "The Gates" and a legendary staging post for caravans and pilgrims arriving from as far west as Timbuktu on the way to the Red Sea.

Burckhardt kept a record of Shendy's thriving slave market. About 5,000 slaves were traded each year. Most were under 15 years of age, the boys fetching $15 each and the girls $25. Of the girls, Ethiopians were prized "for their beauty, and for the warmth and constancy of their affection." All boys were circumcised and given Arab names but, in spite of the greatly enhanced value of eunuchs, the Muslims themselves disliked performing the mutilation. If it had to be done – as when Mohammed Ali placed an order for 200 eunuchs whom he wished to give away as presents – the job was passed on to a couple of Christian Coptic priests. It was a rare trader who did not sleep with the girls who passed through his hands.

produced a translation of *Robinson Crusoe.*

He spent eight years on the Nile as a solitary nomad, observing tribes like the Shaiqiya, a mysterious people who appeared to be neither Nubian nor Arab and in some respects resembled the Mameluks. He encountered the few Mameluks who survived the Battle of the Pyramids against Napoleon's army and the subsequent massacre by Mohammed Ali. They had been able to maintain a luxurious standard of living by systematically plundering villages. Burckhardt found a colony of Mameluk fugitives living on river rafts, their slaves keeping the overhead awnings cool with buckets of water.

For all his preparations in Cambridge, Bur-

Burton and Speke

In everything that has been written about Richard Francis Burton, the reader can sense the author taking a deep breath before plunging in. Moorehead is typical: "Almost too much was contained here in one man." He was not especially tall – about 1.8 metres (5 ft 11 in) – but he looked and was immensely strong, a brilliant swordsman who did not need even a sword to put down single-handed a mutiny on a ship in which he happened to be a passenger. He had, as the poet Swinburne remarked, the brow of a god and the jaw of a devil, together with an enormous moustache and, most riveting of all, "questing panther eyes".

His erudition was beyond belief; he was an authority on a wide range of subjects, including anthropology, history, geography, botany, geology, meteorology, economics and, somewhat notoriously, erotica. He wrote and spoke well over 30 languages and reckoned he could master any new one in six weeks. Not content with obscure languages most people had never heard of, he lived with a troop of monkeys to compile a kind of monkey dictionary.

John Hanning Speke, whose name in the context of the Nile is usually mentioned in the same breath as Burton's, was very different. He was six years younger, tall, fair and elegant. He was passionately fond of hunting, practically the only subject in which Burton could not work up any interest. Although by no means prudish, Speke hardly drank and never smoked.

They were both in the British Indian Army but met by chance in Aden. Burton was passing through on his way to explore Abyssinia and Speke at once changed his plans to go with him. They were lucky to survive the experience. Their camp was rushed by Somali tribesmen at the dead of night and one of their party was killed instantly, but Burton fought like a tiger in spite of massive injuries to his jaw. Speke was first stabbed in the arms and legs and then transfixed with a spear. In the melee he was dragged away unconscious, miraculously to escape certain execution and catch up with Burton some time later. Both recovered from appalling wounds to volunteer for service in the Crimea and, when that war was over, they put their minds to finding the source of the Nile.

Knowing the futility of trying to sail or walk up the river to its source, they elected to start in Zanzibar and cut across Africa in search of snow-capped mountains, lakes or anything else that might look like a good bet. They travelled in caravan behind a guide in ceremonial headdress and beneath the red flag of the Sultan of Zanzibar. When struck by malaria, as they frequently were, they travelled in hammocks.

Eight months on, the caravan drew up on the shores of Lake Tanganyika. Burton surmised that any river flowing north from the lake could well be the Nile. Travelling in two canoes, they found a river but it flowed into the lake, not out of it, and in any case at 770 metres (2,535 ft) above sea level they were lower than known levels of the Nile elsewhere. They paused to reconsider their position. Burton was not feeling well and anyhow wanted to write up his notes. It was agreed that Speke, who had just recovered from a bout of ophthalmia which had virtually blinded him, should proceed ahead to look into reports of a larger lake some three weeks to the north.

LEFT: the great traveller and Arabist Richard Burton.
RIGHT: John Hanning Speke, whose relationship with Burton ended in tragedy.

The great disagreement

The lake Speke found was the fulfilment of his dreams. "I no longer felt any doubt," he later wrote, "that the lake at my feet gave birth of that interesting river, the source of which has been the subject of so much speculation, and the object of so many explorers." He hurried back to tell Burton and found him still nursing an ulcerated jaw. Burton was unmoved. According to him, "we had scarcely breakfasted before (Speke) announced to me the startling fact that he had discovered the sources of the White Nile... The fortunate discoverer's conviction was strong; his reasons were weak..."

Speke could not prove that the lake was the source, and until he did Burton was sticking to his theory that the Nile sprang from the Mountains of the Moon, wherever they might be. The most he was prepared to concede was that Speke's lake, which they agreed to call Lake Victoria, flowed into the Upper Nile. They agreed to drop the subject for the time being and undertook the trek back to the Indian Ocean on reasonably friendly terms. Burton had a few things to attend to in Zanzibar so Speke took an earlier passage back to England, the agreement being (Burton claimed) that he would make no reference to their findings in Africa until Burton rejoined him.

Speke tells the world

In the event, Speke immediately told the Royal Geographical Society that he believed he had found the source. The news caused a sensation. Money was made available so that without delay he could lead another expedition to confirm his findings, and he was well-advanced in planning the expedition, with no role for Burton, when the latter returned – lean, haggard – and ignored. No one was terribly interested in his report on Lake Tanganyika or his objections to Speke's claim. His place on Speke's next expedition would be taken by another Indian Army officer, Captain James Grant.

Speke and Grant took a year over the journey inland from Zanzibar, spending a month with a convivial king whose fat wives were turned one way and another so that Speke could measure their impressive dimensions with a tape. When it was time to go they were advised that the country ahead was in a state of civil war and that it would be necessary to receive permission to progress from a King Mutesa whose court was a six-week walk away. While Speke went ahead to negotiate, Grant, who had hurt his leg, remained with the king.

Etiquette at the court of King Mutesa was unpredictable. Speke was required to shoot four cows to prove that his presents of pistols actually worked. A rifle required more stringent testing. The king handed it to a boy and told him to find some man to try it on: "which was no sooner accomplished than the little urchin returned to announce his success, with a look of glee such as one would see in the face of a boy who had robbed a bird's nest, caught a trout, or done any other boyish trick… There appeared no curiosity to know what individual human being the urchin had deprived of life." The king reciprocated with gifts of young girls whom Speke passed on to his porters as wives.

The search for Speke

Mutesa withheld permission to proceed for nearly five months, a delay which prompted Sir Roderick Murchison at the Royal Geographic Society in London to get in touch with Samuel Baker, then big-game hunting in the Sudan, to ask him to search for Speke and Grant.

In the meantime, Speke and Grant went off to investigate reports they had picked up at Mutesa's court of a large river flowing north from Lake Victoria. If true, it would lend considerable weight to Speke's theory. With his bad leg, Grant could not keep up with the impatient pace of the march and agreed that Speke should again go ahead. On 21 July 1862, Speke was finally convinced by the discovery of a broad river about 65 km (40 miles) north of the lake. It was, he wrote, "the very perfection of the kind of effect aimed at in a highly developed park, with a magnificent stream, 600 to 700 yards wide, dotted with islets and rocks…"

The countryside abounded in crocodiles, hippopotamuses and hartebeest. He told his porters that they were looking at the very cradle of Moses and ought to shave their heads and bathe in it. They reminded him that they were Muslims.

It was still necessary to establish that the river in question did indeed flow from the lake. Marching upstream for a week, Speke was at last satisfied. The river made a spectacular exit, rushing out of the lake over what Speke named the Ripon Falls after an earlier president of the Royal Geographical Society. "It was a sight that attracted one for hours," he wrote. "The roar of the waters, the thousands of passenger-fish leaping at the falls with all their might; the Wasoga and Waganda fishermen coming out in boats and taking post on all the rocks…"

Instead of going back the way they had come, Speke's plan was to head directly north, which meant they would leave the meandering course of the river from time to time. They would pick it up again to meet a boat which by prearrangement had been sent south from Khartoum to await them, always assuming they were still alive. The rendezvous had to be vague because the proposed route through what is now Uganda was uncharted territory.

More than two years after their departure from Zanzibar, Speke and Grant heard welcoming rifle shots and the sound of a drum and fife band. On the

IN THE LAP OF LUXURY

When Baker received notice to look for Speke he was big game hunting in the Sudan with his young, Hungarian-born second wife and provisions supplied by Fornum & Mason of London.

Baker was disappointed to call it off, and even more so when Speke said he had positively identified the source. Thinking that Speke and Grant might be dead, he had been nursing that ambition himself. Speke confided, however, there might be a second source, a large lake known locally as Luta Nzige, and he gave Baker a map of their route. Baker immediately began to recruit a team of porters who were willing to run the risk of being caught up in a war raging along the proposed route.

strength of rumours of two white men in the vicinity, a column of Egyptian and Nubian soldiers in Turkish uniform had come out to greet them. Speke's priority was to send a cable back to London: "Inform Sir Roderick Murchison," it said, "that all is well, that we are in latitude 14° 30" upon the Nile, and that the Nile is settled."

A second source?

At Gondokoro, he ran into Baker and his wife preparing themselves for their rescue mission.

LEFT: King Mutesa, with whom Speke stayed during his second expedition.
ABOVE: Mutesa's capital, Buganda.

Speke and Grant returned to a rapturous reception in England. Speke addressed a capacity audience at the Royal Geographical Society, was widely interviewed by the newspapers and rushed his preliminary findings into print. Burton disputed his discoveries, but was willing to concede, as before, that the Nile flowed from Lake Victoria. He pointed out that Speke had not circumnavigated the lake to find out whether it was itself fed by a river, in which case the source of the Nile lay wherever that river originated; that there was another river, Burton was sure, and of course that it would flow from his Mountains of the Moon.

Burton's objections had some supporters, one

of whom was Dr David Livingstone. "Poor Speke," the doctor wrote, "has turned his back upon the real sources of the Nile." Others joined the Burton bandwagon, one reviewer tearing into Speke's account of his journey. The careful measuring of the fat wives, he said, was disgusting, not what Speke called "engineering". "We believe none of our readers ever met with or ever heard of such a piece of 'engineering' as this, and we dare say will never wish to meet with such another."

PRIZE FIGHT

Notice that Burton and Speke would appear on the same platform at a meeting of the Association for the Advancement of Science in Bath stirred the sort of excitement associated with prize fights.

phy). A note was handed round in silence. Presently my friend Mr Findlay broke the tidings to me. Captain Speke had lost his life on the yesterday, at 4 pm, whilst shooting over a cousin's grounds. He had been missed in the field and his kinsman found him lying upon the earth, shot through the body close to the heart. He lived only a few minutes and his last words were a request not to be moved."

According to those present, however, Burton did not receive the news as stoically as his

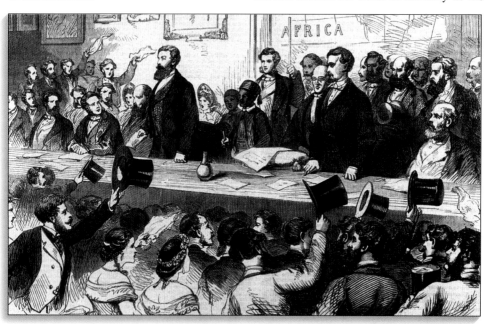

Tragic news

The acrimony between Burton and Speke built up over a solid year. Burton was reported as saying, "I don't wish to have any further private or indirect communication with Speke".

But eventually the men agreed to appear together at a meeting of the British Association for the Advancement of Science in Bath. Several hundred geographers and scientists gathered for the debate which was due to start at 2pm on 16 September 1864. Burton himself recorded what happened on the day: "Early in the forenoon fixed for what silly tongues called the 'Nile Duel' I found a large assembly in the rooms of Section E (Geography and Ethnogra-

account suggests. He staggered visibly about the platform and sank into a chair "with his face working". He was heard to moan "By God, he's killed himself!" But he managed to pull himself together long enough to deliver a hastily-substituted paper on Dahomey. On getting home, his wife said, "he wept long and bitterly". All she could make out was the same word repeated over and over again: "Jack".

Baker's progress

Deep in the heart of Africa, Baker and his wife did not hear of Speke's death, which was officially "accidental", the coroner allowing the possibility that Speke was standing on a low wall when he lost his balance and, in falling, discharged the gun.

Conditions were worse than they feared. Not only was there a war swirling around them and rampant malaria, but they were suspected wherever they went of being slave traders, although matters improved when Baker started wearing a tweed suit. In African eyes he now resembled Speke, and him they trusted.

The suit worked wonders. "I climbed up a high and almost perpendicular rock that formed a natural pinnacle on the face of the cliff, and waving my cap to the crowd on the opposite side I looked almost as imposing as Nelson in Trafalgar Square... Upon landing through the high reeds, they immediately recognised the similarity of my beard and general complexion to that of Speke, and their welcome was at once displayed by the most extravagant dancing and gesticulating with lances and shields, as though intending to attack, rushing at me with the points of their lances thrust close to my face, and shouting and singing in great excitement."

Mrs Baker's waist-length blonde hair was as mesmerising as her husband's tweed suit. Tribesmen brought their families to watch when she washed it, and it gave the trigger-happy King Mutesa ideas. The king had stubbornly refused to supply porters as long as he had reason to believe that Baker, who had already given him shotguns, beads, carpets and so forth, had more presents up his sleeve. "We shall be nailed for another year in this abominable country," Baker despaired, "ill with fever, and without medicine, clothes or supplies." Thus Mutesa one day appeared to have had a complete change of heart, Baker could have his team of porters and proceed. Moreover, he wanted him to take an attractive virgin for company. The quid pro quo was simply that the king should have Mrs Baker.

Baker drew his pistol and, holding it at the king's chest, threatened to shoot him there and then. Mrs Baker, admired by her husband above all because "she was not a screamer", was dreadfully ill with malaria, but on learning of King Mutesa's proposition she rose from her sick-bed and "withered him with an outburst of furious indignation." Faced with the combined wrath of the Bakers, the king dropped the idea. A team of porters and a guide materialised the following day.

Discovering Lake Albert

On 13 March 1864 their guide announced that on the following day they would see the lake that Speke had sent them in search of.

Baker had promised to allow himself three cheers on reaching the lake but in the event he was dumbstruck. "I led the way, grasping a stout bamboo. My wife in extreme weakness tottered down the pass, supporting herself upon my shoulder, and stopping to rest every twenty

paces... A walk of about a mile through flat sandy meadows of fine turf interspersed with trees and bush, brought us to the water's edge. The waves were rolling upon a white pebbly beach: I rushed into the lake, and thirsty with heat and fatigue, with a heart full of gratitude, I drank deeply from the Sources of the Nile." He named it Lake Albert, after Queen Victoria's consort.

Next to him stood the faithful Mrs Baker, "pale and exhausted – a wreck upon the shores of the great Albert lake that we had so long striven to reach. No European foot had ever trod upon its sand, nor had the eyes of a white man ever scanned its vast expanse of water. We

LEFT: Speke addressing an audience at the Royal Geographical Society, London.
RIGHT: Samuel Baker dressed as a pasha.

were the first and this was the key to the great secret that even Julius Caesar yearned to unravel, but in vain."

It took them two months to return to King Mutesa and, in case he had dreamt up some other evil in their absence, Baker thought it prudent to put on a show of force. Off came the tweed suit; on went a kilt, sporran and Glengarry bonnet. Their arrival produced a bizarre twist: the "king" was actually someone else; the man with designs on Mrs Baker was merely a stand-in who had been given the job as long as suspicion remained that the Bakers were slave traders bent on capturing the king.

The Bakers returned to Gondokoro after an absence of two years. They rode into town on oxen with guns firing and a Union Jack fluttering – but there was no one to meet them. They had long been presumed dead. A warmer welcome awaited them in Khartoum, but it was not until reaching Cairo that Baker was able to realise a dream that had haunted him for the past five years he had been in Africa: a decent glass of Allsopp's pale ale.

On the voyage back to England he wondered whether the expedition had all been a dream, but "a witness sat before me; a face still young, but bronzed like an Arab by years of exposure

THE REDOUBTABLE MRS BAKER

Never would Mrs Baker's stamina be more tested than in her expedition with her husband. Crossing an area which was half-river and half-swamp, Baker looked back to see her "sinking gradually through the weeds, while her face was distorted and perfectly purple. Almost as soon as I perceived her, she fell, as though shot dead." It took eight men to drag her to safety. She was apparently dead "with teeth and hands firmly clenched, and her eyes open, but fixed." Mrs Baker was unconscious for three days. Baker nursed her for a week before he, too, collapsed. When he recovered some hours later so had she. They recuperated for two days and pressed on.

to a burning sun; haggard and worn with toil and sickness, and shaded with cares, happily now past; the devoted companion of my pilgrimage, to whom I owed success and life – my wife." Before even reaching England, he was awarded the Geographical Society's gold star and a knighthood soon followed. Officially he became Sir Samuel Baker; to the public "Baker of the Nile".

Dr Livingstone

Baker's discovery of Lake Albert actually confused the issue of the true source of the Nile. Were the lakes Albert and Victoria in any way connected? On 22 May 1865, Sir Roderick

Murchison ended a eulogy of Speke with the announcement that the Society had resolved to clear matters up once and for all. The man they had chosen for the job was a 52-year-old missionary, Dr David Livingstone.

Livingstone said that he did not really want to go back to Africa. He had gone out as a medical missionary 22 years earlier and carried out prodigious exploration in the southern and central regions. On the other hand and for all the fame his books had given him, he felt no compulsion to remain in Britain. Both his wife and eldest son were dead; the younger children were taken care of. He was physically fit with

leaned towards Herodotus and the theory of the river rising from fountains at the bottom of high mountains.

Like many of the other explorers before him, Livingstone chose to start from Zanzibar and planned to travel through unexplored country below Lake Tanganyika, south of the usual caravan routes. "Never can there have been a journey which was founded upon so many misassumptions as this one," says Moorehead. "It was a search for the source of a river in a region where it did not exist; it was an anti-slavery expedition that had no power whatever to put down slavery; it was the march of a man

only occasional bouts of stiffness in the shoulder, where on a previous expedition he had been attacked by a lion.

The invitation from the Society had the appeal, perhaps, of the old dog prevailed upon to show the youngsters a few tricks. Personal considerations apart, the trip would present him with another opportunity to advance his crusade against slavery. On the matter of the source of the Nile, he had liked Speke as a person more than Burton but, like Burton, he

who believed that he alone, unarmed and unsupported, could pass through Africa, and that was almost impossible." One way or another, Moorehead concludes, "it is astonishing that he did not die much sooner."

Three years down the line, most of Livingstone's teeth had fallen out, he had contracted malaria which could not be treated because he had lost all his medicines, and nearly all of his men and animals, and he had achieved next to nothing. A river he reached after incredible hardships was not the Nile but the Congo.

He was in these desperate straits when one of his porters "came running at the top of his speed and gasped out, 'An Englishman! I see him!'"

LEFT: Mr and Mrs Baker on the move.
RIGHT: David Livingstone cutting his way through Africa.

Immortal words

The visitor himself should now be allowed to take up the story. "As I advanced slowly towards (Livingstone) I noticed he was pale, looked wearied, had grey whiskers and moustache, wore a bluish cap with a faded gold band around it, had on a red-sleeved waistcoat, and a pair of grey tweed trousers. I would have run to him, only I was a coward in the presence of such a mob – would have embraced him, but that I did not know how he would receive me. So I did what

moral cowardice and false pride suggested was the best thing – walked deliberately up to him, took off my hat, and said, 'Dr Livingstone, I presume?' 'Yes,' he said, with a kind smile, lifting his cap slightly."

The background to this meeting was a journalistic assignment. Henry Morton Stanley, the English-born *New York Herald*'s man in Paris, had been assigned to cover the opening of the Suez Canal in 1869 and to write a piece on Nile cruises such as would interest tourists. He was then to proceed to Jerusalem, Constantinople, the Crimea, the Caspian Sea, Persia and India. Only after all this should he think of "looking around for Livingstone". This he duly did.

DEPTHS OF DESPAIR

"The impression of being in Hell" destroyed Livingstone's will to continue. He was reduced to begging for food and his only comfort was the Bible.

Having been rescued, it did not occur to Livingstone to turn back home. Instead, the two of them went off to investigate a few ideas that Livingstone had concerning the source of the Nile. This involved a walk of some 960 km (600 miles). Only then did Stanley seem to feel the pressure of a deadline and go home.

Livingstone had to wait several months for the reinforcements which Stanley had promised to arrange at the coast. Within days of their arrival, however, he was on the go again, hoping to establish that the source of the Nile was a stream that ran into Lake Bangweolo. Eight months into his investigations, he began to fear that the river concerned was again the Congo, not the Nile. He did not have to live long with the doubt: on 1 May 1873 his boys entered his hut. Apparently kneeling across his bed in prayer, Livingstone was dead.

On learning of Livingstone's death, Stanley resolved to settle the issue of the Nile source personally. Africa had never seen anything like the expedition he put together: 365 men, 8 tons of stores and a steel boat which came apart in sections. It was conducted like a military campaign. The column did not pause for casualties, and any hint of African opposition was put down with force. The boat was lowered into the water as soon as they reached Lake Victoria. After a voyage of 1,600 km (1,000 miles) lasting 57 days, Stanley had proof that the lake had only one outlet, Ripon Falls.

The riddle is solved

There were still a few loose ends to attend to, but for all practical purposes the argument was over and it remained only to award the garland to the solver of the great geographical secret. "Speke," Stanley wrote, "has now the full glory of having discovered the largest inland sea on the continent of Africa, also its principal affluent as well as its outlet. He also understood the geography of the countries we travelled through better than any of those who so persistently opposed his hypothesis…"

Unfortunately for Speke himself, this recognition was posthumous. ❑

LEFT: Henry Morton Stanley consults a map.
RIGHT: the historic meeting of Dr David Livingstone (on the left) and Henry Morton Stanley.

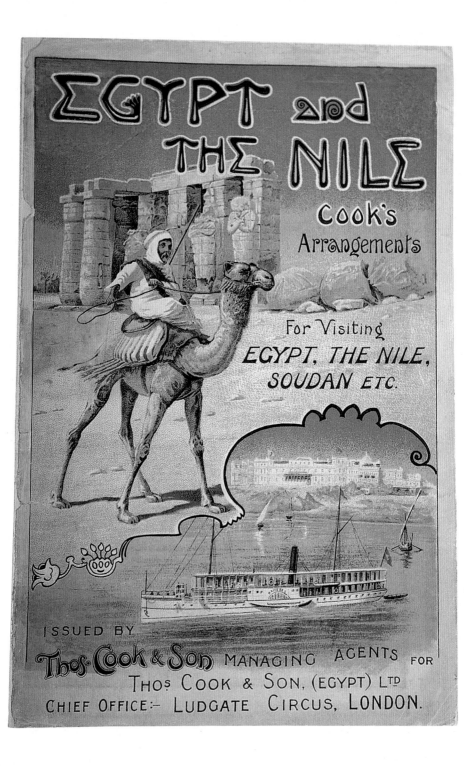

EGYPT and THE NILE

Cook's Arrangements

For Visiting
EGYPT, THE NILE,
SOUDAN ETC.

ISSUED BY

Thos. Cook & Son MANAGING AGENTS FOR
Thos Cook & Son, (EGYPT) Ltd
CHIEF OFFICE:- LUDGATE CIRCUS, LONDON.

THE HISTORY OF NILE CRUISING

Egypt is the Nile and the Nile is Egypt, so if you want to see more
of the country than the Pyramids, it had best be from a boat

Thomas Cook, a somewhat strait-laced printer from Leicester, England who went into tourism in the 1840s as a means of diverting people from drunken idleness, recognised in 1869 that by far the best way to see the sites of Egypt was by boat. It was only along the river that Egypt had ever really been habitable. Everything was built along the river, and ordinary houses depended on bricks made out of Nile mud. The huge blocks of limestone and granite used to build the temples and pyramids could be easily transported by the river; on land, they had to be hauled over desert sand by vast armies of men.

The Great Pyramid of Khufu had in fact been in existence for more than 1,000 years before Egyptians were introduced to any refinements in land transport. The chariots of the invading Hyksos in about 1600 BC demonstrated the possibilities of the wheel, an invention which the Egyptians had taken only as far as the potter's wheel.

Ancient Egypt did not need the wheel to enjoy efficient transport and communications. These two elements, added to the agricultural windfall provided by the annual inundation, were the key to the creation in 3000 BC of a nation-state.

Early days

In those days navigation on the Nile was efficient but not foolproof. Barges drifting down from Aswan with granite blocks for the pyramids dragged a sizeable stone from the stern to keep them pointing in the right direction, and broad, upturned prows evolved to simplify dislodging after inevitable groundings on sandbanks. Sails, originally square but later "lateen", or triangular, under Arab influence, had to be disproportionately large or at least set high to catch wind passing above the shelter of high banks. A stiff breeze made them a handful.

LEFT: Thomas Cook pioneered the cruise business.
RIGHT: Thor Heyerdahl's *Ra*, made of papyrus like the Nile's earliest cruisers.

Modern recreation

Thor Heyerdahl of *Kon-Tiki* fame set out to show that the papyrus raft which was the starting point for Nile craft (the baby Moses occupied a tiny version in the bulrushes) could have been developed into an ocean-going vessel capable of reaching places such as Sri Lanka, a

voyage mentioned in Pliny. Heyerdahl's first experiment in the Mediterranean failed when *Ra I* became waterlogged, but in *Ra II* the next year, 1970, he was halfway across the Atlantic Ocean before the bindings came apart.

Heyerdahl had copied the design from ancient drawings, collected papyrus reeds from Lake Tana (the Ethiopian source of the Blue Nile) and brought in craftsmen from Lake Chad to put the boat together by traditional means. The voyages were not totally successful but he felt he had proved the point. Some experts argue that Heyerdahl set his sights unnecessarily high and that wood, more plentiful in ancient Egypt than at present, would have made up a significant content of craft which nevertheless retained the old, "papyriform" shape.

The early passenger boats on the Nile had a cabin which left enough room on either side for oarsmen. To judge from the amount of deck-scrubbing depicted in tomb paintings, a premium was put on cleanliness. Another curiously recurring feature of these paintings is the ship's boy in the process of being thrashed. This could almost be construed as an early form of advertising, a reassurance to passengers that no stone would be left unturned in the interest of their comfort, and that comfort would not be compromised by an inept or lazy crew.

DESIGNER SAILS

Early sails resembled venetian blinds made of papyrus, but suitable materials were soon found and sails became works of art painted in rich colours and embroidered with the emblem of the king's soul.

The boats in common use were one-man papyrus canoes for fishing and fowling (the latter with a throwing stick resembling the boomerang but with the important difference that it did not come back) and "white-water" sport over the cataracts. However, they were not all small: ships used by the military or for cargo attained lengths of more than 120 metres (400 ft).

A BOAT FIT FOR ROYALTY

The royal solar boat discovered in 1954 near the Great Pyramid at Giza is a marvellous sight: 44 metres (143 ft) long and 5.9 metres (19½ ft) wide, it displaces 45 tonnes and would have had about 38 cm (15 inches) of freeboard amidships, both prow and stern rising well clear of the water. The hull is made of boards stitched together with twisted hemp and leather thongs which shrank with water contact and thus made caulking unnecessary. The captain occupied his own little "cabin" towards the bow, the greater part of the boat being given over to the opulent royal quarters and a long canopy. It is clear from the way the thongs have cut into the wood that the boat was

actually used, but how and why is debatable. Six pairs of oars would not have provided much propulsion, so they might have been used for steering and the boat either towed or pulled along by ropes on land.

Unsuitable conditions in the modern museum displaying the solar boat are yet another example of the dilemma that haunts much of Egypt's history, the choice between preservation and tourist revenue. Unfortunately, the museum is in the path of heat waves bouncing off the pyramid, and the modern air-conditioning system is quite unequal to what the ancients achieved with 16-ton slabs of limestone and gypsum plaster seals.

The solar boat

The royal boats were in a class of their own, symbolic of the boat which took the sun-god Re across the heavens, and hence the potentially misleading term "solar boats" – nothing to do with solar energy. No example of the boats known to have been buried with the pharaohs was found until 1954 when the young Egyptologist Kamal el-Mallakh cleared away rubble on the south side of the Great Pyramid at Giza and found the entrance to what proved to be an air-tight boat chamber.

> ### ONE-WAY RIDE
>
> Ancient Euphrates river craft used hides stretched on wooden frames. They drifted down to Babylon before being dismantled, the pieces piled on the backs of asses brought along for the strenuous walk home.

the other accessories. What was singularly lacking, though, were instructions on how to put the thing together. It took several false starts and 10 years to work out the puzzle, and the solution may now be admired in the purpose-built museum at the foot of the Great Pyramid *(see box, page 36)*.

Medieval craft

By the Middle Ages there were reputed to be around 36,000 ships working the Nile, the Italian monk Frescobaldi reporting that "there was such a great

quantity of boats that all those that I have ever seen in the ports of Genoa, Venice and Ancona put together, would not come to one third (their) number, not counting the double-decked ships." Cairo was then one of the world's great commercial centres, with slaves, gold, ivory, and spices coming down the river to connect with traders operating across the Red Sea.

Prising it open he was struck by a blast of hot air. "I closed my eyes and I smelt incense," he wrote, "I smelt time… I smelt centuries… I smelt history itself." For the first time in 4,800 years, sunlight broke the darkness of the pit and revealed first the tip of a steering oar and then the magnificent prow.

The sealing of the chamber had worked so well that the wood looked "fresh and new". The boat, however, was largely in kit form, 1,224 pieces of wood carefully stacked in 13 layers, together with rigging, baskets, matting and all

The Arab historian Abd el-Latif remarked on ships with "a wooden chamber over which is elevated a dome with windows, and in the daytime furnished with shutters, and which give a view over the river in each direction. There is in this chamber a private cabinet and latrines, and they decorate it in various colours, with gilding,

LEFT: solar boat in the tomb of Ramesses I.
ABOVE: the end of another hard day on board.

and the most beautiful varnish." In the end, of course, these beautiful designs had to yield to changing circumstances. The *dahabiyya* was replaced by the paddle-steamer, which in turn was replaced by the modern, diesel-powered cruise ship. Steel is more practical than wood, as wood was more practical than papyrus.

Modern craft

The Egyptian nobility had always treated themselves to grand river craft; lesser beings travelled a lot more modestly. The modern cruise ship is in the tradition of the former, the ubiquitous *felucca* of the latter. Until recent security problems in Egypt it was still possible to hire a *felucca*, an Italian term applied loosely to any kind of pleasure boat, and explore the Nile independently, but to do so was to miss out on the grander scale of things.

Perhaps inspired by the example of Gustave Flaubert in 1850, the late William Golding tried an independent cruise in recent times and ended up writing a bad-tempered book

SAIL AND RETURN

The cruise-ship deckchair is a fitting place in which to reflect on the fact that sailing is never easier than on the Nile. The prevailing wind blows a craft upstream, the current brings it back.

THE GRAND OLD HOTELS ALONG THE NILE

It was usual for early tourists, travelling on *dahabiyyas*, to decamp to hotels when the boat docked at Aswan and Luxor. As a result, Egypt has several grand hotels dating from these times. The Winter Palace on the waterfront at Luxor was opened in 1905 and became almost as famous as any landmark in the city. In addition to hosting an unbroken stream of suitably qualified guests in the royal suite, the hotel was the headquarters for archaeologists exploring ancient Thebes (Luxor), and the ghosts of men like Howard Carter still hover in the bar.

The Old Cataract Hotel in Aswan has a glorious view from its eyrie on a granite bluff. It opened in 1899 and was immediately so popular that overflow guests had to be put up in tents. Its showpiece was and is the dining room. Its Mameluk-style ceiling rises in four sweeping arches to form a 22-metre (75-ft) dome. Both the Winter Palace and the Cataract have splendid surrounding gardens.

The most sadly missed of Egypt's historic hotels is Shepheard's in Cairo, which had a ballroom modelled on the pillars of Karnak. A guest once wrote that "even the lavatories have something monumental about them... you feel as if you were sitting in the central chamber inside a pyramid." The hotel was destroyed during riots in 1951; the present Shepheard's Hotel stands on a different site.

about the experience. His crew were forever jumping ship to look up relatives, and his skipper was argumentative about where they should moor for the night.

Flaubert and Maxime du Camp, the photographer, travelled as far as Wadi Halfa, although they were as interested in the brothels along the Nile as in its famous ancient monuments. Flaubert was particularly taken by a certain Kuchiouk Hanem: "a regal-looking creature… with slit nostrils, enormous eyes, and magnificent knees; when she danced there were formidable folds of flesh on her stomach." Both men caught venereal diseases.

Christie's famous *Death on the Nile*) but at the time scorned by traditionalists who preferred the elegant *dahabiyya*, a traditional Arab sailing vessel. Napoleon commandeered *dahabiyyas* for his Nile expedition and named his flagship *L'Italie*.

The 19th-century traveller and writer Amelia Edwards, whose *A Thousand Miles up the Nile* became a travel classic, did for the *dahabiyya* what *Death on the Nile* later did for the paddle-steamer. The redoubtable Miss Edwards joined a Miss Marianne Brocklehurst and her nephew Alfred of Cheshire for her voyage to Abu Simbel, the two parties travelling in sep-

Thomas Cook, a militant abstainer, would not have approved. In his eyes, the secret of a good holiday was not to have to haggle over prices. He therefore charged his clients a lump sum for passage, accommodation, board and the services of a guide. Naturally, he made no provision for alcoholic drinks.

Travellers' tales

Cook introduced the paddle-steamer, romantic in retrospect (with no small thanks to Agatha

LEFT: *dahabiyyas*, Arab sailing vessels.
ABOVE: *Ramesses I*, one of the first paddle steamers on the Nile.

arate boats. They made leisurely progress, pausing to collect innumerable objects and to allow Alfred to pursue his futile dream of bagging a crocodile. "Too clever for him," Miss Edwards remarked.

The two spinsters managed to acquire a mummy, but even stuffing it into a tight locker could not contain the terrible smell. Worried about being caught in illegal possession, they gave up after a week and tipped "the dear departed" over the side. At Abu Simbel Miss Edwards cleaned the faces of the statues of Ramesses II, "one of the handsomest men not only of his own day but of all history." The noble features had acquired unsightly white spots as the result of an artist applying plaster to take a cast. These were touched up with coffee, "gallons a day".

Books like hers caught the popular imagination and soon hundreds of *dahabiyyas* were plying for trade on the Cairo waterfront: "boats with six cabins and boats with eight; boats provided with canteen, and boats without; boats that can pass the cataract and boats that can't; boats that are only twice as dear as they ought to be." Miss Edwards ploughed back the royalties she received from her book into the Egypt Exploration Society and an Egyptology chair at Cambridge University.

CRUISE BACK IN TIME

The short cruise between Aswan and Luxor presently takes three days, often with extra days tacked on at either end. On the way, the boat usually stops at Kom Ombo, Edfu and Esna. It would be a criminal waste to allow fewer than three days for the temples at Luxor (Thebes) and the attractions of the west bank (the Valley of the Kings, Queen Hatshepsut's Temple, etc). A few seven-day cruises continue as far north as Nag Hammadi, allowing passengers to see Dendarah and Abydos, but, sadly, very few now go all the way between Aswan and Cairo, with the result that the great sites of Middle Egypt, such as Tall al-'Amarnah and Bani Hasan now see very few tourists.

Modern style

The steam engine and then the diesel forced the pace of change, but in the 1870s, just as Thomas Cook was getting his new business off the ground, something else was going on. Egypt was at last getting proper roads and feeling, for the first time, the full impact of the wheel. Nonetheless, a cruise remained the best way to see Egypt.

The present type of cruise-ship was introduced in 1959. It is evident from their shape – like vast floating hotels – that today's cruise ships are made with the passenger in mind. They are not designed for rough weather or choppy seas. Some are built overseas in Italy or the UK, but even these do not sail to Egypt under their own steam; they wouldn't cope with the conditions of a sea-journey (they don't need to be sea-worthy, as the Nile only experiences rough weather, say, once a year). Instead they come in pieces as cargo on far larger vessels.

Cruising today

In 1975 there were only a couple of dozen boats on the river of the size and standard of today's cruisers; by the beginning of the Gulf War in 1991 the number had increased to over 200, Today there are about 250 boats, most of them travelling between Luxor and Aswan. Some cabins may be small bordering on claustrophobic, but in general the standards of accommodation, food and entertainment are good. Most boats have a small pool, and the bar staff cheerfully go without sleep for as long as passengers are likely to need their attention. Some of the better cruises employ a resident Egyptologist to hold lectures and answer questions.

However, cruising is not as romantic as it used to be. Prices have come down considerably since the 1980s and the river is now very crowded. When the boats dock in Luxor and particularly in Aswan, passengers may have to walk through several other boats to reach the shore, and the view out of the window may often be another boat rather than the Nile. Another problem is the low water levels of recent years, combined with the small, slow lock in the barrage at Esna. The lock can be closed for several days when the water is low, in which case cruise operators are obliged to bus passengers to a different boat on the other side of the barrage. ❑

LEFT: the sound of a gong signals dinner.

Vodka with Pyramids: the Cruise Business

In the pleasantly cool hours of the evening, as you settle by the pool on the roof of your cruise ship with a glass of something mildly intoxicating in your hand, spare a moment to ponder the industry you are part of. The pedigree of Nile cruising is as long as that of the temples upon the river's banks. Egyptian pharaohs cruised up and down the river to survey their kingdom and Cleopatra took Caesar for a magnificent river cruise as part of her seduction of the Roman emperor.

The fact is that most of inhabited Egypt is visible from the Nile, and here the old philosophical tenet that the world only comes into existence when you can actually see it is curiously applicable. Nothing is hiding beyond the horizon except sand, and sometimes even that creeps close to the river bank, squeezing civilisation out into a narrow, thin line of green.

The more substantial Nile cruisers comprise around 50–80 cabins and a staff of 80 for a passenger complement of around 100. Only six or seven of the staff are actually ship's crew, usually distinguishable by their *gallabiyas* (traditional dress). The captain is only in charge of the technical operation of the boat and has no jurisdiction over the passenger areas.

Each Nile cruiser has the equivalent of a hotel manager, who is the overall master of the boat. He will have moved into the cruise business from onshore hotel management, and it is to him that the captain answers. The two will have very different backgrounds – the hotel manager coming from urban middle-management and the captain coming from agricultural stock; indeed, the captain is likely to be rank lower than the chef in the ship's pecking order.

Observant passengers may sometimes notice members of the crew conducting odd rituals, such as throwing bread or salt on to the water, or hooting of the ship's horn for no apparent reason; as with any water-going people, the crews of the Nile boats are superstitious, and pay homage at various shrines on the river-bank in order to keep luck on their side. Beaching a Nile cruiser is a very embarrassing business, an occurrence that every captain dreads. Scraping the bottom is not infrequent, but just occa-

sionally a boat gets so stuck – usually in the shallows near Edfu – that it has to apply to the Cairo Board of Navigation to have more water released into the river so that it can float free. In an incident like this the captain is unlikely to survive in his job unless he has a very good excuse.

Catering is a prime concern on a cruise ship, just as eating is a prime occupation. The bigger ships have a kitchen staff of around 15, who make all their own bread, cakes, pastries and so on, on the boat. Most of the meat and groceries are bought either in Luxor or Aswan, and are supplemented by fresh vegetables, fruit and cheese which is sometimes bought at the stops en route.

The crew on the passenger side work shift systems, and are paid a salary plus a bonus which depends on the bar takings and room occupancy rate. Every 45 days they usually get two weeks off. As a rule, they earn better money on cruise ships than they would in the equivalent quality of hotel onshore, and so such jobs are sought after. The work is varied and the scene – passengers and places – is always changing.

For the passengers, reclining with a cocktail on the top deck while watching the sun set brilliantly over the Nile, the combination of dry history, sumptuous self-indulgence, a delicious winter sun, and an endless unrolling of landscape makes this the holiday of a lifetime. ❑

RIGHT: fancy-dress night on a Nile cruise.

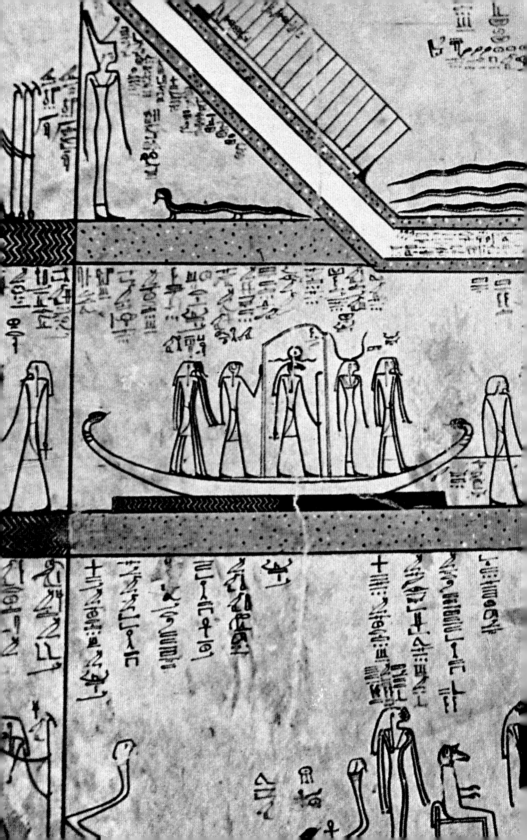

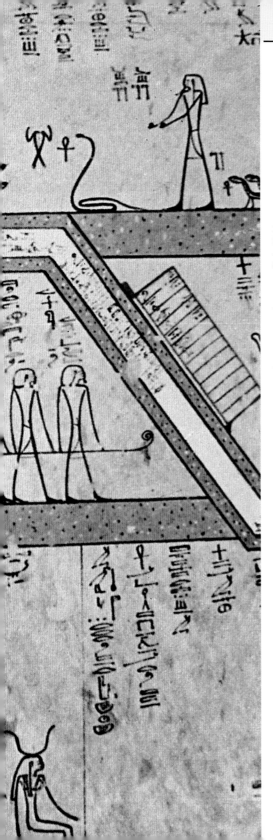

THE PYRAMID BUILDERS

The Old Kingdom pyramids are
astounding feats of engineering

Like the egg – or, for that matter, the original Coca-Cola bottle – the Egyptian pyramid has a purity of line which not only makes it instantly and universally recognisable but belies the fact that, as a design exercise, a pyramid is nowhere near as simple as it looks. There are 87 pyramids of different shapes and sizes, as well as in various stages of repair, along a 60-km (100-mile) stretch of the Nile, but it is the trio of large pyramids on the Giza plateau near Cairo that fill the imagination even of those who will never see them.

Another dimension

The classic pyramid has four sides, not three, and the sides are not equilateral triangles. After a number of false starts, the builders settled on sides which rise at an angle of 52°, aesthetically more pleasing than the shallower angle one builder resorted to but not so steep as to create concern about earth tremors. For the mathematically-minded, the chosen angle happens to mean that the ratio of the pyramid's height to the perimeter of its base is the same as that of a circle's radius to its circumference.

The more comprehensible statistics of the Great Pyramid of Khufu (Cheops) are awesome: for a start, it covers 5.4 hectares (13 acres) at its base – about seven American city blocks – and is as high as a 40-storey building. It contains more stone than all the cathedrals and churches of England put together and its height as a purely stone structure has only been exceeded by the spires of Cologne cathedral. In its heyday it had a gleaming coat of polished limestone, and Pliny, the Roman historian, mentions locals who slid down the sides to entertain tourists, presumably for a little *baksheesh*. The limestone mantle was all of 2.4 metres (8 ft) thick and the blocks were mated with such precision that the cracks were all but invisible.

As feats of engineering, the pyramids are prodigious beyond comparison, which makes

LEFT: tomb painting of the pyramid builders.

it all the more fantastic that they are not the triumphant summation of ancient Egyptian civilisation but, if anything, the start. They are the products of the so-called Old Kingdom, specifically the Third to Sixth Dynasties.

First efforts

The pyramids, of course, did not spring up in a cultural vacuum. The pickings of recorded Egyptian history are so rich that satiated historians have, by and large, passed lightly over developments before about 3000 BC when Upper and Lower Egypt were united by conquest under a single king known in legend as

Menes but whose real name, from what can be deduced from scanty written evidence, was almost certainly Narmer. Under whatever name, it was he who established a new capital at a convenient meeting point between the previously divided kingdoms, at Memphis, not far from modern Cairo.

During the First and Second Dynasties, which is to say for about five centuries after the union of Upper and Lower Egypt, the burial arrangements for the king and nobility became steadily more elaborate. Perhaps because grave robbers were already making a mockery of the most carefully contrived defences, the monu-

THE GREAT IMHOTEP

With the arrival of the Third Dynasty, there emerged an architect, Imhotep, of such genius that he was later deified by the Greeks. Imhotep recognised the difficulties but also the advantages of building in stone rather than relatively flimsy mud-brick. One Egyptologist has painted the alluring picture of Imhotep building a square but otherwise fairly conventional *mastaba* slab for his patron, King Zoser, and then, the king being in robust health, wondering whether he would not have time to put a slightly smaller slab on top of it. With the king still in peak condition, there was ample time for another... and so on. When Zoser did die, the Step Pyramid, tiered like a wedding cake, awaited him.

ment to a departed king and his actual grave were not necessarily in the same place, and it is still not absolutely clear which was which. It would appear that all eight kings of the First Dynasty and at least some of the Second were buried in tombs cut into rock at Abydos, the centre of the Osiris cult, not far from Luxor, while their monuments were erected at Saqqarah, near Memphis, but there are experts who argue that it was the other way round.

Either way, the inspiration for the first pyramid was in the mud-brick *mastabas* of Saqqarah. Originally large but unremarkable oblong slabs, these developed into monumental buildings, still made out of mud-brick, with stylised facades sufficiently reminiscent of Mesopotamian palaces to encourage some experts to postulate that the architects were not recent immigrants to Egypt.

The Bent Pyramid

The evolution of the straight-sided pyramid had to overcome a number of early examples of "back to the drawing board". The dissatisfaction of King Snofru may explain why three pyramids are attributed to him. At Dahshur, 8 km (5 miles) south of Saqqarah, the architect started boldly with sides rising at 54° but, for reasons that may be to do with religious sym-

(possibly following earth tremors) while the temple was still under construction. The project was abandoned.

The only part of King Snofru that found any lasting peace in the resting places he had so assiduously constructed was (and even this is not certain) his severed, mummified foot.

The achievement of Cheops

If all Snofru's diligence was ultimately frustrated, the preoccupation with pyramid design in his household came to fruition in his son, known to him as Khufu but to posterity by his Greek name, Cheops. Technically a god him-

bolism and aesthetics, let the top tail off at 43° – hence the Bent Pyramid. The Northern Pyramid was designed with a gentle incline.

A precipitous 75° was risked on the Maydum Pyramid, the intention being to build it in steps and then make the sides come true with polished limestone inserts. In keeping with what later became common practice, the pyramid was to have an adjoining mortuary temple. As usual, there is a dissenting minority among Egyptologists, but it seems the incline was altogether too ambitious and the sides collapsed

LEFT AND ABOVE: different views of the Great Pyramid of Khufu (Cheops).

self, his secular ambitions evidently antagonised the priesthood, a recurring conflict which was to boil over practically into civil war in the New Kingdom. The vilification of the priests was so pervasive that, judging by Herodotus, the echoes were still rebounding 2,000 years afterwards. Cheops (Khufu), he heard, "plunged into all kinds of wickedness", not stopping at steering his daughter into prostitution to raise money for his immortal monument, the Great Pyramid at Giza. It may be closer to the truth to add that Cheops also locked up the temples and put the priests out of business.

The effort that went into the Great Pyramid was immense. Herodotus describes shifts of

100,000 men taking 10 years just to build the enormous causeway, 18 metres (60 ft) wide, from the water's edge to the plateau. Apart from the fact that only the desert nomads ventured any distance from the river, pyramids were built within easy reach of the Nile to simplify the last leg of the journey that brought blocks of granite, some weighing as much as 70 tonnes each, 800 km (500 miles) down the river from Aswan – a feat achieved on reed barges. However, to be too close to the river would

Pyramid of Khafre

Perhaps out of filial piety, Khafre kept his pyramid 3 metres (10 ft) lower than his father Khufu's, although, because it is built on slightly higher ground, their relative sizes can be deceptive.

On the inside

The internal workings of the pyramid are a story in themselves. It seems that the original plan was to have a burial chamber beneath the pyramid with access via a descending passage from the north face. The passage had already been lined and polished when it was decided that the chamber ought to be higher, roughly in the centre of the pyramid itself. This entailed a second passage ascending from the first. The ascending passage was enlarged

have exposed the site to annual flooding, so they were kept at a respectful distance and serviced by a canal. The blocks were then dragged along the causeway on sleds.

The building site of 5.4 hectares (13 acres) was first levelled with incredible precision and the floor plan laid out on a north–south axis. Herodotus maintains that the casing blocks were stacked on top of one another with a derrick, the inner core being topped up with whatever was at hand. The final layer of polished limestone, he says, was started at the top from a ramp which had gradually been built up. As the mantle progressed, the ramp was whittled down to ground level.

at its extremity into a "Grand Gallery" which in turn led to the burial chamber.

Two narrow shafts from the chamber to the outside of the pyramid were at first assumed to be for ventilation, but it now seems more feasible that they were aligned for astronomical purposes. Once the king was buried, granite plugs kept in readiness in the Grand Gallery were slid down the ascending passage to seal it off to further visitors.

In Mark Antony's time, Roman tourists were able to enter the descending passage through a hinged stone in the north face and scribble their graffiti on the walls of what was at first intended to be the burial chamber. Very little about the pyramids then appears in print until AD 820 when Abdullah Al-Mamun, son of the Caliph of Baghdad, Harun Al-Rashid (of the *Arabian Nights*), assembled an army of engineers and labourers to break into the Great Pyramid. Their path eventually crossed that of the descending passage and they arrived at one of the granite plugs. Unable to budge it, they burrowed a difficult detour which, in the end, delivered them to the burial chamber. It contained nothing but an empty sarcophagus. They vented their frustration by hacking at the magnificent granite interior.

Plundered for stone

The limestone exterior of the pyramid was still intact in the 13th century when Abd-al-Latif, the Arab historian, paid a visit. He was amazed at the spectacle of colour, apparently a combination of original decoration and subsequent graffiti artists. To make copies of the inscriptions, he said, would have filled 10,000 pages. Sadly, his Arab contemporaries were not as impressed by the crowning glory of the limestone. The mantle was ripped off and carted across the river on camel trains to build palaces and mosques in Cairo, amongst which the Sultan Hasan Mosque was one of the notable beneficiaries. The tip of the adjacent Pyramid of Khafre (Chephren), Khufu' son and successor, is all that remains to give visitors a slight impression of how the pyramid would have looked with its mantle intact.

The Sphinx is not now as enigmatic as it was when buried in sand up to its eyebrows, but there is still doubt about who the human face on the lion's body belongs to. Because it is carved from a natural outcrop at the foot of Khafre's causeway, it is generally thought to be him. The Egyptians seemed never to rate the beast highly, and Herodotus does not mention it at all. It was certainly worshipped at one point as a god in its own right: the stele between its paws is a tribute from King Tuthmosis IV of the much later 18th Dynasty.

The third pyramid

On Menkaure (Mycerinus), Khafre's brother and heir, Herodotus at last finds a good word to

say about the pharaoh's of the Fourth Dynasty: "... he opened the temples and permitted the people, who were worn down to the last extremity, to return to their employments and to sacrifices... he made the most just decisions of all their kings."

In any case, Menkaure was content with a much smaller pyramid. Howard-Vyse, a 19th-century British colonel, whose family sent him off to do some exploring in Egypt, used gunpowder to blast his way into Menkaure's pyramid. He recovered a sarcophagus but it was lost when the ship transporting it to England sank in the Bay of Biscay. ❑

THE FIFTH DYNASTY

After the Fourth Dynasty, the rest of the Old Kingdom is rather anti-climactic. The Fifth Dynasty apparently felt unequal to the task of matching the architectural achievements of their predecessors and perhaps to avoid unhappy comparisons chose to conduct their building activities some distance south of Giza. Their pyramids – some of which can be seen at Dahshur and al-Fayyum *(see page 266)* – were smaller and rather slapdash. During the Middle Kingdom there was a revival in pyramid-building around the 19th–18th centuries BC. Examples can be seen at Dahshur, including the Black Pyramid of Amenemhet III, built in black mud-brick.

LEFT: the Sphinx and the Great Pyramid as first seen by Napoleon and his team of *savants*.
RIGHT: a fanciful depiction of the boyhood of Khufu.

Pyramidology and Pyramidiocy

I n about 1850 Pasha Abbas I described the pyramids as "an ugly, useless pile of stones." He was unimpressed or possibly even unaware that the Greeks had ranked them among the Seven Wonders of the World. Medieval Arab rulers were no less disappointed than he that the burial chambers had long been robbed of their treasure, but they were convinced that there were undiscovered chambers containing maps of unknown parts of the world, navigational charts and the secret of weapons that never rusted. No one, they argued, not even the most extravagantly morbid pharaoh, would have invested so much effort in just a tomb.

Abbas, a discredited member of Egypt's last dynasty but nevertheless an indirect descendant of the pharaohs, would not have found many in contemporary Europe who shared his contempt. Following the publication of the 24-volume *La Description de L'Egypte* by Napoleon's *savants*, the Egyptian style in jewellery, clothing and furnishing was all the rage internationally.

"Pyramidologists" were pursuing all sorts of wonderful theories about the pyramids, although those who pushed their fancy too far risked being demoted to "Pyramidiots". Even the Astronomer Royal for Scotland had to watch his step. "The whole of Professor (Piazzi) Smyth's theory about the Great Pyramid," wrote a fellow member of the Royal Society, "is a series of strange hallucinations, which only a few weak women believe, and perhaps a few womanly men, but no more."

In London, John Taylor, editor of *The Observer*, was caught in a dilemma. A gifted astronomer and mathematician, he had studied the Great Pyramid of Khufu (Cheops) and come to an astounding conclusion. The builders, he decided, "knew the Earth was a sphere; and by observing the motion of the heavenly bodies over the earth's surface, had ascertained its circumference, and were desirous of leaving behind them a record of the circumference as correct and as imperishable as it was possible for them to construct."

Taylor's problem was his profound faith in the literal truth of the Old Testament. He believed that Adam had been created in exactly 4000 BC and that the Flood had occurred in 2400 BC. In marvelling at the sublime mathematics of pyramid design, he was quite ready to accept that the Great Pyra-

mid had been built in 2100 BC. What he could not reconcile was how, in just 300 years, the brains and labour required could have recovered from mankind's watery grave.

The pyramid had other peculiar properties too. Patent No. 91304 in Czechoslovakia was rushed through to protect the commercial possibilities of mysterious forces swirling around pyramid-shaped objects. The product in question was a cardboard contraption known as the "Cheops Pyramid Razor blade Sharpener". Sir W. Siemens, a manufacturer of electrical appliances, on the other hand, was a thoroughly reputable British inventor. He took his guide up a pyramid to prove that a wine bottle wrapped in a

moist newspaper and held above his head would emit a shower of sparks. When it did, the official witness let out a howl, hoisted his *gallabiya*, and bolted.

The Curse of the Pharaohs is only one of a long line of demonic powers guarding the sanctity of the royal tombs. They do not seem to have bothered early Roman visitors because Strabo, who took a Nile cruise in 24 BC, described his party crawling down the descending passage of the Great Pyramid by the light of flaming torches.

In the Middle Ages, however, the Arabs were put off by reports of an enormous naked woman with big teeth whose lust no male intruder could decline or escape. If he survived at all, it would be as an insane wreck. It is conceivable that this insatiable woman was loosely based on the daughter whom Khufu, builder of the Great Pyramid, is reputed to have prostituted in order to defray building costs. She was installed in a special chamber and encouraged to charge each of her clients the cost of one block of finished limestone, 2½ million of which were needed before the pyramid was finished.

In 1638 John Greaves, a young astronomer at Oxford University, was prepared to run all these real or imagined risks in order to settle a teasing mystery of the type which would later distress the editor of the *Observer*. The pyramids were too well built simply to have been thrown together, so the architects must have drawn up plans with detailed

measurements. What, he wondered, was the unit of measurement they used, and how had the Egyptians arrived at it? Was it essentially practical, like the three grains of barley which originally made up the English inch, or had the Egyptians been capable of arriving at an abstract one like a fraction of a degree of longitude?

Wriggling "like a serpent" down the same descending passage that Strabo and party had followed, Greaves measured anything and everything that looked like a calculated length. Frequently recurring lengths would therefore be a unit or con-

ABOVE: the mystery of the Pyramids of Giza captured at sunset.

venient multiples of a unit. He soon had enough data and observations to fill a book.

Pyramidographia, published in 1646, caught the attention of Sir Isaac Newton. Using Greaves's figures, he arrived at the length of what he called the "profane" or Memphis cubit, which enabled him to interpret the geographical degree as quoted in the classical authors and so move closer to his theory of gravitation. The role of the pyramids in his theory is not as widely known as perhaps it ought to be.

The search for other examples of applied mathematics in the pyramids then extended to *pi,* the ratio between the diameter and the circumference of a circle. This had traditionally been credited to Pythagoras, the Greek geometrician who lived about 500 BC. Modern computers have now calculated this incommensurate number to 10,000 decimal places, but it was only 1,100 years after Pythagoras that a Hindu mathematician, Arya-Bhata, worked out the fourth decimal. Mathematicians were agog at what seemed like evidence that the pyramid builders had reached at least the second decimal 2,000 years before Pythagoras.

All this was meat and drink to Napoleon's *savants* who cleared sand and rubbish which had all but buried most of Egypt's pyramids in order to measure the external dimensions more accurately and unlock further mathematical sensations. While they pored over their findings, the young general, still some way from crowning himself emperor, insisted on spending some time alone in the Great Pyramid's burial chamber.

He emerged from the chamber white in the face, pointedly refused to answer questions and told his staff that the matter was never to be raised. Only towards the end, when he was in exile on St Helena, did he nearly bring himself to discuss what happened with a trusted companion. He held himself back, however, and shook his head. "No," he remarked. "What's the use? You'd never believe me."

Conjecture about the hidden purpose of the pyramids never ceases. Some of the discoveries are beyond dispute. Clearing the base of the Great Pyramid has established, for example, that the perimeter of the 5.4-hectare (13-acre) site is level to within a tolerance of 2 cm (¾ inch). It has also confirmed that, like most pyramids, the axis is aligned on true north with an astonishing degree of accuracy. Such findings have led a new generation of pyramidologists to suggest that what were long thought to be access or ventilation passages into the centre of a pyramid were actually designed to time the moment of a star's transit across the sky. ❑

GRAVE ROBBERS AND CURSES

Through the years, the tombs of the pharaohs have been prone to desecration –
despite ingenious defences and inscriptions warning violaters of dreadful death

The Curse of the Pharaohs, a built-in feature of almost every B-film about Egypt, is distinguishable from kindred phenomena like the Bermuda Triangle in containing at least a grain of truth. Pharaohs, priests and *felaheen* (peasants) alike were forever putting curses on people for all sorts of reasons, and in a superstitious way they often worked. But Hollywood's favourite curse, that of Tutankhamun, is another matter.

Tomb curses ranged from short and snappy – "He who enters here will have his neck wrung like a chicken" – to graphically detailed. A vizier was not content simply to see the culprit die. He would first have to endure a jet of fire playing on his head, starvation, social ostracism, the death of his children, the violation of his wife before his eyes – and that was just the beginning.

The curse that the cinema-going public learned about was reputed to have killed more than 20 people involved in the violation of Tutankhamun's tomb in 1922. The first victim was Lord Carnarvon, Howard Carter's patron and partner. His death was attributed to a mosquito bite or, better, a scarab, the belief that the scarab, ubiquitous in Egyptian mythology, was a kind of scorpion rather than the prosaic dung beetle that it was.

King Tut's curse

The dread secrets of Tutankhamun's tomb were unmasked in dramatic announcements over a period of five years, and with popular interest running high, newspapers and magazines as well as the film industry made the most of the story. It did not serve their interests to quote doctors who said that Carnarvon had been in poor health for years and had died of pneumonia. It was more rewarding to recall the words of a philosophical peasant who was said to have

been seen loitering at the tomb-site and heard to mumble: "These people are looking for gold but they will find death." A death-bed repentance was put into Carnarvon's mouth and solemn significance attached to a power failure that switched off the lights in his Cairo room 10 minutes before he expired.

Carter ridiculed the whole idea of a curse, but even he admitted to a slight shudder when a servant reported that he had gone to investigate the sudden silence of Carnarvon's pet canary, always a lusty singer, and found it fast disappearing down a cobra's throat. An Egyptian official engaged a snake-charmer named Mussa to ensure that there were no further mishaps with snakes. The official dropped dead.

Death will come on swift pinions

In due course it was virtually impossible for anyone connected with Carter's work to suffer any kind of misfortune or to die without fingers pointing rigidly at the curse. The wording

LEFT: Luigi Mayer's illustration of exploring a passage in the Great Pyramid.
RIGHT: the reopening of Tutankhamun's tomb by Howard Carter and Lord Carnarvon was said to trigger a curse.

was quite specific: "Death will come on swift pinions to those who disturb the rest of the Pharaoh." It sounded authentic, but when sceptics asked to examine it, it transpired that no one had actually seen the inscription. The truth was that, while almost all the tombs did carry some curse or another, Tutankhamun's did not.

An ancient activity

The robbing of tombs is as old as the tombs themselves. Pharaohs who proclaimed their own divinity were not deterred by the posthumous powers of their predecessors. Not only did they empty tombs of valuables, but they also often threw out the coffin and reserved the space for their own, adding insult to injury by tampering with the cartouche to give the impression that they had built the tomb as well.

The pyramids were a maze of false passages and man-traps designed specifically to foil robbers, but of course these could hardly be concealed from the workforce who built them. In claiming that he alone had super-

SECRET IS SAFE

Switching to the discreet tombs of the Valley of the Kings was a tacit admission by the pharaohs that the pyramids, supreme expressions of self-aggrandisement, could never be wholly secure graves.

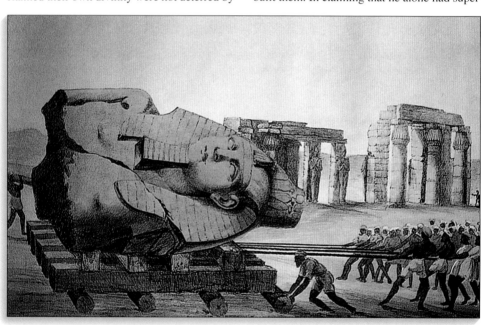

MEDICINAL MISTAKES

In the 19th century, the popular belief that mummies, especially when ground like pepper, had wonderful medicinal properties created a brisk trade in them, so brisk in fact that supply could not meet demand and not a few common criminals in Europe would have been less than flattered to know that their mortal remains were being ground up and passed off as genuine ancient Egyptian. Had the innocent recipients of the supposedly ancient powders possessed an inkling that most of a real mummy's body was made up of mud and saw-dust padding, they may not have been so eager to part with their money.

vised the building of Tuthmosis I's tomb – "No one else knew where it was or ever heard about it" – the architect Ineni was referring to an unmarked tomb in the Valley of the Kings, the security of which lay in its secret location, not its strength. Even so it was not done without slaves, and Ineni skips over the point that his 150 slaves were murdered as soon as the job was done.

The earlier pyramids could not have been more obvious targets. Medieval Arabs applied their engineering skills to the challenge presented by the Great Pyramid. They hacked a large hole in the wall and crawled inside like ants, but when they entered the burial chamber they discovered they were not the first.

Crime and punishment

The 20th and 21st Dynasties, by which time the Valley of the Kings was known and the pharaohs were looking for a new location, seem to have degenerated into a running battle between robbers and loyal necropolis guards who would surreptitiously move the contents of the tombs around to hide them.

When the tomb-robbers were brought to book, justice was harsh, unless they were well-connected. Records show that a carpenter Tramun, a stonecutter Hapi, a water-carrier Kemwese, a peasant Amenheb and a slave Ehenufer who confessed, under considerable duress, to taking "all the gold from the mummies of the God and the queen" were lashed until their palms and the soles of their feet turned to pulp and then executed.

Supply and demand

The history of grave-robbing in Egypt reflects the changing value of antiques. Gold and jewels would appeal to any thief in any age, but it is to be wondered whether a serious scholar such as the Roman Strabo would have attached incalculable value to something like the Rosetta Stone if he had felt inclined to line his pockets with "souvenirs". He reported that at the time of his visit there were 40 empty royal tombs which visitors could enter, and perhaps by then the obvious targets for grave robbers had been exhausted.

Moribund or dead, the business picked up as Egypt was drawn into the European orbit by rivalry between France and England at the turn of the 19th century. Works by Napoleon's *savants* created a craze for anything Egyptian, and peasants became aware that there was cash to be made out of odds and ends in the sand which would previously have been ignored.

"Collectors" such as Giovanni Belzoni, a former circus strongman, used his strength and knowledge of hydraulics (or, failing that, a battering ram) to cart off supposedly immovable objects such as the Young Memnon, whose size had left it unmolested on the ground at Luxor for thousands of years. The race to scoop up anything and everything – or pull it down – for

LEFT: Belzoni's men removing the head of Memnon from Luxor.
RIGHT: today's art of imitation.

LIVING ON A GOLD MINE

The village of Qurnah still stands on the necropolis of Thebes. The authorities have long tried to relocate the villagers, but they say they do not wish to leave, putting forward many different reasons.

---

sale to collections in Europe and America resulted in lurid confrontations between arch-competitors such as Belzoni and Bernardino Drovetti, the Italian-born French Consul in Egypt. Drovetti's riposte to Belzoni's battering ram was dynamite.

Resident robbers

The demand for objects of antiquity did not go unnoticed in the village of Qurnah near the Ramesseum on the west bank at Luxor, where certain atavistic instincts ran deep. No

one was better acquainted with the nooks and crannies of the Valley of the Kings than the descendants of those who had worked on the tombs to begin with. Save for the flow of affluent tourists, Qurnah was an unlovely place to live but the inhabitants were attached to it.

The appearance of some illustrated papyri on the European market in 1871 worried the Antiquities Service in Cairo. Not only was the quality superb, but the papyri appeared to belong to a period that had until then yielded very little. The suspicion was that someone had stumbled on a tomb about which the Service knew nothing. It was almost certainly near Luxor, so it was to Luxor that an obliging American collector was despatched with a brief to behave rich and hungry for important pieces.

Within days the agent was tipped off that he could usefully call on the Abd er Rassul family in Qurnah. After the formalities, items for sale were produced, rubbish at first but steadily improving in quality. What the agent and the Service did not then know was that it had been there for some 10 years, a tomb whose contents were sustaining a large part of the village. Only the Rassuls knew its location but, acting as

> **GRAVE GUARDIAN**
>
> In 1912, Howard Carter had to deal with a gunfight between rival gangs – the Rassuls included – over a burial site. He quietened them by threatening to push the lot of them into the tomb concerned.

wholesalers, they had co-opted the village as their sales team.

The agent's suspicions were sufficient to have the brothers Ahmed and Hussein Abd er Rassul brought in for questioning. Whatever happened to them during the three months they helped with enquiries (the *courbash*, or hippo-hide whip, was still virtually a civil servant's badge of office), the brothers emerged tightlipped.

Muhammed, the head of the family, was not as resilient and in due course led an Antiquities Service representative, the archaeologist Emile Brugsch, on a walk which took them past Hatshepsut's temple at Deir al-Bahari. Climbing a path up the north cliff, Brugsch was assailed by the most appalling smell. This turned out to be a sign that they had reached their destination, a donkey's carcass left rotting in the sun. Close by, was a hole which the tottering Brugsch squeezed through to begin a descent of 15 metres (50 ft) at the end of a rope. At the bottom, a passage about 1.2 metres (4 ft) high disappeared into the rock.

Noble gathering

Trying to keep a candle alight, Brugsch felt his way along the passage. In places, chambers had been cut into the sides, and Brugsch gradually identified the contents in speechless disbelief. Almost any coffin would have been an exciting find, but the names on these defied an Egyptologist's imagination: Tuthmosis III, Ramesses II, Amenhotep I, Seti I. The only explanation for such a galaxy to be assembled in this unprepossessing place is thought to have been an especially turbulent period when all royal tombs were threatened and loyal subjects gathered up as many coffins as they could and removed them in total secrecy to a common grave for safe-keeping.

The objects found with the kings could have put the whole of Qurnah into the lap of luxury for the rest of time. As it was, Muhammed was rewarded with £500 and the case against the brothers was dropped. Brugsch arranged a guard of 300 men to see the find safely down to boats waiting on the Nile. The operation took two days and was enlivened by local women shrieking and tearing at their hair. Charitable observers compared their performance with the traditional mourning for a dead king; others ventured that it might have been despair at the loss of a such a nice windfall.

Almost 30 years later, in 1902, Carter was the Inspector of Antiquities at Luxor and in that capacity was called upon to investigate a robbery at the tomb of Amenhotep II, the only royal mummy left in its original burial chamber. An armed gang had forced their way past the watchmen, pulled the king's body out of the sarcophagus and dumped it on the floor. Using a police dog, Carter followed footprints from the scene of the crime – to the front door of the Abd er Rassul family. Charges were brought against them, once again unsuccessfully. ❑

LEFT: Anubis, the jackal-headed god of embalming.

Smuggling Today

The Egyptian Government has made it very clear that it is illegal to export any antiques without a valid licence issued by the Department of Antiquities. There have been several cases of custom officials being over-vigilant, including one concerning an American family in Sinai during the 1990s, who were arrested for smuggling antiques. In this particular case, experts brought in later confirmed the family's claim that they had bought the bag of scarabs for near to nothing in a tourist bazaar. All too often, however, people are caught smuggling the real thing.

A recent case involved a sculpted head of Queen Meryet (13th century BC) that was smuggled into London. The putative English owner however claimed that the head was a fake that he had bought as a curiosity. The staff of the British Museum did not take long to declare its authenticity and the piece was handed over to the Egyptian ambassador to the UK, who remarked: "This handover is a manifestation of the mutual cooperation between our governments and their fight against the illegal and sinister trade in stolen cultural artefacts."

In 1999 a load of antiquities bound for Jordan was intercepted in the Red Sea port of Aqaba. Objects and sculptures from Pharaonic and Roman Egypt, including scarabs, ushabti statues and hieroglyphic carvings, were shipped as diplomatic luggage to protect them from discovery. The trade in Egyptian relics is so profitable that they now attract the kind of dealers who smuggle arms and drugs (which were also found in the Aqaba consignment). In 2000 an Egyptian furniture dealer was arrested for smuggling minor Egyptian artefacts, hidden in his furniture, with a value of $15 million.

The international art and antiques markets have always been quick to snap up anything Egyptian – and for a time it was easy to supply the insatiable demand as there was plenty coming on to the market. Even the Egyptian Museum in Cairo had a shop selling off surplus stock. When the government decided to protect their valuable heritage, things became a lot more difficult.

However, you can still find ancient Egyptian jewels, statues and carvings in respectable antiques shops and auction houses in Europe and the United States, so where do they come from?

RIGHT: the smashed tomb of Ramesses IV.

The trail of illegal antiques starts where it began – in the tombs in Egypt. The looters are often Egyptians who live in remote parts of the country and know of necropoli or isolated temples that have never been excavated.

It is often not even a matter of theft. The earth is so rich in ancient material that when local people build a house or work their land they are quite likely to stumble across some small ancient artefacts. When they take them to a local dealer they will get some cash, though this will be a fraction of the price eventually fetched on the western market.

The Egyptian architect Hassan Fathy, who built New Qurnah to rehouse those living on top of the

Theban necropolis, said in his book *Architecture for the Poor*: "The peasants had fallen a natural pray to the dealers in the city, who, being alone able to communicate with unscrupulous foreign buyers, were able to exploit the villagers' delicate position and buy their valuable produce for far less than its real value.

Eventually the diminishing returns from tomb robbing forced them to take even greater risks until at last there was an unparalleled scandal. A whole carving in one of the tombs – a well-known and classified ancient monument – was cut out of the living rock and stolen. It was as if someone had stolen a window from Chartres or a column or two from the Parthenon." ❑

REBEL DYNASTY OF THE NEW KINGDOM

A pharaoh purged from history for his controversial beliefs left a gap in the accepted chronology that would remain hidden for 3,000 years

B y the time Nile Valley cruising became really popular 100 or so years ago, the hunt for "antique souvenirs" even in the remotest spots had become a profitable business for *felaheen* who could unearth or manufacture them. The discovery of some rotting wooden chests filled with small clay tablets was therefore a minor windfall for a peasant woman scraping manure from an abandoned archaeological site known as Tall al-'Amarnah.

The tablets were just what customers wanted, the size of a biscuit and therefore easily popped into a pocket or handbag. Many of the tablets chipped or broke as she scooped them into her sack but that hardly mattered: in fact, a modicum of wear and tear made them look all the more authentic.

The mystery of Tall al-'Amarnah

Her find was brought to the attention of experts in Cairo but, over stretched by amazing discoveries pouring in from all over Egypt, they were not unduly excited. The site in question was a mystery. It had been thoroughly excavated by a Prussian team sponsored by King William Frederick IV as early as 1843 when *felaheen* were noticed by an earlier generation of tourists to be in possession of a considerable quantity of glassware, statuettes and pottery, artistically unusual and attractive objects but in nearly every case broken. The Prussians had uncovered the remains of a sizeable city but it, too, had suffered from more than the passage of time. It gave every indication of having been deliberately and comprehensively razed.

The more the skilled Prussian team investigated, the deeper the mystery. To begin with, the site was about halfway between Cairo and Luxor where the uncompromising sands of the Eastern Desert reached all the way to the river. When the Nile flooded, the water broke across the opposite bank; the city side was forever high, dry and barely fit for human habitation, so why was it there? Next, there was clear evidence of temples, palaces, public buildings and private housing of an exceptionally high standard, many with swimming pools. It seemed impossible that historians had not turned up any references to the site, which as a feat of construction must have been on a par with the building of a pyramid.

Obliterated from history

Most perplexing of all was the fanatical manner in which every pictorial or written reference to the notables who controlled the city had been obliterated. Those notables cannot have been less than kings or queens, yet wherever their names and images had once adorned the interior of ransacked tombs there were only the gouge marks of chisels. In one particular instance, a chisel had followed the outline of a human figure with such precise malice that it had gone right through the gypsum surface to leave an almost perfect silhouette in the limestone beneath.

No statue had been spared. The Prussians had found a nose here, a toe there, lips and even a woman's severed breast, but not nearly enough

---

THE 18TH DYNASTY

Lasting as long as it did, ancient Egypt inevitably had high and low fortunes, and in retrospect they were never higher than during the 18th Dynasty, the mainstay, together with the Setis and Ramesses of the 19th and 20th, of the New Kingdom. It was during the 18th Dynasty that the normally placid and hitherto inward-looking Egyptians were fired by imperial dreams which they pursued as determined warriors. The military assertiveness tailed off after a few generations and stopped completely, if it did not actually go into reverse, under controversial Amenhotep III. Thereafter the New Kingdom went into decline, although not without some brisk rearguard actions waged by the Ramesses.

to assemble a likeness. They had admitted defeat, and nothing had happened since to enlighten the resident experts in Cairo.

The tablets uncovered by the woman were neatly inscribed but mostly in an incomprehensible form of cuneiform. Where there might have been references to a Pharaoh the name, if it was a name, made no sense. Thanks to an Egyptian historian named Manetho, who lived at the time of the Ptolemies, the experts had a chronological list of kings since the earliest times.

expertise to make his fakes plausible. Back into sacks they went and, with official blessing, on to the stalls of unfussy souvenir salesmen.

QUEEN NEFERTITI

Despite being smashed, the image of Nefertiti's face has overtaken even the Sphinx as the biggest money-spinner in the tourist-based souvenir industry.

Rebel king

The ghastly mistake was discovered in time to recover only 377 examples of what have become known as the Amarnah Letters. They were inscribed in cuneiform because they had been written to the king of the mysterious city by the subject kings of Nineveh, Babylon, Canaan and Mitanni during the 18th Dynasty

Although there were hazy intermediate periods between 30 dynasties subsequently grouped together and called the Old, Middle and New Kingdoms respectively, the dates themselves meshed, so creating a system that appeared to be watertight. To suggest that it would now have to be dismantled to accommodate a previously overlooked king was tantamount to taking a group of eminent mathematicians aside and whispering in their ears that, on the matter of squares of the sides of a right-angled triangle, poor Pythagoras had got it all horribly wrong.

The woman's tablets, therefore, were considered to be the work of a forger with insufficient

when Egypt was at the zenith of its imperial power. The king concerned was therefore neither an imposter nor some trifling monarch of an intermediate period. The question remained: who was he, and what was he doing in Amarnah rather than in Thebes, whose dominance of contemporary Egypt was a distinguishing feature of the 18th Dynasty?

The letters unlocked the world's best kept secret. The king concerned was Amenhotep IV (afterwards Akhenaten) who, like some of Stalin's rivals after the Russian revolution, had been simply purged from the pages of history. In his case, though, the illusion lasted more than 3,000 years. Those responsible were remarkably efficient. As borne out by the evidence at Amarnah, every public reference to him was smashed. The hole in the 18th Dynasty caused by his summary expulsion was papered over for historical purposes by doctoring the dates of a successor. The odd mention in subsequent records went no further than dark and nameless hints of unspeakable heresy.

The first individual

As a picture of the facts emerged, the reprieved Amenhotep IV was given a tumultuous welcome by the academics. Some scholars drew parallels with Jesus Christ, others opted for the Prophet Muhammed. "The first individual in history," declared another. While theologians pondered the implications of the monotheism Amenhotep propounded – a single God with definite ideas about right and wrong – the imagination of a broader public was captured not so much by the king but by his queen and his younger half-brother.

They were Nefertiti, the immortal beauty, and the boy-king Tutankhamun. The special irony in Nefertiti's case was that her face – gouged and smashed in a frenzied campaign to ensure that it went irrevocably into oblivion – has survived as the most durable and recognisable Egyptian, queen or commoner.

United by the invader

The impetus for a growth of Egyptian militarism was the humiliating occupation of Egypt by the Hyksos for three centuries. They came from "somewhere in the east", and kept to themselves in fortresses, not so much administering the land as helping themselves to whatever they wanted through the long arm of raiding parties. They ventured out on horse-drawn chariots, armed with bronze swords, neither of which the Egyptians had seen before. Any reluctance to meet their wishes was settled with brutal finality. The Pharaohs continued to live in their palaces in Thebes but only under sufferance.

Having inspired Egypt's scattered and fractious noble families with a sense of common purpose, Ahmose I (also K ahmose) managed to nurse popular resentment through what must have been a difficult and dangerous gestation

until he had an army capable of engaging the Hyksos. His ultimate victory depended on chasing the invaders well beyond Egypt's northern border, and this campaign seems to have opened his eyes to the possibilities of turning the tables. Quite soon, harassed kings would pay large sums to persuade the Egyptians to go home and never come back.

The immense wealth of the 18th Dynasty, and hence the means to turn Thebes into the grandiose capital of the world, was based on a subtle form of international blackmail which recognised the price a victim would pay before insurrection became a more attractive alternative.

THE HYKSOS

The Hyksos were Semitic "rulers of foreign lands", feared invaders believed to have come from Syria or Palestine. They conquered Lower Egypt and part of Upper Egypt in the 17th century BC. The introduction of the horse-drawn chariot has been attributed to them and probably helped them achieve military dominance. From the evidence of inscriptions and pottery they seem to have deferred to the indigenous culture and gods of Egypt and taken Egyptian names. The invaders established tribute or trade relations with the Babylonians and the Minoans. No great buildings of the Hyksos kings have survived, although traces of some temple restorations remain at Bubastis.

LEFT: drawing of Nefertiti driving through Thebes by Fortunino Matania.
RIGHT: head of Nefertiti in the Eyptian Museum, Berlin.

Tuthmosis III applied this principle to the hilt. Between 1490 and 1486 BC, he swept through all the neighbouring countries and advanced into Asia Minor. The titles he accumulated reflect his progress: first the "Hero of Seventeen Campaigns", then "Conqueror of Three Hundred and Sixty-Seven Cities", finally "Founder of the Egyptian Empire". His awed subjects heard tales of the intrepid king wrestling personally with an enraged elephant. There was harder evidence of his success in the arrival of barges and

DAY OF THE DEAD

This occasion in Thebes marked the joyous reunion of the dead with their descendants. Oil lamps were hung on doors to help groggy spirits who might otherwise have difficulty locating their graves afterwards.

ambition. He eventually returned to discover that in his absence he had been usurped.

The usurper, moreover, was his aunt, the dowager Queen Hatshepsut, who preferred now to be known as "King" and, to that end, had taken to wearing male clothing and a false beard, albeit the gold variety which was a traditional symbol of royal authority. She evidently liked the look of the beard because she is seen wearing it in a number of official portraits. She also ordained a statue which put her face, with beard, on the body of a scaled-down sphinx. "The world's first feminist," a modern biography notes approvingly.

The "Napoleon of Egypt" took this sudden reverse sitting down. He applied himself to pottery and, on the evidence available, seems to have become rather adept at it. His formidable aunt remained on the throne for a further 18 years, time enough to build what many regard as the Nile Valley's most awesome temple, the one which bears her name at Deir al-Bahari on the west bank opposite Luxor. She may in the end have died of natural causes or, more likely, Tuthmosis's patience ran out and he nudged her in the direction of the pharaohs' occupational hazard, the careless sip from a poisoned chalice.

Erasing Hatshepsut's memory

Hatshepsut's death released Tuthmosis's coiled energy. While one set of workmen embarked at top speed on belated monuments to himself, others went about pulling down everything related to her. He spared the temple, but was unhappy about her two enormous obelisks inside. When no amount of heaving could budge them, he settled for a wall which at least plastered their repulsive presence out of sight, and the obelisks did not see the light of day again until modern times.

caravans at Thebes loaded with booty and the tribute negotiated with newly subject kings. Tuthmosis paused between conquests to erect monuments to his trail of victories. Some of these still stand, although not where he intended or could possibly have imagined: one is in New York City's Central Park, with others in London, Rome and Istanbul.

Royal usurper

Preoccupied abroad, Tuthmosis failed to pay sufficient attention to what was happening at home. The treasures he repatriated were put into the custody of the priesthood of Amun, a provision which conferred power as it nurtured

Tuthmosis introduced an annual "Feast of Victory" as a belated celebration of his earlier triumphs. The festivities lasted 11 days in what must have been an already tight calendar of public holidays. Thebes' Day of the Dead (see panel above), for example, carried on throughout the night, while the most prolonged celebrations were in honour of Thebes's favourite goddess, Opet the hippopotamus. The climax of a month of revelry saw the image of Amun, who had assumed the position of the supreme god in Thebes, leave his sanctuary in the Karnak Temple for a fantastic procession through the city by river to the "Harem of the South" temple (the Temple of Luxor). What happened when god and royal retinue disappeared into the temple was a secret known only to those entitled to be there.

Godly hierarchy

The strict observation of religious obligations may well have been made daunting by the sheer weight of numbers of the gods. Beliefs evolved with regional variations from the basic

religious observance. They were the necessary medium through which dealings with the gods were conducted. To grant or withhold that service from petitioners could in certain circumstances be construed as power over life or death.

The priests naturally demanded payment for each and every transaction they concluded and this, together with the sale of magic charms for every conceivable purpose, constituted colossal revenue. The rewards awaiting a priesthood able to attract adherents to its particular god were as enticing as modern businesses find the prospect of a larger market share. It was the manner in which the priests of Amun pro-

conception of a father-sun and mother-earth (later expanded to include a son, thereby forming a trinity) whose divinity permeated everything, animate and inanimate, which had been created out of a watery nothingness. While a rock was in this sense semi-divine, attention was focused on some 2,000 various gods with whom a more rewarding relationship could be maintained.

The priests had every reason to insist on strict

Left: sphinx of Queen Hatshepsut from Deir al-Bahari, Thebes.
Above: mosaic from Tall al-'Amarnah illustrating the very different style of the rebel dynasty's art.

HOMAGE TO AMUN

It seems Amun underwent a curious transmogrification into Min, a god whose powerful sensuality was credited to eating large quantities of lettuce. The proceedings were enlived by young priestesses who performed a dance which honoured, if it did not imitate, the revered hippopotamus. The time and money needed for such fine entertainment was provided not only by the wealth flowing in from abroad but also by the effortless availability of life's necessities for those on the higher rungs of the social ladder. As long as the Nile flooded reliably every year, the cultivation of crops required no more than short, timely bursts of activity.

moted their vested interest that was to bring about the confrontation which convulsed the 12th Dynasty.

It is possible that the real explanation for Tuthmosis III's lame surrender to his bearded aunt was that she had cultivated the backing of the priesthood while he merely commanded the army. The fear of the priesthood increased over the generations and communicated itself to children who were growing up in the palace nursery in the days of Tuthmosis's great-grandson. The children were the future Amenhotep IV and Nefertiti, the daughter of the then king's principal architect.

Puppy love

Romantic novelists and even purportedly serious biographers can be sensed as near swooning over their word processors as they tackle a plot involving a young prince (shy, sensitive but good at games) and the daughter of a commoner ("a golden slip" with "wide and innocent eyes"). At first they play together like brother and sister. With the furtive exchange of childish kisses they experience a pubescent premonition of love. And so it comes about that they ascend hand-in-hand to the throne and are proclaimed King and Queen of Egypt. "The will of the sun!" declares a biographer bringing her chapter to a breathless close.

The gruffer version of events simply states that the prince Amenhotep was crowned in 1369 BC at the age of 16, his wife Nefertiti was a year younger, and they already had a child. They were initially co-regents, sharing the throne with the ailing Amenhotep III.

According to some interpretations, the king later discarded Nefertiti in favour of a homosexual half-brother, although there is a possibility that the half-brother was in fact Nefertiti in some kind of light disguise, perhaps a play on gender roles reminiscent of Hatshepsut.

Change of god

Amenhotep IV was no warrior king, but to a questioning frame of mind he added fearless tenacity of purpose. He began by chipping at the authority of the priesthood with the ordering of modest temples to a lesser god, better known in the northern city of Heliopolis than in Thebes, with whom he felt a close affinity, Aten. Although Amun had associations with the

HEAVENLY CREATURES

The River Nile had its own roster of gods, principally the hippopotamus and the crocodile. Towns along the river adopted their own particular favourites from lesser echelons. These creatures were given temples where, soothed by hymn-singing, they slithered or wriggled about with rings in their ears (if they had ears) and jewelled bracelets round their legs (if they had legs).

At the end of their pampered lives they were put to rest in a private cemetery. Local loyalties could lead to conflict; war was declared between neighbouring towns and villages over the status of a particular beast. Sacred in one, in the other it was blasphemously caught and

eaten. The Hyksos invaders of about 1600 BC offended Egyptians with gratuitous jibes at the holy hippopotamus, but in Thebes, where the beasts in question were pampered in an artificial lake, there were paintings and sculpture which also showed how the hippo was hunted. It was crept up on, lassoed and played out on a line. Hunters then rushed up to get in their shots with javelins attached to lines. The instinct of this enraged pin-cushion was to find deep water, whereupon a tug-of-war commenced. The hippo would be hauled into a boat, break free, and the process would be repeated until the animal was exhausted.

sun, Aten's were exclusively so, and the god was portrayed with a sun-disc on his head. One of the last glimpses of the young king (with his queen Nefertiti) before the storm broke was included as a painting in the preparation of a tomb for the vizier R amose in the Valley of the Kings, where it can still be seen today.

At 18 years of age, Amenhotep IV probably did not feel quite ready to confront the priesthood head-on, preferring instead to build a haven where he could worship Aten as he saw fit. The site cho-

> **IDENTITY CRISIS**
>
> Thebes the capital of ancient Egypt (now Luxor) should not be confused with Thebes of Boeotia in ancient Greece, a rival of Athens from around 519 BC.

Moving the capital

This immense undertaking required the concerted effort of most of the builders, craftsmen and artisans living in Thebes, a haemorrhage that could not have gone unnoticed by the priesthood of Amun. Barges brought granite down from Aswan and timber up from the Mediterranean. The king seems to have restrained himself while his father remained in Thebes, probably too old and ailing (and perhaps still too loyal to Amun) to decamp to the new city.

sen was halfway between Thebes and the Old Kingdom capital of Memphis. It was, of course, Tall al-'Amarnah, the first city to be designed and built from scratch. It was laid out against the barren backdrop of the desert in an oblong about 3 km (2 miles) long and 1 km (½ mile) wide. It included palaces, temples, a grid of streets broad enough to allow four carriages abreast and – a major innovation much imitated since – a working-class neighbourhood of neat, identical little houses.

On his death in 1361 BC, however, an undeclared war broke out between pharaoh and priests.

The first shot fired was the declaration that the king would henceforth be known as Akhenaten in honour of the sun-god. This was quickly followed, possibly as a pre-emptive measure, by orders that all the temples to Amun and other gods in Thebes were to be closed, the priests dismissed and public references to all gods but Aten removed. One of the pillars at Karnak still shows signs of the defacement of Amun's name, an inadequate indication of what was evidently an orgy of destruction by troops who were loyal to the king.

LEFT: Hatshepsut's mummy.
ABOVE: Akhenaten and Nefertiti depicted in the Tall al-'Amarnah style, playing with three of their children.

The new order

A stalemate lasting several years followed. The priests, denied the right to wear their traditional leopard-skin capes and deprived of a living, went underground. Akhenaten, for his part, was content to retire to Tall al-'Amarnah and forget about them. His rejection of the old religious order brought about a comparable revolution in the arts. Instead of the stylised presentation of the human form, artists experimented with distortions of the body, often grotesque, which would not have been out of place in the 1920s.

This artistic licence extended even to the

way in which the royals were portrayed: Akhenaten seen slouching on his throne or standing with a fat belly and spindly legs; his eyes heavily lidded, his lips bulbous. The most intriguing – and leading to speculation that Amarnah might have tolerated sexual experimentation – show the naked king without male sexual organs but with pendulous, almost female breasts. It was the radical departure in all departments of art which produced the puzzling "antique souvenirs" in the early part of the 19th century.

Diversions at court seem to have deprived Akhenaten of the will to rule in all but a token way. It was either that or a pacifist nature which

caused him to ignore letters from his subject kings in the north warning him of encroachments on the empire and imploring him to lead his army against them. These, indeed, are the letters which, when found by the peasant woman in 1887, were very nearly lost again through the failure to recognise the import of the cuneiform script.

Once the letters had rescued Akhenaten from the oblivion into which the avenging priests had conspired and nearly managed to thrust him after his death in about 1353 BC, Egyptologists were able to piece together a more rounded biography. The gap in the chronology of kings had been papered over, it was discovered, by bringing forward the date on which Haremhab, a former army general, seized power, and fitting it some years after his death.

Akhenaten's death

On the precise circumstances of Akhenaten's death, the trail runs cold. He may have been poisoned; he may have died young (he was probably 32) of a complaint, according to theories based on the elongated shape of his head, associated with excessive in-breeding. In any event, the state in which the Prussian team found Tall al-'Amarnah at the beginning of the 19th century and what was discovered by archaeologists who rushed back to the site to sift through the evidence ever more finely, leaves no doubt about the sheer ferocity with which the supporters of Amun sought to redress the balance.

It was left to the Swiss archaeologist Ludwig Burckhardt and a Briton, Howard Carter, to fit the most spectacular pieces to a fascinating jigsaw. Burckhardt was aroused from an afternoon nap on 6 December 1912 by his foreman who had caught a glimpse of flesh-coloured plaster on an object buried in the sands of Amarnah. It was a magnanimous gesture on the part of the foreman towards a man who was about to realise the fruits of a two-year search. As Burckhardt's practised hand flicked away grains of sand, Nefertiti's features slowly, triumphantly emerged from a 3,000-year-old grave. ❑

LEFT: limestone statues of Akhenaten and Nefertiti, now in the Louvre.
RIGHT: carving showing the royal couple and one of their children worshipping Aten.

RAMESSES THE BUILDER

The great, immodest king of kings, creator of the colossal temple at Abu Simbel,
may well have presided over the beginning of the end of the Egyptian Empire

All the representations of Ramesses II – and they far outnumber those of any other Pharaoh – are of squared shoulders, a head held high, and an expression of immense self-satisfaction. It is all the more ironic, therefore, that it should have been an unrecognised statue of him, toppled face down in the sand, that the poet Percy Bysshe Shelley should have immortalised as an ignominious example of a god with clay feet. The poem is *Ozymandias*, Ramesses' coronation name:

I met a traveller from an antique land
 who said:
Two vast and trunkless legs of stone
Stand in the desert...
... And on the pedestal these words appear:
"My name is Ozymandias, King of Kings:
Look on my work, ye mighty, and despair!"
Nothing beside remains. Round the decay
Of that colossal wreck, boundless and bare
The lone and level sands stretch far away.

Shelley was wrong because a great deal remained: Abu Simbel, the Ramesseum, the temple of Karnak, the temple of Abydos, parts of the temple of Luxor, six temples in Nubia, and others which Ramesses usurped in his name. Recent excavations have uncovered a string of fortresses that he built along the Mediterranean coast. All were lavishly adorned with statues and fulsome tributes to himself, an exercise in self-aggrandisement that makes modern despots look coy.

Hard reign

It cannot be denied that Ramesses II led a full life. He ruled, initially as co-regent, for 67 years, lived for 90 or so, waged 20 wars, oppressed the Israelites (it was from whom Moses fled), married officially three times but maintained an active harem of more than 200 women, had more than 100 sons and about 60 daughters, and by the girls he added to his innumerable grandchildren.

LEFT: a head of Ramesses II at the Ramesseum, Luxor.
RIGHT: the great man's mummy.

"One of the handsomest men not only of his own day but of all history," gushed the normally reserved Amelia Edwards, a 19th-century Nile traveller. She devoted some time to removing white spots from the faces of his enormous statues at Abu Simbel, but even on such close acquaintance she would have been pushed to

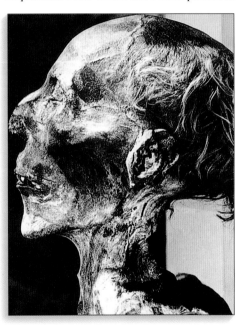

THE VICTOR OF QADESH

On his defeat of the Hittites, Ramesses II claimed: "I became like the god Mentu. I hurled the dart with my right hand, I fought with my left hand; I was like Baal in his fury against them. I had come upon 2,500 pairs of horses; I was in the midst of them; but they were dashed to pieces before my steeds. Not one of them raised his hand to fight; their heart shrank within them; their limbs gave way... As crocodiles fall into the water, so I made them fall; they tumbled headlong one over another. I killed them at my pleasure, so that not one of them looked back behind him, nor did any turn round. Each fell, and none raised himself up again."

recognise the features when his coffin was opened some years afterwards. Admittedly well beyond his prime when he died, Ramesses II had rotten teeth and a large, hooked nose which sculptors scrupulously overlooked. His heart was evidently in a bad way and he had serious arthritis in one hip.

His greatest battle was fought against the Hittites near Aleppo in Syria in the fifth year of his reign, about 1285 BC. Pentaour wrote a Homeric epic that dwelt on Ramesses' single-handed battle with 2,500 Hittite chariots; the king liked the thought so much that he recorded the details of the Battle of Qadesh over and over again on his many monuments, most graphically on a wall of his temple at Karnak in Thebes.

CONFLICTING REPORT

A version of the Qadesh peace treaty in the Hittite capital of Baghazkoy claimed victory not for the great Ramesses, but for the home side.

Enemy of Israel

The references to (unnamed) Ramesses in the Bible are less flattering. He made Israel "sigh" and "groan" (Exodus ii.) and in so doing attracted the unfavourable attention of God. He put the Hebrews to work in the fields "with rigour" and

THE RAMESSEUM

On the west bank at Luxor (ancient Thebes) stands the Ramesseum (see page 225), a temple serving the cult of Ramesses II and containing another account of the Battle of Kadesh. This rendition is embellished with the wretched Hittite prince being dangled upside down by his ankles, apparently to shake out water swallowed when he was dumped in the Orontes. The most striking piece in the Ramesseum, publicised by the poet Shelley, is the broken statue, "Ozymandias" being Ramses's coronation name. It is estimated that in its pristine state, the statue, the largest ever cut from a single piece of granite, weighed around 1,000 tonnes.

it is supposed that they made up a substantial part of the forced labour that built his monuments.

Place in history

Ramesses II, son of Seti I, was of the 19th Dynasty (New Kingdom). His rule followed the religious upheaval fomented by Akhenaten and the boy-king Tutankhamun. His father was instrumental in the drift away from Luxor towards the Delta, and Ramesses accelerated the process by building a permanent palace at what had been a summer residence in the old Hyksos capital of Tanis.

That much was known, and Napoleon's troops thought they had located the palace city near the

Delta town of San al-Hagar, but because of the connection with the Old Testament and the forced labour and subsequent exodus of the Hebrews, confirmation of the site became a matter of archaeological excitement at the end of the 19th century. The old Egypt Exploration Society offered one mud-brick, the product of Hebrew hands, for each £1 subscription to their newsletter that helped fund their work. Money poured in.

Ramesses' fame as a builder is associated not with the New World he sought to establish in the Delta but with the "Old" he strained to leave. He was only a contributor to the temple of Karnak – from the New Kingdom onwards many kings added personal touches – and tried to magnify his work by usurping the hypostyle hall, which was actually begun by Ramesses I and completed by Ramesses II's father, Seti I. Ramesses attempt to claim it has his own can be seen in the way his cartouche has been superimposed. It is on a wall outside the hall that Ramesses emblazoned his account of the Battle of Qadesh.

Ramesses II was similarly only one of a number of contributors to the temple of Luxor, but he assumed pride of place with the front pylons (another report on the Battle of Qadesh) and four colossal statues, two standing and two seated. The obelisk that is now in the place de la Concorde in Paris was one of a pair that originally stood near the statues. As in Karnak, Ramesses usurped the work of one of his predecessors, in this case that of Amenhotep III.

Despite his excessive self-glorification, Ramesses could, however, justly claim all the credit for temples in Nubia, in particular for his masterpiece at Abu Simbel which also celebrates the victory at Qadesh. Four colossal statues of the seated king guard the entrance to a 54-metre (180-ft) hall cut out of solid rock.

Love conquers all

A second temple at Abu Simbel is a clue to the reality of Ramesses' ostentatious reign. It was dedicated to his Great Royal Wife, Nefertari, who was actually one of the despised Hittites, though by all accounts he loved the beautiful Nefertari deeply. He married her 13 years after the Battle of Qadesh and some his-

torians are inclined to believe that the union was a gesture of conciliation towards people he was unable to subdue.

Ramesses II had inherited the vast Egyptian Empire built up by Tuthmosis III. "From and after the conclusion of peace and alliance between Ramesses and (the Hittites)," says the historian George Rawlinson, "Egyptian influence in Asia grew vague, shadowy and discontinuous… we may say that her Asiatic domination was lost, and that Egypt became once more an African power, confined within nearly her ancient limits."

If, as now appears fairly certain, Ramesses

did preside over the beginning of the dissolution of the Egyptian Empire, Shelley's poem may make an unintended point rather well. But perhaps the ultimate irony for a king whose fantastic building activity should at least have provided a secure and dignified grave, was that, along with the mummies of other pharaohs, his body had to be hastily removed from his tomb in the Valley of the Kings to save it from robbers during the breakdown of the New Kingdom in the 12th century BC, following the rise of the so-called Sea Peoples. It was later recovered from what amounted to an anonymous mass grave in the cliff above Queen Hatshepsut's temple at Deir al-Bahari. ❑

LEFT: a fallen head of Ramesses at Memphis.
RIGHT: an upright version at the Temple of Luxor.

CLEOPATRA AND THE PTOLEMIES

A charming lover and a deadly politician, the famous
Queen of Egypt was the last ruler of a great dynasty

In October 48 BC, Julius Caesar had the world at his feet. The only obstacle to complete control of the Roman Empire had been removed with the defeat, in Greece, of rebellious military elements. The rebels' leader, Pompey, had slipped away with the intention of rallying support in Egypt. In response to this threat Caesar sailed into Alexandria with a fleet of 35 vessels carrying what remained of his two legions of infantry and 800 cavalry.

He need not have bothered. Pompey had been murdered as soon as he stepped ashore and, according to some accounts, Caesar was presented with his severed head when he arrived shortly afterwards. So what kept him in Egypt when there was pressing business at home? According to his official despatches, Caesar was not prepared to brave the contrary winds that blew at that time of year, and he wanted to look into an Egyptian royal squabble.

His decision to linger in Egypt may have owed more to gossip about the young Queen Cleopatra than to contrary winds. At the tender age of 21, Cleopatra badly needed an ally, preferably a powerful foreign one, to help her in assorted familial struggles. The previous year a Roman ambassador had found himself in her arms being coaxed round to her point of view.

Caesar in his prime

The 54-year-old Caesar was in his prime, appearances notwithstanding. His hair was thinning and his features were beginning to look gaunt – a bitter pill for one who by reputation "appeared among all victories to value most those over beautiful women". These conquests were, in the words of a commentator, "necessary relaxations in the course of the most arduous public affairs".

A century later St Chrysostom wrote that Cleopatra was "exceedingly beautiful", had "the sweetest of voices" and "every charm of conversation". In the saint's opinion, Cleopatra

possessed the wherewithal "to ensnare even the most obdurate and elderly man."

Wiles and wickedness

Whatever her physical qualities, Cleopatra was certainly wily. "While it was on her sex that she relied when she desired to effect a great

stroke", one historian wrote, "she never neglected the possibilities of bribery combined with an occasional assassination, when it seemed safe to employ the assassin's aid."

Given her involvement in the death of two brothers and a sister, and her spiteful execution of a harmless Armenian king whom she had held captive for several years, Cleopatra "well merited the title of murderess". The historian believed that her crimes were mitigated by the qualities she showed in being a good mother to her children.

To be fair to Cleopatra, her family had hardly set a good example. "If the Ptolemies, at this period in their history, had been able to

---

LEFT: Cleopatra emerges from a rolled-up carpet and confronts Caesar. **RIGHT:** witch or seductive beauty?

produce a good woman," a critic sighed, "it would have been a miracle." Her father was generally recognised as a notorious example of a consistently rotten dynasty. Famously debauched, he would dance in public to the sound of cymbals. As soon as he woke up, he would get drunk again as quickly as possible.

History's displeasure

The Ptolemies are said to have produced just two kings "at which history can point with pleasure", and yet, during the course of their 300-year dynasty, Egypt was the richest country in the world. When Alexander the Great died in Babylon, one of his generals inherited his Egyptian conquest; crowned in 305 BC, he was known as Ptolemy the Saviour. He and his successors wanted the best of both worlds: they accepted the divinity accorded to the Egyptian crown, but remained resolutely Greek. Alexandria was a Greek capital with Greek institutions and had a fleet manned by Greek mercenaries.

The one critical function that, as expatriate

THE LITERATE QUEEN

The Ptolemies' cartouches were in hieroglyphs, which in general they could not read. Cleopatra seems to have been the only Ptolemaic ruler able to understand them.

THE REAL CLEOPATRA

Cleopatra's contemporaries were much taken by her seductive voice and witty repartee. It seems she was an accomplished linguist, capable of conversing with Egyptians, Ethiopians, Hebrews, Arabs, Syrians, Medes and Parthians. We don't really know what she looked like because her adversary, Octavian, destroyed most of the statues and portraits of her after her death. But there has been lots of uncomplimentary conjecture about the size of her nose. "All that we can feel certain about," wrote a Victorian historian, "is that she had not a short nose."

An exhibition devoted to Cleopatra at the British Museum in London brought to light 10 previously unrecognised Egyptian-style images of this endlessly fascinating queen. In depictions on coins and statues sculpted during her lifetime, she appears to be more a caricature-like witch than a seductive beauty, with a very long neck and the sharp features of a bird of prey. In the view of Plutarch, it was quite possible to gaze upon her without being bowled over, which suggests that, even then, a reputation for beauty preceded the reality. As for the big nose, it is said to represent strength of character, which is probably what the 17th-century French philospher Pascal had in mind when he wrote: "If Cleopatra's nose were shorter, the shape of the world would have been different."

Greeks, the Ptolemies could not perform, was the collection of taxes. The priests had a monopoly in that area and so, to propitiate the clergy, the Ptolemies remained stoutly orthodox in religious matters. They ingratiated themselves with the priesthood by building some of the finest temples – which can still be seen – in the Nile Valley, at Dendarah, Edfu, Kom Ombo and, especially, on the island of Philae. A few Greek flourishes intruded on the traditional design, but the Ptolemies took pains to be depicted on the walls in Egyptian costume rather than in the Greek apparel which they customarily wore. At the tail end of the dynasty, Cleopatra was too late to be depicted in the temples in more than one or two places.

History has two popular versions of the first meeting between Cleopatra and Caesar. One has her being dumped at his feet in a sack as a trick to evade the pickets who surrounded the palace where Caesar was staying. The other has her choosing a seductive outfit and bursting in on him in the middle of the night. Either way, by morning Caesar was firmly on her side.

Institutionalised incest

The problem of their romance, as Cleopatra would have explained to the emperor, was that she and a younger brother had inherited the throne jointly. She was then 18, her brother 11. They were also husband and wife, a form of institutionalised incest commonly practiced among Egyptian royalty to keep the regal blood pure. Cleopatra was the product of perhaps a dozen consecutive incestuous unions and seemed none the worse for it, although there was more than a touch of insanity among her family.

This particular incestuous marriage was a disaster from the outset. On reaching the age of majority (at 14), her brother, Ptolemy XIV, reneged on the principle of a shared throne, which he wanted for himself. On being told of Cleopatra's confirmation as queen, Ptolemy went reeling through the streets, howling cries of "Betrayal!". He tore his crown from his head and petulantly smashed it to the ground.

A history written by Caesar describes what happened next as some kind of disturbance in

Alexandria, which he dutifully suppressed. In fact, it seems that the population were for Ptolemy and against Cleopatra, but Caesar scarcely mentions her. Nor does he relate anything about taking time off to visit the sites of Egypt. According to Appian, he went off "to explore the country and to enjoy himself with Cleopatra in other ways."

A luxury cruise

With an escort of 400 ships, they cruised in a double-decker floating palace, 90 metres (300 ft) long and 14 metres (45 ft) wide. They were propelled by banks of oarsmen and by a

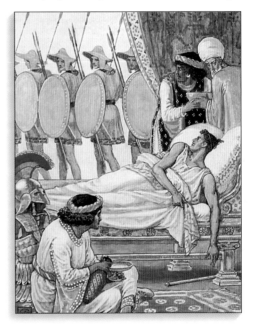

30-metre (100 ft) linen sail fringed in purple. Meals and entertainment were provided for up to 60 guests, who stretched out on couches in a saloon panelled in cypress and cedar. Guests stayed in private cabins and, as the mood took them, they frequented chapels dedicated to Aphrodite and Dionysus. The lower deck contained a mock cave made out of slabs of stone and lined with gold.

The cruise lasted nine months, after which Caesar decided that he had to return to Rome. He was not long gone when Cleopatra gave birth to a son, whom she named Caesarion. Caesar did not acknowledge paternity, although it is thought that a desire to see the child moti-

LEFT: the *Feast of Antony and Cleopatra*, from the studio of Francesco Tevisani.
RIGHT: the *Death of Alexander the Great*, conqueror of Egypt in 332 BC.

vated his invitation to Cleopatra to visit Rome soon afterwards. Travelling with her was her young brother and new husband, Ptolemy XV, who was aged about 11.

Roman society took to Cleopatra and her relations with their emperor much as the British did to Mrs Simpson's claims on King Edward VIII, or Americans did to Aristotle Onassis's designs on the widowed Jackie Kennedy.

"I detest the queen," wrote Cicero after meeting her. "Her insolence... I cannot recall without

The Egypt to which she returned was suffering from a low flood. And, although she may not have realised it, tales of Egypt's wealth had whetted Roman appetites. But for the time being Rome was preoccupied by a civil war between forces loyal to Caesar's memory and a republican movement. As the war moved towards a victory for the former, Cleopatra received an invitation from one of the triumphant generals. He was dealing with commitments in Syria, he said, so he suggested she visit him there.

a pang." As for the young Ptolemy, he was "an unprincipled rascal". Caesar rubbed salt into these misgivings by placing a statue of her right next to the hallowed temple of Venus.

Ides of March

It was whispered that he intended to discard his wife, marry Cleopatra, assume the title of King of Egypt and move the imperial capital to Egypt. Caesar's assassination on the Ides of March 44 BC, was not unrelated to these rumours. It is said that Cleopatra poisoned her brother before leaving Rome in a hurry. She defiantly made Caesar's illegitimate son co-regent and named him Ptolemy Caesarion.

Plutarch describes her arrival in Syria in a ship with purple sails and a gilded stern. The oars were plated with silver and glinted as they moved to the music of flutes, pipes and harps. She stretched out on the deck "like Aphrodite... reclining under an awning bespangled with gold, while boys like painted Cupids stood on either side fanning her. Marvellous odours from many censers wafted to the land..."

Mark Antony

The general who savoured this agreeable sight was Mark Antony, who was certainly free for dinner. "Every dish was golden and inlaid with precious stones, wonderfully chased and embossed... She, smiling, said she made him a present of everything he saw." Did he want to come again? He did, night after night.

When it was time to reciprocate, Antony's hospitality was pathetic. Cleopatra saw that he was no polished courtier like Caesar but a rough and ready soldier. Yet "she fell at once freely and boldly into the same manner toward him." Thereafter his interest in government, according to Appian, "began to dwindle". Octavian (later known as Augustus and, with Marcus Lepidus, a partner of Antony's in the ruling triumvirate) was more blunt: "He has been bewitched by the accursed woman."

It seems that Antony's invitation to Cleopatra to join him in Syria may have had a longer history than her weakness for representatives of Rome. He evidently remembered seeing her as a young girl when he was a junior officer with huge personal debts and a propensity for debauchery on an assignment to Egypt.

Descent from a demi-god

Even his enemies, however, conceded that Antony had good points. Cicero described him as a handsome brute, built like a gladiator, with an impressive beard, broad forehead and an aquiline nose that was, according to his family, evidence of their descent from the demi-god Heracles. Antony cultivated this glorious connection, keeping the image alive by hoisting his tunic high to accentuate his bulging thighs, and by wearing an unusually large sword.

While Antony was being drawn into Cleopatra's personal problems, the triumvirate's position in Rome was deteriorating fast. His co-rulers appealed to him for help but their request fell on deaf ears. "He suffered himself to be carried off by Cleopatra to Alexandria," wrote Plutarch, "there to stay and amuse himself like a boy in holiday-time."

At last, "with difficulty, like a man aroused from sleep and a drunken debauch", Antony agreed to lead a campaign against the Parthians in Asia Minor. He was shocked on reaching Athens to find his wife, the popular Fulvia, looking for him. He apparently accused her of abandoning her duties in Rome and they parted on bad terms. She was soon dead – "a willing

victim to disease on account of Antony's anger." Antony was by all accounts "much saddened".

He did not see Cleopatra for three years and in the meantime remarried. The new wife was Octavia, sister to Octavian. It was evidently a happy marriage and relations with his brother-in-law were good. They split the empire between them, Octavian taking the western half and Antony the eastern. Egypt fell within Antony's sphere of responsibility. Ominously, "that great evil which had long slept, the passion for Cleopatra which seemed to have been lulled and charmed into oblivion by better considerations, blazed forth."

Antony and Cleopatra's reunion saw their earlier positions reversed. Now proving the extent of his generosity, he made her a present of Cyprus, Phoenicia, the Arabian shores of the Red Sea and chunks of Syria, Cilicia and Judaea. Her response was to ask for more of Syria, a tract that belonged to King Herod. He thought not but, by way of compensation, gave her the Gardens of Jericho.

The interlude ended with Antony again called away to war, this time in Syria. The war went badly, and he was driven back to the beaches near Beirut, demoralised, unable to pay his troops and drinking heavily. Both the women in his life set out to rescue him with money and

LEFT: the Ptolemaic temple of Philae.
RIGHT: according to most accounts, Cleopatra had a large nose.

reinforcements. Cleopatra got there first and, learning that Octavia was en route, "pretended to be desperately in love with Antony." The source, Plutarch, says she went on hunger strike, assuming an expression of burning passion whenever Antony was near, and of dejection when he had other things to do. Meanwhile Octavia had orders from Athens to go home.

Octavian was angered by Antony's insulting behaviour towards his sister, and by his gifts to Cleopatra. Then there was news that Antony, back in Egypt with Cleopatra, had staged a triumphant party in Alexandria to celebrate a victory over the Armenians. Triumphs were the

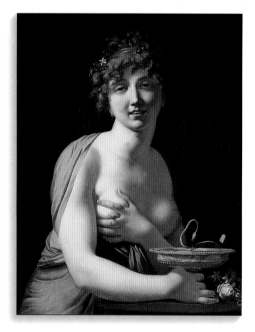

prerogative of Rome. Cleopatra, dressed in a preposterous costume of hawk head and cow horns, watched the party from a golden throne. Octavian assumed that both lovers were mad.

Octavian declares war on Antony

Antony discarded Octavia, ordering her out of their house. Octavian declared war on his brother-in-law but he had to find Antony and Cleopatra, who had gone, with the Egyptian army, to winter in Greece. The battle was a fiasco. Antony deserted his men and took refuge aboard Cleopatra's ship where, realising what he had done, he is said to have sat in silence on the prow for three days, head in his hands.

As Cleopatra's vessel approached Alexandria, and it became obvious that Octavian was not immediately pursuing them, Antony's mood improved. Cleopatra, on the other hand, seemed to sense that the end was nigh. She experimented with poisons, testing them on condemned prisoners until she settled on the asp, whose bite "brought on drowsy numbness, with no spasms or groans, but with a gentle perspiration over the face and a dulling of the senses". She took her preparations to the logical conclusion by building a tomb for herself in Alexandria.

A tale of two suicides

The final act has been portrayed with many a historical infelicity – in the Hollywood movie the asp's fangs become lost in Liz Taylor's ample bosom – but the truth is as follows.

Octavian's army burst through Alexandria's defences with minimal opposition, although Antony personally fought bravely. Antony left the battlefield only to be told that Cleopatra had committed suicide. He went straight to his rooms, handed his sword to his servant Eros and asked to be run through with it. The faithful Eros could not do it; instead he fell on the sword himself as if to demonstrate how it ought to be done. Antony followed suit but made a mess of it. He was writhing on the floor when word came that Cleopatra was, after all, still alive.

Antony was carried to her and winched up to her window in a litter. "Never was there a more piteous sight," wrote Plutarch, who claimed to have spoken to an eyewitness. "Antony was hauled up, stained with blood and wrestling against death, stretching out his hands towards Cleopatra as he hung in the air." She pulled him in and he died in her arms.

Cleopatra did not then clasp the asp, despite the legend. It seems that she attended Antony's funeral and lived for some time afterwards. She did eventually commit suicide – possibly through fear of an Octavian triumph that could well result in her imprisonment – perhaps availing herself of the asp. Before doing so, she had the opportunity to meet Octavian. According to Plutarch, she hoped to the end that, if only Octavian would come into her arms, she would be able to persuade him of her point of view. He wouldn't, so she couldn't. ❑

LEFT: Cleopatra administers the fatal bite of an asp.
RIGHT: two of the greatest lovers in history.

"Thou art the armourer of my heart."

ANTONY AND CLEOPATRA.

THE MAMELUKS

Originally slaves who made their name as royal bodyguards, this elite group rose to become rulers of Egypt and overseers of a prosperous trading empire

The Mameluks are best remembered in the West today for the heroic futility of their performance at the Battle of the Pyramids in 1798, when they charged Napoleon's formidable artillery and were mown down. Their obscurity is undeserved and surprising because, in the words of the soldier-historian Glubb Pasha John Bagot, for example, the empire they created in Egypt was "a historical prodigy, a unique curiosity among civilised states." It was, in short, a sequence of some 50 military autocrats drawn from a frequently replenished pool of young boys kidnapped or imported as slaves from distant foreign lands.

In this system there was no conception of hereditary succession, or none that worked. On the death of a former slave who had become a powerful ruler, his wealth went to the Treasury and his land was redistributed. His succession was determined by whoever could demonstrate the most telling combination of ambition, ruthlessness and ability. "But by far the most amazing factor in this extraordinary story," in Glubb's opinion, "is that all these unique peculiarities made no difference to the rise and fall of their empire".

The Battle of the Pyramids

By the time Napoleon invaded Egypt, the Mameluks' heyday was a thing of the past. They were no longer rulers as such – the country had long been dominated by Ottoman pashas – but behind the scenes they exercised considerable influence as landowners with their own private armies. The French invasion stirred atavistic instincts in the Mameluks. They had not fought a major battle for nearly 300 years but were acutely conscious of their traditions. They had been one of the finest fighting forces in the world, an elite body of cavalry whose only idea about going into battle was to charge.

The rules of modern warfare had changed; theirs had not.

Under the steady gaze of the Sphinx, and armed with gold-inlaid weapons, the Mameluk army entered the battlefield of Imbaba at 2pm on 21 July 1798. Resplendent as Mameluks always had been in silk and satin robes, they rode on

TWO MAMELUK DYNASTIES

The Arabic name Mameluk, a synonym for slave, means "possessed". There were two Egyptian Mameluk dynasties: the Bahri (1250–1382) were Mongols and Turks recruited as bodyguards by the Ayyubid sultan al-Salih, and they in turn recruited the Burji (1382–1517), mainly Circassians, as their own bodyguards. Their rule over Egypt and Syria included what is now Jordan, Israel, Lebanon and western Saudi Arabia. The Mameluks benefited from a highly organised civil service and judiciary. They achieved great prosperity through trade and commerce which spread out across Africa as far as Guinea and Mali, and as far east as Java.

LEFT: the Mameluks fighting the French in the Battle of the Pyramids.
RIGHT: Mameluk soldiers were known for their sumptuous dress, even on the battlefield.

gold saddles, and carried their personal wealth in money and jewels in their saddlebags. Some 6,000 medieval warriors were confronted by several times their own number, and Napoleon's infantry was backed by modern artillery.

Muslim and French forces had clashed in similar circumstances on the banks of the Nile more than 500 years earlier. On that occasion crusaders led by King Louis IX had squared up to a Syrian army under Saladin (Salah ad-Din ibn Ayyub), the founder of the Ayyubid dynasty that went on to

NAPOLEON WHO?

When Napoleon arrived on the coast of Alexandria, the Mameluk commander, Murad Bey, had never heard of him. The Tuscan consul, Rosetti, put him right.

but the French square-formations did not yield. Riders galloping up close behind piled into the mêlée. Others wheeled and headed straight for the cannons, which blew them to pieces. "The first wild charge having failed to break the squares", wrote Glubb, himself a fine desert commander, "there was nothing else the Mameluks could do but ride from square to square, being shot."

The carnage over, the French broke ranks to scoop booty that must have surpassed their dreams. Only 1,000 Mameluks survived.

create the Mameluk troops. The French were annihilated and, to save his life, Louis was compelled to pay a king's ransom of 1 million gold dinars. Ayyub stayed in his tent throughout the action. It transpired that he was dead, a victim of tuberculosis. The measures taken to conceal his death were indicative of the Mameluks' Achilles heel.

In 1798 the Mameluk commander, Murad Bey, waited until the enemy's infantry was within striking range of his horses and sounded the charge. Mameluk cavalry at full tilt had once overwhelmed even the Mongols, but times had changed. The leading horses crashed into the French infantry with tremendous force

Monopolising the trade route

Conditions had been very different when the Mameluks came to power six centuries earlier. Egypt, then under the Fatimid Arabs, had managed to sit out most of the protracted struggle between Muslims and waves of European crusaders in Asia Minor and on the eastern shores of the Mediterranean. In fact, the country had profited from the turmoil around Baghdad by inheriting, and then monopolising, the lucrative oriental trade route. The resulting prosperity attracted the covetous attention of predators. The crusaders never allowed their ostensibly religious mission to obscure commercial opportunities, but on this occasion they were beaten to Egypt by their illustrious enemy, Nur-ad-Din. The army he sent to occupy Cairo in 1169 included a Kurdish mercenary destined for even greater renown – Saladin.

Kidnapped children

Saladin's bodyguards, conspicuous in yellow tunics, were drawn from the ranks of the first Mameluks. They had been bought, or more likely kidnapped, as children aged from six to 10, from nomadic tribes living on the steppes of Asia Minor and the shores of the Black Sea. Distinctively non-Arab, they grew up to serve as bodyguards.

A Mameluk was expected to fight – and if necessary die – for his patron, though not for the army, the state or even the patron's heir when he died. In the latter event, a Mameluk was at liberty to join another army, or give up soldiering altogether. There were cases of Mameluk soldiers who, upon their retirement, went into business. They could become masters and owners of other Mameluks, and those with units of 10, 100 or 1,000 men bound to them as they were to their patrons were honoured with the appropriate rank. An Emir of a Thousand, who might be an Arab noble or an elevated Mameluk, was the equivalent of a colonel.

A private Mameluk army was essential for anyone with aspirations to power, especially given the Byzantine nature of the struggles between powerful families. Only Mameluks did not have the family or tribal ties that invariably compromised a native soldier's loyalty. In this the Mameluks were comparable to those Nubian soldiers who, at other times in Egypt's history, were employed for similar reasons. They too had a reputation as fierce fighters.

Al-Salah-Ayyub, who used his Mameluk army to such devastating effect against King Louis IX's crusaders, had perfected the system. Of all the boys he imported from various markets, the best were 1,000 Qipchaq Turks whom he installed in a castle on Rawdah, an island opposite Cairo. They became known as Bahri Mameluks, or "white slaves of the river". It was they who, in the odd circumstances of their patron's death in 1249, showed the flaw in a system that turned servants into gaolers.

LEFT: the mighty Saladin, the founder of the Ayyubid dynasty that produced the Mameluks.
RIGHT: a Mameluk soldier in action.

Turan Shah

Ayyub's heir, Turan Shah, was viewed by the Mameluk officers as an intolerable hooligan who drank too much and boasted of plans to promote some dubious Syrian cronies over their heads. Such talk was unwise because he was not protected by the loyalty which had been his father's due. He had only been in office a few months when a Mameluk soldier burst into his tent and ran him through with his sword. A shocked Turan Shah somehow survived and was trying to wade to safety across the Nile when he was overtaken by other Mameluks who had no compunction in finishing him off.

The leaderless Mameluks – who, it seems, had a relatively relaxed attitude towards women – were generally in favour of recognising the sovereignty claims of Ayyub's widowed queen, a former slave-girl named Spray-of-Pearls. Indeed it was she who had drawn up the battle orders while Ayyub lay dead in his tent. But the more conservative Arabs were appalled. "If you have no man, I'll send you one," wrote the Caliph of Baghdad, who remembered Spray-of-Pearls as the slave-girl he had sent to Ayyub as a present.

> ### CULTURAL CENTRE
>
> It was under the Mameluks that Cairo became a cultural centre, and the country a haven for any number of Muslim artists.

consider themselves as free agents. Displaying a cavalier disregard for their former reputation as firm upholders of discipline, they ran amok in Cairo. "This truculent soldiery became a terror to the inhabitants," in the words of one Stanley Lane-Poole, a rare European authority. "They indulged their licence in atrocious acts of violence, pillaged innocent houses, and raided the public baths for women. After Turan Shah's murder," he wrote, "it was but a short step to the throne, and for the next 130 years the colonels of this

The most distinguished Mameluk general, Aktai, offered to lend the arrangement respectability by marrying Spray-of-Pearls. She agreed, with the proviso that he first divorce his existing wife. This he did, but he had no intention of curbing his wandering eye, and Spray-of-Pearls, it transpired, was exceedingly jealous, even though she could barely stand the sight of her new husband. Unsurprisingly this conjugal nightmare ended violently. Spray-of-Pearls murdered Aktai in his bath before she in turn was battered to death with wooden clogs by the slave-girls of Aktai's former wife, who threw her body over the walls of the citadel.

On Ayyub's death the Mameluks began to

celebrated regiment, and their descendants, rapidly succeeded each other as sultans."

Rival factions

Rapid the succession certainly was – on average every five years, and sometimes just weeks. The common people learned how to recognise all the portents of a power struggle, and how to act accordingly – shuttering their shops, rushing home and locking themselves in. Rival Mameluk factions would then open proceedings by attacking the houses of their rivals and carrying off the women and children. Pitched battles in the street brought arrows and spears raining from roofs and windows. "These things were of constant occurrence," Lane-Poole observes, "and the life of the merchant classes of Cairo must have been exciting", as must the lives of the majority, labouring classes. There were occasions when a nimble Mameluk was able to play rival factions off against one another, thus creating some, albeit temporary, stability, but for the most part there was little convincing central authority.

Sultan Baybars al-Bunduqdari

The most energetic of the Mameluk sultans was Baybars al-Bunduqdari. As a boy he was big for his age but had fetched only a trifling £20 be found for them". To ensure that his decrees were observed, he travelled incognito and often alone to every corner of an empire which, owing to his brilliant campaigns against the previously invincible Mongols and the various crusader strongholds, covered a large part of West Asia.

Polo in Cairo and Damascus

Baybars's ability to hold the empire together was facilitated by superb communications. He boasted of roads which enabled him to play polo in Cairo and Damascus in the same week. Urgent matters were expedited with astonishing speed through the use of pigeons – whose beaks and

on the market because of a cataract in one eye. He compensated for this deficiency in a number of ways. He set an example to his men with an exhausting daily routine of martial arts on the training field. On one occasion he swam the Nile both ways wearing a breastplate.

Although he enjoyed a drink, and ultimately probably died of alcohol poisoning in the course of a victory celebration, Baybars al-Bunduqdari closed all wine shops. He also banned brothels and imprisoned prostitutes "until husbands could

LEFT: Mameluk exercises in the square of Murad Bey's palace in Cairo.
ABOVE: a map of Alexandria dating from 1575.

AHEAD OF THEIR TIME

The Mameluks were keen sportsmen. They built a horse-racing course in Cairo and played a robust game of polo. Their records contain apologies for absences from official events due to injuries sustained on the polo field.

Those Mameluks who suffered serious injuries were treated in the Maristan hospital. Completed in 1284, the hospital was way ahead of its time. There were wards for every known disease, laboratories, baths, kitchens and a lecture room for interns. Musicians wandered the wards playing a medley of soothing melodies, and 50 full-time scholars were on hand to recite uplifting passages from the Koran on ways to cope with pain and discomfort.

legs were branded to identify them as carriers of the royal mail. Birds were kept in readiness at key positions, especially frontier posts, within flying range of home bases, at which point messages written on a special kind of thin paper were transferred to another bird for the next stage.

The Circassians

The complexion of Mameluk rule in Egypt changed in 1382 with the rise of the Circassian (or Burji) Mameluks, many of whom were Mongol or Greek. When an emir

LAST OF THE LINE

The Ottomans banned the trade in boys who might otherwise have replenished the Mameluk ranks, so the survivors of the Battle of the Pyramids were the last of the line.

in the next world by building mosques, colleges, hospitals." Compared with their predecessors, however, they lacked military prowess, and the northern parts of the empire were under increasing pressure from, among others, the infamous Turkoman Black Sheep and White Sheep sects.

Coupled with the threat posed by the combined Sheep, were the exploits of the Portuguese explorer Vasco da Gama, who sailed round the southern tip of Africa in 1498 and reached India. The opening of the sea route to India killed the

died – a frequent, and often sudden, event – "the son kept the throne warm whilst the leading nobles fought for the succession; and when the best man won, the 'warming pan' was put away." One poor pawn in this process, Timurbugha, was deposed, reinstated and deposed again all on the same day. The presence of large numbers of Mongols and Greeks meant "it was impossible to allow women to appear in the streets" not even, it seems, on ceremonial occasions.

"Personally," says Lane-Poole, "some of the second line of sultans [Circassian Mameluks] were men of considerable culture... They were also good Muslims, fasted... abstained from wine, made pilgrimages and insured their place

Mameluk monopoly over trade passing between Europe and the East, which had previously provided a lucrative tax revenue on account of its passage through Mameluk territory.

Naval threats

To make matters worse, Portuguese ships entered the Red Sea and began plundering the Egyptian coast just as a naval threat was also growing in the Mediterranean. For the Mameluks, war at sea was beyond comprehension, and beneath their dignity. And they did not have the timber that would have enabled them to build ships. The deserts that had protected Egypt's borders for so long were suddenly inadequate.

Within five years of da Gama's historic voyage, the Mameluk administration was all but bankrupt. All along the Nile, the anarchic tendencies of the Mameluks were exacerbated by the sultan's inability to pay them.

The Battle of Chaldiran

The end was brought closer by the Battle of Chaldiran, fought between the Ottomans and Persians in 1514. The Ottoman army relied on its Janissaries who, like the Mameluks, were foreign boys reared as fighters. The Janissaries tended to be kidnapped Christians who were compelled to "take the turban". Although the

the sultan!" he cried. "Let me go somewhere else. Choose another sultan!"

Qansuh, then 76, knew his duty, however, and after numerous insults – the heads of friends and relatives being delivered to him in baskets and so on – he led his grumbling army north to engage the Ottomans in Syria. The Mameluks went into action with one of their thundering charges. They were acquitting themselves well when Qansuh was convulsed by a stroke. Paralysed on one side, and with his mouth hanging open, he tried to drink some water and fell off his horse. Officers ran to his assistance but he was already dead. Almost at

Janissaries had developed infantry tactics to unprecedented levels of effectiveness, the Ottoman triumph was nevertheless a dazzling surprise. Unfortunately for the Mameluks, the victorious Ottomans were now free to give them their undivided attention.

The venerable Sultan Qansuh al Ghori, plagued by bankruptcy and mutinous young Mameluks, stripped his palace of its treasures to pay the arrears owed to the Mameluks, but they merely asked for more. "I never wanted to be

---

LEFT: Mameluk tombs, Cairo.
ABOVE: Muhammed Ali had the last of the Mameluks massacred, after inviting them to the Citadel.

BAD LUCK PLAYS A PART

In September 1502, the impoverished Egyptian sultan managed with the greatest difficulty to scrape together 12,000 dinars to calm Mameluk tempers. The money was sent under guard to Cairo on a mule. On entering the gates of the citadel, the mule was stolen and the cash was never recovered.

The sultan had no more luck when it was decided that, in the name of modernisation, the Mameluks ought at least to look into the possibility of equipping the army with artillery of the type favoured by European armies. However, at the first test firing of guns cast in Egypt, they all disintegrated.

once, the Ottoman army swept over the position and his body was lost among the casualties.

The Ottoman leader sent a note to Qansuh's successor "If you do not submit," he threatened, "I will come to Egypt and kill all the Turks [he considered the Mameluks "Turks", whereas his own subjects were "Ottomans"] and rip open the belly of every pregnant woman." Not for nothing was he known as Saleem the Grim. The ensuing battle in Cairo was a desperate affair with no quarter given. The streets were said to have been littered with the headless bodies of Mameluks and Ottomans alike.

Qansuh's successor, the young Toman Bey,

resisted fiercely and, rather than accept defeat, retired north to continue a guerrilla campaign. Before long he was caught and paraded through Cairo on a packhorse (in itself an insult to Mameluks, who bred and rode magnificent horses) on his way to the gallows. He recited the first chapter of the Koran three times, turned to the hangman and said: "Do your work."

End of the empire

The Mameluk Empire was formally ended by Toman's execution in 1517 but, of course, there were still Mameluks around when Napoleon invaded in 1798. It seems that about 5,000 Mameluks survived the Ottoman takeover.

Their rehabilitation began with the restoration of their right to appear armed on horseback. With a substantial empire to the north, though, the Ottomans had overreached themselves in Egypt, which was in a chaotic state. The pasha appointed to run the country was increasingly grateful for the Mameluks, who were as willing as ever to provide loyal mercenary services.

Egypt moved further and further away from the focus of Suleiman the Magnificent's titanic struggle with the Habsburg Empire in Europe. "By the 18th century," writes H. Wood Jarvis, "the pasha had grown to be a cipher and the Mameluke Governor of Cairo... was the real master of the land. Disputes between rival beys [as former sultans came to be known] continued as before the Turkish conquest."

The fatal charge

The Ottoman Empire went into a steep decline after Suleiman's death, and a succession of French kings cast their covetous eyes over Egypt. The French invasion had to wait, however, for the revolutionary zeal of the young Napoleon. The French army landed 38,000 men at Alexandria on 1 July 1798. The elderly Ibrahim Bey had little choice but to ask his Mameluk associate, Murad Bey, if the Mameluks could be organised to resist them. It was in this context, then, that at 2pm on 21 July and under the gaze of the Sphinx, Murad Bey sounded the fatal charge. It wasn't long after the Battle of the Pyramids that the French were thrown out of Egypt by the British. Britain was not yet interested in running the country, so the Ottomans resumed control, reasserting their presence with a garrison which consisted mainly of Albanian units, including a certain Muhammed Ali.

Ali seized power in 1805 – Europe was preoccupied with the Napoleonic wars and not inclined to intervene. Only the Mameluks opposed Ali. In 1811 the future "Father of Egypt" indicated that he was willing to listen to their views and they accepted his invitation to a meeting in Cairo. The assembled Mameluk princes entered the citadel and were filing down one of the narrow streets when the way ahead was blocked. Before they understood what was happening, they were butchered to a man. ❑

LEFT: Muhammed Ali, the father of modern Egypt.
RIGHT: Muhammed Ali and his followers assembled outside the Citadel.

THE FRENCH ON THE NILE

Napoleon nursed grand plans for Egypt. He wanted to oust the Mameluks,
turn Cairo into a Paris on the Nile and to conduct an exhaustive cultural survey

Countless battles have been fought along or for control of the Nile, usually both, but history's "official" Battle of the Nile was actually neither. It was a naval battle fought between Britain and France in Aboukir Bay, near Alexandria, on the night of 1 August 1798, and although it dragged Egypt out of centuries of political hibernation, the Egyptians themselves were not involved in the fighting and probably did not much care who won. In the event, the result was a resounding British victory which came close to ending Napoleon's promising career before it had properly begun.

Except by his own messianic standards, Napoleon was already a precociously successful general at only 28 years of age; he had conquered most of Italy and been compared with Hannibal. Nevertheless, he was not quite ready to proceed with his overwhelming objective, which was the invasion of England. India, Britain's imperial crown snatched from France 50 years earlier, was also high on his list but not within reach either. Egypt, in the middle, was perfect. To found a French colony there, he predicted, would make the old enemy England "tremble for the safety of India" and, while it trembled, he could nip back to Paris "and give the enemy its death-blow".

An historical romantic

Under centuries of Mameluk rule, Egypt (like Greece, also part of the Ottoman Empire) had become an obscure, virtually closed society, the neglected monuments largely buried under drifting sand. As a junior officer, however, Napoleon had devoured scholarly works on the East, his interest spread evenly between erudite mathematical theories about the dimensional ratios of the pyramids and the conjugal tricks attributed to oriental women. In Milan, he had made a bee-line for the famous library's

collection of such books, many of which were later found to contain scribbled margin notes made in his handwriting.

He was the supreme historical romantic. Comparisons with Hannibal were satisfying but insufficient: he preferred to think of himself as another Alexander the Great who would liber-

ate noble Egyptians from abominable servitude under the Mameluks, a military oligarchy of self-perpetuating slaves. Under Napoleon's guidance, the oppressed Egyptians would throb with the French Revolution's clarion call for Liberty, Fraternity and Equality.

Financing his campaign

Napoleon's Egyptian campaign was to be financed by unadorned piracy. To top up a fortune in gold and diamonds stolen in Switzerland, his fleet of 13 ships of the line, 14 frigates and hundreds of transports called at Malta, the refuge of the once glorious crusader Order of the Knights of St John. Their glory had faded

LEFT: *The Coloured Monuments of Egypt* by the 19th-century French painter C. L. F. Panckoucke.
RIGHT: Napoleon Bonaparte.

but they retained the priceless plunder of their campaigns, including the Jerusalem treasures. With the collusion of French knights attached to the Order, Napoleon annexed Malta and popped the treasure into his war chest.

The invasion

A wretched sailor, Napoleon was thoroughly sick all the way to Egypt. The fleet arrived off the beach resort in the Bay of Agami and ploughed through violent seas in small landing boats. About 30 troops drowned, and Napoleon himself crawled ashore so wet and exhausted that he passed out on the beach. On coming

round, he went to the head of the column and plodded into the sand in the general direction of Alexandria. His orders to the fleet were to find a suitable mooring and wait.

Bedouin manning a coastal fort put up only token resistance, but even so two French generals were knocked out by stones that bounced down on their heads. The army as a whole fared no more auspiciously on a horrendous, waterless march to Cairo in suffocating heat after taking Alexandria. The Mameluk defenders preparing themselves in the Cairo Citadel imagined that military matters were much as they had been in the Middle Ages, when they had held their own against the crusaders.

After three days, the French caught first sight of the enemy, a cavalry detachment which Murad had personally brought down the Nile from Cairo in armed *feluccas*. The French troops must have wondered what to make of them. They were mounted on magnificent horses decked out for battle. Typically, the soldiers themselves were resplendent in yellow turbans, streaming robes worn over a coat of chain mail, billowing red pantaloons and matching slippers.

Each man had a pair of pistols tucked into an embroidered shawl around his waist, a mace, a scimitar and a carbine. The only disappointment for the amazed French was, perhaps, that Murad failed to live up to the rumour that he went into battle on a white camel. The French for their part were in thick serge uniforms designed for Europe, although at the moment of this first encounter many had stripped and were cooling off in the waters of the Nile.

The Mameluks broke off quickly on this

FITTING IN WITH THE LOCALS

While the *savants* prepared to immerse themselves in Egyptian antiquity and the study of exotic creatures like the hippopotamus, Napoleon hastened to assure the sceptical Egyptians that, as a product of French revolutionary atheism, he was above the religious differences between Christian and Muslim. "When I am in France I am a Christian," he declared, "when in Egypt a Muhammedan." He tried to drive the point home by appearing in public in Arab costume, sitting cross-legged at banquets to eat with his fingers, and advising his guests to give equal weight to the Koran and Thomas Paine's *The Rights of Man*. As a concession to the troops, though, he sent an urgent

shopping list to Paris: comedians, ballet dancers, marionettes, 100 prostitutes, 200,000 pints of brandy and one million pints of wine.

As a gesture of cultural reciprocity, bemused Egyptians were expected to wear cockades in their turbans. Although Napoleon had issued orders that his troops were to respect the mosques and refrain from looting, the hands-off policy was impossible to enforce. "Cairo has become a second Paris," one Egyptian complained. "Women go about shamelessly with the French, intoxicating drinks are publicly sold and things are committed of which the Lord of Heaven would not approve."

occasion to mull over the experience of infantry who kneeled to fire muskets while the artillery kept busy over their shoulders. The second encounter a few days later was a combined operation: the armed *feluccas* challenging the gunboats which were keeping pace with the French advance while the wheeling cavalry tried to cancel out the unexpected resilience of the French square with mounting recklessness. The casualties were rather higher than before on both sides, but the action

grand entrance into the city to a fanfare of trumpets, he installed himself in a sumptuous Mameluk palace and began to draft his orders.

MAMELUK OUTRAGE

The first reaction of the Mameluk commander, Murad Bey, to news of a French invasion was outrage. "His eyes became red and fire devoured his entrails," but he soon calmed down and looked forward to slicing up Frenchmen "like watermelons".

Cultural survey

The French contingent included 167 intellectuals and scholars, the "living encyclopaedia" whose task, put simply, was to learn and record as much about Egypt and its ancient monuments as they possibly could. Their number included every conceivable discipline from astronomy to zool-

still served as no more than a rehearsal for the monumental Battle of the Pyramids that occurred a week later.

The dénouement at Imbaba – "the last great cavalry charge of the Middle Ages" – is referred to in the Mameluk chapter of this book *(see page 79)*. The Mameluk survivors retired into the desert to fight, as we shall see, a running battle along 1,130 km (700 miles) of the Nile, but Napoleon's victory gave him Cairo and an opportunity to put into practice the idealistic side of his mission to Egypt. Having made a

LEFT: Murad Bey, commander of the Mameluks.
ABOVE: a gathering of the *savants*.

ogy, and none was more colourful – or destined for greater fame – than Dominique Vivant Denon, impoverished minor aristocrat, failed lawyer, temporary diplomat, antiques dealer, archaeologist, interior decorator, street artist, pornographer, friend of Voltaire and also, more relevant to his inclusion in the party, of Josephine, Napoleon's wife.

The battle of Aboukir Bay

Exactly one month after reaching Egypt, the French fleet was still lying at anchor in Aboukir Bay and on 1 August Sir Horatio (later Lord) Nelson of the British Royal Navy, having searched the Mediterranean high and low, at last caught up with it. He wasted no time, sailing straight at the ships, many of whose crew were ashore. at the time

After a ferocious battle lasting all night, the French fleet was all but destroyed. Worst of all, *L'Orient,* the flagship containing all the stolen Swiss gold and Knights of St John treasure, blew up and sank. Admiral de Breuys went down with it, as did the son of an officer immortalised in the poem which opens with "The boy stood on the burning deck". In the

> **THOROUGHLY SHOCKED**
>
> Denon made excursions to see the Great Pyramid. He also had a look at Cairo's nightlife, describing the dancing girls as displaying "a gross and indecent expression of the ecstacy of the senses.

original version, by a Mrs Hemens, it continues with "when all but he had fled", and so on. British Royal Navy ratings ever since have provided many variations on the original, most of them unprintable.

Bonaparte had no way of knowing about the disaster for another week. He had been out riding when the news reached Cairo. A companion described how he dismounted, walked away and was heard to mutter. "So the navy has gone... Is this the end?" The entry in Denon's diary reads: "On the morning of July 31, 1798, the French were masters of Egypt, Corfu and Malta; thirty vessels of the line united these possessions with France." "On the following day," he continued, "the Army of the East was imprisoned in its own conquest."

Implementing plan B

For someone cut off from home and penniless to boot, Napoleon seemed to bounce back with remarkable fortitude. "Oh well," he remarked, "this upset will urge us on to greater things. Egypt used to be the centre of civilisation. We shall have to recreate the Egyptian Empire..."

A letter to his brother Joseph in France paints a rather different picture. "In two months it is possible that I shall be back in France, so find me a house where I may spend the winter alone. I am sick of humanity: I need solitude and isolation. Greatness wearies me, emotion chills me, my passion for glory has vanished. At twenty-nine years of age I am worn out. I mean henceforth to live in a country house, but never will I share it with her. I have no more reason to live." The "her" in question was of course Josephine. He had just heard the latest from Paris – Josephine, in the words of a popular song, "was at it again".

Murad, the fugitive Mameluk commander, heard about the loss of the fleet too and took it as the cue for a guerrilla campaign. In order to repair the damage to his military standing, Napoleon felt he needed something more spectacular than a counter-insurgency campaign against a slippery foe. The conquest of Syria appealed, and he decided that one of his generals, Desaix, could look after Murad and at the same time escort the team of *savants* up the Nile.

> **PARIS OF THE EAST?**
>
> After the disaster of Aboukir Bay, Napoleon had no idea how long he would be stuck in Egypt, so he began pondering over how he could smarten up the country. He thought of relaying the streets of Cairo along Parisian lines, ordered his engineers to dust off plans for a Suez canal, bewildered the locals with a bureaucracy that sought to replace bribery with taxation, stopped people from burying their dead outside their houses, and insisted on every household hanging a lamp in their doorway at night. One of his *savants* laid on a demonstration of balloon air travel and introduced farmers to the efficacy of the windmill.

Desaix's Expedition up the Nile

The expedition assembled for the Nile trip consisted of 3,000 infantry, 1,000 cavalry, about 100 guns travelling by boat and, where necessary, by camel train. "The scenes they saw along the Nile were not quite the same as those we see now," says Alan Moorehead *(The Blue Nile)*. "…The villages, though smaller, have not altered much in the intervening years, but the ancient temples were then very different. Many were half-buried in sand, and successive gen-

> **FIDDLING THE FRENCH**
>
> Egyptian merchants were pleased to find that the French soldiers paid their asking prices. Gleeful bakers produced a special French loaf which was smaller than normal and contained a fair proportion of sand.

record the phantasmagoria and sometimes provided a squad of soldiers while Denon fell behind the column to make the sketches that electrified the 24 volumes of *La Description de L'Egypte,* a runaway success when eventually they were published between 1809 and 1813.

More than once Bedouin looking for stragglers opened fire as Denon sat at his easel. Moorehead describes the interruptions: "No sooner would he begin a sketch or start to trace an inscription than the trumpet

erations of Arabs built mud-brick houses among the crumbling walls, throwing out their rubbish everywhere. No one cared for these old columns and statues, no one could read the hieroglyphics on the walls. The mummies hidden in their hundreds in underground caves were of interest solely because the resin with which they were impregnated could be extracted and sold in the Cairo market. The fallen obelisk was simply another rock."

The military did their best to accommodate the *savants* in their attempt to absorb and

would sound the advance, and he would have to scramble back on to his horse and hurry after the others.

"It was intensely frustrating. He was like the enthusiast who, having come miles to see a painting, is turned out of the museum by the closing bell – except that here he never knew whether he, or any other trained observer, would ever be able to come back again."

Murad dropped back along the river all the way to Philae, south of Aswan. The longer the French lines of communication were stretched, the easier it was for him to double back through the empty desert and cut them. Thieves entered the French camp at night and even got away

---

LEFT: Dominique Vivant Denon, one of the *savants.*
ABOVE: Denon measuring the Sphinx.

with Desaix's horse. He quickened the pace of the campaign and there was less time than ever for Denon to pause in places like Dendarah, Esna, Edfu and Kom Ombo.

At Luxor, however, the ordinary soldiers were so impressed by the temples that they spontaneously stopped, grounded their arms and went off to do a bit of sight-seeing. Desaix and Denon themselves rode around the temple site together, little expecting to come under a hail of javelins and stones from troglodytes who were living in the

NUBIAN NUDES

Denon thought the Nubians exceptionally barbarous – the men went round stark naked while unmarried women wore no more than strips of leather "to tranquilise all the alarms of modesty".

mishes and complaints to Napoleon that "we are naked, without shoes, without anything…" that Desaix felt he had the situation under control.

Denon returned to Cairo loaded with drawings and notes but also with some disappointments: he had set his heart on capturing a baby crocodile to take home, but had failed.

Added to Denon's wonderful tales was the excitement created by the discovery of the Rosetta Stone in the Delta. Scholars realised the Greek inscription at the bottom of the stone was proba-

ruins and resented the intrusion. "A war with gnomes," Denon snorted.

The column reached Aswan, 955 km (587 miles) from Cairo, on 1 February 1799. Murad and the Mameluks had melted mysteriously away beyond the First Cataract and, if it was true that Sesostris III, a Middle Kingdom Pharaoh, had once cleared a passage through the barrier for his punitive expeditions into Nubia, the French could not find it. The French force rested in the town and Denon had more time to look around. The inhabitants of the ruins, however, were no more welcoming than the troglodyte gnomes of Luxor had been.

It was not until July, after any number of skir-

bly a translation of the hieroglyphs above, but of course it would be some years before the code was finally cracked (see page 303).

Distractions overseas

News of Napoleon was not so satisfying. His expedition to Syria had been a disaster, and there was disturbing intelligence of an imminent Turkish landing at Alexandria. Murad had reappeared in the vicinity of Cairo and had reportedly climbed the Great Pyramid to signal his arrival to his wife Fatima who, having paid a colossal ransom for her freedom, was on friendly terms with Napoleon. He was furious when a French soldier beat up her chief eunuch.

Murad shadowed at a discreet distance as Napoleon led his men to meet the Turkish threat. The Battle of Aboukir was some sort of consolation for the loss of the French fleet and the setbacks in Syria. The Turks were driven into the sea with huge losses. One of them, actually an Albanian tobacconist turned mercenary, was extremely lucky to be pulled out of the water by Napoleon's *bête noire*, the British admiral Sir Sidney Smith, who was watching from a small boat. The rescued man was Muhammed Ali, and it was he who would drive the final nail into the Mameluk coffin. In the meantime, Murad saw that no further help

saviour, there was only one man for the job.

His real destination when he left Cairo was kept secret even from his travelling companions, who included Denon, several of the *savants* and a captured Mameluk whom Napoleon planned to exhibit in France. He promised La Bellilote, a woman who had helped him forget Josephine, that he would be back in a fortnight. Officially, they were embarking on an inspection trip of the Lower Nile, but in Alexandria the passengers transferred to two French frigates for the voyage to France. A month after his arrival home, he was the dictator.

His generals were left behind in Egypt to

would be forthcoming from the Turks and he slipped back into the desert.

Returning home

Napoleon's satisfaction was short-lived. The news from France was terrible: political chaos in Paris, an army retreat in Italy, his garrison in Malta blockaded. His incorrigible opportunism, however, told him that the débâcle could be manipulated to advantage. If France needed a

LEFT: *The Cairo Revolt*, 1798. Detail from a painting by Anne Louis Girodet-Trioson.
ABOVE: attack by Turkish gunboats in the *Battle of Aboukir*, a painting by the Reverend Cooper Willyams.

cope with new Turkish threats as best they could. In 1801, however, Britain was in full cry against France and sent troops to bolster the Turks. There was some French resistance in Alexandria, but Cairo fell without a struggle. Britain offered the French transport back to France but at a price: the Rosetta Stone and one or two other interesting artefacts.

Having got to know the French and deciding that, on the whole, they preferred the Mameluks, the Egyptian population wondered what would happen next. The British did not try to persuade Egypt that they were there for the country's own good. On the contrary, their presence was just a means to an end. ❏

THE BRITISH ON THE NILE

Queen Victoria's influence in northeast Africa was increased by the intrepid leadership of three men – Sir Samuel Baker, General Gordon and Lord Kitchener

An Egyptian nationalist tract at the end of the 19th century stated: "The power which becomes the absolute master of the Nile Valley becomes virtual sovereign of Africa... the Holy Land and the Red Sea. The Suez Canal is an integral part of Egypt and commands the route to India, China and Australia... England already controls the Mediterranean and it is vital to the Powers of Europe that she should not command also the trade routes of Africa... Thus the British occupation of Egypt is a menace..."

Fifty years earlier Lord Palmerston, the British Prime Minister, had equated Egypt with an inn on the road between Britain and India. There was no wish to own the inn, he declared, merely to ensure that it was "well-kept, always accessible" and able to furnish the traveller with a suitable standard of "mutton-chops and post-horses".

Lord Cromer, the symbol of the British occupation of Egypt, produced his own refinement that Britain did not govern Egypt, it only governed the governors of Egypt. The mechanics of government were convoluted. Supreme power lay ostensibly with the Sultan of Turkey, the head of the Ottoman Empire. On the ground, it was exercised by the Khedive, one of the Muhammed Ali dynasty and as such not an Egyptian but a Turkish-Albanian who usually could not speak Arabic. British army personnel and civil servants in Egypt were officially on loan to, and paid by, the Khedive, but the Khedive took his orders from the likes of Lord Cromer, whose title (Resident, Consul etc) was anything but Governor.

The occupation

British troops occupied Egypt in 1882, and government records show that in the following quarter century British statesmen said solemnly that Britain had no interest in having – and

would shortly be leaving – Egypt on no fewer than 72 occasions. The reason for landing in 1882 was to put down on behalf of Turkey the Arabi nationalist revolt, in which the Khedive himself was also to some extent implicated.

The justification for British involvement in Egypt was very flexible, and in the 1860s it bent

smoothly to the cause of gaining some international respectability for the Khedive Ismail. He was expecting half of Europe's royalty for the grand opening of the Suez Canal and it could do him no harm to be associated with a crusade against slavery. "My country is no longer in Africa; we are now part of Europe. It is therefore natural for us to abandon our former ways..."

It seemed not to matter that Ismail himself was a massive slave-owner or that he had given state contracts to slave-hunters in the Sudan. There was no doubting Ismail's sincerity in one respect, and that was his willingness to let the anti-slavery drive add large chunks of new territory to his pseudo-empire.

LEFT: detail of George Arnold's painting of the explosion of the French gunship *L'Orient* in the Battle of the Nile.
RIGHT: British troops keep watch on the Nile.

Anti-slavery mission

Ismail met the man he wanted to lead his anti-slavery campaign at a fancy dress ball. He was Sir Samuel Baker, the worthy Victorian explorer whom we have met in the section of this book dealing with the search for the source of the Nile. Ismail offered Baker £40,000 for a four-year contract, the title "Pasha", and virtually unlimited expenses. Within a year Baker had assembled one of the most amazing armadas ever to sail up the Nile: nine steamers and 55 sailing boats to carry a force of 1,700 men, including 200 cavalry, two artillery batteries and a personal bodyguard in scarlet uniforms and

fezzes whom he called the Forty Thieves. The Egyptian contingent among the ordinary troops was an unknown element, mostly comprising criminals released from prison for the purpose. The fleet was accompanied by hundreds of camels loaded with extra equipment. The intention was to establish a base at Gondokoro, a place that Baker knew and hated from his explorer days.

The armada refloated

The armada got only as far as the infernal Sudd. The channel that nowadays enables paddle steamers to negotiate the jungle of swamp, weed and papyrus in three days did not exist. The boats reached a point where they could neither advance nor retreat, added to which the Nile fell suddenly so that they were all left hard aground. Baker ordered his men out of the boats to pack sandbags sufficient to build a dam across the river. Five days later, and at the sound of a bugle, the sacks were dropped in rows between piles and the boats were refloated.

Thereafter, things got worse. While Baker had once been able to overcome tribal suspicion that he was just another slaver himself by donning a tweed suit, the hostility of the tribes and, of course, the Arab traders was implacable. He came under a hail of poisoned arrows at Gondokoro, and before long 1,100 of his men, mostly the jailbirds, deserted with 30 of his vessels. The Forty Thieves and his Sudanese troops, however, proved loyal and efficient. Baker annexed the country around Gondokoro in the name of the Khedive and called it Equatoria. With greatly reduced forces, Baker was nevertheless able to mount operations deep into what is now Uganda. They frequently saw action, but Baker persevered until his contract had been fulfilled to the letter; slavery was overcome.

"A paternal government extended its protection through lands hitherto a field for anarchy and slavery… The White Nile, for a distance of 1,600 miles from Khartoum to Central Africa, was cleansed from the abomination of a traffic which had hitherto sullied its waters. Every cloud had passed away, and the term of my office expired in peace and sunshine. In this result, I humbly traced God's blessing."

Gordon's turn

Baker's campaign against the slave trade was in reality nowhere near as successful as he

THE SLAVE TRADE

In the 1860s the slave trade in the Nile region was bigger and more profitable than it had ever been. It was practised in and around the Sudan, vast areas of which were owned by the Khedive himself, who had inherited them from Muhammed Ali. The Khedive had also been responsible for issuing state contracts to slave-hunters. In total around 15,000 licensed Arabs took some 50,000 slaves out of the Upper Nile every year. The traders ranged from individuals with a couple of donkeys to the commanders of large private armies with rights to anyone they could capture in areas as large as 233,000 sq. km (90,000 sq. miles).

believed (it simply moved away from the river), nor was Ismail satisfied with his contribution to the size of the Egyptian empire.

Casting around for another European to succeed Baker, his eyes lit on Colonel Charles Gordon. He was already a legendary figure, a pious and fearless soldier seemingly indifferent to the normal distractions and comforts of life. He proved his eccentricity at the outset of his dealings with Ismail: offered £10,000 a year, Gordon would not accept more than £2,000. His brief was to establish a chain of forts down the White Nile from Gondokoro to the source in Buganda, annex Buganda and start a steamer service on Lakes Albert and Victoria.

Gordon was fortunate to find an open channel through the Sudd which enabled him to reach Gondokoro, 1,600 km (1,000 miles) south of Khartoum, after a voyage lasting 25 days. He was dismayed by what he found: in a year, the discipline of Baker's regime had degenerated under Egyptian officials into anarchy. The troops were paid not in money but in spirits and in slave-girls shipped from Khartoum. Gordon dismissed the Egyptian officials; their European replacements, however, suffered terribly from malaria and the heat.

According to Charles Chaille-Long, an American who fell out with Gordon, the latter was frequently depressed, sitting in his tent "with a hatchet and a flag placed at the door to indicate that he was not to be disturbed for any reason whatever; until at last the cloud would lift, the signals would be removed, and the Governor would reappear, brisk and cheerful."

Whether or not Gordon sulked in his tent, with or without the purported brandy and soda, he tackled his assignment with prodigious energy. Where the river proved to be totally unnavigable, he had his ships dismantled and carried around the obstacle piece by piece, and in this way he was eventually able to put two ships on to the waters of Lake Albert, although for the moment Lake Victoria remained out of reach. The forts he built, a dozen altogether, formed a chain stretching 960 km (600 miles)

LEFT: the British taking tea on top of the pyramids.
RIGHT: Ismail Pasha Ayyub, the corrupt Governor-General who preceded General Gordon.

"CHINESE" GORDON

Colonel Charles George "Chinese" Gordon's nickname derived from his former glittering military exploits in China.

from Fashoda almost to the Equator. After two-and-a-half years, perhaps because he felt he could achieve no more in the circumstances, Gordon resigned.

The circumstances which defeated Gordon were associated with Ismail Pasha Ayyub, the Egyptian Governor-General who presided over a system of bribery and extortion that, according to Alan Moorehead, was "wonderfully complete, even by Egyptian standards." Barely a month after Gordon's return to England – long enough for him to be recommended

for the post of Governor of Bulgaria – he received a telegram from the Khedive Ismail pleading with him to return as Governor-General of the whole Sudan.

The man he was to replace, Ismail Pasha Ayyub, did not surrender his position gracefully, although it was his sister who smashed every window in the Governor-General's palace in Khartoum and slashed the furniture to bits. Compared with the kind of meal the outgoing Governor-General had laid on, Gordon stipulated that lunch would last no longer than 10 minutes. He lived alone in the palace, "a strange little unpretending man with eyes like blue diamonds."

Gordon Pasha

Gordon worked tirelessly for the benefit of his charges. A channel was cut through the Sudd and his improvements in Khartoum moved an Italian to say that the city reminded him of Milan. His work in and around Khartoum was only the tip of his labours; he was forever disappearing on a camel to settle some distant dispute personally and often alone. He organised punitive expeditions against the Arab slave-lords; one alone resulted in the release of 10,000 slaves. He

GORDON MALIGNED

"Some thought him mad," the pro-Egyptian Wilfred Blunt wrote of General Gordon, "others that he drank, and others again that he was a religious fanatic."

appointed Europeans to administer the various provinces that made up his domain.

Gordon himself was especially concerned by news from Cairo, where it was becoming apparent that the Khedive's well-known financial difficulties were assuming absurd proportions and that his European creditors had run out of patience. In June 1879, Ismail was deposed, his last act being to scoop up what cash was left in the Treasury, about £3 million, and sail into exile in his yacht.

"Do not fret about Ismail Pasha," Gordon wrote, "he is a philosopher and has plenty of money. He played high stakes and lost... I am one of those he fooled but I bear him no grudge. It is a blessing for Egypt that he is gone." In July, Gordon himself resigned his Governor-Generalship, and few people among the Anglo-French administrators who were trying to untangle the country's financial mess were honestly sorry.

Rebellion breaks out

The Arabi revolt that followed *(see page 113)* was the manifestation of long-dormant Egyptian nationalism, although few commentators admitted this at the time. The British government asked the Ottoman Sultan to send in a Turkish general to restore discipline in the Egyptian army. The Sultan despatched Dervish Pasha, an aristocrat with experience in handling rebellious Ottoman minorities, who instantly compromised his authority by accepting a £50,000 bribe from Tewfik, the new Khedive, but in any case he was too late.

A serious riot in the streets of Alexandria led to the death of at least 50 Europeans and several hundred Egyptians. Agitators were reported to be roaming the streets with the cry "O Muslims, kill the Christians." On 11 July 1882, the British Navy bombarded Alexandria; on 13 September the Egyptian army was defeated in an hour or two at the battle of Tel al-Kebir.

Rebellion had been brewing in the Sudan, too, first against the Egyptian presence and then decisively against the prospect of rule, direct or indirect, by the occupying British. The unrest centred on a curious figure who had emerged on Abba Island in the Nile, about 240 km (150 miles) south of Khartoum.

Puritan values

Muhammed Ahmed Ibn al-Sayyid Abdullah, the Mahdi, claimed to be the Prophet Muhammed reincarnate. His family background was uncertain, but everyone who met him agreed with the observations of an Austrian priest who commented on an appearance that was "strangely fascinating... a man of strong constitution, very dark complexion, and his face always wore a pleasant smile." Nor was there any doubt about the Mahdi's ability to inspire his followers. As the British forces were landing at the Suez Canal, he was laying siege to Al Obeid, a sizeable town with a formidable Egyptian garrison.

Al Obeid fell to the Mahdi, and from his new residence in the town he issued a proclamation: "Let all show penitence before God, and abandon all bad and forbidden habits, such as the degrading acts of the flesh, the use of wine and tobacco, lying, bearing false witness, disobedience to parents, brigandage, the non-restitution of goods to others, the clapping of hands, dancing, improper signs with the eyes, tears and lamentations at the bed of the dead, slanderous language, calumny, and the company of strange women. Clothe your women in a decent way, and let them be careful not to speak to unknown persons. All those who do not pay attention to these principles disobey

force was dangerously low on water supplies in the ferocious heat.

This ramshackle troop was wandering south of Al Obeid when it was set upon by some 50,000 of the Mahdi's supporters. Only 200 or 300 survived, and with that the whole of Sudan erupted. The mood in England changed from a reluctance to become involved to the feeling that the whole Nile was threatened and someone would have to do something about it. "If you want some out-of-the-way piece of work to be done in an unknown and barbarous country," Sir C. Rivers Wilson remarked to the British Prime Minister, "Gordon would be your man."

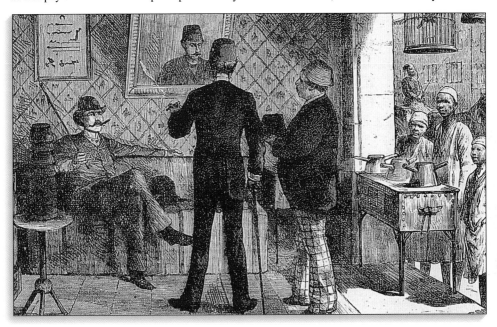

God and His Prophet, and they shall be punished in accordance with the law."

The Egyptian government's attempt to bring the Mahdi to heel was a disaster. A force sent up the Nile to deal with him looked good on paper: about 10,000 troops under a competent British Indian Army officer, Colonel William Hicks. In reality, some of the soldiers were jailbirds, transported in chains, others were wearing chain armour and exotic helmets, the guides turned out not to know the way, and the entire

LEFT: riots in Alexandria in the 1880s prompted rigorous search-patrols by British marines.
ABOVE: a British gentleman trying on a fez.

Mahdi and Gordon

In semi-retirement, Gordon was restless and was looking for action. Jobs in India, China, South Africa and Mauritius had not suited him, and he had gone off to Palestine for Biblical studies. He was on the point of accepting the Belgian king's offer of the governorship of the Congo when the Sudan blew up.

The British government's instructions were not to conquer the Sudan, merely to evacuate the (Egyptian) government that looked as if it might soon be trapped there. Gordon left the Cabinet Office and went directly to the railway station for the journey to Egypt. He was about to board the train when he remembered he had only a few shillings in his pocket. Sir Garnet Wolseley, one of the ministers seeing him off, fished in his pocket for change which, not amounting to much, he topped up with his pocket-watch and chain.

Appointed Governor-General again, Gordon went to work at characteristic full speed. On arrival in Khartoum, he ordered the city gates to be flung open and invited anyone who wished to join the Mahdi to do so. Prisoners of war, debtors and men who had long served their sentences were set free from the city jail. Records

> ### SHARP TACTICS
>
> During the siege of Khartoum, Gordon sprinkled the southern flank liberally with spiky "crows' feet" and broken bottles to deter the bare-footed Arabs.

of old debts were burned. He appointed a "Council of twelve Notables, Arabs" to help him with administration, and started to plan how to "smash up" the Mahdi.

Gordon bombarded Sir Evelyn Baring, his superior in Cairo, with telegrams, 20 to 30 a day, which provided a running and often contradictory commentary on the ideas cascading through his mind. Recoiling under the weight of these telegrams, Baring adopted a policy of allowing them to pile up during the day and then, when he had finished other business, going through them all at once. The patent contradictions cancelled one another out, some were answered, and a summary was forwarded to London.

"I am most anxious to help and support you in every way," Baring telegraphed to Gordon after wading through a particularly large and contradictory pile, "but I find it very difficult to understand what it is you want. I think your best plan will be to reconsider the whole question carefully, and then state to me in one telegram what it is you recommend, in order that I can, if necessary, obtain the instructions of Her Majesty's government."

Not even Baring, however, welcomed the day when the telegraph went dead. The tribes north of Khartoum had risen for the Mahdi. Khartoum, and Gordon, were suddenly cut off, and for 10 months – from March 1884 until January in the following year – the wire was silent. The only messages received from Gordon were written on tiny scraps of paper smuggled out of the city by native runners.

Under siege

Khartoum was besieged by about 30,000 Arabs, but two sides of it were protected by the White and Blue Niles which kept snipers out of range. The garrison in Omdurman fort guarded the northern approach; the southern, facing open desert, had a deep trench which ran for 6 km (4 miles) between the branches of the river. He could send out raiding parties to bring in cattle and maize, and his boats could sail up and down the river with relative impunity. On 22 March, Mahdi envoys were admitted to Gordon's palace to ask whether he would like to become a Mahdi follower and to offer him the necessary costume. Gordon made his response clear by throwing the garment to the ground.

Nevertheless, Gordon's predicament caused considerable consternation in London. "It is alarming," Queen Victoria declared to one of her ministers. "General Gordon is in danger; you are bound to try and save him… you have incurred fearful responsibility." The cry was taken up at mass meetings, and prayers were said in churches. The Foreign Office dithered, instructing Cairo to pass on a message to Gordon to the effect that troops would not be sent to Khartoum and that he ought to abandon while he could. If he chose to stay, "he should state to us the cause and intention with which he so continues." Gordon's laconic reply, which took some months to reach London, ended: "I stay at Khartoum because Arabs have shut us up and will not let us out."

In the end the government relented. The general who was given the job of rescuing Gordon was, with sweet irony, the very same man who had handed over his spare change and pocket-watch at Charing Cross station: Wolseley.

"There is a fated quality about the events of the next six months," writes Alan Moorehead, "an air of pure and certain tragedy that lifts the story out of time and space so that it becomes part of a permanent tradition of human courage and human helplessness... Each of the three main protagonists – Wolseley coming up the Nile with his soldiers, Gordon waiting and watching on the palace roof in Khartoum and the Mahdi with his warriors in the desert outside the town – behaves precisely as he is destined to do, and it is wonderfully dramatic that these three men, who were so perfectly incapable of understanding one another, should have been thrust together in such desperate circumstances and in such an outlandish corner of the world."

Relief expedition

Meanwhile Gordon's solitary life in the palace took on a surreal quality. He ate alone and spent hours on the roof with his telescope, monitoring activity in the enemy lines. The long vigil was electrified by news that Wolseley was on his way. Guns were fired, Gordon scampered about renting houses for English officers and placing orders with butchers and bakers on their behalf.

He smuggled out secret messages advising the advancing Wolseley on the best tactics: "Parties of forty or sixty men, swiftly moving about, will do more than any column... The time to attack is the dawn, or rather before it (this is stale news), but 60 men would put these Arabs to flight just before dawn, which one thousand would not accomplish in daylight... I do hope you will not drag on that artillery: it can only produce delay and do little good."

Meanwhile, however, the ship which had taken away the last European contingent had struck a rock and been disabled, passengers and crew were massacred, and information gleaned from documents taken off the bodies persuaded the Mahdi to close for an attack.

Left: the last known photograph of General Gordon.
Right: artist's impression of General Gordon's fatal defiance of the Mahdi.

The shelling of Khartoum

The attack on Khartoum began on 12 November. Rounds from a gun trained on Gordon's palace generally bounced off the stone walls, but the quickening barrage caused alarm in the city. There was still no sign of the relief column and no way of knowing when it would arrive. "Now mark this," Gordon wrote in one of his last communiqués, "if the Expeditionary Force, and I ask for no more than 200 men, does not come in 20 days, the town may fall; and I have done my best for the honour of my country. Goodbye. C.G. Gordon."

About two weeks after he wrote this message

(which had not yet been delivered), the advance guard of the expedition began a final advance on Khartoum. A force of 100 British troops with 2,200 camels were within 160 km (100 miles) on 30 December. On 18 January, after a first contact in which the Arabs suffered 1,100 killed, the British column was 37 km (23 miles) away, but a low river and problems with the steamers' engines delayed the advance.

On 28 January the leading ship ran the gauntlet of heavy artillery fire from both banks to reach the junction of the White and Blue Niles, at which point the town was clearly in view. Ten months after Gordon had first called for assistance it had arrived, although doubts were stirred in the men's minds by Arabs who called out from the bank that they were too late and Gordon was already dead.

Meanwhile Gordon had been putting on a show of defiance by not only refusing to barricade the palace windows but inviting the Arab gunners to aim at a bright lantern beneath which he had his meals. The signs of an imminent assault almost made him crack. "What more can I say," he protested, flinging his fez away, "I have nothing more to say, the people will no longer believe me, I have told them over and over again

WAR LORD

As a famous military commander, Lord Kitchener was the ideal choice for the "Your country needs you" recruitment poster of World War I.

in their path. No wild animals ever behaved as the Arabs did in that one short hour before the dawn; they killed their victims regardless of whether or not they surrendered, and without distinguishing between men, women and children."

Gordon had stayed up writing until midnight and was woken by the sounds of the fighting. He went up to the roof in his night clothes and lowered a gun to fire at the Arabs who were surging towards the palace. He then went back to his room, changed into his white uniform,

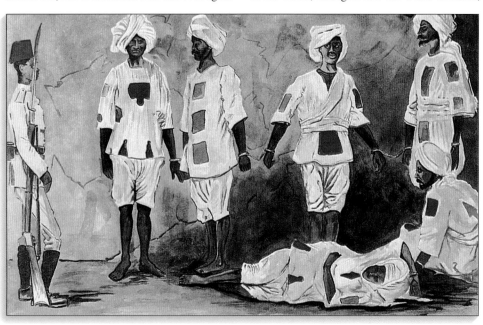

that help would be here, but it has never come, and now they must see I tell them lies." With that he gave the commandant permission to open the gates, if he chose, to let the residents join the rebels. "Now leave me to smoke these cigarettes," he concluded.

The palace falls

Some 50,000 Mahdi supporters crept up on the city that night, crossing the ditch where it had filled with mud. In the early hours, they broke in. "Before any sort of resistance could be organised," writes Moorehead, "the streets were filled with a tide of screaming fanatics who hacked with their spears at every human being

took up a revolver and sword and stood at the head of the stairs in "a calm and dignified manner, his left hand resting on the hilt of his sword." A mob hurled their way through the palace and up the stairs. To one who cried out, "O cursed one, your time has come," Gordon is said to have made "a gesture of scorn". The General was speared to death. His head was cut off and sent to the Mahdi in a handkerchief.

The relief column reached the city three days after Gordon's death and came under furious fire. Wolseley applied to London for permission to launch a counterattack but, with Gordon confirmed dead, this was refused. The column withdrew down the Nile. London's policy, for the moment, was to "let the Sudan stew in its own juice."

With the fall of Khartoum, the Mahdi seemed to lose much of his messianic zeal. According to prisoners, he retired across the river to Omdurman and grew fat with his large harem. It was a style of life that lowered his defences, either against disease or, according to another version, against poison administered by a vengeful woman. He outlived Gordon by just five months.

The shock caused by Gordon's death in England was not assuaged when the Mahdi's successor, Khalifa Abdullah, wrote to Queen Victoria summoning her to come to Omdurman to submit and turn Muslim. It was later estimated that during the Khalifa's rule about three-quarters of the Sudan's population of about 9 million were exterminated. Nevertheless, Britain could not find the will to avenge Gordon's death until 1895.

Kitchener settles old scores

One of the first signs of British determination was the requisitioning of all Thomas Cook's pleasure cruisers on the lower Nile for an expedition which was to be commanded by General Herbert Horatio Kitchener. A famously unemotional man, he led a force of 20,000 which tore apart an attack by Emir Mahmoud, one of the Khalifa's generals, in a preliminary battle, and as he rode along the British ranks afterwards, men raised their helmets in the dark and cheered him. He was, said an officer who watched him closely, "quite human for a quarter of an hour." The words were written by a promising young soldier with Kitchener's army, Winston Churchill.

Kitchener was at Omdurman on 1 September 1898. His men could see the Mahdi's tomb and beneath it, on the sand, what appeared to be a *zeriba,* a defensive wall made of branches and bushes. "Suddenly," wrote Churchill, "the whole black line which seemed to be the *zeriba* began to move. It was made of men, not bushes… "

The Arabs held their attack until the following night, when 50,000 warriors, many armed with only spears, charged into the teeth of the British artillery. A war correspondent described "a torrent of death", bodies piling up in mounds so that within an hour or two there were 10,000 casualties strewn all over the battlefield. Of these, the British losses amounted to 400.

After a break for lunch, Kitchener examined his conquest. The Mahdi's tomb had already been somewhat damaged by bombardment, now his body was dug up, decapitated, and thrown into the Nile.

In England, celebrations greeted news of the victory. Queen Victoria, if she had thought about it, could have worked out that, but for one small detail, she now ruled the Nile from the Mediterranean to the Mountains of the Moon. ❏

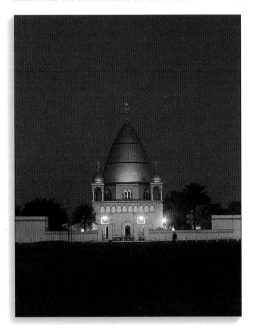

KITCHENER OF KHARTOUM

Horatio Herbert Kitchener (1850–1916) was 1.9 metres (6 ft 2 in) tall, a paler version of the explorer Richard Burton in that he was an excellent horseman, was interested in archaeology and related subjects, and spoke a number of languages. Unlike Burton, however, he had no interest whatsoever in women and he despised journalists. In conquering the Sudan, his organisation of supplies and the devastating use made by his men of the recently invented machine gun enhanced his reputation as an efficient and fearless commander, making him a popular hero. Seeing action in the second Boer War, he later became Secretary of State for War. He drowned in 1916.

LEFT: prisoners at Wadi Halfa.
RIGHT: the Mahdi's tomb in Omdurman.

ENCOUNTER AT FASHODA

*French and British interests in Africa collided head-on at
a hellish, swamp-bound outpost on the Nile*

In 1898, the wounds of Waterloo reopened and England and France were once again baring their teeth at one another. Britain particularly wanted to rule an African corridor from the Cape to Cairo and France yearned for one that cut a swathe on the other axis between the Atlantic and Indian Ocean. They would collide, anyone

cleanse Egypt of its repulsive British presence.

The race to occupy Fashoda began. The nearest British and French bases, the starting blocks, were at Cairo and Brazzaville respectively, both 3,200 km (2,000 miles) away.

The British advance on Fashoda was the task of Horatio Herbert Kitchener, Sirdar (Comman-

could see, in the Sudan, but that was a vast territory. The precise point where the two putative corridors met was nothing but a derelict, mudbrick Nile fort on the edge of an indescribably awful swamp, at a place called Fashoda.

Fashoda came to be pinpointed because the French believed that a dam here would present Egypt to France on a plate. Britain had other plans: the opening of the Suez Canal had made the country an attractive proposition and they didn't want the French anywhere near Egypt.

The proposed dam at Fashoda would hold Egypt to ransom. The Nile could be shut off completely or, by suddenly pulling the plug, the waters could be released as a tidal wave to

der-in-Chief) of the Egyptian army, a towering autocrat, recently celebrated as the defeater of the Mahdi at Omdurman.

The French contingent

His opponent, in Brazzaville, was Jean-Baptiste Marchand, a captain of marines and veteran of several "pacifications" who loathed Englishmen.

In 1897, by which time the British had taken Dongola and were extending their railway southwards, Marchand and his team of 12 Frenchmen and 150 Senegalese troops left Brazzaville with 13,000 pieces of baggage, not a few of them taken up by a selection of wines, and travelled by steamer up the Congo. With the prospect of intermittent rivers and streams ahead, they had packed into their luggage a number of small metal whalers which could be supplemented by native canoes. They had barely started overland when they chanced upon what looked like a huge stroke of luck. Stranded by falling water in the M'Bomu River they came across a 30-ft steamer called the *Faidherbe*. Marchand decided they must have it.

The *Faidherbe* did a wonderful job towing them along in their boats. When the keel began

GENERAL MARCHAND

Marchand moved stiffly, his military bearing hampered by an elbow wound, a legacy of pacification. Restlessly energetic at the best of times, it was said that he twitched in the unforgiving climate of Africa.

to abandon the little boat which had served them so well. They would take the *Faidherbe* with them, even if that meant cutting it up into portable slices. The cutting and slicing duly followed, but that still left the boiler. If the boiler were cut up, the *Faidherbe* would never steam again.

"They all gathered around the cylindrical, intractable object weighing over two tons," says Patricia Wright in her book *Conflict on the Nile.* "There was nothing for it: the boiler would have to be rolled. If it

dragging on rocks, however, the hard work began, the repeated process of unloading everything, towing the *Faidherbe* over the obstacle and reloading. There was great relief when the M'Bomu deepened again to take them merrily to within 210 km (130 miles) of the Upper Sueh, which they believed connected with the Nile.

Marchand may not have known that those 210 km included dense jungle and substantial hills, but in any case he was extremely reluctant

LEFT: the Anglo-Egyptian fleet heading upriver.
ABOVE: the *Faidherbe*, Marchand's brave boat, being dragged from the river.
RIGHT: British gunboat being hauled up the cataracts.

were to be rolled then a path would have to be cut and logs laid so as to make a rough road." A thousand dubious porters were recruited to negotiate the new track.

Eventually they reached the Sueh, and they set about reincarnating the *Faidherbe*. But despite starting well, the Sueh widened until it ceased to be a river. "I try in vain to find a horizon," one of the Frenchmen wrote in his journal. "There is not even a tree, nothing but marsh; silent, unforgiving in its uniformity beneath an unyielding sky."

The faithful *Faidherbe* could go no further unless some kind of channel could be found, and even then only when rains brought up the water level. Marchand sent off a party to look for any means through the marsh. The further they went into it, the worse the conditions were, an impossible combination of neither enough water to float a canoe nor firmness underfoot to support a man's weight. "Often there was no water at all, just thigh-deep mud flipping with half-dead fish and reptiles, everywhere enclosed by stifling, airless heat and clouds of mosquitos."

Eventually they spotted a mountain in the distance. "A mountain means land, real earth

SLEEPING IN SLIME

The resourceful Senegalese found an answer to the problem of marshland mosquitos by sliding into the muddy slime at night with only their nostrils protruding.

without marsh, without endless muddy sludge, without reeds, without papyrus," the French officer wrote in his journal. "Land which one can walk on, can sleep on without sinking, on which one can live as a man again." He was emboldened to the conclusion that "the Nile is before me – Fashoda within my grasp!"

Heart of darkness

After nine weeks in hell the advance party struggled back to the camp, but as there was no question of the main party or the *Faidherbe* itself trying to go where the reconnaissance party had been until the water level rose, they were still stuck. After several weeks of frustration, they

set off as soon as the water rose to a level that suited the canoes. The first part of the journey went remarkably well. Game was plentiful, excessively so in the case of hippos, and the chef devised a very acceptable sauce for sautéed elephant trunk.

Their good progress brought them ever closer to the dreaded marsh described by the scouts, the Sudd. When at last they reached it, the worst of the stories they had heard came true. They were lucky to cover a mile in an afternoon through the solid vegetation, and at night the mosquitos descended in vengeful clouds. The hippos also became a constant menace.

On 10 July 1898, after several weeks of misery, the party's doctor was at last able to make the diary entry they all longed for. "We pass an old Dervish redoubt and then all at once round a bend in the river a group of high, sparse palms appear, behind which stretch some imposing but slashed and ruined walls… 5 o'clock, in the name of France, we take possession of Fashoda!"

The former slaving post was in ruins: piles of broken stones, the odd dismembered arch. Nevertheless, they had brought champagne across Africa for the occasion and nothing was going to stop them from toasting Fashoda.

But although Marchand had won the race, it was not inconceivable that with a much larger force Kitchener might arrive at any moment, brush them aside, and claim to have got there first. In fact the first enemy were the Mahdi, who attacked the French from two steamboats and were duly repulsed after an exchange of fire.

The French were worried: they had already used much of their ammunition on the Mahdi, who were certain to return. Four days later someone spotted the telltale smoke of a vessel approaching. The Mahdi? Kitchener? Neither. It was a sight which brought tears to their eyes. With its siren screeching joyful greetings, there was the faithful *Faidherbe*, with a few welcome reinforcements and supplies.

Letter from the enemy

A month passed before two sentries reported that the Mahdi were back. Everyone turned in early that night in readiness for a dawn attack. At 11.30 pm, however, two couriers approached. They had a letter addressed to "The Commandant of the European Expedition at Fashoda". It was signed: "Herbert Kitchener, Sirdar".

The letter was polite and to the point. Kitchener wrote that he had come across a group of Mahdi who reported the battle they'd had with Marchand, and, wishing to learn more, he intended to visit Fashoda the following day.

"Mon Général," Marchand replied, "I have the honour to acknowledge receipt of your letter dated 18 September 1898... I shall be the very first to present the sincere good wishes of France to General Kitchener, whose name for so many years has epitomised the struggles of civilisation..." If Kitchener called, he would be happy to welcome him "in the name of France".

The generals meet

In the morning, Kitchener and Marchand met privately on one of the British boats. Marchand had possession of Fashoda and no intention of leaving. Kitchener, on the other hand, had the means to take it from him – five gunboats, 2,500 Sudanese troops, 100 Highlanders, machine guns and artillery – but no wish to use them.

After initial awkwardness, the two men agreed that both sides would occupy the area. Accordingly, the British set up a flagpole on a mudbank next to the fort, fired a 21-gun salute and ran up not the British flag but the Egyptian. It suited all concerned to maintain that Kitchener was technically there on behalf of not the British but the Egyptian government, and with the permission of the French – who wouldn't anyway have been able to stop him.

In the French officers' mess Kitchener listened with interest to the story of their hideous journey through the marsh. the French were keen to impress on him how well they had settled in and presented him with a large basket of flowers and fresh vegetables. Kitchener saved his bombshell for the moment of departure. The French government was in tatters, he said, ripped apart by the Dreyfus scandal. He did not believe they would have the time or the inclination to back up Marchand.

The two parties lived side-by-side on the "glob of mud" through the stifling heat of the Sudanese summer. Eventually, word came from the British government insisting on controlling all movement on the river. It also said that a boat was on its way "to undertake the evacuation of Fashoda by French troops." Paris had too many of its own problems to deal with at home.

Forced farewell

Marchand could never afterwards bring himself to speak of the evacuation. The British gave a farewell dinner for the French. The two outposts had remained on fairly amicable, albeit wary, terms. On one point, Marchand was adamant: the *Faidherbe* would leave with them too. The doctor recorded the departure in his diary: "It is done, we have passed by the English

camp towed by the *Faidherbe*. Their Sudanese presented arms, the officers saluted with their swords, the band played Marseillaise, we raised our hats, and so we passed, we passed sadly by."

But the wood was poor and the pressure in the *Faidherbe*'s boiler was low; the boat was also heavily overloaded. At one point a British gunboat had to give them a tow. On reaching rapids, the *Faidherbe* could go no further. The engine expired, the hull was split in a collision with a rock. Two whole days were devoted to constructing a dry dock. The *Faidherbe* was dragged into her final resting place and given a solemn farewell. "Our brave little ship," the doctor noted. "May she rest in peace!" ❏

Left: Horatio Herbert Kitchener in Egypt.
Right: Kitchener and Marchand meet in Fashoda.

THE LAST PHARAOHS

*From the brutal Muhammed Ali to the gluttonous King Farouk, the final,
eccentric dynasty of Egyptian autocrats was no match for British imperialism*

After an absence of 2,000 years, pharaonic rule returned in the unlikely form of a half-dead Albanian tobacconist. In 1799 an Ottoman army arrived to save Egypt from Napoleon. As the Turkish and French armies clashed at Aboukir Bay, the British admiral Sir Sidney Smith was offshore in a small boat.

Sir Sidney thought the Turks might have won the day had they not succumbed, as usual, to the tactically unsound practice of breaking ranks and dashing forward to collect the heads of fallen soldiers. "A barbarous custom", Sir Sidney observed primly. The French retaliated with such venom that the Turks were driven into the sea, and Sir Sidney found himself surrounded by shoals of Turkish troops. He fished out one who reached his gig on the point of drowning and handed him over to one of the crew for artificial respiration. As the man came to, Sir Sidney was struck by the bushiness of his beard and the piercing glint in his grey eyes.

It was only by luck, then, that the career of Muhammed Ali, an Albanian orphan who had worked in the tobacco business before joining the army, did not end then. Sir Sidney had rescued the founder of one of history's most eccentric dynasties. Ali returned to Egypt as soon as Turkish suzerainty was restored, this time as second-in-command of the Turkish army's Albanian division. In mysterious circumstances, his commanding officer's head flew out of a Cairo window and came to rest in a gutter. Automatic promotion made Ali the governor of Cairo.

Humiliation of the British

Ali used guerrilla tactics, in addition to more conventional forms of warfare, to establish his authority. And a brilliant cavalry charge on the British force of 7,000 troops sent to deal with him resulted in a resounding victory that was perhaps the greatest humiliation the British army had suffered in the east. A grim procession of 500 British prisoners was prodded along to

the Cairo slave market. The route was lined with the heads of their dead comrades.

Having seen off the British threat, Ali invited the Mameluk princes in the south to Cairo to join Ali in a glorious send-off for his son, Toussoun, who had been given the task of taking the holy cities of Mecca and Medina.

Massacre of the Mameluks

The guests arrived on horseback, resplendent in their jewelled robes and armour. "After a time", wrote an Italian mercenary, "according to Eastern custom, coffee was brought, and last of all the pipes, but at the moment when these were presented, as if from etiquette, or to leave his guests more at their ease, Muhammed Ali rose and withdrew." The Mameluks were invited to take up a place of honour in the centre of the procession. Trapped between gates, they were mown down from above.

The massacre ended an epoch that stretched back to Saladin and the Crusades. Ali became an autocrat. He expropriated all farming land and

---

LEFT: the young Farouk with his ministers in France.
RIGHT: Muhammed Ali, a strong but brutal ruler.

could thus charge whatever he liked for the crops. He became the sole proprietor of factories (and all manufactured goods), and took control of all imports and exports. His crash programme of industrialisation was supposed to bring Egypt up to European standards.

Ali's violent excesses tend to be forgotten due to his status as the father of modern Egypt. The army he created was genuinely Egyptian rather than a collection of slaves and hirelings, and he used it to devastating effect. He and his elder son Ibrahim

> **AN INTELLECTUAL ELITE**
>
> Under the aegis of Muhammed Ali, Egypt's Bulak Press became the most illustrious publisher in the Arab world. Its books played a key role in creating an intellectual elite.

conquered Arabia, including Mecca and Medina; he sent his younger son Ismail up the Nile with a force of 5,000 to seize Sudan, but tribesmen killed Ismail in his tent. Ali's reprisals cost 50,000 Sudanese lives.

Ibrahim conquers the Levant

Egypt was part of the Ottoman Empire and, to begin with, Ali was a loyal subject-ruler. But before long his own ambitions on that empire surfaced. Ibrahim swept across Sinai to take Palestine, Lebanon and Syria right up to the Turkish border. The sultan deposed Ali as pasha of Egypt, but Ibrahim took Konia, the ancient Ottoman capital, and was soon within striking distance of Constantinople. France and Britain took opposing views. The French supported Ali, with whom they hoped to do business, if he could only sew up both the Suez and Euphrates overland routes to the east. Britain sided with the Ottomans, if only to prevent its old enemy, France, from doing just that.

Treaty of London

Britain's Commodore Napier was despatched with six ships to Alexandria, where Ali lived in his new Ras el Tin Palace. "If your Highness will not listen to my appeal to you against the folly of further resistance", Napier threatened, "My God, I will bombard you, and put a bomb right where you are sitting!" Ali was robbed of his conquests but the Treaty of London recognised him as ruler of Egypt under nominal Turkish suzerainty, with the rights of succession to his eldest son.

Ali lost an empire, but founded a dynasty. And Egypt was back on the tourist map. In 1841, the same year in which Ali initiated the construction of his mosque, Samuel Shepheard, a British farmer's son who ran away to sea, took the first steps towards the establishment of the hotel in Cairo that bears his name.

The dynasty ran into difficulties when Ali's mind began to fail. The co-regent during his debility was Ibrahim, the soldier-son who had campaigned so well on his behalf. Hot after a hard day in the saddle, Ibrahim contracted pneumonia while cooling off under an upturned bucket of iced champagne. Even thus weakened, he could not resist a young Circassian slave girl who arrived as a present from his mother. Getting to know her finished him off.

Ibrahim was succeeded by his nephew, Abbas, a morose recluse. It was Abbas's idea to dismantle the pyramids, which he described as "ugly, useless piles of stone", to provide stones for a Nile barrage. He was eventually strangled by two slave boys.

Abbas's successor, Said, was a fat child who grew up to weigh 160 kg (25 stone). He was as gregarious as Abbas had been reclusive, but he too had a strange sense of fun. In addition to decapitating misbehaving shaykhs, he liked to challenge guests to join him, candle in hand, as he waded through loose gunpowder.

Said was open to new ideas, and the idea that appealed to him most was that of a Suez canal, which was the brainwave of a French engineer, Ferdinand de Lesseps. Almost immediately the scheme went wrong and for the first time Said began to lose weight. He had given de Lesseps a concession without realising that he himself would have to put up a large proportion of the enormous capital required. Nor did he foresee Britain's strenuous objections: the canal would create a new avenue of trade to the detriment of the British-controlled Cape sea route to India. A skeletal Said died of worry in 1863, with an overdraft of £10 million.

Ismail, the moderniser

His successor, Ismail, was "one of the most bewildering personalities in history", according to the historian Hugh McLeave. Lord Milner called him a "depraved ogre", others saw him as "a maligned but enlightened spirit". His charm and prodigal hospitality soon mitigated reservations about his unfortunate looks and unconventional etiquette.

Ismail's favourite saying was that Egypt – which, like Ali, he saw as his private domain – was a part of Europe. Beyond his preoccupation with the Suez Canal, he sought to improve the country in every possible way. The American civil war put a premium on the price of Egyptian cotton and he could afford massive expenditure on public works. He expanded the railways, adding 1,600 km (1,000 miles) of track, built lots of palaces, and 60 sugar mills, extended canals to increase the amount of arable land, opened 6,000 schools, and created the city of Ismailia.

The appearance of modern Cairo was largely determined by Ismail. It was he who laid out boulevards modelled on the rue de Rivoli and created out of wasteland and old native quarters the modern city centre. The famous palace on Gazirah Island, sensitively preserved as the heart of the modern Cairo Marriott Hotel, was built in less than six months for the visit of France's Empress Eugénie, one of dozens of foreign dignitaries invited to the opening of the Suez Canal. The hotel is worth visiting to see what Ismail thought a billiard saloon ought to be.

The canal's grand opening in 1869 was plagued by problems. A mountain of fireworks ignited prematurely and nearly demolished Port Said. A police launch ran aground in the path of the 68-ship procession and had to be blown up by de Lesseps himself. A new opera house was ready, but *Aida*, which Ismail had commissioned Verdi to write, was not; the guests heard *Rigoletto* instead.

Six years later, the national debts exceeded £100 million, and Britain and France forced Ismail to accept their own financial experts. Ismail, whose powers were reduced to those of a constitutional sovereign, organised a military riot, whereupon Britain and France appealed to the sultan of Turkey, Ismail's nominal superior, to assert his authority. The ensuing telegram from the sultan was addressed to "The ex-

Khedive, Ismail Pasha". Four days later he boarded the yacht *Mahroussa* for exile in Italy, having pocketed all the cash left in the Treasury.

Tewfik, Ismail's 27-year-old weakling son, was quite unequal to the chaos he inherited, least of all to the challenge thrown down by Ahmed Arabi, a junior army officer who resented the influence of foreigners in Egypt. In 1881 Arabi ringed the Abdin Palace with 2,000 troops and demanded reforms. "I am the khedive", Tewfik retorted, "and shall do as I please". To which, by his own account, Arabi replied: "We are not slaves and shall not from this day be treated as such." Tewfik appointed him Minister of War.

On 10 July 1882, Admiral Sir Beauchamp

LEFT: Abbas, Ibrahim's nephew and successor.
RIGHT: Said, the initiator of the Suez Canal.

Seymour sailed into Alexandria and gave Tewfik and Arabi, who were occupying a harbour fort, 24 hours for Arabi's resignation. Foreign ships in the harbour beat a hasty exit, saluting the British flagship on their way out to sea. The admiral's band returned the compliment with the appropriate national anthem.

Bombardment of Alexandria

At dawn on the following day, the bombardment of Alexandria began. It went on all day and by evening there were 2,000 Egyptian dead and the fortifications were demolished. The city itself was blackened, not only by British gunfire but also by looters who ransacked the commercial centre. Tewfik threw himself on the mercy of the British and declared Arabi to be a rebellious *persona non grata*. The minister of war was swiftly rounded up by the British army.

Shopkeepers replaced pictures of Arabi with ones of the khedive, and Britain's Coldstream Guards manned the new garrison in the Cairo Citadel. *The Times* reported the celebrations in honour of the victorious British army: "Tewfik in state takes the salute from the 18,000 British who have replaced him on the throne while Arabi from his prison window in the same

square watches the defile of the army which scattered to the winds, in 20 minutes, his ambitious labour of the year." Tewfik died in 1892.

Installed by the British

The outbreak of World War I found Tewfik's successor, Abbas II, visiting Constantinople in what Britain considered an attempt to curry favour with Turkey, which had entered the war on Germany's side. Britain decided that "Egypt will henceforth constitute a British protectorate". Abbas was deposed and Fu'ad, his sixth son, was placed in his stead.

Fu'ad married his cousin, Princess Shevikiar – he was short of cash and she was rich – and

ODD APPEARANCE, ODDER HABITS

Ismail's face was pitted by eczema and sprouted tufts of ginger hair, but it was his eyes that were his strangest feature. They pointed in different directions and tended to revolve – "keeping an eye on Upper and Lower Egypt", it was said. Perhaps to put guests at their ease, he tried to keep one or the other eye closed. Unfortunately such good intentions were undermined by his habit of removing his boots in company and, sitting cross-legged, playing with his toes. Not that this seems to have inhibited his pursuit of women. His harem contained 3,000 Turkish and Circassian women, although one commentator suggests this was "an exercise in self-promotion rather than self-gratification".

both lived to regret it. His obsession with cleanliness, so admired by the British, seemed to have stemmed from an unfortunate incident in the Khan el-Khalili bazaar, when someone emptied a bucket of slops on his head. He stalked his palace for bad smells. When he cornered one, he attacked it with a burst of *eau-de-Cologne*. For her part, Shevikiar decided to run away from the harem.

Fu'ad's decision to divorce Shevikiar led to a showdown with her hot-headed brother, Seif ed-Din. On 7 May 1898 ed-Din was passing Cairo's Khedival Club when he spotted Fu'ad chatting to a fellow member out on the balcony. The two princes met face to face, in the Silence Room. Fu'ad took one look at ed-Din's revolver and took up a flimsy defensive position behind a table. The two men circled the table warily, the tempo increasing until it became a sprint. Two fellow members of the club dived under the leather sofa, a Russian visitor locked himself in a toilet and the minister of war climbed the curtains. All the while ed-Din tried to get a shot in. One bullet hit Fu'ad in the side, one in the throat, one in the thigh. On running out of bullets, ed-Din was arrested.

Doctors operated on Fu'ad where he lay. They removed two of the bullets but decided the one in his throat was too close to an artery. It remained there for the rest of his life, giving his voice a high metallic whine.

The trial of ed-Din sent shock waves across the world. The criminal prosecution of an Egyptian prince was unprecedented, and ed-Din's sentence of five years' hard labour was sensational. He was eventually sent to a lunatic asylum in England. His grievance raged unabated for 26 years when, with the help of two of the asylum attendants, he escaped.

Fu'ad and Britain's Foreign Office launched an international manhunt. The prince managed to reach Constantinople, where he settled on legal proceedings in an effort to recover his fortune, which had been appropriated by Fu'ad. The appropriation of ed-Din's inheritance was

EXILE IN SWITZERLAND

After Britain deposed Abbas II, the former Egyptian king lived out his exile in Switzerland, where he died, having written *The Anglo-Egyptian Settlement* in 1930.

but one step in Fu'ad's accumulation of fabulous wealth. By compulsory purchases, at a fraction of the market price, or by diverting an irrigation canal from the estate of a reluctant vendor, he came to own a seventh of the nation's cultivable land. The police ensured that his produce reached the market and was sold before that of the competition.

Fu'ad's son, Farouk, was brought up in palatial quarantine, in the Kubbah and Abdin palaces in Cairo and in Ras el-Tin and Montazah in Alexandria. Kubbah, his principal

home, featured a 1.6-km (1-mile) long drive through 28 hectares (70 acres) of lakes and exotic gardens to a moated, 400-room palace. His doting father spared nothing on the boy's comforts – boats in the lake, camels and horses in the stables, mountains of toys – not least because he wanted to keep him within the high palace walls, away from any unwonted contact with boys of his age or indeed Egyptians in general.

The young Farouk

Farouk grew up with the idea that football was played by kicking a ball and then waiting while a servant ran after it and replaced it at his feet. When he swam, an escort of sailors paddled

LEFT: the Prince of Wales's visit to the opening of the Suez Canal in 1869.
RIGHT: the rebellious Arabi, who was appointed Minister of War by Tewfik.

along on either side. Given an airgun, he tried it out by smashing every ground-floor window in the palace. Queen Nazli, his mother, complained that he was forever locking her maids up in cupboards and hiding the key.

Given that his only playmates were his sisters Fawzia, Faiza, Faika and Fathia, Farouk came to frequent the servants' quarters. Many of the servants were Italian – Fu'ad had a weakness for Italian mistresses. Farouk learned their language and formed far-reaching friendships.

RULE OF CONTEMPT

Fu'ad had little time for his subjects: "Don't ever expect good faith of the Egyptians," he once commented. "They don't understand what it is."

An English education

When Farouk was 14, illness gave his father a brush with death and the heir to the throne's further education became a matter of urgency. So he sat exams to get into English private schools. He would sit nibbling his pencil as he had done in the palace, waiting for someone to supply the answers. The palace tutors had given him a distinction in every subject, but the headmaster of Eton was less accommodating. Farouk failed the entrance exam to the Royal Military Academy at Woolwich but he was admitted in the capacity of "Gentleman Cadet".

Farouk did well at Woolwich, where he was known as Prince Freddie. An 18-room mansion

in Kingston-on-Thames with a staff of 20 and the occasional reception at Buckingham Palace set him apart from the other cadets, but he pitched into the life and cheerfully carried out mundane chores, such as cutting up oranges for the commandant's wife.

Farouk was recklessly putting a horse through its paces in Richmond Park when he was told of his father's death. "I'll just do three more rounds of jumps..." he said. "You'll do nothing of the sort," replied his English tutor. "We can't have two kings of Egypt dying on the same day." The new king was 16 years old.

On his accession, Farouk owned a tenth of Egypt's cultivable land outright and had control over twice as much again. He had £45 million in the bank, five palaces, two sea-going yachts, more than 100 cars including 10 Rolls-Royces, a squadron of aircraft and any number of royal villas and rest-houses throughout the kingdom.

A menace on the roads

Farouk had never even visited Luxor or the pyramids. And, despite a penchant for quoting the Koran, he loved picking pockets, and was a menace on the roads. His fleet of cars painted a distinctive shade of red, he indulged not only in speeding, but in shooting at the tyres of cars he overtook. Horns fitted to his cars simulated the sound of a dog being run over. On the first sign of a royal-red car coming their way, pedestrians and other road-users would dive for cover. Farouk had a newspaper editor imprisoned for running a story about the ambulance that followed him everywhere to pick up casualties. In 1943 he drove a Cadillac into a tree and took three weeks to recover from the injuries.

Those close to Farouk were also alarmed by his eating habits. He seldom went to bed before dawn and never without a bedtime snack of caviar, chicken or steak, several ice creams and a half-gallon of fruit juice. Breakfast, at noon, began with a course of boiled eggs, 30 at a time, brought to his bedside on a tray. By the time he had eaten three or four, the rest were cold, so they were replaced with a fresh tray of 30. And so it went until he was ready to tackle subsequent courses, which were permutations of lobster, steak, lamb chops, chicken, quail and pigeons. Hungry again by mid-afternoon, he would consume a lunch as big or bigger than breakfast, followed by dinner at a conventional hour. Hunger between meals was staved off with a bag of toffees that he carried everywhere. Knowing the family tendency towards obesity, Fu'ad had kept him on a diet throughout childhood. Farouk made spectacular amends and was beginning to balloon at 18.

Several theories have been put forward for Farouk's gluttony, but the consensus points at a complaint which has biographers groping for euphemisms: "nature had dealt shabbily with him", "a certain lack of sexual development…"

The determination with which Farouk tried to compensate for this handicap could be mischievous – he would pop an ice cube down the dress of a curtsying woman – or lethal. One of Farouk's aides shot a young army captain dead to prevent him from entering his wife's bedroom when Farouk was there.

On more than one occasion, trysts in his car came to grief. He and a female friend were waylaid by robbers when parked in a country lane near Helwan. They were stripped of their valuables and Farouk, whom the robbers had not recognised, was about to have his throat cut when the gang leader told his men to "leave the fat pig – he's not worth the trouble of killing". The gang member were duly rounded up and executed, all bar their leader. He was given 100 lashes for calling Farouk "a fat pig" – and £1,000 for sparing his life.

All the king's women

Farouk was not impotent, although there were some conspicuous dissenters among the 5,000 women whom, it was fancifully claimed, Farouk could have called on as expert witnesses. A number of mistresses deserted him and made no secret of his performance's shortcomings. A sympathetic aide once tried to comfort him with the observation that "some people are better endowed by nature than others" and he ought to admit his weakness to himself.

Farouk's long-suffering queen, Farida, was a popular figure whom he had married in 1937. She had given him three daughters but no son. That, coupled with paranoid suspicion that she,

too, was having affairs on the side, persuaded Farouk to divorce her. He then took up with a starlet whom he might have married but for the insuperable difficulty of her Judaism. In 1949 his advisers suggested that a royal marriage would draw public attention away from the military humiliation Egypt had suffered by the creation of Israel. Reluctantly he agreed, but first he had to find a suitable woman.

Farouk's favourite jeweller recognised in one of his customers the sort of woman Farouk liked. She had the light skin of a Circassian and a baby face that contrasted with a well-developed body. Unfortunately, she had entered the shop with her

fiancé to select an engagement ring. While the couple busied themselves with trays of rings, the jeweller made a furtive call to Farouk. Within half an hour Farouk, having seen her through the window, raised his fingers in a gesture of approval. The jeweller removed the chosen ring from the girl's finger and replaced it with a monstrous diamond. The nonplussed fiancé protested that it was out of his price range. The jeweller intimated that he was out of luck. "By command of His Majesty," he murmured. Narriman, a girl from Heliopolis, thus became Egypt's last queen.

Farouk's other great passion was gambling. He often spent all night at the casino tables, and as long as he was there no one was allowed to leave.

LEFT: King Fu'ad, whose divorce from Princess Shevikiar nearly led to his death.

RIGHT: the wedding of the young King Farouk and his first wife Farida in 1937.

He was a bold gambler but he rarely won and at times he resorted to desperate measures to change his luck. On one occasion at the Automobile Club, a favourite haunt, he opened the betting at £10,000 on a draw which had given him three kings. The stakes mounted rapidly. When he was called, his opponent laid down a full house. Farouk showed his three kings and set about raking in the chips. "But Your Majesty," the opponent protested, "my hand beats yours. You have only three kings."

"No," replied Farouk, "I am the fourth king."

AN ABSENT BRIDE

The 17-year-old Narriman was not present at her own wedding to the 31-year-old King Farouk. She was married by proxy, in accordance with Egyptian tradition.

equally casually asked whether the ambassador too might be replaced if he misbehaved. "I suppose so", came the reply.

In February 1942 the war in North Africa was going badly for the Allies. So Farouk, in common with many of his subjects, began to cover his bets in case Germany took over Egypt. But the government was deadlocked, with Farouk favouring a pro-German candidate for prime minister. Lampson supported the nationalist Wafdist, Nahas Pasha; his back-up plan involved the

In the circumstances, it is not surprising that men went into hiding when it was known that Farouk was looking for partners. If necessary, and regardless of the hour, he would drive to some luckless victim's house and park outside, leaning on the car horn until the victim got out of bed and followed the red car back to the casino.

Britain had tolerated young Farouk's foibles. The attitude of its patrician ambassador, Sir Miles Lampson (later Lord Killearn) was typified by an exchange at the bar of the Automobile Club.

"The boy is misbehaving," he remarked to one of the princes, about the king. "If we decided to make a change, would you be prepared to take over the crown?" The prince lit a cigar and

WINSTON'S WATCH

Winston Churchill was dining with Farouk during World War II when Churchill, wishing to drop a hint that time was short, reached into his pocket for his watch. It had gone. Churchill was in no mood for pranks. The watch had been given to his ancestor, the Duke of Marlborough, by Queen Anne after his victory at Blenheim. "Your Majesty," Churchill growled, "I want that watch back as quickly as it can be arranged." "When did you last see it?" asked Farouk with a show of innocence. "A little less than an hour ago." Farouk left the table saying that he could guess who the culprit was. In 10 minutes he was back, with the missing watch dangling from his hand.

overthrow of Farouk. With this in mind, Lampson told Farouk that "unless I hear by six o'clock tomorrow (the 4th) that Nahas Pasha has been asked to form a cabinet, your Majesty must expect the consequences."

Farouk rejected the ultimatum and British tanks and infantry moved into Abdin Square. Farouk was at his desk when Lampson burst into his study. The ambassador thrust a document at the king. "Isn't it rather a dirty piece of paper?" Farouk asked. Lampson, squinting due to a troublesome sty in one eye, told him to read it and sign: "We, King Farouk of Egypt, mindful as ever of the interests of our country, hereby renounce and abandon for ourselves and their heirs of our body the Throne of the Kingdom of Egypt..."

Farouk had his pen on the paper when he looked up almost in tears. "Won't you give me another chance, Sir Miles?" Lampson would have preferred to see the back of Farouk, but he waived the technical breach of the ultimatum and allowed the king to ask Nahas Pasha to form a government. The new government duly took its place and within days Farouk was back at his favourite table in the Auberge des Pyramides club, joking with the very soldiers who had been about to remove him from the palace.

Nationalist resentment

Farouk's submission mortified the Egyptian army's officer corps, including the nation's future leaders, Nasser and Anwar Sadat. But Farouk saw out the war and resumed his wily plotting against any Egyptian government that attempted to curb his increasingly autocratic tendencies.

Nationalist resentment after the war focused on both Farouk and the British occupation of the Canal zone. In 1952 the British moved against the Ismailia barracks of the Buluk Nizam (auxiliary police), which had been the springboard for attacks on British installations, and 46 policemen were killed.

Meanwhile in Cairo a row between a policeman and a dancer in the Badia Cabaret club led to a brawl that set off the explosive atmosphere in the city. Mobs threw petrol bombs at cinemas and the Turf Club, a Mameluk innovation that

had become the haughty symbol of British Egypt. Ten members were burnt alive. Lesser symbols of Western decadence – bars, nightclubs and, most prominently, Shepheard's Hotel – were torched.

American meddling

Farouk was content to let Cairo burn for a while – a pretext for dumping the government – before sending in the army to restore order. Farouk banked on the army's loyalty, but he reckoned without Nasser's vision of the future.

US intelligence almost certainly urged Nasser and his "Free Officers" to strike at the "depraved

and dissolute weakling who was allowing Communism to take a grip on Egypt." With the connivance of Britain and the US, the coup passed bloodlessly. Farouk was wakened in the Montazah Palace in Alexandria with the news. Once again he had an abdication document placed in front of him; this time there was no reprieve and he sailed, penniless, for Italy.

On 17 March 1965 Farouk took his girlfriend, a hairdresser named Annamaria Gatti, to dinner. As usual, he started with a dozen oysters, followed by lobster thermidor, roast lamb and a huge helping of trifle. He lit a cigar, his face turned puce and he reached for his throat. At 45 he was dead. ❑

LEFT: King Farouk at the age of 26.
RIGHT: Farouk in Naples after his deposition. His companion is an opera-singer whom he had promised to marry.

Spy Stories of World War II

Cairo was never a city for secrets: the bazaars buzzed. The sheer volume of apparently sensational material swilling about made spying a sinecure, but the spies themselves were victims like everyone else. Even secret Rustum Buildings, headquarters of the super-secret British Special Operations Executive, which ran resistance movements in enemy-occupied territory, were nonchalantly familiar to every Cairo taxi driver.

Into this cauldron in early 1942 stepped an ostensible Egyptian known as Hussein Gafaar. His real name was John Eppler, he was German, and he was Germany's hand-picked Man on the Nile.

On paper, Eppler's spy credentials were excellent. Born in Germany, he had moved to Alexandria with his mother while still a boy. His mother later married an Egyptian who adopted young John, made him a Muslim and renamed him Hussein Gafaar. After an education in Europe, he returned to Egypt and on the strength of a generous allowance from his step-father became yet another elegant, unemployed man about town. As a future spy, it didn't matter much that he spoke English with an exotic accent. The Allied forces included so many émigré volunteers that Eppler could lounge about in a British uniform without arousing suspicion.

Nationalist sentiments were naturally anti-British so there were always plenty of Egyptians, up to and including King Farouk, who were willing to help the Germans, especially when it looked as if they might win. Farouk resisted official British requests to dismiss his Italian servants, who were privy to everything that went on in the palace and accordingly kept Mussolini informed. These were the servants who in his childhood had fixed his train set and slipped him sweets and cakes when he was supposedly on a strict diet.

Mussolini had pencilled in Egypt as part of his new Roman Empire. The Italian Air Force was ordered to soften up Cairo in advance of an invasion from Italian forces in Libya, but the order was quickly withdrawn when Churchill threatened to bomb Rome.

With Mussolini out of the way and the German Afrika Korps' entry into the desert war, Eppler's moment arrived. He had been taken to Germany for training and in the spring of 1942 was ready to return, but the only practical route to Cairo began in Libya. This entailed a slog of 2,700 km (1,700 miles) across the Sahara, a jolting prospect for someone whose previous travels had been short hops between nightclubs by taxi. Count Ladislous Almasy, a desert explorer, was seconded from the Hungarian Air Force to lead Operation Salaam.

Almasy, who had hated the air force and wanted only to return to his beloved desert, steered Eppler and Sandy, his wireless operator, to the outskirts of Assyut on the Upper Nile. There they took their leave, Almasy retreating into the desert while Eppler and Sandy walked into town carrying large suitcases, one stuffed with money and the other with wireless equipment.

In Cairo, Eppler rented a luxurious houseboat on the Nile near the Zamalik bridge. While Sandy set about installing his equipment under a radiogram in the mahogany bar, Eppler nipped off to look up old friends, in particular a belly-dancer named Hekmet Fahmy. She was on the friendliest possible terms, she said, with a number of British officers, one of whom worked in intelligence. With that, Eppler thought his job was all but done. It only remained to let the whole belly-dancing sorority know that a suitcase of British and Egyptian currency awaited disclosure of their pillow talk with British military personnel. Eppler could relax. He acquired a Rifle Brigade uniform and set off for the bright lights.

Back at the houseboat, Sandy, masquerading as an American, laboriously encrypted Eppler's signal to the effect that he was on base and open for business. The code was based on Daphne du Maurier's *Rebecca*, and somewhere out in the desert a German in earphones had his copy of that book open in readiness. The message was tapped out and, via an aerial generously but unwittingly provided by one of Hekmet's "friends", a British Army major, Sandy had the satisfaction of receiving an acknowledgement from the distant desert.

Eppler's second message did not go off as sweetly; at any rate, the acknowledgement was not forthcoming. The two agents prodded at their transmitter but could see nothing wrong with it. They decided to seek expert advice and were given the name of an Egyptian signals officer. The expert, when he turned up at the houseboat, was a certain Anwar Sadat. The future president of Egypt was appalled at what was going on in the spies' nest. It seems that Eppler felt he ought to maintain close physical contact with his network of belly-dancer agents. "A place straight out of the *Thousand and One Nights*," Sadat later wrote, "where everything invited indolence, voluptuousness and pleasures of the senses." He told them there was nothing wrong with the transmitter and stormed out.

The loyal Hekmet persevered in their interest. According to a fictionalised account of one incident (by Leonard Mosley in *The Cat and the Mice*), she invited a British major to join her for a drink on the houseboat before he went off on an important mission. One drink led to another and, of course, the major dutifully passed out. Eppler and Sandy rummaged through his briefcase to discover that it contained top secret information which (of course) could have settled the outcome of the war, at least in North Africa. Eppler and Sandy filtered their windfall through *Rebecca* and sent it off. They waited for an acknowledgement from the desert, but none came. They tried again; same result. It later transpired that if anyone was picking up the signal, it was a British counter-intelligence operation hundreds of kilometres away.

Having exhausted their Egyptian currency, the Germans opened up bundles of English £5 notes. Their crisp condition should have warned Eppler that they were counterfeit, albeit expertly printed in Germany.

With or without benefit of the red-hot information lifted from the comatose British major, Rommel was at that juncture steamrollering towards Cairo. His progress was not unmitigated good news for Eppler because the prospect of a British defeat decimated the value of his £5 notes on the black-market. In any case, the British forces in Egypt were paid in Egyptian pounds and British notes were a rarity. Field Security, as British counter-intelligence was known, was soon paddling up the stream of fivers flowing into the city flesh-pots. They then uncovered another clue in two German wireless operators picked up in the desert. Although neither man spoke English, they had a copy of *Rebecca* in their possession. The case against Eppler was clinched by a new girl inducted into Eppler's harem, who worked undercover for Field Security.

The houseboat was raided in the early hours of

a morning in mid-July. While Sandy hastened below to open the stopcocks and sink the boat, Eppler grabbed the best weapon he could lay his hands on. Unfortunately, this was a pair of rolled-up socks and they were not wholly convincing as the "grenade" which Eppler lobbed at the policemen as they battered down the stateroom door.

In the event, the two spies owed their lives to Sadat, but only by default. The British decided that they could hardly shoot them without shooting Sadat as well, and that would have been too provocative. Sadat was nevertheless stripped of his rank and sent to a detention camp. Eppler and Sandy were sent to a prison camp, there to contemplate a sour reverse in their fortunes. ❏

LEFT: Anwar Sadat went on to become president.
RIGHT: the British take Egypt.

THE REPUBLIC

Since becoming a republic, Egypt has had three presidents – Nasser the populist,
Sadat the pragmatist, and Mubarak, who treads a fine line between the two

On 26 July 1952 Egypt was declared a republic. Its prime minister and head of the army was General Naguib, who had led the coup against Farouk, although power was wielded by the nine officers of the Revolutionary Command Council, among whom Colonel Gamal Abd an-Nasser was a main player.

The years after the revolution saw many political intrigues and a power struggle among the Free Officers. When Naguib was implicated in an attempt on Nasser's life, he was put under house arrest, after which Nasser became the acting president.

Nasser was officially appointed president in 1956. Within the first months of his presidency he forced British troops to withdraw from the Suez Canal zone and, in the process, became a hero in his country, as the man who could protect Egyptian independence. Encouraged by his success he started looking for ways of financing an ambitious project to build the High Dam at Aswan, which would provide Egypt with sufficient water and electric power to cope with its snowballing population.

The success of Nasser

When Nasser accepted military help from the Soviet Union, the United States refused to provide the much-needed funds for the dam. In July 1956 Nasser decided that the only solution to his problems was to nationalise the Suez Canal, at that time still owned by a company with a majority of foreign investors, and use the revenue to finance the dam. This move prompted an immediate reaction from Britain who together with France and allied with Israel, invaded Sinai in October 1956. The United States stepped in to help Egypt, foreign troops were pulled out and for the first time in its history the canal was fully under the control of the Egyptians. Already a national hero, Nasser came out of this Suez crisis as the champion of Arab nationalism.

Looking back at the reforms Nasser undertook during his presidency, it is easy to understand his popularity in the country. One of his first important acts was to end feudal ownership of land, redistributing the estates of big landowners among the *fellaheen* or peasants. Private property was confiscated from foreigners, members

ROOTS OF THE MUSLIM BROTHERHOOD

When the State of Israel was declared in May 1948, Egypt decided to join the other Arab states in a war that ended in ignominious defeat of the Arab armies. There were many rumours about the ineffective organisation of the army and that the soldiers were fighting with defective arms. This chaos created the perfect climate for opposition parties to flourish, including the Muslim Brotherhood, one of whose members had killed the prime minister in 1948. As a result of the assassination, the government cracked down on fundamentalists: the Brotherhood founder and leader Hassan al-Banna was killed, many supporters were arrested and the party was outlawed in Egypt.

LEFT: posters of presidents Mubarak and Sadat.
RIGHT: President Gamal Abd an-Nasser.

of the royal family and from the rich in general. Bank accounts, land, houses, furniture, jewellery and even books belonging to 4,000 families were seized, in an effort to deprive the old upper classes of their capital assets and political influence. Nasser also built the Aswan Dam, which not only supplied water and energy but also provided more cultivable land and allowed Nasser to develop, almost from scratch, an industrial base. He immediately took action to improve the health care system by developing a

TRIBUTE TO NASSER

A measure of Nasser's popularity was the extent to which he was mourned after his death. It was estimated that more than 3 million people turned out to watch the funeral cortege.

Egyptian airforce on the ground, and in six days (the Six-Day War) had occupied the Golan Heights, Gaza, Jerusalem, the West Bank and the Sinai. Israeli troops crossed the Suez Canal and were ready to march to Cairo. Only a ceasefire quickly worked out by the United States and the Soviet Union prevented further disaster. A humiliated Nasser offered to resign immediately, but popular demonstrations in the streets forced him to stay. He remained president until his death in 1970.

wide network of village health centres, and life expectancy rose considerably as a result. His reforms were equally radical when it came to education, especially education for girls.

The Six-Day War

Less than 10 years later, however, in the summer of 1967, Nasser made a disastrous miscalculation in foreign policy. When Israel invaded Syria, Nasser made the decision to help his Arab ally by demanding that UN troops leave the Sinai and then sending troops to block the Israeli port of Eilat. The Israeli response was swift, and on 5 June it launched a sneak attack on Jordan, Syria and Egypt, wiping out the entire

Sadat's open doors policy

On Nasser's death, his vice-president, Anwar Sadat, another Free Office, became president. He did not have Nasser's charisma, and was never as popular as his predecessor, but he was just as radical when it came to making reforms. Sadat cut the close links Nasser had built with the Soviets and turned Egypt towards the West.

To begin with, Egyptians doubted his ability to lead their country, but he won their respect by launching a new Arab-Israeli war in 1973. Even though the October War was not the ultimate victory the Egyptians claimed, some advances were made and it proved that Egypt was again a force to be reckoned with. It also gave Sadat enough prestige to ignore the cry for Arab unity. In November 1977 he shocked the Arab world, not least the Egyptians themselves, by being the first Arab leader to visit Israel. Throughout the Arab World this was seen as a betrayal of the common cause and a sign of his weakness, but in the end it led to the US-sponsored peace agreement signed at Camp David in 1978.

The response of the rest of the Arab world was to expel Egypt from the Arab League, and withdraw its ambassadors from Cairo. But in return for making peace Egypt received from the west the second-biggest financial aid package after Israel. Sadat's open door policy attracted foreign investment and created great wealth – but only for a minority. The downside was massive inflation, a widening gulf between rich and poor and a massive haemorrhage of Egypt's brightest men and women to the oil-rich Gulf states. When, in 1977, Sadat abolished food subsidies there were riots across the country.

To deal once and for all with the leftist movements in the country, Sadat encouraged Islamic revivalism by lifting repression of the Muslim Brotherhood. However, it was this move that proved to be his final downfall: he was assassinated by one of its members during a military parade in October 1981.

The Hosni Mubarak years

Once again one of the original Free Officers took up the reins of power – Hosni Mubarak, who remains Egypt's president today. As president, he is the head of state and of the army, and can appoint government ministers.

Mubarak has been called the most democratic leader Egypt has ever had, but despite cautious liberalisation he is still often criticised abroad for not offering real democracy to the Egyptians. Although a diverse press is tolerated, censorship is the norm, particularly when the government is being criticised or there are reports of human rights violations. Amnesty International has nothing good to say about human rights in Egypt.

A national referendum in 1999 asked: Do you want Mubarak to stay on as president? It came as no surprise that Mubarak was endorsed for his fourth six-year term, as the election process is considered far from democratic.

LEFT: President Sadat is greeted by Begin in 1977.
RIGHT: Mubarak, in power since 1981.

The president still struggles against Islamic fundamentalists; even though many of their leaders are imprisoned, they continue to threaten the government (so far Mubarak himself has survived three assassination attempts), as well as tourism, which is vital to the economy. In the 1990s terrorist attacks by the Islamic Group (Al-Gama'a al-Islamiya) targeted several tourist sites, as well as cruise boats and tour buses, causing tourism – Egypt's biggest foreign earner – to plummet. The government reacted with a harsh crackdown, and the hanging of convicted terrorists was resumed for the first time since Sadat's assassination.

On an interntional level, Mubarak has been a key figure in the Middle East Peace process, treading carefully to maintain Egypt's fragile ties with Israel and its relationship with the United States (from which it still receives massive financial support) and with the rest of the Arab world. In 1990 Egypt was readmitted to the Arab League, and its headquarters have moved back to Cairo.

At home, the freeing of exchange rates, the easing of import controls and the creation of an Egyptian stock exchange have helped the middle classes, Their support of Mubarak and their ability to stimulate the economy are considered key to Egypt's future prosperity. ❑

TAMING THE NILE

*Control of the annual flood has always
been the key to the country's prosperity*

E gyptian civilisation relied on a paradox: at
the hottest, driest time of the year, in what
would otherwise have been one of the least
habitable places on earth, the Nile would break
its banks with an ocean of water and rich silt.

All a farmer had to do was to wait for the
flood to subside. Then he could scatter a few
seeds, let his pigs trample them into the mud,
and sit back to wait for the first of as many as
three crops in a season. "The Egyptians", wrote
Herodotus, "gather in the fruits of the earth with
less labour than any other people". With subsistence more or less taking care of itself, the
pharaohs had a pool of underemployed labour
without which their unparalleled achievements
along a 1,600-km (1,000-mile) ribbon of river
bank would not have been conceivable.

There were, however, one or two circumstances that could upset the system. If the flood
was too low, the amount of arable land could
shrink disastrously; if too high, it washed away
settlements that were supposedly on safe
ground. Moreover, the secret of two or three
consecutive crops was in having water on hand
to refresh silt which would otherwise turn to
stone in the searing heat. Thus control of the
Nile was a challenge to Egyptian ingenuity.

Early engineering

A real understanding of the annual inundation
was not apparent until 5,000 years after the
first concerted effort to tame the river. This
bold attempt is credited to Menes, the first king
of a united Upper and Lower Egypt who, in
about 3000 BC, is said to have successfully
diverted the river in order to build the new
capital, Memphis, on reclaimed land.

Another example of early Nile engineering
was that of a "native queen" named Nitocris
who cunningly built an underground apartment
with a secret channel leading to the river. She
was accordingly able, it is said, to invite a
group of guests to dinner only to pull the plug
and drown the lot of them, on the grounds that

LEFT: the High Dam at Aswan.

they were suspected of murdering her brother. Immediately after the fateful gathering, so the story goes, she committed suicide by throwing herself into a room full of ashes.

The aquatic engineering feats of the pyramid builders were inspired by rather more practical considerations. Enormous granite blocks were floated down the river from Aswan on reed barges. The pyramids were generally built high above the flood plain so special canals were dug to reduce the distance over which the blocks had to be dragged on sledges. A curious lapse in the technical precocity that produced the pyramids was the failure to recognise the potential of the wheel, a concept already known to potters and shipwrights, for land transport.

Free labour

Prisoners of war supplemented local labour, especially during the Middle Kingdom years (2040–1640 BC) at the tail end of the pyramid period. According to Herodotus, Sesostris III was notably aggressive and showed his scorn for cowardly enemies abroad by depicting them as female genitalia on the columns he left behind as memorials to his conquest. His prisoners were put to work on a network of canals that served to increase the amount of

THE ASWAN DAM

The Aswan Dam created the world's largest artificial lake, the 6,000-sq-km (2,300-sq-mile) Lake Nasser, which stretches into Sudan. Its purpose was to protect Egypt from droughts or floods in Ethiopia and Sudan, as well as to provide water resources and cheap power needed by a rapidly growing population. The 280,000 hectares (700,000 acres) of land already cultivated could be harvested more than once a year, and more than 400,000 hectares (1 million acres) of desert land have been reclaimed for cultivation. But the cost was high.

Lake Nasser wiped out Nubia; some 100,000 Nubians lost their land and most of their culture when they were resettled around Aswan and upriver. The dam traps the silt that formerly enriched the fields, so farmers now rely on chemical fertilisers, which enter the food chain and exhaust the soil. The perennial irrigation has caused soil salinity requiring extra drainage systems, which in turn provide breeding grounds for mosquitoes and bilharzia-carrying snails. This salinity of the soil, rising water tables and greater humidity also threaten the ancient monuments. The lack of silt deposits in the Delta area make the coastline more vulnerable to erosion. And some scientists claim that Egypt is now more susceptible to earthquakes due to the changes in climate.

arable land. His impatience with the enemy in Nubia to the south was such that he cleared a passage for ships through the First Cataract, enabling him to mount successful punitive raids. It is difficult to visualise where and how Sesostris managed to do this, now that modern dams have altered the level of the river and put paid to the annual inundation.

King Amenemhet appreciated the extra crops that could be wrung out of the silt by efficient irrigation so he initi-

> ### ODE TO KHALEEGA
>
> As a source of poetic inspiration, the Khalig canal was second only to the Nile: "Where bright Khaleega, like a spotted snake, Past meads and gardens trails her glittering coil."

for triremes to pass abreast, and it reduced the fearsome overland journey to a comfortable four-day cruise. Some 120,000 labourers died for the project, Herodotus noted, but it was only completed by Darius, the Persian conqueror, not long before Herodotus's visit.

Roman improvements

The Romans, like the Persians and Greeks before them, improved the waterways of Egypt, and built a Red Sea canal that began near modern Cairo. At the time they considered

ated a bold programme of canals and reservoirs. The 32-km (20-mile) dam wall he built across the oasis lake in the al-Fayyum was still functioning a millennium later, when Herodotus wrote: "The water in this lake does not spring from the soil... It is conveyed through a channel from the Nile, and for six months flows into the lake, and for six months out again into the Nile."

Herodotus was also impressed by a canal that joined the Nile and Red Sea. It was wide enough

---

LEFT: building the Aswan Dam.
ABOVE: Abu Simbel temple was relocated above the rising Lake Nasser.

but rejected the idea of a Suez canal because the Red Sea was thought to be 6 metres (30 ft) higher than the Mediterranean. (This was one of the objections put to de Lesseps when he resuscitated the plan in the 19th century.) The Arabs continued the good work: the Khalig canal dissected the capital they built at Cairo.

Napoleon's complaint

The Mameluks neglected the waterways but Napoleon, who arrived in 1798, wanted to clear the canals and repair the hydraulic machine that lifted water into a tower to supply the citadel. "The Mameluks never fixed anything" he said. Napoleon planned a series of dams along the

Nile but, like a proposed Suez canal, they did not materialise before his enforced departure.

Incompetent heirs

The good work done by Muhammed Ali, who rose from the French defeat to establish a new Egyptian dynasty, was undone by a succession of incompetent heirs, and in the middle of the 19th century a British resident in Cairo was moved to observe that the city's canal was "only pretty during the four months when the Nile fills it", while for the rest of the year "bright Khaleega is a gutter of mud and the home of noisome smells."

The entrance to the canal was opposite the Nilometer on the island of Rawdah in Cairo. Nilometers maintained at key points along the river from pharaonic times measured the rise of the water and, in particular, signalled the level (16 cubits) at which the farmers had to start paying tax on the land they worked. "The government," said the British resident, "of course used to take care to publish a falsified measurement before the due time, and thus induce the peasants to begin payment."

The town crier, accompanied by a boy, would make his rounds with the latest news about the level. "Five digits today," he might cry, "and the Lord is bountiful!" To which the boy would

respond with "Bless ye Muhammed!" The real excitement happened on the day on which the government declared "Full Nile" as a prelude to cutting the dam and letting the water into the Khalig canal. With scores of small boys forming a procession, the town crier would improvise lines to stir a rich man into producing a tip. The boys' chorus would proclaim: "Paradise is the abode of the generous", or "God has given abundance". An unsympathetic response was likely to bring a quick change of tune: "Hell is the abode of the niggardly".

Virgin sacrifices

The annual cutting of the dam was observed with a tradition going back to pharaonic times: a young virgin was thrown into the river as a sacrifice. The victim was symbolised by a "Bride of the Nile" earth tower erected in front of the dam. The river rushed in to consummate the union when the dam was breached.

A huge celebration took place on the eve of the great day. "All that night, nobody sleeps," wrote the long-suffering British resident. "The constant firing of guns... the beating of drums... the discharge of rockets, and general babel of noises would render the desire abortive... It is like Venice in the old carnival time, only the voices and dresses are changed, and we cannot help feeling that, like the carnival, this ceremony belongs to an older state of things and an older religion. As we gaze upon the crowd we feel dimly that the priest of Isis ought to be there."

Early next morning, Cairo's governor checked the progress made on the breaching of the dam. A holy man read a "turgid" document, whereupon purses of gold were flung about. A roar went up as the Nile was let in. "Reserve and decency are thrown to the winds," the Briton noted, "and all the world goes bathing."

By 1833 Muhammed Ali had been persuaded by the Frenchman Mougel Bey into adopting a scheme to regulate the water level over the delta. The scheme faltered due to lack of funds, but was revived by a British administration looking to rescue the ailing economy from Ali's heirs.

Sir Colin Scott-Moncrieff, the canal expert brought in from India to find another solution, noted wryly that Mougel Bey's project, idle for 50 years, still employed a large workforce which did nothing but draw their pay, "a duty which they performed with praiseworthy regularity." A number of packing cases from England turned out to contain electric lighting. Henceforth, Scott-Moncrieff announced, the workers could look forward to labouring night and day. The dams were completed in 1891.

The next major Nile project on the British agenda caused an outrage: a proposed dam at the First Cataract would drown the island of Philae. Though the island was only 450 metres (1,500 ft) long, it was the site of Egypt's finest Graeco-Roman works, notably the Temple of Isis. The height of the dam was lowered to answer these objections. Over the years its height was gradually increased.

The island was initially partially submerged for half of the year; later, all but the tip of the temple of Isis remained under water. Tourists viewed the site from boats as if it were a coral reef. Ironically, the limestone monuments were impervious to water; with the added protection of a layer of mud, the immersion probably did them good, although it did erase some wall painting. The dam facilitated an increase in the number of acres under crops and, together with the higher yield produced by perennial irrigation generally, the increased revenue easily exceeded the cost.

UNESCO to the rescue

The decision in 1960 to build the High Dam at Aswan would have sandwiched Philae in destructive currents between the new dam and the older British dam downstream. A UNESCO rescue plan resulted in the nearby, higher island of Agilqiyyah being blasted into a semblance of Philae, after which the monuments were dismantled block by block and reassembled on their new home.

For all the unfortunate side effects, a tamed Nile has removed the uncertainties which, at least 7,000 years ago, began with questions of the river's source and durability. In the 12th century, conditions when the Nile threatened to fail were described thus: "The air was corrupted, the plague and contagion began to make itself felt, and the poor, pressed by the famine which struck them always, ate carrion, corpses,

dogs, and the excrement and filth of the animals... We entered a city and found nothing alive, neither on the earth nor in the air..."

Linked to control of the Suez Canal, the Aswan Dam was the apex of Nasser's dream for the future. It was an undertaking of pharaonic proportions: 30,000 Egyptians worked day and night for 11 years under Soviet supervision after Britain and the US withdrew their support in protest at Nasser's nationalist politics. ❏

> **CELEBRITY OPENING**
>
> The grand opening of the first Aswan Dam in 1902 attracted many of the international celebrities of the day, including the younger brother of King Edward VII and Winston Churchill.

> **POPULATING THE DESERT**
>
> President Hosni Mubarak inaugurated the ambitious Toshka Irrigation Project in 1997 in the hope of finding a solution to the debilitating over-population of the Nile Valley. Whereas today a mere 5 percent of the country's landmass is populated, the irrigation project is set to raise that figure by up to 25 percent.
>
> The largest pumping station in the world will pump water from Lake Nasser to irrigate the desert area of Toshka, northwest of Abu Simbel. Although the results recorded by experimental farms set up by the government have been encouraging, many sceptics doubt the eventual outcome.

LEFT: the Archimedean screw, a method of irrigation still in use today.
RIGHT: the *shaduff* in action.

THE NILE IN THE CINEMA

The river and its surrounding history have provided a rich source for some memorable epics of the screen

There were films about the great past of Egypt in the earliest days of cinema. Mark Antony and Cleopatra were on the Italian screen before World War I; Helen Gardner played Cleopatra in 1911, Theda Bara played her in 1917, and everyone in those primitive days was busy with Biblical tales involving the conflict between Egypt and the Children of Israel. Of course, these were all silent films in black-and-white. It was when the talkies arrived, and colour, that the spectacular fictions of history held the day.

It was the stage which led the way. In the restless gap between the wars George Bernard Shaw looked with new eyes on the vagaries of history; but his own plays were guarded: he would not abandon them to the caprices of the screen. He was won over at last by the persuasive voice of Gabriel Pascal. Pascal came from Hungary, and he brought a mood of irony new to the British screen; he prevailed on Shaw to yield. *Pygmalion* became a film; so did *Major Barbara,* and in 1945 Pascal directed a version of *Caesar and Cleopatra.* The lively cast was led by Vivien Leigh as the young Cleopatra; Claude Rains played Caesar; Stewart Granger was there, so was Basil Sydney, and Flora Robson appeared as Ftatateeta. In its day it was the most expensive film ever made in Britain.

But it disappointed. If you wanted spectacle it was there, but only in fleeting moments. Shaw is not the place for spectacle: Shaw is the place for irony, for an antidote to romance, and somehow the ironic comment on the absurdities (and the horrors) of history had evaporated in amiable romance. Nor was Egypt in the film; the huge, heartless landscape played little or no part.

The home of romance

The baldness of *Caesar and Cleopatra* as a piece of visual art was to allow irreverence into

PRECEDING PAGES: in search of the source, from the film *Mountains of the Moon.*
LEFT: Mankiewicz's *Cleopatra*, with Elizabeth Taylor.
RIGHT: Cecil B. de Mille's *The Ten Commandments.*

a story of classical history: theatre was used to it, but cinema, at any rate where Cleopatra was concerned, was the home of romance. In another way, too, the film was making changes. To an Anglo-Saxon audience, if not to Continental watchers, Egypt in close view rather than in the compressed vision of the silent screen

was unfamiliar territory. Biblical influence and years of Old Testament teaching had impressed on the public an image of the Israelites crossing the Red Sea under Egyptian pursuit. The cinema, always searching for a good story (and where could it find better narrative material than in the Book of Genesis?) had repeatedly clutched the idea of a hostile Egypt.

Cecil B. de Mille made two versions of *The Ten Commandments,* the first in 1923; the second was to come more than 30 years later. Naturally, though, the theme of the enslaving Egyptians still held true. This time there was a new insistence on the background of history; there was emphasis as well on the part played by the Nile itself. The tale of the birth of Moses cannot exclude the presence of the river: the Pharaoh decrees that every newborn Hebrew boy must die, one mother wraps her child in bulrushes and entrusts his cradle to the water, and it is the Nile which carries him away to the rescuing hands of the Pharaoh's own daughter.

The De Mille film was not to be the last of the cinema's famous version of the stories of the Old Testament, and in memory at least it has survived: by the force of its convinced maker. It had a distinguished cast: Charlton Heston played Moses; Yul Brynner played the Pharaoh Ramesses, and Edward G. Robinson and Cedric Hardwick were among the cast. In publicity the film was described as a record of a struggle for freedom: struggles for freedom were high fashion in the cinema of the time, and the piece was popular.

But tastes were shifting. There was Rome to be considered as well as Israel, and there was Egypt itself. In 1934 De Mille made a *Cleopatra* film with Claudette Colbert as the queen, but it made no lasting impression; another name would take over. In 1953 Joseph L. Mankiewicz made a version of Shakespeare's *Julius Caesar* with John Gielgud as Cassius and Marlon Brando as Mark Antony; in 1963 he wrote and

LIZ AS CLEO

In Joseph L. Mankiewicz's spectacular screen version of the Antony and Cleopatra story (made in 1963), Elizabeth Taylor appeared as the queen herself and Richard Burton, who was enjoying with her a relationship closer than publicly permitted on the screen, was *the* Mark Antony. But Miss Taylor, whose stunning physical beauty was sometimes allowed to overshadow her natural gifts as a player, was not at her best; personal preoccupations, perhaps, got in the way of a rendering of the great historical tragedy. In the end, it was Rex Harrison's portrayal of Julius Caesar that impressed the critical audience of the day.

directed the version of the Cleopatra story which is generally remembered today. It was fabulously expensive and had a dazzling cast, including Elizabeth Taylor and Richard Burton.

The spectacle was splendid – in particular Cleopatra's entry into Rome was admired – but the film was four years in the making. There were endless interruptions, including the illness of Elizabeth Taylor herself; and when at last the opening came the public, too, was starting to feel exhausted. History and two appalling wars had left audiences ready for another kind of spectacle, a spectacle with reality behind it.

There was something else. Archaeology, once the precinct of the learned, became popular.

Discoveries in the Mediterranean made young people think of excavation; the Tutankhamun discoveries focused interest on Egypt; and fantasies, disguised as learning, occupied the cinemas. Not that they had ever quite vanished.

The early years of the 1930s brought Germany's extraordinary horror-thrillers: *The Cabinet of Dr Caligari* came in 1920, but it had followers later on, before Hitler, and in America, too. In 1932 *The Mummy*, directed by Karl Freund, was one of the funerary leaders: other mum-

MUMMY DEAREST

It is natural that Egypt should be the frequent source of funereal fantasy films. After all, the country devoted the most urgent attention to the preservation of the body in its science of mummification.

The burial places of Egypt caught the imagination of the thriller-writer. Bram Stoker wrote *The Jewel of the Seven Stars*, a tale of a man unlucky enough to find the tomb of a murderous Egyptian queen: the spirit of the woman, dead for thousands of years, haunts him and takes possession of his daughter. The story has been used on the screen on two occasions: first in 1971 in *Blood from the Mummy's Tomb*, second in 1980 in *The Awakening*, which was directed by Mike Newell. Egyptian ghosts die hard, it seems.

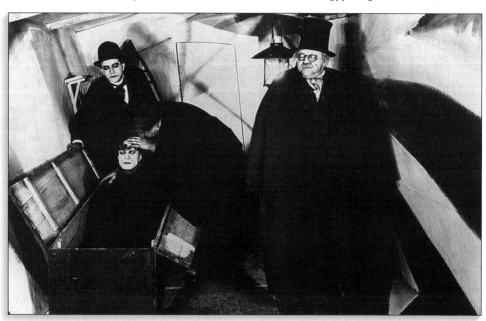

mies equally threatening appeared in Britain, where in the 1970s Hammer horror films had a vogue. In these films there are reminders of the themes of the past. In 1956, for instance, Jean Simmons and Victor Mature appeared in *The Egyptian*; it was a story of a medical student and a military cadet who, centuries before Christ, accidentally save the life of a future pharaoh. But to touch a pharaoh was a criminal offence. Sooner or later ghosts would rise from the relics of history, the vengeful dead would threaten the incautious living.

The background of contemporary Egypt is less familiar through the cinema than the images of remote history. But the Nile, lodestar of tourists, still haunts imagination, still serves the novelist. Now and then it is the Egypt of the comfortable traveller which we see on the screen – usually with murder thrown in. *Death on the Nile*, say the posters; the screen has recorded more than one multiple murder, including a case by Agatha Christie, that industrious chronicler of the geography of crime. There was a *Death on the Nile* in 1978, with the popular Peter Ustinov as Hercule Poirot; it was made in Britain, but with an international cast that included Bette Davis.

LEFT: De Mille's *Cleopatra* with Claudette Colbert.
ABOVE: *The Cabinet of Dr Caligari.*

Egypt's own story

Egypt has also contributed to the list of cinema directors. *The Night of Counting the Years* was an Egyptian film made by an Egyptian, Shadi Abdelsalam; it was produced by Italy's distinguished Roberto Rossellini; it won France's George Sadoul prize in 1970. The narrative deals with fact; it begins in 1881, when the authorities in Cairo were surprised to find that valuable objects from the 21st Dynasty had been appearing on the black market. Archaeologists were sent to investigate and it was found that a mountain tribe had passed on from generation to generation the secret of the tomb they had discovered; the sale of the objects had proved a source of income in times of need. Now there was disagreement; one of the sons of the family concerned was horrified by what he regarded as sacrilege; and there was murder – a body was thrown into the Nile.

Archaeology thus once again played a part both in cinema and in the history of Egypt. The film was shown in London and at several international festivals; it may not be an outstanding example of cinema, but it has importance as part of Egypt's own story.

Nile adventure

And now the screen moves into another area of adventure: the Nile is still concerned, but not Egypt. In the 1850s two men set out on a dangerous expedition. They hoped to find the source of the Nile. One of the two men was John Hanning Speke; the other, Richard Francis Burton, is better known as the author of an unexpurgated English version of *The Arabian Nights*.

The first expedition ended in disaster. But the explorers persevered; funds were raised; and the result was the discovery that the great lake named Victoria is now accepted as feeding the Nile. The tale is told in *Mountains of the Moon*, directed and part-written by Bob Rafelson in 1990. It is a tale of adventure, but it is also a record of history. It enquires into the lives and characters of adventurers and thus contributes to the annals of cinema. In these days of air travel it is easy to forget the explorers of little more than a century ago. The cinema reminds us, as it revives for us the fantasies as well as the poetic truths which human minds have woven around the terrors of the past. ❏

RIGHT: Peter Ustinov in *Death on the Nile*.

WILDLIFE

The banks of the Nile teem with birds,
especially during the migration seasons

Despite the great cities that line its banks, and the growing number of dams that harness it, the Nile in many ways belongs to the flora and fauna that proliferate along its shores and in its waters. The mild weather and rural expanse through which the river runs – unpolluted – offer a great habitat for wildlife.

In parts of Uganda and the Sudan the variety of wildlife remains as it was centuries ago, but in Egypt this is not the case. In pre-pharaonic times Egypt was a savannah on which leopards, cheetahs and lions roamed freely. Herds of elephant, buffalo, oryx and gazelle fed on the wild grasses and drank from the river. In the Nile, crocodiles and hippopotamuses foraged from source to outlet. But with environmental changes and the growth of civilisation, by which man began to dominate the Nile valley, local animals were pushed further and further south.

Animal gods

The ancient Egyptians seemed to like the natural world – many of their gods were associated with animals: Sobek, god of al-Fayyum and Kom Ombo, was linked to the crocodile; Anubis, god of the dead, with the jackal; Thoth, god of wisdom, with the ibis. Hieroglyphic symbols included depictions of animals, birds, flowers and trees. Houses were decorated with paintings of flowers, and public buildings had pillars and colonnades in the form of papyrus and lotus.

By the time of the New Kingdom many of the Nile's indigenous species – elephants, giraffes, monkeys – were disappearing from Egypt. The hippopotamus took longer to make its journey south. Hippos outlasted ancient Egypt and the Islamic medieval period and were quite a novelty for European travellers of the Middle Ages. Their vivid descriptions must have thrilled the people back home. Hippos still lived in the delta in 1685, and a lone specimen was sighted in Aswan in 1816. By the 20th century, of the great creatures, only crocodiles remained in Egyptian waters. Now

LEFT: homeward-bound birds.

they too are gone. The construction of the Aswan Dam in the 1960s pushed the crocodile into the Sudan, though a baby croc sometime gets churned through the dam's sluice gates.

The long migration

By contrast the country is still home to a tremendous variety of birds, whose numbers are swollen each winter as they are joined by additional species migrating to escape the winters of Europe and western Asia. Known as the Palaearctic-African Bird Migration, this massive movement begins in August and can last until early December. The birds take to the air following a variety of migratory paths that take them over the Maghreb, Egypt, Saudi Arabia, Iraq, Iran and parts of Russia. Some birds travel nearly 2,000 km (1,240 miles) before they reach their journey's end south of the Sahara. They come in their thousands but are often so exhausted by their journey that they are vulnerable to predators.

Birds of prey

Raptors (hawks, eagles and vultures) make their way south following land routes. These paths, sometimes known as flyways, begin in eastern Europe and Asia Minor. They follow the east-

EGRETS AND IBIS

One of the most common residents of Egypt is the cattle egret. This graceful white bird can be seen in fields, along canals and at the river's edge foraging for food. A cattle egret sometimes perches on the back of a water buffalo to peck at ticks and other pests. Many people confuse the cattle egret and its cousin the common egret (the former has yellow legs and bill while the latter has black legs) with the sacred ibis. But the ibis, symbol of Thoth, the god of wisdom, and raised by the thousand as sacrificial birds (4 million mummified ibis were found in one king's tomb), no longer finds the habitat suitable in Egypt. It can still be found in the Sudan.

ern shore of the Mediterranean, move south over Israel and Jordan and cross the Gulf of Aqaba to the east of Sinai. From Sinai the migrating birds cut west over the Red Sea gulfs to the Egyptian coast, turn south and head to Safaga. At Safaga they turn west again and soar over the Red Sea Mountains to Qena along the Nile. At Qena their journey continues south and, as they pass Luxor, Esna and Aswan, some birds settle, wintering on the Egyptian Nile. Others continue to lakes nearer the source and some go as far as South Africa.

Two of the most exciting birds to be seen in the green areas along the Nile are the little green bee-eater and the hoopoe. The former can frequently by seen perching on telephone wires, from which it looks out for insects. Its light green feathers appear almost brown at a distance, but on closer viewing its delicate lime-green plumage can be seen. The ochre-bodied hoopoe is so spectacularly adorned that it cannot be mistaken at any distance. It has an orange and black feathery crown that opens like a fan when it is excited, and black and white striped wings.

Another garden resident is the Nile Valley sunbird. Once a year the male – resplendent in

ANCIENT HUNTERS

There is nothing new about the sport of hunting. The ancient Egyptians killed birds and other animals for fun – they would use different techniques, such as snare nets, when hunting for food.

Purple plumage

Of the resident birds that enjoy the shores of the Nile, the most colourful and elusive is the purple gallinule, a stunning bird with blue, purple and green plumage and a red beak and legs. It is half the size of a duck but just as plump. Another stunning bird about the same size as the purple gallinule is the spur-winged plover, which has black, white and brown feathers. According to legend it once helped the crocodile by cleaning its teeth. Both migrant and resident is

exotic iridescent purple-green plumage, yellow breast and long, slender tail feather – goes courting. Of African origin, this small bird is found in various habitats all along the Nile, from the lush Delta area to the desert. The sunbird is most frequently seen in flower gardens, particularly when hovering around trumpet-like flowers as it pierces the corolla and sips the nectar. In winter the sunbird, along with other resident birds, shares the gardens with migrating wheatears, warblers and finches.

LEFT: a bee-eater and a flamingo.
ABOVE LEFT: a heron about to take flight.
ABOVE RIGHT: papyrus still grows along the Nile.

the grey heron, a tall, elegant, shy bird that wades knee deep along the river's banks.

The water birds arrive in winter. Migrants include the white pelican, white stork, spoonbill, greater flamingo, and numerous species of gull and duck. The sight of these birds flying over the Nile is a spectacular one: gulls follow boats, foraging for food, flocks of pelicans and storks fly high overhead, and the flamingo, graceful long neck outstretched and black striped wings flapping gracefully, flies at eye level past cruise boats.

Among the birds of prey that can be seen all year round are the kite, black-shouldered kite, and kestrel. If your luck is in, you may see one of these birds hovering in the air as they hunt for field mice or insects. Talons at the ready, the legs come down, toes spread out. Then they plunge, disappearing into the grass. In a second the prey has been killed and they fly off to a safe place to eat their catch.

Ornithologists' delight

Crocodile Island in Luxor is a good year-round site for bird-watching. The hotel Mövenpick Jolie Ville has made a special effort to cultivate and preserve the island's natural environment and a variety of birds can be seen in winter and summer alike. Aswan is a nature lover's

In recent winters flamingos have returned to the western shores of Lake Qarun. It is hoped that other species will follow.

Shooting game

Given its abundance of wildlife, it's no surprise that the Nile Valley became a destination of game hunters. The white hunter with his wide-brimmed hat supplanted the intrepid explorer and his pith helmet in the first half of the 20th century, when the wholesale slaughter of some of Africa's finest animals began.

Unfortunately the Nile area still attracts hunters, despite the imposition of environmental

paradise. Any place along the river's edge is good for watching hundreds of birds; Salugah Island, now a protected natural area, is the best.

Lake Qarun in al-Fayyum is a spectacular natural habitat. The salt-water lake is situated in a pastoral environment with desert along its northern shore and farmland to the south. Protected by newly enforced laws, water birds winter in this area in the tens of thousands, with Senegal thick-knees flying in particularly graceful formations. At the shore of the lake smaller birds, from sandpipers to spotted shanks and pips, flutter. At night thousands of gulls roost in backwaters; during the day, accompanied by coots, grebes and an impressive variety of ducks, they dot the shores.

restrictions. Today's hunters tend not to be the imperialists of yore but rather individuals looking for a way to feed their families. Gulf Arabs for instance train falcons to catch prey.

But for the most part, today's visitors, motivated by curiosity about our fellow creatures rather than the will to kill, come armed with nothing more lethal than binoculars and cameras. In recent times, local environmental agencies have prevented European hunters from shooting birds on illegal hunts in Egypt. ❏

ABOVE: tomb paintings such as this hunting scene give us a very good impression of the kind of wildlife around in Ancient Egypt.

Flourishing Flora

Most of Egypt's population lives in the Nile Valley, but few towns have been built on the rich soil near the river; most are on the fringes of the desert. A trip down-river runs through the heart of agricultural land. Along the river, between acacia and tamarisk trees, are fields of sugar cane, banana groves and palm trees.

There is a variety of native acacia (mimosa) trees, all of which bloom with tiny yellow flowers. The largest, the Nile acacia, rises high above the river. The smallest is the sweet acacia known as *Acacia farnesiana* due to its abundance in the gardens of Rome's Villa Farnese. Its flowers are the famous *cassie* flowers used in perfumes and cosmetics – their fragrance fills the air when they bloom in the late autumn. They are particularly common around the monuments of Abu Simbel.

The delicate tamarisk with its blue-green feathery blooms, the thick-trunked mulberry with its light green leaves and edible fruit, the wind-breaking casuarina with its long pine needles, and the tall eucalyptus with its camphor-producing light green leaves also grace the shore of the Nile, as does the sycamore, the ancient Egyptians' tree of love.

Sugar cane is not native to Egypt but was introduced by Muhammed Ali early in the 19th century. Cane fields exist all along the Nile – a government decree stipulates that all farmers must grow sugar cane. The cane is harvested in November and shipped on narrow-gauge railways to government-owned factories, also located along the Nile. The cane is processed from December to June, when the sweet smell of molasses fills the air. In addition to refined sugar, Egypt's only refinery produces molasses, alcohol, yeast and vinegar.

The banana is also an import, probably brought to Egypt in the Middle Ages. The plant has a short life, yielding its fruit for only three years, after which it must be destroyed and a new one planted.

The date palm is the country's most important and prolific tree. From Aswan to the delta, in Sinai and the western desert, the palm provides farmers with food, shelter and income. A tree takes six or seven years to bear fruit; once mature it will produce for over 100 years. When it no longer bears fruit, the top can be transplanted to create another tree.

There are a variety of date trees in Egypt, each of which bears a different kind of date, which are

categorised as dry, semi-dry, or soft. Dry dates are crimson, crunchy and astringent. Orange coloured dates are semi-sweet and can often be seen drying in the sun, thousands of them spread on the ground. Brown and black dates are usually soft and sweet.

Palm trees must be pollinated by hand each spring; the female can be pollinated for only two weeks a year. At harvest time (September) the farmer climbs the palm tree and picks each date by hand. By the end of November the harvest is over and the tree is carefully pruned of dead branches.

The giant fronds, which can be 7 metres (20 ft) long, are weaved into baskets and mats. The leaf ribs

are made into crates and furniture such as chairs, tables and beds. The residue is turned into sawdust.

The fibre that grows at the base of the leaves is combed, kneaded, and woven into sturdy rope while the fruit stock is cut and converted into brooms. One often sees a number of these orange stocks lying on roadways where the weight of passing vehicles softens the thick, firm branches.

When a tree is no longer useful the trunk is cut and trimmed to serve as roof beams in mud-brick houses or as pathways and canal footbridges. There was a time when date wine was fermented from the sap. Though this tradition has ceased, when a tree is felled, the delicious heart of the palm is often still eaten as a treat.   ❏

RIGHT: harvesting the date palm.

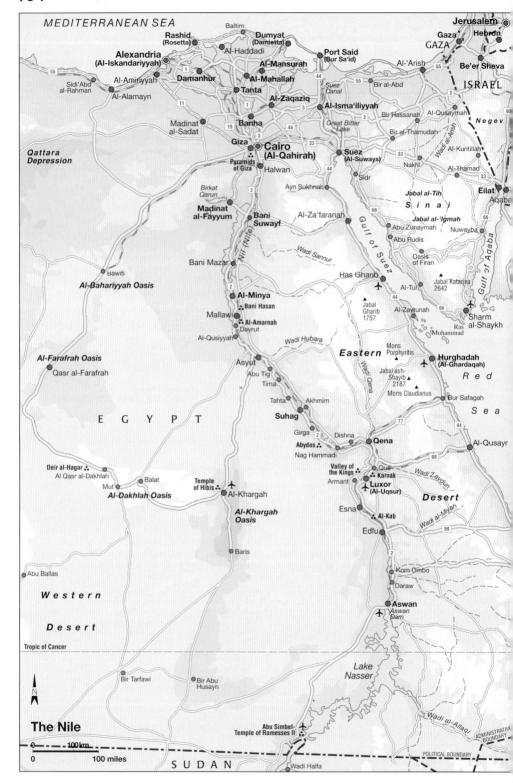

MEDITERRANEAN SEA

Jerusalem

Baltim

Rashid (Rosetta)
Dumyat (Damietta)
Gaza
Hebron
GAZA

Alexandria (Al-Iskandariyyah)
Al-Haddadi
Port Said (Bur Sa'id)
Al-'Arish
Be'er Sheva

55

Sidi 'Abd al-Rahman
Al-Amiriyyah
Damanhur
Al-Mansurah
Al-Mahallah
Suez Canal
Bir al-Abd
ISRAEL

Al-Alamayn
Tanta
Al-Zaqaziq
Al-Isma'iliyyah
Bir Hassanah
Al-Qusaymah
Negev

Madinat al-Sadat
Banha
Great Bitter Lake
Bir al-Thamudah

Qattara Depression
Giza
Cairo (Al-Qahirah)
Suez (Al-Suways)
Nakhl
Al-Kuntillah

Pyramids of Giza
Halwan
Sidr
Al-Thamad

Birkat Qarun
Ayn Sukhnah
Jabal al-Tih
Eilat
Aqaba

Madinat al-Fayyum
Bani Suwayf
Al-Za'faranah
Sinai

Jabal al-'Igmah

Ras Gharib
Abu Zunaymah
Nuwayba

Bani Mazar
Wadi Sannur
Abu Rudis
Oasis of Firan

Al-Bahariyyah Oasis
Bawiti

Ras Gharib
Al-Tur
Jabal Katarina 2642

Al-Minya
Bani Hasan
Jabal Gharib 1757
Al-Zaytunah
Sharm al-Shaykh

Mallawi
Al-Amarnah
Dayrut
Ras Muhammad

Al-Qusiyyah
Wadi Hubara
Eastern
Mons Porphyritis

Al-Farafrah Oasis
Asyut
Jabal ash-Shayib 2187
Hurghadah (Al-Ghardaqah)

Qasr al-Farafrah
Abu Tig
Tima
Mons Claudianus
Red

E G Y P T
Tahta
Akhmim
Bur Safagah
Sea

Suhag
77

Girga
Dishna
Qena
Al-Qusayr

Deir al-Hagar
Abydos
Nag Hammadi
88

Al Qasr al-Dakhlah
Balat
Valley of the Kings
Karnak
Wadi Zaydun

Mut
Temple of Hibis
Al-Khargah
Armant
Luxor (Al-Uqsur)
Desert

Al-Dakhlah Oasis
Esna
Al-Kab
Wadi al-Milah

Al-Khargah Oasis
Edfu
99

Baris

Abu Ballas
Kom Ombo

Western
Daraw

Desert
Aswan
Aswan Dam

Tropic of Cancer

Bir Tarfawi
Bir Abu Husayn
Lake Nasser

N

The Nile
ADMINISTRATIVE BOUNDARY

100 km
Abu Simbel-Temple of Ramesses II
POLITICAL BOUNDARY

0
100 miles
S U D A N

Wadi Halfa
Wadi al-'Allaqi

PLACES

A detailed guide to the Nile, with principal sites cross-referenced by number to the maps

Most Nile cruises travel the historically-rich stretch of river between Aswan and Luxor, a basic cruise of 208 km (130 miles) which takes three days to complete but which is sometimes supplemented with a trip further down-river to Abydos and Dendarah. In summer, it is possible to cruise the whole length of the river to the south of Cairo (upriver, because the Nile flows due north), a total distance of 900 km (558 miles). No cruise boats travel north of Cairo into the Nile Delta, partly because of the difficulties of navigation but also because the ancient monuments that once stood on these lands have since been washed away by centuries of Nile flooding, and little remains that is worth seeing.

The river bank varies from parched desert near Aswan – which can be as much as twice as hot as Cairo – to highly fertile agricultural land in Middle Egypt and the Delta. Because of the river's history of annual floods, most of Egypt's towns outside Cairo (with the notable exceptions of Luxor and Aswan) are situated on raised land on the edge of the floodplain. As a result, the impression that many cruise passenger get of Egypt is of a green and pleasant land occupied by farmers and fishermen, temples and tombs. Pumping stations, occasional factories – built since the upriver dams stopped the flooding and supplied power for electricity generators – and rare road bridges only hint at the rest of the country's modern economy.

Luxor, a small provincial town, and Aswan, a market town and a gate to Africa, have retained a lot of their charm, despite the ever expanding tourism industry. But Cairo, the Mother of the World, is where western cruise passenger are most likely to get a taste of modern Egypt. Cairo is a monument to Islamic architectural achievement in which 17 million Egyptians struggle to make a living; the history of Cairo begins where the temples and tombs of the Nile river leave off, and its history is still in the making. While the pharaonic tombs along the river are empty tourist destinations, the Islamic tombs of Cairo – the cities of the dead – are homes to one million of the living.

Upriver, south of Aswan, the Nile disappears behind the dam into the Sudan and beyond, dividing into White and Blue Niles at Khartoum. Between them, these rivers complete another 5,600 km (3,500 miles) through inaccessible territory into central Africa. For most travellers this has to be a journey of the mind. ❑

PRECEDING PAGES: the granite blocks of a Nile temple; fishing on the Nile in Upper Egypt; seed beds on the riverbank; harvesting sugar cane.

NUBIA AND LAKE NASSER

Map
on page
161

As cruises on the Nile are curtailed by security concerns, cruises on Lake Nasser, the great reservoir created by the Aswan Dam, are increasing in popularity

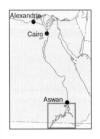

In 1972, Nubia, an arid stretch of land of about 22,000 sq. km (8,500 sq. miles) between the Sudanese border and the Egyptian town of Aswan disappeared under the largest artificial lake in the world, Lake Nasser. The Nile was tamed once and for all by the building of the High Dam, which created the vast lake, but the Nubians paid a high price. Though the world community rallied to saved most of the ancient monuments, including the spectacular Sun Temple built by Ramesses II at Abu Simbel and the impressive temple in Philae, by dismantling them block by block and transplanting them elsewhere on the shores of the lake, some 800,000 Nubians lost everything else. They lost their lands, much of their culture and their ancestral homes, as they were relocated, mainly to Aswan, Kom Ombo and to Kashem al-Girba in Sudan, but also to Cairo, Alexandria or abroad.

Although Nubia was strategically important as a buffer zone to the ancients, historically the Egyptians have always looked down on Nubia as a vast barren area, and its loss was considered inconsequential. However, a growing realisation of the cultural value of what had been destroyed gathered momentum during the 1980s, and in the late 1990s a new Nubian Museum, backed by international interest and funds, opened its doors in Aswan *(see page 173)*. Dedicated to the memory of Nubia, it houses a collection of ancient Nubian artefacts and a section on lost Nubian traditions.

PRECEDING PAGES:
the Temple of Abu Simbel on Lake Nasser.
LEFT:
visiting Abu Simbel.
BELOW:
Wadi as-Subu.

Ancient Nubia

To understand the drama of the Nubian diaspora it is necessary to understand the importance of ancient Nubia. Known as Kush, the area stretched from south of the First Cataract until well into modern Sudan. The area protected Egypt's southern frontier and was an essential gateway for the Egyptian trade with Africa. Around 1550 BC, the Theban pharaohs turned their attention to conquering Kush. However, this was not an easy task and it took them over a century to subdue Lower and Upper Nubia, and southern Nubia never fell under the Egyptian yoke. From the middle of the 18th Dynasty Upper and Lower Nubia were ruled by a viceroy appointed by the Egyptian pharaoh and a process of Egyptianisation ensued.

During the New Kingdom the Nubians worshipped a deity in ram-form, which the Egyptians accepted as another form of their god Amun. From that point on the Nubians played a more important role in Egypt. They participated in the large religious festivals, such as the Opet festivals, and numerous Egyptian temples were built in Nubia. These temples are basically Egyptian in design and style, but also incorporate local Nubian elements and are often also dedicated to

local gods. Most of the 25th Dynasty Kushite pharaohs were of Nubian descent, and some archaeologists even believe that Cleopatra was a Nubian woman from Wadi Halfa on the Sudanese border – *kilu baba tarati*, the possible derivation of Cleopatra, is Nubian for "Beautiful Woman".

As Nubia was a largely barren land, it is not surprising that the Nile played a crucial role in the life of the Nubians. Their small riverside villages, each usually comprising one extended family, were supported by growing corn, melons and a few vegetables, fishing and cultivating date-palms, which provided a nutritious source of food, fibre for ropes and wood for construction and furniture. They depended on the river spiritually, too. They would petition the water spirits when they needed a favour, and the river played an integral part in most of their celebrations. The imposing Egyptian-style temples were scattered in between the villages, often flanked by the villagers' simple white-washed shrines, dedicated to local saints.

When the warrior-pharaoh Ahmose conquered the gold-rich lands of Nubia in around 1500 BC, he laid the foundations for the immense wealth of the Egyptian Empire of the New Kingdom and the glorious rebuilding of Thebes.

The Nubians

Despite their plight in the modern world, the Nubians have managed to retain their distinct identity and are immensely proud to be Nubian. They rarely marry Egyptians, even when they live in Cairo or Alexandria, and as is discernible from the many Nubian boatmen in Aswan, they speak their own language, which is totally different from Egyptian. Other elements of traditional Nubian culture survive in the villages on Elephantine Island and neighbouring islands – many women, for instance, still wear the Nubian-style dress of a black transparent gown over a brightly coloured dress. Wedding celebrations last over a week, and include performances by Nubian musicians.

BELOW: the *Nubian Sea* at Kalabasha.

CRUISING ON LAKE NASSER

In 1993 an old *dahabiyya*, the MS *Eugénie*, was renovated and decorated in style to take passengers on luxurious three-, four- and seven-day cruises on Lake Nasser, stopping to visit the salvaged temples on the shores of the lake, which, with the exception of Abu Simbel, were rarely visited by tourists.

Now five boats all offer similar cruises: four five-star boats – the *Eugénie* and the *Qasr Ibrim* run by Belle Epoque Travel (tel: 02-516 9656), the *Nubian Sea* operated by High Dam Cruises (tel: 02-361 3680) and the *Prince Abbas* (tel: 02-332 3384) – and the four-star *Tania,* run by Hamed al-Chiaty (tel: 02-342 0488). All the boats are smaller than the average Nile cruisers, with 50 or 60 cabins, all equipped with air-conditioning, and a small pool.

Cruises generally start in Abu Simbel with a visit to the temples at dawn, before most of the day-trippers have arrived. Depending on the itinerary taken, further stops are made at the remote sites of Qasr Ibrim, Amadah, Ad-Darr, Wadi as-Subu, Dakkah, Muharraqah and the Tomb of Pennut, as well as the temples of Kalabshah and Bayt al-Wali and Qertassi nearer to Aswan. The experience is quite different from a Nile cruise, but no less magical. Views over the lake are spectacular.

Following the diaspora, the Nubians were much in demand in Cairo as door-men, cooks and servants, as they are known for their honesty and reliability. Many used their earnings to give their children a better education, with the result that many Nubians have entered tourism, commerce and even politics.

Map on page 161

Saving history

After it became clear that the creation of Lake Nasser would submerge all the Nubian monuments, Egypt and Sudan asked the world for help. The response was immediate. In the largest archaeological operation ever undertaken, 30 countries worked against time to save what they could, which in the end totalled 23 temples. The monuments were dismantled block by block and relocated elsewhere. Most found a new home on the shores of the lakes, while a few are now housed in museums around the world.

The biggest challenge for archaeologists was saving Nubia's most magnificent monument, the two temples of Abu Simbel which, unlike most of the other temples, were not freestanding but cut into the rock face. The temples were hand-sawed into more than 1,000 blocks, and rebuilt on an artificial hill above the lake. The reconstruction was almost perfect: every year on 22 February and 22 October the dawn rays of the sun illuminate the inner sanctuary, to revive the cult statues, just one day later than the original plan.

The temples at Abu Simbel

The temples of **Abu Simbel** ❶ (daily winter 7am–5pm; summer 7am–6pm; admission charge for each temple) count among the highlights of Egypt's many ancient monuments. Ramesses II built his temples of the sun god Re-Harakhte,

Not all the temples found homes on the shores of Lake Nasser. Some were relocated abroad, including the Temple of Dabod, which is now in Madrid, and the two Roman temples of Tafa which were sent to the Rijksmuseum in Leiden, Holland.

BELOW: moving Abu Simbel.

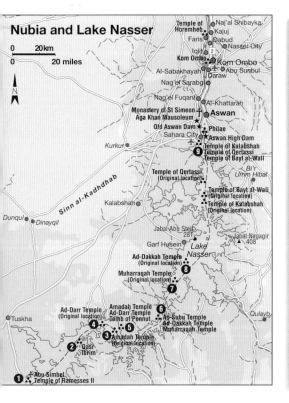

The smaller of the two temples was built for Ramesses' beloved chief wife Nefertari and is dedicated to the cow-goddess Hathor.

BELOW: the Temple of Ramesses II at Abu Simbel.

and his wife Nefertari to intimidate visitors from the south by flaunting Egypt's might and glory. It was known as "Hut Ramesses Meryamun" (the Temple of Ramesses beloved of Amun).

A good road leads from Aswan to Abu Simbel and, providing the route is not closed for security, taxis (which travel in convoy in case of breakdown) and buses can complete the journey in around 3½ hours (the tourist office in Aswan can advise on bus timetables and taxi fares). There is also a daily plane from Luxor and Aswan, but this is a lot more expensive and unless you plan to stay the night (there are two hotel, *see Travel Tips*) allows only a short time at the site, especially if the flight is delayed. If you do take the plane try to get a seat on the left-hand side to ensure great aerial views of the temple.

The facade of Ramesses II's temple, flanked by four huge seated colossi of the pharaoh, each 21 metres (69 ft) high and surrounded by other members of his family, is a spectacular sight. The rock-cut Hypostyle Hall is lined by eight large Osiride (with a crook and a flail) figures of Ramesses which support the roof. The walls are decorated with superb reliefs depicting the king's military campaigns, including the Battle of Qadesh against the Hittites, as well as wars against the Libyans and Nubians. The detail on the northern wall reliefs is extra-ordinary; filled with activity, they show more than 1,000 figures, marching, fighting, riding or capturing enemies. The ceiling is adorned with flying vultures, with stars and the names and titles of the king over the side aisles.

Behind the Hypostyle Hall a smaller pillared hall decorated with scenes of ritual offerings leads to the sanctuary carved 55 metres (180 ft) deep into the rock. The rear niche contains damaged statues of Ptah, Amun-Re, the deified Ramesses and Re-Harakhte the sun-god.

Outside the temple, on the way to the temple of Nefertari, a small door opens into the rock face. Here inside the belly of the rock is a section of the massive high-tech structure that supports the temple, a revealing insight into the mechanics of the rescue operation.

The smaller **Temple of Queen Nefertari** was dedicated to the sun god's wife Hathor. Nefertari was the most beloved of the wives of Ramesses II and throughout the temple, on pillars and walls, and even in the sanctuary, the names of the royal couple are linked in their shared dedication to the goddess. Testimony to Ramesses' love for this wife is set down along with his titles: "Ramesses, strong in *maat* (truth), beloved of Amun, made this divine abode for his royal wife, Nefertari, whom he loves." The facade is flanked by statues of Nefertari and Ramesses II with their children standing between them. The Hypostyle Hall has Hathor-headed columns, and reliefs of the royal couple confronting the gods. A damaged cow-statue of Hathor adorns the sanctuary.

Further temples

Most of the other monuments on the lake, except for Philae and Kalabshah, have open access. As yet there is no road to them, so the only way to reach them is by boat, perhaps on a lake cruise *(see page 160)*.

Fifteen kilometres (9 miles) north of Abu Simbel, the imposing Roman castle of **Qasr Ibrim ❷** still stands in its original location, but it is now an island rather than a hilltop, as the rest of the settlement lies beneath the lake. Originally it was one of three massive peaks (the others lie below water) and it seems likely that the Romans, Saladin, the Ottoman sultans and Muhammed Ali all stationed troops here. Ongoing excavations on the site have revealed letters and

Map on page 161

TIP

A daily sound and light show is held at Abu Simbel, beginning at 6pm in winter and 8pm in summer.

BELOW:
the Hypostyle Hall, the Temple of Ramesses II, Abu Simbel.

legal documents, in Egyptian, Coptic, Greek and Old Nubian; the latter has so far not been deciphered.

Further north on the lake is a group of three monuments. The small temple of **Amadah ❸**, built by Tuthmosis III, retains many of its painted reliefs, as well as some important historical inscriptions describing military campaigns. Ramesses II built the rock-cut **Temple of Ad-Darr ❹** in a similar style to that of Abu Simbel but without the colossi in the front. The third monument is the **Tomb of Pennut ❺**, the local 12th-century BC governor, which was moved here from Anibaaah, 40 km (25 miles) south.

On the western shore further north is another group of temples. The most complete is **Wadi as-Subu ❻** (Valley of the Lions), named after the avenue of sphinxes leading to a temple built by the Viceroy of Kush for Ramesses II. The court has 10 statues of the king carved into pillars. The front bit of the temple was built in the usual sandstone, but the antechamber and sanctuary were carved into the rock. The central niche was decorated with reliefs of Ramesses worshipping the gods Amun-Re, Re-Harakhte and his deified self, but those made way for depictions of the king making offerings to St Peter when the temple was later converted into a church.

The neighbouring **Temple of Muharraqah ❼** was built during Roman times, and dedicated to both Isis and Serapis. The **Temple of Dakkah ❽**, dedicated to Thoth, the god of wisdom, and built by the 3rd-century Nubian king Arganani, was expanded by the Ptolemies and Romans, but never finished; the pylon is undecorated but the interior has some fine reliefs.

The temple of Philae also presented the archaeologists with a serious challenge as the whole complex had to be moved to an alternative island. This temple is

BELOW: Wadi as-Subu temple.

however described under the chapter of Aswan, as it is a standard excursion from there *(see page 179)*.

Map
on page
161

Temple of Kalabsha

Closer to the High Dam is the less visited **Temple of Kalabshah** ❾ (daily 8am–4pm; admission charge), reached overland if the waters of the lake are low or by a boat hired from Aswan's boatyard. This is the largest free-standing temple of Lower Nubia, built during the reigns of the last Ptolemies and the Roman emperor Augustus. Dedicated to the Nubian god Horus-Mandulis and to Isis and Osiris, it is one of the finest examples of Egyptian architecture in Nubia, even though it was never completely finished. A granite entrance gate, now in the Egyptian Museum in Berlin, led to the pylon, which stands at an unusual angle to the rest of the building, followed by a colonnaded courtyard, a hypostyle hall and a sanctuary which was later used as a church. The pharaoh Amenhotep II (1450–25 BC) is depicted in the reliefs as one of the founders of the temple, though most of the current structure was built under the Romans.

Nearby is the 1st-century BC Roman **Temple of Mandulis**, dedicated to the Nubian fertility god. Also used as a church in the Christian era, it has a great ramp leading up to the first Pylon, followed by a court and hypostyle hall with floral columns. The emperor Augustus appears in front of the gods in the sanctuary. The smaller temple of **Bayt al-Wali** (House of the Governor) was cut out of the rock by the Viceroy of Kush in honour of Ramesses II. Here again the victorious pharaoh is depicted in brightly coloured reliefs, leading campaigns in Nubia and Syria, and receiving tributes from his conquered enemies. The temple was used as a church in the Christian era. ❑

BELOW: working at the Temple of Kalabshah.

ASWAN

With its many palm-topped islands, lateen-sailed feluccas and perfect winter climate, Aswan is the ideal place to relax beside the Corniche or mess about in a boat

Map on page 172

n the eyes of many, **Aswan** is the most beautiful of Egypt's riverine cities. It became known for its healthy climate amongst 19th-century tourists, who came in winter to escape Europe's cold weather. Its warm winter temperatures and very dry air were considered especially beneficial for lung conditions. Lady Duff Gordon set a fashion when she travelled to Upper Egypt to seek a cure for tuberculosis in the mid-1800s. After her, came other members of Europe's upper classes. The late Aga Khan, leader of the Ismaili sect of Islam, and his wife the Begum found such peace and beauty in Aswan that they not only built a villa on the West Bank but also chose to be buried in a mausoleum on top of a hill overlooking the river they loved so much. It is said that the Aga Khan would bury himself neck-deep in warm sand as a cure for rheumatism. Summer temperatures in Aswan can reach 48°C (118°F), but during winter it's a pleasant 22–25°C (72–77°F), although the nights can be seriously chilly.

Perfect setting

Situated 132 metres (400 ft) above sea level, 900 km (558 miles) south of Cairo, Aswan is effectively a border town, where Egypt ends and Africa begins. The governorate of Aswan covers approximately 850 sq. km (340 sq. miles), with a population of 1 million. Before the High Dam was built, only about 40,000 people lived in the town itself, but the industrialisation that ensued has swollen the population to around 200,000, which together with the expansion of tourism has transformed the town's character.

The Nile at Aswan, just north of the First Cataract, is thick with river vessels of all kinds and studded with islands of granite. Elephantine Island is the largest of these, with ancient monuments and a Nubian village; Kitchener's Island behind Elephantine hosts the botanical gardens. On both banks, date palms grow down to the river's edge, but beyond them, the hinterland of Aswan is bleak, hot and arid: the sandstone hills of the Eastern Desert are tinted with iron ore and the Western Desert has ochre dunes and limestone hills.

Unlike Luxor, which can seem overwhelmed by tourists and their interests, Aswan somehow manages to shoulder the burden of tourism without letting it dictate its character too much. The market streets are often filled with visitors from the Sudan or tribes from the Eastern Desert as well as with Europeans on package holidays. There are no bridges over the Nile here, so the town has grown almost exclusively on the east bank behind the Corniche, the long riverside promenade, which is usually lined with cruise boats, *feluccas* and restaurants on the Nile side, and by travel

PRECEDING PAGES: the Nile near Aswan. **LEFT:** Aswan from the Old Cataract Hotel. **BELOW:** Nubian boatman, Aswan.

offices and tourist shops on the land side. Several riverside restaurants offer Nubian folkloric entertainment. Inland, running parallel to the Corniche, is the souq, which is particularly active at night.

Furious floods

Before the dams were built, the Nile was interrupted only by the cataracts. Massive granite-toothed boulders torn from the rockface by floods, they lie strewn along a 7-km (4-mile) stretch of the river. When the Nile was low the water was sluggish, and it would flow around these obstacles. But during the annual flood it hurled over them with a roar that classical writers described as loud enough to cause deafness.

When the river flowed through Nubia, between the Sudan and Egypt, the water was confined by sandstone hills, but once it passed the First Cataract and approached Aswan the waters became quiet. The hills on both banks flattened out and, as the water found its level on the floodplain, it deposited a heavy layer of rich alluvial soil. It was this annual replenishment of vital minerals that rendered Egypt so fertile.

Little wonder that the ancient Egyptians, although well aware of the barren and inhospitable land of Nubia lying to the south, saw the churning water around the cataracts below Aswan as the point at which the life-giving waters arose from the eternal ocean; the cataract region was the edge of their world and the source of life. They believed that the cataracts were guarded by three gods: Khnum, the ram-headed god of Elephantine, Satis, his wife, and Anukis, his daughter. Welcoming the flood was Hapi the Nile-god, who was believed to live in a grotto at Biga Island in the midst of the cataracts. Hapi's role was to

BELOW: cruise boats docked along the Corniche.

receive the water with outstretched arms and channel it north to Upper and Lower Egypt, where it flowed into the eternal ocean to the north (the Mediterranean). Hapi is depicted on temple walls as a simple fisherman with a round belly and drooping breasts, symbolising plenty. On his head are aquatic plants and papyrus, and in his hands he holds the fruits of the land.

The ancients prayed and made offerings, so that the gods would be generous and let the Nile rise. They installed a nilometer to measure the annual rise, so that they could plan for the future and calculate taxes on agriculture.

Bridging two cultures

Aswan has been the link between the Egyptian and Nubian cultures for thousands of years. In antiquity Elephantine, the largest of the islands, situated immediately opposite Aswan *(see page 173)*, was known as Yebu or Elephant Land, because it was the trading post for ivory (although another theory for the island's name points to the shapes and textures of the rock formations). The island commanded the First Cataract that formed a natural boundary to the south, and its noblemen bore the title "Guardians of the Southern Gate". During the Old Kingdom (2686–2181 BC), Egypt had a loose sovereignty over Nubia. The Nubians, moving with their herds of sheep and goats, relied on Egypt for grain and vegetable oil. Aware of the rich veins of gold-bearing quartz and iron ore in the seemingly impoverished land to the south, the Egyptians were only too happy to supply their needs.

The princes of Elephantine were a proud and independent breed who lived at a time when the pharaoh encouraged initiative and responsible action; a time when many Lower Egyptians travelled to Upper Egypt to find work, just as today

Map on page 172

BELOW: the Aswan Moon café.

INSPIRED BY NUBIA

Visitors to Aswan who spend time getting to know the local people may be lucky enough to get an invitation to a Nubian wedding in one of the Nubian villages on the islands south of the town. Such visitors are usually amazed and delighted by the harmony of these villages. The internationally renowned Egyptian architect Hassan Fathy (1900–1989) found his inspiration in vernacular Nubian architecture. Writing about his first visit to Elephantine Island in 1941 in his *Architecture for the Poor,* he said: "It was a new world for me, a whole village of spacious, lovely, clean and harmonious houses each more beautiful than the next. There was nothing else like it in Egypt; a village from some dream country, perhaps in the Hoggar hidden in the heart of the Great Sahara – whose architecture had been preserved for centuries uncontaminated by foreign influences, from Atlantis itself it could have been… house after house, tall, easy, roofed cleanly with a brick vault, each house was decorated exquisitely around the doorway with claustrawork-moldings and tracery in mud."

Fathy believed in adapting traditional materials, designs and techniques to create modern, attractive and economical solutions to housing the poor.

Aswan is a good place to buy spices and herbs. Look out for karkadeh *(dried hibiscus flowers) which are used to make a cooling red drink, often served to welcome visitors.*

Upper Egyptians travel to Cairo and the Delta. They held responsible positions that answered to central government, but they also controlled the caravan routes south. With the passing of the Old Kingdom, Aswan's time of glory ended. It was never again to have such prestige, though in the Graeco-Roman period it regained some of its former importance when, in the reign of Ptolemy II (285–246 BC), the popular cults of Osiris, Isis and Horus were brought to Aswan.

Traders' town

Aswan's name stems from the ancient Egyptian *Swenet* meaning "making business" or trade. Indeed, trade is the very essence of Aswan. Its market places are packed with Nubians, Egyptians and tribes from the surrounding deserts, especially the Bisharis of the Eastern Desert. They exchange their produce in the same way as they have for thousands of years.

In Egypt, Aswan is famous for its dry dates, *foul sudani*, peanuts roasted in the hot sand, and *karkadeh*, dried hibiscus flowers which are used to make a refreshing drink. Colourful woven silk-cotton shawls, cotton tablecloths, African amulets and locally used spices such as red chilli pepper *(shatta)*, cumin *(kamoum)*, coriander *(kusbara)* and black pepper *(filfil aswad)* are also good buys. Bargaining here is a less aggressive process than it is in many Egyptian towns, and some products, notably the spices, are fixed-price.

The main sights

The finest relic from colonial times is the **Sofitel Old Cataract Hotel** Ⓐ, at the southern end of the Corniche, with the interior of a fabulous Moorish palace. Tea on the hotel's terrace, overlooking the river and the ruins of Elephantine

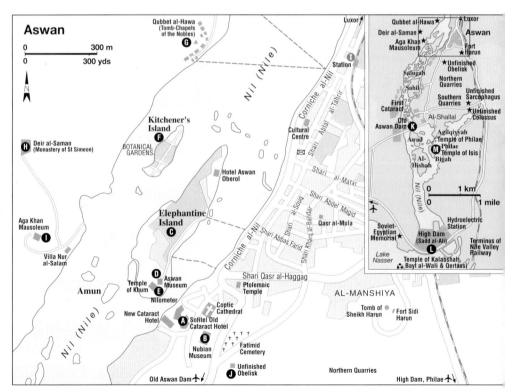

Map on page 172

Island, is an institution, although this is restricted to residents when the hotel is full. Even if you are not staying at the Old Cataract, it is worth poking your head into the hotel's dining room, Club 1902, to the left of the main entrance. For a splurge you can stay in the huge suites of Agatha Christie or King Farouk.

A short walk south of the hotel is the most recent addition to Aswan's attractions, the **Nubian Museum ⓑ** (daily, winter 9am–1pm and 5–9pm; summer 9am–1pm and 6–10pm). This museum, partly funded by UNESCO, was belatedly established to commemorate the long history and rich heritage of the Nubians, much of which disappeared under the waters of Lake Nasser after the building of the High Dam. It is housed in a Nubian-style building and set in a well-tended garden dotted with sculpture, a typical Nubian house, some tombs of Nubian saints, including one of 77 *wali* (Muslim shaykhs), and caves with prehistoric rock paintings brought here from all over Nubia.

Exhibits, covering the area's history from prehistoric times up to the present, are well-displayed and labelled in Arabic and English; a space is devoted to the international operation to rescue Nubia's monuments *(see page 161)*. The first section of the exhibition is devoted to archaeological finds such as jewellery, statues, sarcophagi and other objects, including, in the main exhibition hall, an impressive statue of Ramesses II built by Setau, the Viceroy of Kush. The second section of the museum illustrates Nubian culture and crafts in a series of tableaux.

Enjoying afternoon tea on the terrace of the Sofitel Old Cataract Hotel.

Elephantine Island

Most of Aswan's sights lie on the islands or on the west bank. A boatman or the public ferry will sail you across to **Elephantine Island ⓒ**. The island's small

BELOW: home on Elephantine Island.

TIP

One of the most pleasurable things to do in Aswan is to hire a *felucca* in the late afternoon and either cruise among the islands opposite Aswan or sail down to the First Cataract and Sahil Island. Your captain will probably serve mint tea on the way.

BELOW: the granite boulders of Elephantine Island.

museum ❿ (daily, winter 8.30am–5pm, summer 8.30am–6pm; admission charge) occupies a colonial-style building originally constructed as a resting place for the British engineers engaged on building the original Aswan Dam. The exhibits include Old and Middle Kingdom objects from local sites, treasures from the Heqaib Sanctuary, and various objects of the New Kingdom and Graeco-Roman period. The latter include sarcophagi containing mummies of a priest and priestess of Philae as well as a mummy of the sacred ram. However, many of the museum's best exhibits have been moved to the Nubian Museum south of the Old Cataract Hotel *(see page 173)*. The museum has a pleasant, well-kept garden and a path leads to the ruins of Yebu and an ancient nilometer.

The **Nilometer ❺** may not be as striking as some, but it is still interesting. It consists of a stairway on the river's bank constructed of regular-shaped stones designed so that the water, rising and falling with the ebb and flow of the flood, could register maximum, minimum and average water levels. A text on a wall of the Temple of Horus at Edfu *(see page 191)* tells us that when the river rose to 24 cubits and three and a half hands at Elephantine, there was sufficient water to supply the needs of the whole country.

The level of taxation was also governed by the level of the water, as a higher flood usually resulted in a better harvest. Plutarch, the Greek writer, recorded that the Nile once rose to a height of 28 cubits, or 14.7 metres (47 ft). The Nilometer here was repaired by the Khedive Ismail in 1870. A new scale was established and the ancient construction, unused for centuries, came into use once more. On the walls of the staircase are records in Demotic (fluid hieroglyphic hand) and Greek, showing different water levels.

The Old Town of Yebu, on the southern tip of Elephantine Island, is still

being excavated. Among the monuments are a granite portal that once formed the entrance to a large temple, the foundations of a small temple built by Naktanebos II, the last native pharaoh, Julius Caesar and Trajan (AD 98–117), and blocks from the edifices of earlier temples. The most important piece of restoration is that of the elegant Temple of Satis, goddess of the Cataract Region, wife of Khnum, who guarded the "new water" of the rising of the Nile.

On the other tip of the island is the concrete tower of the Oberoi Hotel and several beautiful Nubian villages set in lush gardens.

Kitchener's Island

Lord Kitchener, British Consul of Egypt, was granted **Kitchener's Island** Ⓕ by the Egyptian government for his campaigns in the Sudan. Kitchener was passionate about botany and imported and planted a large variety of rare African and Indian plants here. Kitchener's mark is also to be seen in graffiti relating to his Sudan campaigns on the walls of the Temple of Isis at Philae, on Agilqiyyah Island near the Aswan Dam *(see page 179)*.

The whole island (daily 7am–sunset, until 6pm in summer; admission charge) is open to the public as a fragrant botanical garden with an impressive collection of palm trees and other exotic plants. It makes a perfect escape from the heat and dust of the town. (If you arrive by *felucca*, your boatman will normally deposit you near the entrance to the botanical garden and then sail around to pick you up from the exit.)

Among the other islands are Amun Island, on which the Amoun Hotel, run by Club Med, occupies a former royal lodge, and, further south, Isis Island, with a much larger holiday resort.

A shady path in the Botanical Gardens on Kitchener's Island, which are planted with flora from all around the world

BELOW:
Aswan fishermen.

Aswan is a good place for spotting wintering birds. Salugah Island, between Elephantine and Sahil islands, has been designated a protected reserve.

BELOW: St Simeon's Monastery.

The west bank

On the summit of a hill on the west bank opposite Aswan is the domed structure of **Qubbet al-Hawa** or "Dome of the Wind". This is not, as is popularly believed, the tomb of a shaykh, but one of several signal posts built in the 19th century, most of which bore the name of a saint or shaykh. Nearby are the **Tombs of the Nobles** (daily 7am–5pm; admission charge), the burial ground of the noblemen from Elephantine. The tombs were hewn out of rock about halfway up the hill, facing the river and approached by a narrow ledge. The group of OldKingdom tombs is especially interesting because the door-jambs bear autobiographical texts written by ancient Egyptians who explored the African continent. A decree by Pharaoh Pepi I (*circa* 2300 BC) refers several times to "the peaceful Nubians", and inscriptions in many of the tombs make reference to them. One of these tombs (No. 34) belongs to a nobleman called Harkhuf who lived in the reign of the 6th-Dynasty pharaoh Merenre (*circa* 2280 BC). Harkhuf styled himself a "caravan leader"; he went on many journeys southwards, perhaps as far as the Sudan and beyond, and he recorded that "never had any companion or caravan-leader done it before".

On each of his travels, Harkhuf brought back precious products: gold, ostrich feathers, animal skins, ivory, ebony, incense and gum. On his fourth expedition, he brought back a "dancing pygmy" for his pharaoh, the young Pepi II, successor of Merenre, who acceded to the throne at the age of six. In his record of the event, Harkhuf states that he sent his messengers ahead of his convoy to inform His Majesty of his gift, to which Pepi wrote back, with enthusiasm, that the pygmy should be guarded so as not to let it fall overboard.

Another example of pioneering spirit and filial devotion can be found in the

Map on page 172

tombs of Mekhu and his son Sabni. A nobleman of Elephantine in the reign of Pepi II, *circa* 2280 BC, Mekhu was attacked and killed by desert tribes while on an expedition in Lower Nubia. When his son Sabni received the news, he mustered a convoy of troops and pack-donkeys and marched southwards to recover the body. The text on Sabni's tomb relates how he duly punished the tribe responsible for his father's death, recovered the body and started his journey home. Meanwhile the pharaoh, who had been informed by Sabni of his intention, had despatched a whole convoy of royal embalmers and mortuary priests along with the necessary oils and linens for the mummification of Mekhu. In an expression of gratitude, Sabni delivered the spoils of Mekhu's convoy to the pharaoh at Memphis.

West of Qubbet al-Hawa, hidden in the flanks of the Western Desert, is the large and well preserved **Deir al-Saman** ❻ (Monastery of St Simeon; daily 7am–5pm; admission free, but tip the guardian). It is dedicated to a local 5th-century saint. The present construction dates from the 7th century, and there is evidence of restoration in the 10th century, but the building is thought to have originated from much earlier times. The monastery was abandoned in the 13th century, either because of lack of water or the threat of marauding tribes. At over 6 metres (18 ft) high, the enclosing wall is fortress-like. The view from the upper level, built over the northern wall, is one of the most picturesque of Egypt's desert scenes.

The **Mausoleum of the Aga Khan** ❶ and his wife the Begum (closed to the public), also in the Western Desert, is another famous landmark. The Aga Khan, the spiritual leader of the Ismaili sect of Islam (he claimed direct descent from Fatima, the daughter of the Prophet Muhammed) liked to winter in Egypt to seek relief from rheumatism. The tomb was built in the Fatimid style with a single dome, one of the most significant developments of Islamic architecture between the 10th and 12th centuries. Its outer walls are of rose granite and the inner walls are of marble embellished with verses from the Koran. Each day a fresh rose is placed on the tomb.

BELOW: local faces.

South of the mausoleum is the island of **Sahil**, dominated by two hills in which over 250 inscriptions from the Middle Kingdom up to Ptolemaic times are carved into the granite rock. These inscriptions record expeditions further south or tell about their safe return. On top of the Eastern hill is the Famine Stele, relating how a seven-year famine during the Old Kingdom was ended by building a temple for Khnum, the god of the cataract. The summit commands great views over the First Cataract.

The unfinished obelisk

On the fringes of the Eastern Desert, in the southern perimeters of Aswan, lie the famous granite quarries, the main source of granite in ancient Egypt. The quarries were exploited throughout the ancient period right through to Graeco-Roman times. The Fourth Dynasty pharaohs who built the pyramids of Giza (2613–2494 BC) were among those who used stone from here. Nine great slabs of granite, 54 tonnes each, were extracted for the ceiling of the so-called King's

The unfinished obelisk, with its fatal crack, still lies in its ancient quarry. The proximity of the quarry to the Nile made transporting such obelisks relatively easy.

BELOW:
the Mausoleum
of the Aga Khan.

Chamber of the Pyramid of Khufu (Cheops); red granite was chosen for the Temple of Khafre (Chephren), and black granite was quarried for the lower reaches of the outer casing of the Pyramid of Menkaure (Mycerinus).

The lofty obelisk of Queen Hatshepsut at Karnak, made of a single block of pink granite, was also quarried in Aswan and transported by river to Luxor. A further **unfinished obelisk** ❶ is still lying in the quarry (daily 7am–5pm) attached to the bedrock. There is no indication for whom it was intended but, had it been completed as originally planned, it would have weighed some 1,162 tonnes, and soared to a height of 42 metres (126 ft). It seems to have been abandoned because of a crack in the stone.

The process by which the stone was extracted is deduced by examining the quarry. Holes are bored along a prescribed straight line, and it was once thought that wooden wedges were driven into these, watered and left to expand so as to split the stone. Recent excavations, however, show that balls of dolerite, one of the hardest types of stone, were attached to rammers and simultaneously and repeatedly struck with great force by the quarry workers until the stone separated. These dolerite balls, some weighing up to 5.5 kg (12 lbs), have been found in their hundreds in the area.

The Aswan dams

South of the quarries is the **Old Aswan Dam** ❸. The first barrage across the Nile was built at the apex of the Delta north of Cairo in 1842. This was soon followed by others: at Assiut in Middle Egypt and at Esna and Aswan in Upper Egypt. The Aswan Dam was erected above the First Cataract between 1899 and 1902 when Egypt was still a British Protectorate. Its height was increased

between 1908 to 1912 and again between 1929 and 1934. With each successive heightening, the thwarted waters increased in volume, threatening monuments and settlements alike. In the 1960s the **High Dam**  or Sadd al-Ali was built by President Nasser with the help of the then Soviet Union *(see page 172)*, necessitating the movement of many ancient monuments that would otherwise have been engulfed by Lake Nasser.

Map on page 172

Excursion to Philae

In between the dams is one of the most important of the monuments that were moved after the building of the High Dam, the Ptolemaic **Temple of Isis** at **Philae** (daily 7am–5pm; admission charge plus boat charge). The cult of Isis flourished here until well into the Christian era and the temple was in use until around AD 550. Bigah Island, believed to be the burial place of the left leg of the god Osiris and the first tip of land to appear out of the primeval waters, was so sacred that only the priesthood had access to it, so it was on the neighbouring island of Philae that the popular cult of Isis developed. The Temple of Isis was developed over more than 700 years by Ptolemaic and Roman rulers who wanted to identify with this Egyptian cult. Fantastic tales were told of the goddess's magical powers. When the evil god Seth chopped his brother Osiris's body into pieces, and scattered them all over Egypt, his beloved wife Isis, the Great Mother of All Gods, searched the land to find them and, using her knowledge of sacred formulae, pieced him back together. Her spells also saved her son Horus from a poisonous snake.

After the first dam was built, the temple was under water for six months of the year, and the rest of the time visitors could sail amongst its ruins by boat, like

"Seen from the level of a small boat," wrote Amelia Edwards of Philae in A Thousand Miles up the Nile *in 1873–74, "those sculptured towers rise higher and ever higher against the sky. They show no sign of ruin or of age. All look solid, stately, perfect."*

BELOW: a Soviet monument, the High Dam.

Carving on the wall.
of the Temple of Isis,
Philae Island.

the traveller Amelia Edwards. The creation of Lake Nasser following the building of the High Dam threatened to submerge the temple completely, so it was
moved it to the nearby island of Agilqiyyah, which was landscaped to resemble
the original site.

Salvaging the temple

The salvage contract to rescue the temple from the water was awarded to an Italian company which started with the construction of a coffer dam in 1977. The
stone blocks (47,000 in number) were then cleaned and stored. Meanwhile, 450
tonnes of granite were blown off the top of the neighbouring island of
Agilqiyyah to accommodate the temples. Some of the granite was used to
enlarge part of the island so as to resemble the shape of Philae.

The stones were then transported to their new home and, in just 30 months,
re-erected. Many of the blocks were replaced in the course of the reconstruction
so the result is rather pristine, but you can still see a water-level mark on the
entrance pylons. The old island of Philae – a sandbank surrounded by the rusty
remains of the coffer dam – is still visible from Agilqiyyah.

Exploring Philae

Today the temple is approached by boat from the Shallal boatyard south of
Aswan, where you can also buy tickets to the temple. The official price for boats
is posted at the dockyard, but this only allows for a one-hour visit so if you want
to spend more time you should negotiate with your captain.

Boats land near the ancient quay and the Vestibule of Nectanebo I, the oldest
structure on the island. Beyond lies a vast court, surounded by elegant colon-

BELOW:
the Temple of Isis.

Map on page 172

nades, in front of the massive **First Pylon** of the Temple of Isis. Taking the small door to the left, you can see the lovely carvings of Isis suckling her baby in the marshes in the 3rd century BC **Birth House**, built by Ptolemy I; this is sometimes cited as the origin of the Christian image of the Virgin Mary suckling the infant Christ. The larger gate, flanked by two granite lions, leads to the **Second Pylon** and a **Hypostyle Hall**. Beyond is the Inner Sanctuary, but the granite shrines are now in European museums. Stairs lead to the upper floor and the **Osiris Room** (tip the guardian to obtain access) with reliefs depicting the story of Osiris and Isis.

A relief alluding to the source of the Nile can be seen in **Hadrian's Gateway**, just to the west of the Temple of Isis. It shows blocks of stone heaped one upon the other, with a vulture (representing Upper Egypt) and a hawk (representing Lower Egypt) standing on top. Beneath the rocks is a circular chamber which is outlined by the contours of a serpent within which Hapi, the Nile-god, crouches. He clasps a vessel in each hand, ready to pour the water towards Egypt and bring goodness to the land. Also here is a beautifully tender scene of Isis looking at a crocodile carrying her husband's body to Biga.

The monuments at Philae, particularly the grand **Trajan's Kiosk**, dating from about AD 100, are covered in graffiti from almost every era of history. A Greek inscription in the Osiris shrine above the sanctuary of the Temple of Isis reveals that even as late as AD 453 Isis was worshipped here by the Blemmys, tribes of the Eastern Desert, long after the edict of Theodosius had declared that pagan temples should be closed. The monuments of Philae, therefore, represent the last outpost of ancient Egyptian tradition on its native soil. Known as the "Pearl of the East", the temple is the only monument dedicated to a single goddess. ❑

TIP

An excellent sound and light show is held at the Temple of Isis; check with the Aswan tourist office for times.

BELOW: the goddess Isis on the pylons of the Temple of Isis.

ASWAN TO LUXOR

The lush riverbanks between Aswan and Luxor are peppered with Ptolemaic temples, one or two of them right on the river bank

Map on page 186

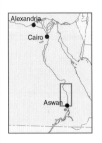

The river journey between Aswan and Luxor is a popular route for cruise boats, which usually spread the journey over three or four days. Village life along the Nile – particularly picturesque in this part of Upper Egypt – can be viewed from the comfort of a sun-lounger, and there are occasional stops to visit the Ptolemaic temples of Kom Ombo, Edfu and Esna, which are all well preserved and notable for their detailed reliefs. Such modern cruises have an ancient pedigree. Greeks, Macedonians, Carians and Persians visited Egypt for pleasure from as early as the 6th century BC. Then came Roman emperors and their ladies, many of whom also went river cruising, followed in the 19th century by European aristocrats.

At one time this trip was also possible by *felucca* in around five days. Though uncomfortable (passengers slept on board and the captain did the cooking), this was a popular option among young travellers, who often negotiated directly with the boatmen in Aswan. However, security concerns mean that this is not currently feasible, though restrictions may ease in the future.

It is also difficult to travel by taxi because of a government requirement that all foreigners travel in armed convoy *(see page 234)*. You should check with the tourist office to see if such restrictions are in force; if they are, you will need to join the first convoy of the day, and will only be able to visit one temple – probably Edfu – joining the second convoy to continue your journey north. There is no accommodation between Aswan and Luxor, and restaurants are few and far between, so take a picnic.

PRECEDING PAGES: carving of the gods Sobek and Horus, Kom Ombo. **LEFT:** a guardian stops work to pray. **BELOW:** freewheeling in Edfu.

South to north

The ancient Egyptians did not, as we do, orient themselves towards the north, but towards the south, the source of the flood which was the bearer of life. In sailing from Aswan, you are therefore moving northwards from Egypt's "first" Upper Egyptian province, which extended from the cataract region to a mountain chain north of Kom Ombo known as Jabal as-Silsila. From there, the 2nd to 4th provinces extended as far as Luxor. The nome capitals (chief towns of each province) acted as centres for local administration and housed the temples of the major deities of the region.

This is a fascinating part of Upper Egypt, where ancient monuments and early Christian settlements stand side by side with modern factories producing goods ranging from fertilisers to molasses. Though agriculture was probably introduced into the Nile valley in about 5,000 BC, a farmer today is probably almost as hard-working as his counterpart in ancient times. He rises with the sun and retires early (though electricity has brought television to many rural areas), tends his land with a wooden plough, transports produce by don-

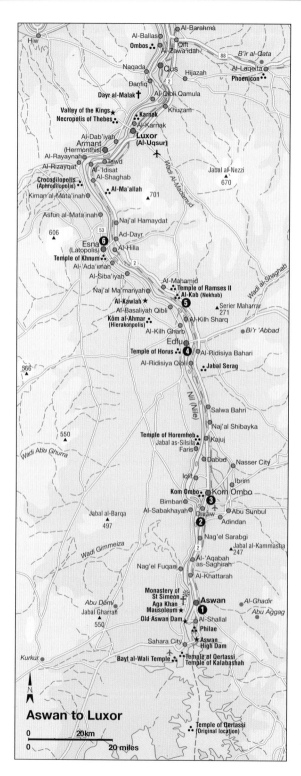

Aswan to Luxor

0   20km

0   20 miles

key, and draws water by a water-wheel driven by buffaloes. In rural Egypt there have been few technical advances for thousands of years.

The sun and the universe

In a largely rainless country the sun is an insistent presence and it is no wonder that it was so central to ancient Egyptian beliefs. The sun was seen to sail across the heavenly ocean in a barge each day, from the pink-speckled dawn to the fiery sunset. With the last rays of the day, it transferred to another barge that continued the voyage through the underworld, bringing light to its darkened spheres. During the sun's absence the northern stars, the ones that never set, were "the eternal ones", the place of the afterlife.

The ancient Egyptians had a delightful and imaginative concept of the universe. They saw their world as confined in something like a large box, with a narrow, oblong floor with Egypt as its centre. The river, arising from the eternal ocean in the south flowed towards the eternal ocean (the Mediterranean) in the north. The sky was conceived like an iron ceiling sprinkled with suspended stars. The people who lived within this protected area were *remej*, quite simply "people". All others were "sand wanderers", "desert wanderers" or people of the hill country. In other words, they were not the inhabitants of the flat land, the fertile, god-given land of Egypt.

The Ancient Egyptians also devised explanations about the environment. The land was Geb the earth-god who, in the beginning, was locked in an embrace with Nut, the sky-goddess. Then Shu, representing the atmosphere, emerged from the primeval waters and separated the two by slipping between them and raising Nut aloft in his outstretched arms to her new abode. Geb was left on the ground where the crops sprouted from his body. Geb and Nut were father and mother of four deities: Osiris, associated with the Nile and the fertile lands bordering it, Isis his wife, Seth, the god associated with the desert, and Nepthys his wife.

Map
on page
186

Camel market

As the river pushes north of **Aswan ❶**, it leaves behind the granite rocks that are characteristic of the area. The desert here comes virtually to the riverbank, tinted with red ochre from iron mines. But after this arid beginning, the river-banks become more fertile at the village of **Daraw ❷**, on the eastern bank of the Nile, where, if you are lucky, you may catch sight of a caravan of camels kicking up the dust or crossing the river on the ferry. Daraw is the end of the Darb al-Arbaeen or the Forty Days Road, one of the last surviving desert routes, running from Darfur and Kordofan in Sudan, through the Libyan Desert to Dongola, and then further along the Nile. The camels, which in Egypt are used as beasts of burden and for meat, are sold in Daraw's weekly camel market (Souq al-Gimaal; Tues 6.30am–2pm and, in winter only, Sun am), where many are then transported by road to the Birqash camel market in northwest Cairo.

Although the Daraw market attracts an increasing number of tourists it is still an exotic sight. It is best to visit the market before 10.30am, when the Sudanese traders are at their liveliest. There is plenty to look at, and visitors are welcome to join the traders in the makeshift cafés under the tents.

A temple for crocodiles

The river now takes a curve to the west and, on the eastern bank, an imposing temple stands proud. It is the Ptolemaic temple of **Kom Ombo ❸** (daily 7am–5.45pm; admission charge), constructed on what must be one of the most picturesque locations in Egypt. The town of Kom Ombo is some distance inland and the temple has been left in splendid isolation, unlike many others which have been swallowed up by recent construction. The temple, which was cleared

Right up until the end of the 19th century crocodiles infested this part of the Nile. In ancient Egypt crocodiles were worshipped in areas where the Nile was particularly dangerous, such as at Kom Ombo and in the cataract region south of Aswan.

BELOW:
playing dominoes
in a local café.

BELOW: the camel market, Daraw.

by the Antiquities Department in 1873, is in an excellent state of preservation, despite some earthquake damage in 1992 and the fact that the river, which runs extremely fast at this point, has washed away part of the temple. A special pier enables vessels to moor immediately beneath it.

The ancient city of Ombos probably owed its foundation to the strategic importance of this site, on a hill *(kom)* commanding both the Nile and the trade routes from Nubia to the Nile valley. Yet the town attained no great prosperity until Ptolemaic times (332–30 BC) when it became the capital of a separate province. Construction of the Great Temple of Kom Ombo began under Ptolemy V *(circa* 205–80 BC*)*, and was continued by Ptolemy VIII and XII (Neos Dionysos), but was finished under the Roman emperors Tiberius, Domitian Caracalla, Geta and Macrinus.

The temple was not dedicated to a single deity, as was usual in ancient Egypt, but to two unrelated gods: Horus the Elder, or Harouris, and Sobek, the crocodile-god, a partnership that is particularly odd when you consider that reliefs at Edfu *(see page 191)*, a little to the north of Kom Ombo, depict the evil Seth in the guise of a crocodile being killed by Horus. The reason for this may have been because the Ptolemies saw how many of Egypt's traditions were presented in dualistic terms (a double crown for the pharaoh, who was called "Lord of the Two Lands" – Upper and Lower Egypt), and saw nothing unusual in building this double temple to two hitherto unrelated deities. The gods are given equal billing in the temple and occupy symmetrical halves.

The temple is entered via a massive gateway built by Neos Dionysos, with, on the right, a small chapel of Hathor which is now home to some mummified crocodiles found in a nearby cemetery. Hundreds of these mummified crocodiles were

discovered in 1960 during the construction of the Aswan to Kom Ombo road, but the unpleasant smell became so overpowering that most of them had to be removed. It is thought that a crocodile was kept in the small square pool in the middle of the courtyard.

The temple complex was built on traditional lines with an entrance pylon, open court, hypostyle hall and sanctuary, but most of the first pylon, forecourt and birth house have slipped into the Nile. As it was dedicated to two gods, there is an invisible division down the middle of the temple: the right side is dedicated to Sobek, while the left side is dedicated to Harouris. Two separate doorways lead past halls and antechambers to the twin sanctuaries where the sacred statues of the deities were kept. Two different sets of priests would have attended the sanctuaries.

The entrance of the temple leads into the **Hypostyle Hall**, which is noted for its grand columns with foliage capitals, and has walls decorated with fine reliefs of Neos Dionysos appearing in front of the gods. The **Second Hypostyle Hall** is older and shows well preserved reliefs of Ptolemy V making the usual offerings. The sanctuaries are mostly ruined but between the entrance doors is a superb relief of Ptolemy VI and his wife receiving a palm frond from both Sobek and Horus.

Between the two sanctuaries is a hidden corridor – now exposed – that was built into the thickness of the wall. This secret place could only be approached from a chamber situated immediately to the rear, where a portion of the floor could be raised to admit a priest to a passage below ground level. A priest whispering through the wall at the worshippers in the sanctuaries must have played an important part in the oracular power attributed to the two deities.

Map on page 186

BELOW: herding the camels to market.

Detail in the sandstone temple at Kom Ombo.

Behind the sanctuaries is a stairway leading up to the roof, which offers a good view over the complex and its surroundings. On the north wall of the corridor look for a relief showing a display of what are taken to be surgical instruments. This is often upheld as evidence of the immense sophistication of medicine in ancient Egypt. In fact, although the medicine of the ancient Egyptians was advanced for its time, there were also great gaps in their knowledge. It was believed, for example, not only that the heart was connected to the stomach but also that it was the source of human intelligence. During the process of mummification, therefore, the brain was discarded.

Sandstone belt

North of Kom Ombo the range of hills known as the **Jabal as-Silsila** appears on the eastern bank, roughly halfway between Aswan and Luxor. This is the point at which the boat leaves the first province of Aswan, which geographically belongs to the sandstone belt of Nubia, and enters the limestone plateau of the rest of Egypt. The sandstone used at Thebes during the New Kingdom came from here. Prior to the New Kingdom most temples were built of mud-brick and quickly perished.

According to legend, the range was called Jabal as-Silsila ("Hills of the Chain") because the Nile was once closed against river traffic at this point by a great chain that stretched across it. The legend even points to two curiously shaped rocks that supposedly anchored the chain. In reality, the chain probably refers to the sandstone ridge that the Nile needed to break through in order to continue its journey north. Ancient rock-cut temples to Hapi, the god of the inundation, and Sobek, the crocodile god, were built at this spot. The remains

BELOW: the temple at Kom Ombo.

of these can still be seen on the east and west banks, and they are well worth exploring. Ancient graffiti and stelae litter the sites.

Edfu and the Temple of Horus

The next port of call is the provincial town of **Edfu ❹**. Its name is derived from the Coptic Atbo which, in turn, derived from the ancient name Tbot. The Greeks, who gave the site great importance, knew it as Great Apollinopolis.

The focus of interest at Edfu is the **Temple of Horus** (daily, winter 7am–4pm, summer 7am–5pm; admission charge), on the west bank of the Nile (*calèches* or horse carts usually transfer visitors from the river to the site and great numbers of these await the daily arrival of cruise boats); if you are driving, cross the river just past the village of Al-Ridisiya Bahari. This cult temple was built over a period of 180 years, from 237–57 BC, during the Ptolemaic era. Yet it follows all the rules of classic pharaonic architecture. It is unquestionably the best preserved temple in Egypt, not least because it was completely covered by sand until the 1860s, when the French Egyptologist Auguste Mariette undertook the massive task of excavating it.

A visit to the temple provides a clear picture of the layout and decoration of the archetypal Egyptian temple – an entrance pylon leading through to an open court with a 32-columned colonnade, a hypostyle hall and an inner sanctuary that would have contained a statue of the deity. The entrance is now at the rear of the temple, but it makes sense to walk its whole length and start a visit at the **Pylon**, which is notable for its large carvings of Ptolemy XII (Neos Dionysus) slaying his enemies in front of Horus and Hathor.

Horus, to whom the temple was dedicated, was the falcon (hawk) god, known

Map
on page
186

BELOW: reliefs on the columns of Kom Ombo.

in one form as Horus of Behedet. He was foremost a sun-god (often depicted with the solar disc over his head) but also a protector of kings and a guide to the dead in the underworld. Edfu was a cult centre since it was believed to be the spot where Horus fought with his uncle Seth for power over the world *(see page 179)*. Two large granite falcon statues of Horus stand at the entrance to the temple, while a pair of majestic statues of Horus as a hawk guard the gateway into the hypostyle hall. The deity is represented in reliefs throughout the complex, either as a man with a falcon's head, or as a solar disc with outspread wings. Throughout the temple, inside and out, the walls, pylons, corridors, halls, antechambers, sanctuary and inner chambers are embellished with reliefs that are considered among the most beautiful in Egypt, despite being partially defaced by early Christians, who particularly targeted faces and hands lest the images should come to life to haunt them.

The inner wall of the pylon, in the vast **Court of Offerings**, records the Festival of the Beautiful Meeting, when Horus joined his consort and sister Hathor at her temple in Dendarah. On the back walls of the first **Hypostyle Hall** are some superb reliefs illustrating the temple rituals. Off the Hypostyle Hall, a small room is known as the **House of the Morning**; it was here that the pharaoh would purify himself before performing temple rituals. Horus's statue was kept in the **Sanctuary**, which also contained his sacred barge. Around three sides of the sanctuary, separated from it by an ambulatory, is a series of shrines reserved for certain rites or dedicated to various other deities, all adorned with reliefs and showing traces of their original colour. Note also (in the east ambulatory) a nilometer, used for measuring the height of the annual inundation and setting taxes for the year, and, in front of the temple, a "birth house", or *mammisi*, a fea-

BELOW: women of Edfu take cover.

FARMING IN ANCIENT EGYPT

The annual flood was the source of remarkable fertility, but unless the waters of the inundation were retained for times of need, the fertility of the soil would last for only a few months. Without the farmer to create and mend water channels to carry the moisture to the outlying fields, the land would have yielded no more than the wild grain collected by the hunter-gathering communities of pre-dynastic times. The full exploitation of the Nile was only achieved through unremitting toil. The first season was the *akhet*, the inundation, which started with the rising waters in June and reached its height by July, the start of the New Year. Within a few weeks the water receded and the land was soon ready. This was the second season – the *perit* or "going forth" – beginning in mid-November. Although the farmer could simply cast the seed, reliefs show that he frequently turned the soil by means of a hoe or a plough.

The *shemu* (harvest), the third season, began in mid-March. Ceremonies were performed to mark the cutting of the first sheaf of grain and afterwards there were festivals of thanks. Because such festivals related to the reaffirmation of life, it was a time for merry-making and, right into the Persian period in the 6th century BC, it was also a time for the taking of marriage vows.

ture of all Ptolemaic temples in which the birth of a particular god occurred. There are also birth houses in the Ptolemaic temples of Dendarah and Philae.

One of the most interesting series of representations in the Temple of Horus relates to the New Year Festival. They show that each year the pharaoh, accompanied by priests bearing standards representing Egypt's ancient provinces, mounted the roof of the temple (the staircase still exists but is closed to tourists). The king was followed by a long procession of priests of a lower order, chanting and reciting hymns, some shaking sistrums, burning incense or carrying offerings. Priests of a higher order carried two caskets, bearing the statues of Hathor the cow-goddess and Horus the hawk-god, towards the roof.

More priests are shown following the procession. They burn incense to safeguard the sacred statues from evil spirits lurking in the temple. At the top of the staircase, priests with standards welcome the pharaoh who heads the procession. The caskets are placed on the roof of the temple to be revitalised by the rays of the rising sun.

Also depicted on the inner side of the outer walls, on the left side facing the sanctuary, is the second part of the Horus legend, telling the story of the battles against his evil brother Seth, who is represented both as a hippopotamus and a crocodile.

River scenes

As the Nile slips under the bridge at Edfu, it is interesting to note the different kinds of boats in the river. Many are the classical flat-bottomed *feluccas*, transporting produce – mostly pottery, grain, sugar cane and limestone – and sometimes tourists. Sailing northwards, *feluccas* have the flow of the Nile to power

Map on page 186

A granite statue of Horus guards the entrance pylon at Edfu.

BELOW: pylon of the Temple of Horus, Edfu.

A snake charmer in Edfu scans the street for passing custom.

BELOW: fishermen cast their nets.

them, and southbound the prevailing north wind. The smaller boats belong to fishermen who use long nets laid out in a semicircle.

Sadly, there are no longer any *dahabiyyas*, the traditional Arab sailing vessels introduced in the 7th century after the Arab conquest of Egypt. These large sailing boats with cabins were described by the 19th-century British writer and Egyptologist Amelia Edwards as the ultimate in luxury travel on the Nile. Still common in the 19th century, they were used for the first Nile cruises for westerners, introduced around 1830.

On the riverbanks you may catch sight of one of the ancient pumping methods that are still used today: the *shadouf,* a bucket and counterweight attached to the ends of a pile, operated by downward pressure to lift water from one level to another, dates back to pharaonic times; the Archimedean screw comprises a screw thread in a cylinder dipping into the water at an angle of not more than 30 degrees; and the *sakiya* consists of a chain of buckets passing over a vertical wheel dipping in the water, geared to a horizontal wheel turned by a blindfolded buffalo walking in circles. Of course, today there are also numerous electrical pumping devices of all shapes and sizes.

Crops cultivated on the riverside have remained largely unchanged since ancient times. They include vegetables, grains, lettuce, melons, cucumbers, onions, garlic and a sweet red carrot that is particular to Egypt. During pharaonic times flax was the fibre used for weaving, but this became obsolete with the arrival of cotton in the 7th century.

Egyptian farmers have always taken great care of their livestock, which in a poor country is an extremely valuable asset: several tombs have depictions of young farmhands feeding animals, milking them and assisting them in giving

birth to their young. Similar scenes are still enacted all along the Nile today. A farmer giving his charge a bath in a canal or on the banks of the river is a very common sight. Modern Egyptians still house their animals in the courtyards of their homes.

Map
on page
186

Wadi Abbad

The temples between Aswan and Luxor attract huge numbers of visitors, but very rarely visited, and well worth seeing, in the desert about 58 km (35 miles) east of Edfu is the **Temple of Wadi Abbad**, near the village of Redesyeh. Built by Seti I (1318–1304 BC) to serve goldminers and traders en route to the Red Sea, it occupies a spectacular site at the foot of sandstone cliffs and is partly cut into the rock. It has outstanding carved reliefs.

Warrior tombs

The ancient city of **Al- Kab ❺**, on the Nile north of Edfu, is on few river cruise itineraries. But this ancient city, known as Nekhab, once ranked among the chief cities of Egypt and even under the Ptolemies it was the capital of the 3rd province. The site (daily 8am–6pm; admission charge), which lies on the eastern bank, has recently been restored and prepared for tourists. The tombs have been made accessible by stairways and the surrounding area enhanced with trees and gardens.

Al-Kab was most prominent in around 1567 BC during the 18th Dynasty, when two of the city's young men were recruited to fight in the armies of Ahmose and Tuthmosis I. The two youths bore the same name as their pharaoh, Ahmose, who later became known as the "Father of the New Kingdom". The

BELOW:
mill workers pose
for the camera.

first was Ahmose son of Ebana, and the other was Ahmose Pennekhbet. Their tombs, among the most interesting of ancient Egypt, date from after the war of liberation from the Hyksos, a foreign power that occupied Egypt during the 2nd millennium BC. They consequently shed light on an extremely important period in Ancient Egyptian history.

Ahmose Pennekhbet lived through the war of liberation from the Hyksos and the wars that immediately followed. His tomb is a fascinating record of military activities and conquests. The hieroglyphs describe, in somewhat exaggerated prose, how he personally took prisoners, captured horses and chariots, and, on one occasion, killed the enemy because it was less trouble to do this than to take "living prisoners". As an aged warrior, he was appointed to the prestigious post of tutor to the eldest daughter of Queen Hatshepsut "while she was a child upon the breast."

Ahmose, son of Ebana, lived through a similar period of crisis, but his tomb is more significant for its biographical data than its artistic merit. He claimed that he was a "soldier and sailor too" and was also a "warrior of the ruler". The inscriptions describe how he fought "more than what is true" during a campaign in Nubia, and "showed great bravery" in the pharaoh's wars in western Asia. He claimed, furthermore, that he was at the head of the troops under Tuthmosis I, and that his king "beheld my valour" and "presented me with gold in double measure" in recognition of his worth. In his old age, Ahmose was apparently content in his retirement, happily reminiscing about his war years and his honourable record.

BELOW: Temple figures at Esna.

Opposite Al-Kab, on the western bank, is the ancient city of **Nekhen**, an important archaeological site which can only be visited by special permission.

DEFEATING THE HYKSOS

The Hyksos, foreign invaders believed to have come from the region of Syria, conquered Egypt in around 1648 BC. They came with horses and chariots (hitherto unknown in Egypt), swept across the northern Sinai, fortified a stronghold at Tall a'-Deba, south of Tanis in the northeastern Delta, then moved towards the apex of the Delta, from where they surged southward.

The humiliation of foreign occupation came to an end when the young warrior-king Kamose and, later, his brother Ahmose, regarded as the Father of the New Kingdom (18th–20th Dynasties, 1551–1085 BC), started a war of liberation and finally expelled the invaders from the land.

This first unhappy exposure to foreign domination left a lasting mark on the Egyptian character. The seemingly inviolable land of Egypt had to be protected from invasion and to do so meant not only to rid the country of enemies, but to pursue them into western Asia. Out of the desire for national security was born the spirit of military expansion characteristic of the New Kingdom. The later military conquests of Tuthmosis III, in no fewer than 17 campaigns, resulted in the establishment of Egyptian power throughout Syria and northern Mesopotamia, as well as in Nubia and Libya.

The city was the pre-dynastic capital of Upper Egypt, and relics of the earliest kings of Egypt have been found here. These include some of the most famous treasures of the Egyptian Museum in Cairo, including the Palette of Narmer, the pharaoh traditionally known as Menes who unified Upper and Lower Egypt in 3100 BC and brought the whole of the Nile Valley under his domination. The Palette, which commemorates the unification, depicts Narmer about to smash the skull of his defeated enemy.

Map
on page
186

Esna and the barrage

The barrage at Esna was erected in 1908–09 to regulate irrigation as far as Qena, north of Luxor. Today it is a major stumbling block for the cruise industry, as the lock is slow to operate and can take only one boat at a time, so boats must sometimes queue for hours here. Moreover, at times of low water the river authorities sometimes close the lock altogether as it drains too much water from the upper reaches of the river. An Italian-built hydroelectric barrage, known locally as the "Electricity Bridge" was built in the 1990s; it also has a lock that lets vessels through.

Esna ❻ itself is a district capital and the largest town between Aswan and Luxor. Although some of the buildings hint at the prosperity of times long past, the town is rather uninspiring today. Were it not for the temple one would be hard-pressed to recognise this as one of the most important places in Upper Egypt in antiquity and it is also a far cry from the city of brothels and dancing girls as described by the French writer Gustave Flaubert. There is, however, a small camel market in town on Saturday mornings, and some old houses around the temple have kept their beautiful *mashrabiyya* screens.

BELOW: the Temple of Khnum, Esna.

A felaheen (Egyptian peasant) tends his fields. The ancient gods that were worshipped in the Esna region were all associated with agriculture and fertility.

BELOW: farming in the Nile Valley.

The Ptolemaic **Temple of Khnum** (daily winter 6am–5.30pm; summer 6am–6.30pm; admission charge) was almost totally obscured by the modern town until relatively recently, and today it lies in a large depression well below the level of the modern buildings, five minutes' walk from the river. Khnum was a ram-headed creator god said to have moulded man on a potter's wheel, who also guarded the source of the Nile.

The temple was probably as large as the one in Edfu, but so far only the Roman hypostyle hall has been excavated, an exercise begun by Mohammed Ali in 1842, not, it is recorded, for cultural reasons but "in order to provide a safe underground magazine for gunpowder." Mariette completed the task later that century. Literally dozens of houses were removed from its precincts, and the lip of the depression is still crowded with the modern buildings.

The most noticeable part of the temple is the **Hypostyle Court**; its roof is still intact and supported by six rows of four columns, each with elaborately carved capitals. There are 16 different types for the 24 bud- and flower- columns. The walls and columns are decorated with reliefs which may not be the finest in quality but are of considerable interest for their content. They carry scenes of the various Roman emperors depicted as Egyptian pharaohs sacrificing to the gods and carrying out ritual observances, underlining how keen the Romans were to show respect to the Egyptian pantheon, even though they did not enjoy the affinity that the Ptolemies had with the Egyptians.

Among the most interesting is a relief near the bottom of the northern wall showing the Emperor Commodus in the company of the hawk-headed Horus and the ram-headed Khnum drawing in a clap-net full of waterfowl and fish (the Nile perch was a recognised deity here), observed by the ibis-headed Thoth.

The ceiling has an astronomical calendar which is second only to the one in Dendarah for detail and fine execution.

The temple is important because the Emperor Trajan Decius (AD 249–251) is the last Roman name to appear in a royal cartouche (an elliptical sign bearing the name of the pharaoh) in an Egyptian temple. Some of the hieroglyphs here have proved to be indecipherable.

Environs of Luxor

The last stretch of the journey towards Luxor is uneventful. In the background lie the hills of the Western Desert, with a foreground of extensive palm-groves interrupted by the smoking chimneys of brick factories. The town of **Armant**, the ancient Hermonthis, on the western bank of the Nile can hardly be seen from the river, but two summits, known as Jabalian ("two mountains") can be spotted. On the higher of these is the tomb of a holy woman called Shaykha Musa.

Armant is the site of one of many sugar factories in Upper Egypt. This important crop was introduced to Egypt at the beginning of the 19th century by the Khedive Ismail. In spring you will find this part of Upper Egypt a hive of activity as the valuable sugar cane harvest gets underway. Trucks race around delivering the cut cane to the sugar factories, where the juice is pressed, and then convey it to the sugar refineries in the north.

Approaching Luxor, the Nile begins to get wider, and the hills recede to the west and to the east, curving away from the river's bank and leaving broad plains on either side. This was the site chosen for Thebes: few spots in Egypt are so ideally suited for the growth of a great city; few places in the world have bequeathed to us more numerous or mightier monuments. ❑

Map on page 186

The terrace of the Temple of Esna has some interesting graffiti from the Napoleonic era, including the names of some of the soldiers in the army that pursued the Mameluks down the Nile in 1798 (see page 95).

BELOW: sugar plantation between Aswan and Luxor.

LUXOR

*Ancient Thebes rose to pre-eminence during the Middle and
New Kingdoms as the capital of a united Egypt. Its prosperity was
reflected in grand temples, tombs and palaces*

Map on page 204

L uxor, ancient Thebes, is like a huge open-air museum spread over both
sides of the Nile. On the east bank, the town side, are the Temple of Luxor
and the Temple of Amun-Re at Karnak. On the west bank, in the necropolis, or city of the dead, are the Valley of the Kings, the Valley of the Queens,
hundreds of tombs of noblemen, and a semicircle of grand mortuary temples
along the edge of the flood plain.

Luxor lies 675 km (420 miles) south of Cairo. It is often described by Egyptians as a "village" even though it has a population of 100,000 and an international airport where charter flights bring in as many as 2,000 tourists a day.
Unlike Aswan, with twice the population yet no international flights, it con-
ducts very little trade other than in staple foods and tourist services. Funda-
mentally it is a tourists' and farmers' town and once you get past the barrage of
over-pushy salesmen and *calèche* drivers (who actually do offer the best way of
touring Luxor) it is friendly.

From the river the town is almost hidden by the forest of cruise boats and
other crafts which moor, sometimes five deep, for 3–5 km (2–3 miles) along the
east bank, many tied up alongside prestigious hotels. Two or three ferry services
operate between the east and west bank (one of the most convenient operates
from opposite Luxor Temple); taxis and buses take
the road bridge south of town.

Inland from the corniche are the tourist *souq*, full
of kitsch Egyptiana, and behind that the local *souq* for
food and household goods, and the railway station.
Beyond that are the expanding but simple suburbs.

PRECEDING PAGES:
the Temple of
Amun-Re, Karnak.
LEFT: view of Queen
Hatshepsut's
Temple, Thebes.
BELOW: visiting the
tombs at Thebes.

Slumbering Thebes

Unlike Aswan, which bears an aura of what it always
was, a bustling border town, Luxor's monuments
alone hint at its ancient glory. Its name is derived from
the Arabic *al-Uqsur*, "the palaces", a reference to the
ruins that until the 1930s were half-buried in the sand.
Mud dwellings were built by the local people alongside the walls of temples, and dovecotes were erected
beside architraves and pylons. David Roberts's water-
colours of the ancient monuments, painted after his
first voyage to Egypt in 1838, romantically show the
temples with columns toppling, architraves falling,
and once lofty colonnades half-submerged in sand.

Today, the monuments have been excavated and
restored and it is possible to visualise the ancient city
of Thebes, a city that once epitomised the splendour
and magnificence of the ancient world. For over four
centuries the city was unrivalled in Egypt, and for part
of that time it was the centre of the ancient world.

Thebes was of no particular significance for the
first 2,000 years of ancient Egyptian history. It started

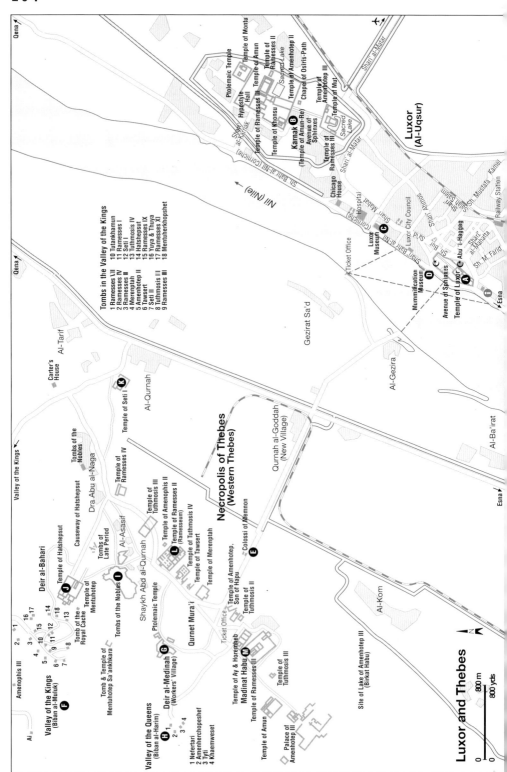

Luxor and Thebes

Tombs in the Valley of the Kings

1 Ramesses VII
2 Ramesses IV
3 Ramesses III
4 Merenptah
5 Amenhotep II
6 Tawsert
7 Seti II
8 Tuthmosis III
9 Ramesses III
10 Tutankhamun
11 Ramesses I
12 Seti I
13 Tuthmosis IV
14 Hatshepsut
15 Ramesses IX
16 Yuya & Thuya
17 Ramesses XI
18 Mentuherkhopshef

Valley of the Kings
(Biban al-Muluk)

Valley of the Queens
(Biban al-Harim)

1 Nefertari
2 Amenherchopeshef
3 Tyti
4 Khaemweset

Necropolis of Thebes
(Western Thebes)

Luxor (Al-Uqsur)

Nil (Nile)

off no different from hundreds of other villages, and its inhabitants lived much as they do in Egypt's isolated rural areas today, in villages of sun-dried mud-brick houses separated by narrow lanes, their lives governed by the agricultural cycle and little else.

During this time the Old Kingdom civilisation (2686–2181 BC) was making headway in the north. Zoser, the builder of the Step Pyramid at Saqqarah, had complete control over the two lands of Upper and Lower Egypt and was developing a sophisticated society. Vessels over 50 metres (150 ft) long were constructed for river traffic, the copper mines in Sinai were exploited, commerce was carried out on the Phoenician coast, cedarwood was imported from Lebanon and slaves imported from Nubia. Ancient Thebes, however, simply slumbered, even when the powerful monarchs of the Fourth dynasty, Snofru, Khufu, Khafre and Menkaure, built the great pyramids at Giza.

Map on page 204

The rise of Thebes

It was only when the unlimited power enjoyed by the pharaohs was partly passed to their officials and local governors sought to establish independence from central government that political awareness developed in Thebes. This time was known as the First Intermediate Period, the Seventh to the 11th Dynasties (*circa* 2181–2133 BC), and it was then that a powerful family of monarchs, whose capital was in Armant near Thebes (today an industrial town just to the south), gained power and started to move northwards. Little by little they extended their authority, annexing local provinces until they they came into conflict with the rulers of the north. A civil war ensued, ending in triumph for the Thebans. Theban supremacy was recognised, Amun-Re was introduced as the local deity and Thebes began to develop and prosper.

BELOW: statue of Tuthmosis III in Luxor Museum.

But the city achieved its prominent place in Egyptian history following the wars of liberation from the hated Hyksos occupation. Tribespeople from the region of Syria, the Hyksos ruled Egypt between about 1786 and 1567 BC, at which point an Egyptian prince called Sekenenre and his son Kamose rose against them. Kamose's brother Ahmose was able to establish the 18th Dynasty, marking the start of what is now known as the New Kingdom, with Thebes at its centre. The Kingdom included the 18th, 19th and 20th Dynasties (*circa* 1551–1085 BC).

After ridding the country of foreign occupation, Thebes began to develop into the seat of a world power such as had never been seen before. Military conquests and territorial expansion went hand in hand with an artistic and architectural flowering of unparalleled grandeur. Greek visitors to Egypt were overwhelmed by the material wealth of the civilisation. Tuthmosis III (1490–1436 BC), was the Napoleon of ancient Egypt. He conducted no fewer than 17 campaigns, resulting in the creation of a vast empire comprising almost all of Western Asia including Palestine, Syria, Phoenicia, the western part of the Euphrates, Nubia, Kush (modern-day Sudan) and Libya.

As a result of military victory, booty from conquered nations and tributes from the provinces of the then known powers poured into the gigantic store-

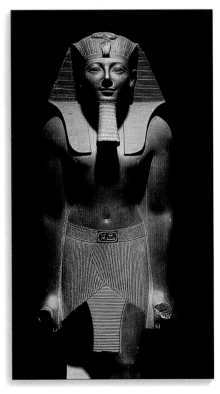

house of Thebes. The greater part of the wealth was bestowed upon Amun-Re, who, with the aid of the influential priesthood, was established as "The King of Gods". The Theban triad, or group of three gods, comprised Amun-Re, usually portrayed as a ram-headed sun-god, his wife Mut and son Khonsu. Both temples in Luxor were built in their honour, Amun-Re resided in the temple of Karnak, while the Luxor temple was known as the "Harem of the South". It was both a duty and a privilege to serve the great god, and successive pharaohs strove to outdo their predecessors in the magnificence of their endeavours.

Decline under Akhenaten

When Amun-Re was dishonoured by Amenhotep IV (Akhenaten), who worshipped the life-giving rays of the full solar disc, the Aten, in place of the ascending sun Re *(see chapter on the rebel Dynasty, pages 57–64)*, Thebes was suddenly overshadowed by Akhenaten's new capital at Tall al-'Amarnah. Reliefs were defaced, shrines destroyed and the image of Amun-Re hacked away. But the god's dethronement was short-lived. Tutankhamun, on succeeding to the throne, restored Thebes as capital and started to repair the temples; Haremhab, Ramesses I, Seti I and Ramesses II continued the work of rebuilding, reconstructing and renovating the temples, to restore the reputation of Amun-Re.

The advent of Christianity brought systematic destruction to the ancient monuments, initially in the tombs and shrines in which early Christians took refuge from Roman persecution. Later on the "pagan" statues were uprooted, sacred sanctuaries mutilated, and attempts made to topple obelisks and colossi to obliterate the visages of the "heathen gods". It wasn't until the 19th century that the pieces were slowly reassembled by modern archaeologists.

When Diodorus visited Thebes in 57 BC, the ancient splendour of the city was still talked about. The citizens told him: "There was no city under the sun so adorned with so many and stately monuments of gold, silver, and ivory and multitudes of colossi and obelisks cut out of one entire stone."

BELOW: a *calèche*, a favourite mode of transport in Luxor.

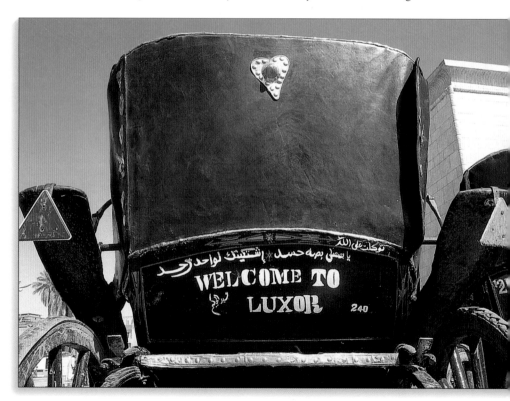

THE EAST BANK

The two main monuments on Luxor's east bank are the Temple of Luxor near the centre of the city and the Temple of Amun-Re at Karnak a little to the north, which were originally linked by 3-km (1¾-mile) long processional avenue lined with sphinxes. Both national temples (as these two are) and mortuary temples (those on the west bank, *see page 223–7*) were generally decorated on the outside with battle reliefs, such as Ramesses II's famous Battle of Qadesh, in which the pharaoh is shown trampling the enemy beneath the wheels of his chariot and capturing the Hittite fortress (this battle is portrayed both on the entrance pylon of the Temple of Luxor and in the Ramesseum on Luxor's west bank).

Maps: 204 & below

Other popular topics are Seti I fighting against the Bedouin tribes of Libya, Palestine and Syria, as seen on the northern outer wall of the Hypostyle Hall at Karnak, and Ramesses III in his naval battle against the "People of the Sea", who were probably Phoenicians, depicted on the northern, outer wall of the Temple of Ramesses III at Madinat Habu.

View of the Court of Ramesses II in the Temple of Luxor.

The Temple of Luxor

The **Temple of Luxor** Ⓐ (daily winter 6am–9pm; summer 6am–10pm; admission charge) was built by the 18th-Dynasty pharaoh Amenhotep III, the great-grandson of the military genius Tuthmosis III, and expanded by the 19th-Dynasty Ramesses II. Most of the complex is well preserved, particularly the wall reliefs, as it was covered in sand and built over by the town until excavations started in 1885. The structure follows the classical pattern of pharaonic temples: the pavement progressively rises and the roof declines from the entrance to the inner sanctuary. Only the pharaoh, or the high priest in his stead, was permitted to enter the darkened inner sanctuary and behold the statue of the deity. Nowadays the temple lies in the heart of Luxor town, and every so often forms the setting for a production of Verdi's *Aida*.

The **Avenue of the Sphinxes** leads straight up to the entrance **pylon**, decorated with the reliefs of Ramesses' victory in the Battle of Qadesh. Fronting the pylon are two seated colossi of the pharaoh and a damaged standing colossus. Dog-headed baboons support a superb **obelisk**, the twin of which has adorned the Place de la Concorde in Paris since 1833. The pylon leads to the **Court of Ramesses II** surrounded by two rows of papyrus-bud columns.

Perched high up to the left of the court, and easily missed at first, is the **Mosque of Abu 'l-Haggag**, the patron saint of Luxor, who is buried on the site. Founded in the 12th century by the Sufi mystic Abu 'l-Haggag, the mosque was built when the temple was almost completely covered in silt and sand. When excavations began on the temple, and houses were cleared away, the local people refused to allow any disturbance of the mosque. Since then the picturesque mosque hangs about 13 metres (40 ft) above ground level, with its foundations exposed.

An annual Sufi *mawlid* (festival) is held to celebrate the saint's day. During the festival several *feluccas* are carried up from the river to the mosque, not unlike in ancient days during the Opet festival *(see*

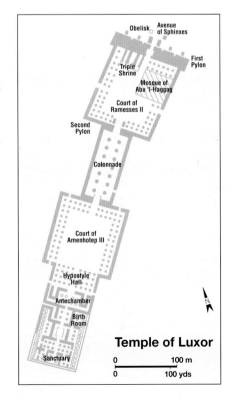

Temple of Luxor

page 208), when the sacred barge was carried up to the temple. This is the largest festival in Upper Egypt; the town is bedecked with flowers during the celebration, and dancing and clapping greets the procession.

On the western wall of the Court of Ramesses II is a beautiful relief of a funeral procession led by 17 of Ramesses II's 100 or so sons. A portal leads into the impressive **Colonnade of Amenhotep III** (1402–1364 BC), of exquisite proportions and a fine example of the architecture of this period. The reliefs on its walls, dating from the time of Tutankhamun (1357–1348 BC), depict the great Opet festival that took place each year at the height of the flood. During the festival the sacred statue of the god Amun-Re was taken out of the sanctuary at Karnak and, amidst great pomp and ceremony, transported in a sacred barge to Luxor to be reunited with the statues of his consort Mut and their son Khonsu. It remained here for a few days of celebrations and festivities, before being returned to Karnak. The occasion offered the people of Thebes a rare opportunity to glimpse the statue of Amun-Re, a chance repeated at the end of the year when a second festival was held in which Amun-Re was carried across the Nile to visit the mortuary temples of the dead pharaohs *(see page 215)*.

Reliefs illustrating preparations for the Opet festival can be seen on the right-hand wall of the temple's colonnade (some of which was reconstructed in the 1970s), including a rehearsal by dancing girls. They show the procession beginning at the gate of Karnak Temple, shown complete with flagstaffs, from which white-robed priests bear the sacred barge of Amun-Re down to the water's edge. An enthusiastic audience claps hands in unison, and it is accompanied upstream by celebrants along the shore; a sacrifice of slaughtered animals is followed by a group of acrobats, and finally offerings are made to the Theban

The Mosque of Luxor's patron saint, Abu 'l-Haggag, perches on top of part of the Temple of Luxor. It is the focus for the biggest festival in Upper Egypt.

BELOW: view from the Winter Palace Hotel.

riad at the Temple of Luxor. On the opposite wall are scenes of the festival's eturn procession. The barges are floated downstream, and the final sacrifice and offerings of flowers are made to the deities at Karnak Temple.

An important discovery was made in the **Court of Amenhotep III** at the end of 1989. When the flagstones were being lifted to check on the tilt of the land and possible undermining of the temple's columns, archaeologists found a hidden cache containing, among other objects, life-size statues of various New Kingdom pharaohs. Many of these are displayed in the New Hall of the Luxor Museum (*see page 212*).

Beyond this court are several chambers, some of which were adapted by the Romans into churches. Alexander the Great added the small end chapel, with reliefs of himself as an Egyptian.

Maps:
Luxor 204
Site 210

The Temple of Luxor is open until 9pm (winter) and 10pm (summer). It is well worth visiting in the evening, when it is flood-lit.

BELOW: Avenue of the Sphinxes, Luxor Temple.

Karnak

The great **Temple of Amun-Re** at **Karnak** ❸ (daily, winter 6am–5.30pm; summer 6am–6.30pm; admission charge) was the great god's chief sanctuary and is much larger and far more complex than the Temple of Luxor, or than any other monument in Egypt. The ancient Egyptians called it *Ipet-Isut* (the "most perfect of places").

It lies 2.5 km (1½ miles) north of the town centre, a 20-minute walk along the Corniche or a pleasant ride by *calèche* (discuss the price with your driver beforehand and be clear about whether you want a one- or two-way trip; if you want your driver to return later, you should count on spending around 2½–3 hours at the temple).

This huge and splendid complex which actually contains many separate

temples, covers 1,300 years of expansion and an area of 80 hectares (200 acres). Beneath its giant architraves and between bulky column and wall reliefs are records of its growth from a modest Middle Kingdom shrine to a magnificent temple of vast proportions. It owes a column to one pharaoh, a pylon to another; an inspiration here, a whim there. But each has the sole purpose of honouring the god, Amun-Re, who would then ensure the builder a long, powerful and glorious life.

Family rivalry was often the chief motivation behind new constructions. Often a reigning pharaoh would alter the royal cartouche of a former pharaoh and thereby take credit for the work of his predecessor (which may be why Ramesses II seems to have been so prodigious in temple building). To add to the confusion, some parts of the buildings were raised from dismantled shrines or the walls of other temples. In the case of Karnak, the matter was complicated further by the degradation of Amun-Re, first at the hands of the rebel pharaoh Akhenaten *(see page 57)* and then by the early Christians.

Karnak's granite colossus of Ramesses II with one of his daughters at his feet. Ramesses had some 60 daughters and actually married three of them.

The Precinct of Amun–Re

The Temple of Karnak is unusually built on a north–south instead of an east–west axis. The largest and most important precinct is the Precinct of Amun–Re, with the Precinct of Mut to the north side, and the Precinct of Khonsu on the west, although the latter are in a poor state of repair and rarely visited.

The site of the car park and souvenir shops outside the temple complex was once a landing stage for a canal connecting the temple to the Nile; from here the builders' and the festival barges came and went, including the barges used in the Opet festival *(see page 208)*. The processional way of ram-headed sphinxes

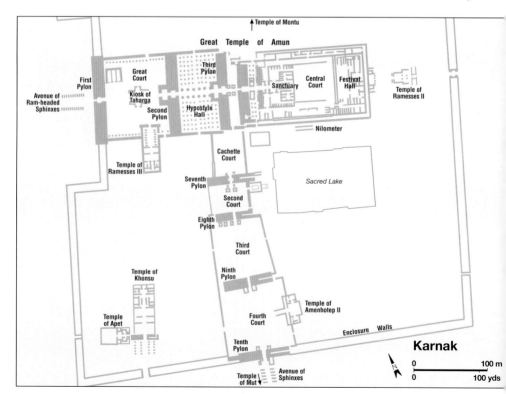

Maps:
Luxor 204
Site 210

with sun-discs on their heads and statues of the pharaoh between their forepaws once led from the river bank to the main entrance, while another row led all the way to the Temple of Luxor.

The two blocks of the massive entrance **pylon**, added by an Ethiopian king, are unadorned and unfinished. Note the mud-brick ramp (a large mass of rubble behind one of the entrance pylons) which was used during the construction of the pylon. It shows that the roughly-shaped stones, heaved into position on ramps, were shaped after their erection, and that the polishing and decoration were performed from the top downwards as the mud-brick ramps were removed layer by layer.

Behind lies the **Great Court**, a vast area of 8,919 sq. metres (95,433 sq. ft), built to enclose several older structures. It was the one part of the temple accessible to the general public. Within it are shrines, believed to have been used during the preparations of the Opet festival, another row of ram-headed sphinxes and a small well-preserved **Temple of Ramesses III**. Its court is lined with Osiride (with a crook and a flail) columns, and reliefs on the walls depict the annual festival. In front of the second pylon stands the granite colossus of Ramesses II flanked by one of his daughters.

Behind this pylon lies one of the highlights of ancient Egypt, the **Great Hypostyle Hall**, covering an area of 4,983 sq. metres (53,318 sq. ft). To support the roof, 134 columns were arranged in 16 rows, with the double row of central columns higher than the others. They have smooth shafts and are 21 metres (67 ft) high, topped with calyx capitals large enough, it is said, to accommodate 100 standing men. The columns are decorated with superb carvings of cult scenes. The overall effect is truly awe-inspiring. It was noted by the *savants* of

Column capitals in ancient Egypt were usually carved with papyrus, palm or lotus motifs. The papyriform columns in the Hypostyle Hall in Karnak are the finest of their type.

LEFT: the Second Pylon at Karnak. **BELOW:** Amenhotep II clutching the key of life.

TIP

The Karnak sound and light show, which is one of the best in Egypt, is held three or four times a night. As at the Pyramids, performances are held in different languages, with English performed every night except Sunday. To get to Karnak in the evening, hire a taxi. You can ask your driver to wait while you watch.

BELOW:
Amenhotep II in the Museum of Luxor.

Napoleon Bonaparte's expedition to Egypt in 1798 that the whole of the cathedral of Notre Dame in Paris could comfortably be accommodated within its walls. At the time of Napoleon it was half-submerged in sand and antique graffiti is clearly visible some distance up the columns.

Work on the Hypostyle Hall was started by Seti I and later finished by his son Ramesses II; note the difference in decoration between the exquisite wall carvings from Seti I's era, in the left wing of the hall as well as on its outer walls, and the much cruder finish by Ramesses II in the right wing.

Beyond the Hypostyle Hall are the badly ruined third and fourth pylons, and further along, one of the two lofty **obelisks** erected by Queen Hatshepsut (1490–1468 BC) – the tip of the second lies near the Sacred Lake. Obelisks were characteristic monuments of the New Kingdom, intended to represent the first ray of light that created the earth. This, the tallest obelisk in Egypt, was erected in the 16th year of the queen's glorious reign. It was carved from a single block of pink Aswan granite of the finest quality and the apex was once covered with a mixture of gold and silver. It was made in seven months, and one cannot but marvel at the skills required to quarry and transport it – it weighs around 323 tonnes – down river to Karnak and then erect it with perfect accuracy on a pedestal.

Behind the ruinous 6th pylon, in another court, are two granite pillars, one carved with lotus flowers, the other with papyrus flowers, representing Upper and Lower Egypt. At the end of the court is a **Chapel of the Sacred Boat** built by the brother of Alexander the Great. Further along lies the **Jubilee Temple of Tuthmosis III** with fine reliefs.

Off the main axis near the Hypostyle Hall are the **Cachette Court**, where thousands of statues were discovered in 1903, the **Open Air Museum**, with more statues, and the **Sacred Lake**. The priests of Amun-Re used the lake to purify themselves in holy water, piped through from the Nile in underground channels. Unfortunately too few of the hewn rocks survived the years to allow genuine restoration of the lake, but there is a pleasant cafeteria on its banks – a good place to ponder over the temple's history.

Further west is the arena for the *son et lumière* shows. Part tour and part spectacle, these offer a brief introduction to the history and mythological traditions of Karnak, including a description of the annual Opet festival. If you attend a performance in winter, be sure to wear warm clothing.

Luxor's museums

On the riverbank about halfway between the temples of Luxor and Karnak is the **Museum of Luxor** ⊙ (daily, winter 9am–1pm, 4–9pm; summer 9am–1pm, 5–10pm; admission charge). This excellent museum was designed by one of Egypt's leading architects, the late Mahmoud al-Hakim, to display important finds from the temples and other local sites. The selection, installation and illumination of the collection were done with the assistance of New York's Brooklyn Museum, and the difference between this designed environment and the warehouse approach of Cairo's

Egyptian Museum is particularly marked. The museum offers the opportunity to examine in close up the superb workmanship of the artists and craftsmen.

Some of the larger statues are displayed in the garden and in the recesses of the building's facade. Among them is a representation of Amenhotep II as an archer, from sections of a red granite stela found in the third pylon at Karnak (pylons are often hollow). Amenhotep is depicted driving arrows through a copper target tied to a pole whilst galloping at full speed in his chariot, thus demonstrating his athletic prowess.

Inside the museum, the first focal point is a magnificent cow head of the sky goddess Mehit Weret, covered in gold-leaf, from Tutankhamun's tomb. Walking towards the rear of the main hall, you pass a seated statue of Amenhotep, the Son of Hapu, who was so important in ancient Egypt that he was accorded special prerogatives during his life and was finally deified thousands of years after his death. Also in the main gallery is a huge alabaster statue of Amenhotep III, seated beside, and under the protection of, Sobek, the crocodile-god. Found at the bottom of a water-filled shaft in a canal in Armant, south of Luxor, in 1967, this is one of the most important finds in the Thebes region in modern times. It is remarkable for the harmonious balance between two figures of markedly different scale. As Sobek presents the *ankh* (the key of life) to Amenhotep, the sweep of his arm draws attention to the handsome face of the king.

The upper gallery has two notable exhibits. The first are blocks, carved in relief, from the famous brown quartzite shrine of Hatshepsut, also known as the Chapelle Rouge. These were found in the 3rd pylon at Karnak. Six long-haired acrobats arch their supple bodies in a backbend in the upper register; the lower depicts musicians, including a harpist.

Maps:
Luxor 204
Site 210

Detail showing a harpist in a carving of dancers and musicians in the Luxor Museum.

BELOW: Mehit Weret depicted as a cow with the sun disk between her horns.

Another highlight of the museum is part of the famous "Akhenaten Wall", an 18-metre (54-ft) wall reconstructed on the upper floor of the museum from some 300 of the 6,000 blocks of Akhenaten's sun temple, extracted from Harmhab's ninth pylon at Karnak. These talatat, as the decorated and uniform sandstone blocks are called, were discovered by a team of French excavators restoring the pylon. They soon realised that the fill inside the pylon had not been deposited in a haphazard manner. Rather, the upper courses had been dismantled and placed in the lowest level with the middle courses on top, and the bottom courses higher up the pylon. This enabled the easy reconstruction of a wall that had been deliberately dismantled 33 centuries earlier.

The museum also contains monuments from the early centuries of the Christian era and to the Coptic period. Among the former objects is a headless limestone and marble statue of the Greek goddess Demeter, an unusual find to have made in Upper Egypt where the worship of foreign gods was not as prevalent as in other areas. There are also examples of so-called Roman portraits, which were painted on linen. One portrait of a man thought to be a Roman officer in a garrison at Luxor was found in a tomb that had been used for secondary burial in the 3rd century.

The **New Hall** displays the cache of 26 statues found in Luxor Temple during excavations in 1989 *(see page 209)*.

Mummy Museum

More or less opposite Luxor Temple, on the river, is Luxor's newest museum: the **Museum of Mummification** (daily, winter 9am–1pm, 4–9pm; summer 9am–1pm, 5–10pm; admission charge). As well as a small collection of mum-

The Ancient Egyptians were expert embalmers. By 1500 BC, when mummification was at its peak, they had developed sophisticated recipes for preserving the body and had a detailed knowledge of the bacterial processes that caused decay. Among the products used to arrest decay were natron, beeswax, myrrh, pine resin and camphor oil.

BELOW: in the souq at Luxor.

in the souq at Luxor.

mies, the museum explains clearly the process of mummification and has a well-documented array of tools and materials used in the ancient art. It also throws light on some of the more essential grave goods that would be buried alongside the mummy *(see also page 222)*.

The east bank's other attractions centre on the Corniche, where riverside cafés offer the chance to watch the sun go down over the west bank and *feluccas* offer cruises. You can also shop in the *souq*, which is at its liveliest in the early evening, when locals pour outdoors to enjoy the cool air, or have a drink on the terrace of the **Sofitel Old Winter Palace Hotel**, a splendid colonial-style hotel overlooking the Nile near the Temple of Luxor.

THE WEST BANK

To explore the tombs and mortuary temples of the west bank you should allow at least two days. Public ferries, leaving from the dock opposite the Temple of Luxor, take locals and tourists across in a matter of minutes, while buses and taxis must take the bridge 7 km (4 miles) south of Luxor town. The temples and tombs on the west bank are spread over a large area, so you will need transport to get around. Taxis are available for hire at the landing stage (ascertain current rates from the tourist office on the east bank before taking the ferry). If the weather is not too hot, then bicycles, which can be hired from most of the larger hotels as well as rentals on the east bank (and can be taken on the ferry), are a pleasant way to get around (make sure you pack plenty of water for the journey).

The central ticket office for all the monuments is on the crossroads past the Colossi of Memnon *(see page 216)*. Be sure to make up your mind in advance which tombs or temples you wish to visit in a day (three or four are probably

Map on page 204

The Sofitel Old Winter Palace Hotel is one of Egypt's grand colonial hotels. Come here for afternoon tea on its terrace overlooking the Nile

BELOW: in the *souq*.

enough) because if you change your mind and want to see an extra monument it will mean coming all the way back to buy another ticket. The monuments are open daily from 6am to 5pm, but be aware that the less visited monuments sometimes close earlier particularly in summer.

Crossing the flood plain

The necropolis starts where the flood plain ends, about 3 km (2 miles) from the river. The area was not always as arid and lifeless as it seems today. Beside each mortuary temple there were once dwellings for the priests and stables for the sacrificial animals, as well as guardhouses and granaries, each with its own superintendent. Surrounding or in front of each temple were lakes, groves and beautifully laid out gardens, and beside the mortuary temples were large palaces where the pharaohs took up temporary residence to supervise the progress of their monuments. Such palaces have been excavated beside the mortuary temples of Seti I, the Ramesseum of Ramesses II, and the temple of Ramesses III.

The approach to the necropolis is marked by two massive, sadly weathered statues known as the **Colossi of Memnon** Ⓔ, 18 metres (54 ft) high, just past which is the ticket office for the west bank sites *(see page 215 for information)*. The colossi are all that remain of what was once the largest mortuary temple, that of Amenhotep III. It was probably damaged from a high flood, and further devastated by Ramesses II and his son Merenptah, who used the fallen blocks to build their own temples. In ancient times, cracks and holes on the northern statue of the two colossi created a musical sound when the breeze blew through them at dawn. Early Greek and Roman travellers explained this in their mythology by claiming that when Memnon fell at Troy he reappeared at Thebes as a singing

Taking Luxor's public ferry over to the West Bank. An early morning start is recommended if you want to avoid the crowds and extreme heat that build up by mid-morning.

BELOW: the Colossi of Memnon.

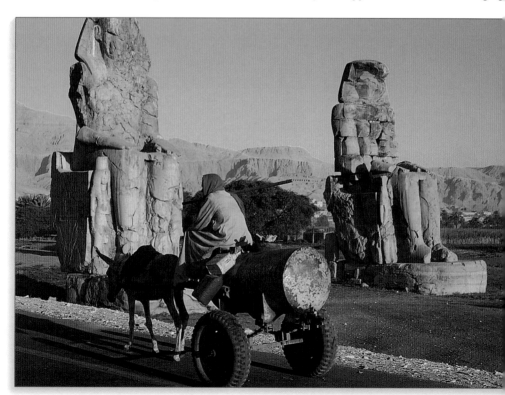

stone statue and each morning would greet his mother Aurora with a plaintive song. Aurora, on hearing the sound, shed tears in the form of morning dew on the cold stone of the statue. But the cracks on the statue were filled in during the reign of Septimius Severus in AD 193 and the sound ceased.

Maps: 204 & below

The Valley of the Kings

The most impressive tombs in the necropolis are those in the **Valley of the Kings ⑤**, known locally as Biban al-Muluk. A road leads northwards from the ticket office, and then forks westwards past Howard Carter's House, up into the mountains where the tombs are hidden in a secluded valley, 2 km (1 mile) from the edge of the flood plain. The valley contains 64 tombs belonging to the pharaohs of the 18th, 19th and 20th dynasties (*circa* 1567–1080 BC). Only nine of these are open to the public, on a rotation system. More may well be discovered, as a new tomb, KV5, the largest found so far and thought to contain 50 of Ramesses II's 52 sons, was found in 1995 and is currently being excavated.

The majestic pyramids of the Old Kingdom were too conspicuous to be secure tombs for kings and their treasure. The later practice of building a monumental funerary temple in one place and discreetly burying the body in another was aimed at throwing grave robbers off the scent.

The tombs were hewn out of the bedrock and decorated with scenes of the journey of the sun-god through the underworld. The deceased pharaoh, absorbed by the setting sun, travelled in the barge of the sun-god through the 12 hours of night, each hour separated from the other by gates guarded by serpents. The solar barge, safeguarded from the hazards of the underworld by protective deities and emblems, finally reached the Court of Osiris. Here the

One way to visit the tombs and temples of Thebes is by donkey.

BELOW: the way to the Valley of the Kings.

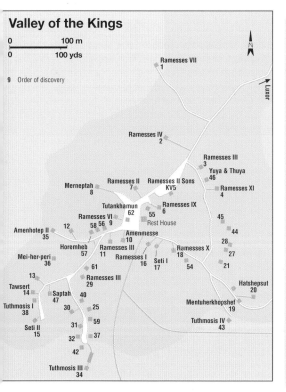

Valley of the Kings

0   100 m
0   100 yds

9   Order of discovery

Ramesses VII 1

Luxor

Ramesses IV 2

Ramesses III 3
Yuya & Thuya 46

Merneptah 8   Ramesses II 7   Ramesses II Sons KV5   Ramesses XI 4

Tutankhamun 62   Ramesses IX 6
Ramesses VI 58 56 9   55   45
Amenhotep II 35   12   Rest House   44
Amenmesse 10   28
Horemheb 57   Ramesses III 11   Ramesses X 18   27
Mei-her-peri 36   Ramesses I 16   Seti I 17   54   21
13   61   Ramesses III 29   Hatshepsut 20
Tawsert 14   Saptah 47   40   Mentuherkhopshef 19
Tuthmosis I 38   30   25
Seti II 15   31   59   Tuthmosis IV 43
32   37
42
Tuthmosis III 34

Discovering Tutankhamun

The awesome sight which Howard Carter made out by candlelight when he opened up Tutankhamun's tomb in 1922 was all the more remarkable because, as royal tombs go, it probably was rather modest. The factor that had allowed it to go unplundered was the occupant's insignificance.

Carter had begun work in 1915 and, with little to show for it seven years later, his patron, Lord Carnarvon, was about to terminate his contract. But on arriving for work on 4 November 1922, Carter was immediately aware that something out of the ordinary had happened. While exploring the foundations of houses that had accommodated the workers on the tomb of Ramesses VI, his diggers had come across a step cut into the rock. By the following afternoon they had exposed a flight of 16 steps and, at the bottom, a sealed door. The seal was merely that of a necropolis guard, not a royal one, but Carter dashed off a cable to Carnarvon and sportingly waited 17 days for him to arrive.

Together Carter and Carnarvon cleared the entrance and at the bottom of the door hit the jackpot. There, still intact, was the seal of Tutankhamun. Beyond the door lay a sloping passage full of rubble. About 9 metres (30 ft) along the passage Carter found another door. "With trembling hands, I made a tiny breach in the upper left-hand corner... widening the hole a little, I inserted the candle and peered in. At first I could see nothing, the hot air escaping from the chamber, causing the candle flame to flicker, but presently, as my eyes grew accustomed to the light..."

To the men's astonishment the tomb was packed with an untidy mess of three gilded beds, two golden chariots, various chairs and stools, two black and gold life-size statues and a huge assortment of objects. That proved to be only the antechamber, and on 17 February 1923 began the exciting job of chipping away at the plaster to find what lay beyond – a massive golden shrine. Carter squeezed around it to find an open doorway which led to the treasury, watched over by a life-size statue of a guard dog. Here a box-like shrine provided the most exciting striptease ever performed. When a way was devised to open it up, it was found to contain another shrine only marginally smaller. It came apart like a Russian doll, four shrines in all.

It took a whole year to reach the fourth and final shrine, which produced a quartzite sarcophagus with a lid of pink granite. "The contents were covered with linen shrouds," Carter recalled, but inside was a coffin in the shape of the young boy-king.

The weight of the coffin was such that a hoist was needed to move it. It contained, in a repetition of the multi-layered shrine, a second coffin. On 17 October 1926, four years after the excavations had begun, this was opened, revealing what made the thing so heavy – a third and final coffin of solid gold, weighing nearly 110 kg (300 lb). The mummy of the king was at last exposed: the now famous mask of gold with inlaid glass and lapis lazuli. The mask had protected the face well but the rest of the body had carbonised. ❏

LEFT: Howard Carter at work.

judge of the underworld, attended by Maat, goddess of truth and justice, and in the presence of 42 gods of the underworld, listened to the confession of the deceased and then watched over the weighing of the heart against the feather of truth. The ibis-headed Thoth, god of wisdom, recorded the verdict. If unfavourable, the deceased was consumed by a terrible animal or consigned to the fires. A favourable verdict gave access to everlasting life.

Some of the royal tombs (Ramesses VI, for example) have burial chambers adorned with astrological signs. The decorations in others (such as Amenhotep II) were made to resemble papyrus texts pinned to the walls, while others again (Seti I) have wonderfully preserved painted reliefs.

Top tombs

The **Tomb of Tutankhamun**, the tomb all visitors to the west bank particularly want to see, is the smallest and, surprisingly, least impressive of the royal tombs in the Valley of the Kings; it is difficult to imagine how the pharaoh's fabulous treasures fitted into it. It was discovered in 1922 by the British archaeologist Howard Carter, working for the wealthy English aristocrat Lord Carnarvon, who was on the point of dismissing him from the project. It was estimated that some 200,000 tons of rubble were moved before Carter finally located the tomb immediately beneath that of Ramesses VI, where roughly-constructed workmen's huts had obscured its entrance.

Whatever had been expected or hoped for, there is no doubt that the tomb's actual contents surpassed their wildest dreams. When Carter first looked into the tomb and was asked by Carnarvon, who was standing behind him, "What do you see?" he replied: "Wonderful things!"

Maps:
Luxor 204
Site 217

...a gasp of wonderment escaped our lips, so gorgeous was the sight that met our eyes: a golden effigy of the young boy-king, of most magnificent workmanship.

–HOWARD CARTER

BELOW: some tombs are hidden in the rock at the top of the valley.

Tutankhamun was the only pharaoh to escape the grave robbers, who were so effective that the priests eventually removed 40 of the royal mummies for safe keeping and reburied them in a cache near the temple of Queen Hatshepsut, where they were finally discovered in 1899.

The **Tomb of Seti I** (indefinitely closed to the public) is a classical tomb that surpasses all others both in size and in the artistic execution of the sculptured walls. Every centimetre of wall space in its 100-metre (300-ft) length is covered with paintings and reliefs executed by the finest craftsmen. The burial chamber (a long descent) contained a sarcophagus made out of a single piece of alabaster carved to a thickness of 5 cm (2 ins) and with the exquisite reliefs filled in with blue paste.

Giovanni Belzoni, a former circus strong-man who originally came to Egypt to market an irrigation pump he had designed in England, discovered Seti I's tomb in 1817. When Turkish officials in Egypt heard of the discovery they headed for Luxor bent on the delightful thought, no doubt, of acquiring priceless treasure. Down the corridors they went, ransacking every corner, only to find to their disappointment that the tomb contained no more than an empty sarcophagus. When Belzoni effected its transportation to England, the trustees of the British Museum considered his price too high and the treasure was without a buyer until 1824. Sir John Soane paid £2,000 sterling for it and it now sits in the museum that bears Soane's name in London.

The lengths to which the kings went to conceal their burial places and fool robbers is illustrated most graphically by the **Tomb of Tuthmosis III**, hidden in a crevice right at the back of the valley and with several twists, turns and traps in its construction.

To find out about the latest excavations in the Valley of the Kings, particularly for a progress report on the excavation of KV5, visit the website of the Theban Mapping Project: www.kv5.com

BELOW: the Tomb of Tutankhamun.

Deir al-Medinah

After visiting the Tombs of the Kings it is interesting to see **Deir al-Medinah G**, the village, in use from the time of Tuthmosis I (1505–1493 BC), where the masons, carvers and painters of the royal tombs lived. The craftsmen recorded their daily life on astraca (pottery fragments) or papyrus, leaving archaeologists an invaluable record of their working practices and wages (in grain), not to mention all manner of notes relating to the details of their everyday activities, from laundry lists to letters. They worked eight hours a day for 10 days, and then came back to the village to work on their own tombs, which were inspired by those of the pharaohs.

With the rise of the Sea Peoples and the gradual collapse of the New Kingdom in the 12th century BC the workmen of Deir al-Medinah lost their livelihoods. Unpaid by the pharaoh, they became desperate and ultimately plundered the very tombs they had built and adorned, including the tomb of the great Ramesses II. They were the first grave-robbers.

The village itself is closed to the public, but a few of the rock-cut tombs are well worth visiting, particularly the well-preserved tombs of Sennedjem and Inherkau. The former shows Sennedjem kneeling before Osiris while Anubis on one side prepares the mummy and on the other guides the dead.

Valley of the Queens

A road leaves from here to the **Valley of the Queens H**, containing the tombs of royal consorts and also of a number of sons of Ramesses III who died young, possibly of smallpox during an epidemic. The most famous tomb is that of Nefertari, the favourite wife of Ramesses II (visits to this tomb are strictly lim-

Map on page 204

Ramesses II adored his chief wife Nefertari and her exquisitely decorated tomb was intended to be a testament of his love. He said of Nefetari, "Just by passing she has stolen away my heart." But his chief tribute to her was the Temple of Nefertari at Abu Simbel, situated alongside his own great temple.

BELOW: the Tomb of Tuthmosis III.

BELOW:
tomb paintings
in the Valley of
the Nobles.

ited and only 200 tickets are available each day). Beautifully restored with help from the Getty Foundation, this tomb has exquisite low reliefs painted on a plaster base; it was opened in 1995 for the first time since its discovery in 1904.

One of the most appealing tombs in the Valley of the Queens, however, is that of prince Amenherchopeshef. The tomb paintings portray the young prince being led by his father, Ramesses III, through the mystical regions of the underworld. Ramesses introduces the boy, one by one, to the various gods of the dead. The reliefs are of fine quality, in beautifully preserved colours.

Tombs of the nobles

Just as the royal tombs in the Theban necropolis provide an insight into the realm of the dead and the pharaohs' vision of the afterlife, the 400 or so **Tombs of the Nobles ❶** reveal aspects of the everyday life of important officials in the New Kingdom. Unlike the kings who wanted above all to conceal their tombs, the nobles were ostentatious and keen for their tombs to be seen.

The **Tomb of Rekhmire**, a vizier under Tuthmosis III and his son Amenhotep II, contains numerous painted scenes of jewellery-making, pottery manufacture and carpentry, as well as a court of law, in which tax evaders are brought to justice. Rekhmire was an outstanding official who was entrusted with so many duties that there was nothing, he claims in an inscription, "of which I am ignorant in heaven, on earth or in any part of the underworld." For many years this tomb was inhabited by a local peasant family, and the wall decorations suffered somewhat. Nevertheless the tomb is a memorial to personal greatness and is, in the words of British Egyptologist James Breasted, "the most important private monument of the Empire."

The **Tomb of Ramose** is also historically and artistically noteworthy. Ramose was the vizier in the reign of Amenhotep III and his son, Amenhotep IV, later Akhenaten, leader of the rebel dynasty that promoted the worship of one god *(see page 57)*. Ramose's tomb provides a unique opportunity to see classical reliefs alongside the "realism" encouraged by Akhenaten. One scene, for example, depicts Ramose standing before his seated pharaoh, who is depicted in the stylised majesty of traditional royal representations; on the opposite wall Ramose stands beneath a balcony on which Akhenaten and his wife Nefertiti stand in an informal posture beneath the symbol of the Aten, a solar disc with rays ending in hands holding the symbols of life and prosperity.

The **Tomb of Nakht**, though small, ranks as one of the finest in the group. The reliefs are executed with infinite charm and are in a good state of repair. Nakht was a scribe of the granaries under Tuthmosis IV and his tomb is beautifully decorated with reliefs of agricultural scenes including ploughing, digging and sowing, as well as stages of the harvest, especially measuring and winnowing the grain, reaping and pressing it into baskets. One of the most delightful scenes shows the nobleman on an outing with his family. He is depicted standing in a papyrus craft spearing fish and shooting fowl while his little daughter holds his leg to prevent him from falling into the water.

Female pharaoh

Just across the mountains from the Valley of the Kings is Deir al-Bahari, the **Temple of Hatshepsut** ❶, one of the most spectacular mortuary temples in Egypt. The temple was built in terraces set against the steep cliffs and it was styled in ancient times as "Most Splendid of All". It was built by the queen's

Map on page 204

Following Hatshepsut's death, after 22 years on the throne, all records of her were erased by Tuthmosis III. She wasn't heard of again until 3,000 years later, when Howard Carter uncovered her tomb in 1903. Reading the name Hatshepsut, he was astonished to note the use of the female pronoun.

BELOW:
Deir al-Bahari.

A home in Qurnah is decorated with images of Mecca, denoting that the owner has completed the haj *(the pilgrimage to Mecca), which all Muslims with the necessary means are required to undertake.*

BELOW: villagers in Qurnah Tarif.

architect, Senmut, who was also her political adviser and, according to graffiti of the time, her lover, though this may have stemmed from malicious gossip. Whatever the truth, he was granted the unique privilege of constructing his own tomb beneath the temple of his queen.

Queen Hatshepsut's famous voyage to Punt, on the Somali coast, is recorded in the carvings on one colonnade. This trading mission was the first time an Egyptian force had been so far for 5,000 years. It was a huge success and, as the carvings show, the army returned laden with ivory, baboons, leopard skins and, most precious of all, incense, an essential ingredient of temple rituals and said to embody the spirit of the deities. Reliefs on the southern colonnade depict the legend of her "divine birth" by the god Amun-Re, who took on her father's appearance and made love to her mother.

This claim was made by the queen to help justify her position to the people. Queen Hatshepsut was of direct royal lineage to the Great Royal Wife of Tuthmosis I, while his other (male) children were from minor wives. Hatshepsut consequently married her half-brother Tuthmosis II, and when he died became regent for her young stepson. But she quickly declared herself pharaoh, and to underline her authority had herself depicted with a male body, a male kilt and a false ceremonial beard. She claimed, as one inscription records, that her father had appointed her as his successor. After her death her stepson and successor, Tuthmosis III, did his best to erase her image.

More mortuary temples

From Hatshepsut's temple you can clearly see the outline of two more mortuary temples: the **Mortuary Temple of Tuthmosis III**, long ago destroyed by a

LIVING ON THE TOMBS

Qurnah, the picturesque village of ochre-coloured houses, where many tour buses oblige you to stop to visit the alabaster workshops, sits right on top of the Theban necropolis. Attempts to relocate the villagers have so far been strongly resisted. Some 30 years ago, the Egyptian architect Hassan Fathy built a model village for the community on the floodplain between the River Nile and the Colossus of Memnon. Although New Qurnah was designed with spacious homes, a mosque, schools, a health care centre and other facilities, the people of Qurnah never agreed to settle there. They chose, instead, to remain where they were on top of the tombs. The reason, it is said, was because they were living on income derived from illegal pillage *(see chapter on grave robbers, pages 51)*, but this is not the whole truth. The people of Qurnah are Arab, and although many such tribes today survive through agriculture, they tend not to mix with the *felaheen*, the Nile valley farmers whom they regard disparagingly as "tillers of the soil". They traditionally live at the edge of the desert. More recently the government has built a new village north of Luxor to relocate villagers, but the "Save Qurnah" campaign was set up to help the people stay, as they are very much part of the landscape.

landslide, and the older **Temple of Nebhetepre Mentuhotep**, who was the first pharaoh to be buried in Thebes. In fact, there are around 30 such temples altogether, though many of them are in a poor state of repair, made worse by rising ground water.

Near Howard Carter's House and the village of Qurnah Tarif, is the little visited **Temple of Seti I** , the mortuary temple built by the mighty pharaoh Seti I, the father of Ramesses II. It is in a ruinous state, but the carvings, although cruder than most carvings in Seti I's monuments, are still among the finest in Egypt. The columns in the Hypostyle Hall, are decorated with superb reliefs of Seti and his ambitious son Ramesses II. In the chapels and the sanctuary beyond are more interesting reliefs.

Ramesses II, that most active of builders, built his mortuary temple, known as the **Ramesseum** ①, opposite the Tombs of the Nobles. Unlike the other still-standing monuments he built, his mortuary temple, which was especially meant to last forever, collapsed because it was built on weak foundations. Although half in ruin, it is a magnificent monument and contains remains of a colossus of king Ramesses II, which is the largest granite statue ever fashioned to such a high standard. Mathematicians who travelled to Egypt with Napoleon's army in 1798 made careful measurements of the chest, upper arm and foot. They calculated that the statue's total height must have been 17 metres (51 ft), and its weight over 1,000 tonnes.

Ramesses II did an extraordinary amount of building during his 67-year reign. He had his state sculptors depict him repeatedly, and there is hardly a pylon, hall or chamber in the temples of Egypt that does not bear his name. His favourite theme was his famous alliance with the King of the Hittites, as depicted on the

Map on page 204

Ramesses II lived until he was 93 years old. He had reigned for 67 years, longer than any other pharaoh. His mummy can still be seen in the Egyptian Museum in Cairo, with wisps of his red hair intact.

BELOW: Madinat Habu.

great pylon that forms the eastern entrance to the Ramesseum. Another series of reliefs concerns the festival of Min. The pharaoh was borne on a richly-decorated carrying-chair, led by priests and soldiers, and followed by his sons and courtiers, to witness sacrifices and to watch the release of four birds which would carry the royal tidings to the corners of the earth.

Further back from the ticket office is **Madinat Habu** , the splendid Mortuary Temple of Ramesses III, which, although built much later, was modelled on the Ramesseum, the mortuary temple of his ancestor Ramesses II. This huge temple is second only to Karnak in size, and it is one of the best preserved and easiest to understand temple structures. It was built on an older structure, as legend has it that this was the first land that appeared from the Waters of Chaos. Centuries after it was built, the temple was surrounded by the town of Jeme, inhabited by a Coptic community.

End a hard day of tomb and temple visiting with a relaxing cruise by felucca.

The enclosure is entered from a gatehouse where stairs lead to Ramesses III's pleasure appartments on the first floor, with beautiful carvings of dancers on the wall. To the right is a small temple built by Hatshepsut on the primeval hill. The gigantic pylons and walls of the temple are decorated with scenes of battles that were fought by Ramesses II and Ramesses III and inscriptions record a battle against the Sea Peoples, who attacked Egypt early in the reign of Ramesses III; it is thought to document the earliest known sea battle. The ultimate success of the Sea Peoples, combined with the exhaustion of the Nubian gold mines, brought down the New Kingdom.

BELOW:
an alabaster
shop in Luxor.

Celebrations and festivals took place in the large First Court, which has an opening to the pharaoh's now ruinous palace to the left. Some of the colours of the fine reliefs are remarkably well preserved. The Second Court was later

turned into a Coptic church, and the Copts carved many crosses on the walls. At the back are three sanctuaries dedicated to the triad of Mut, Khonsu and Amun. It is worth walking around the outer walls, which have some remarkable scenes of Ramesses hunting and fishing, to get an idea of the splendour and grandeur of this temple. To the north is the outline of a sacred lake, and the temple is surrounded by a mudbrick enclosure.

A good way to end a day of sightseeing is to watch the sun go down behind this temple from one of the café terraces opposite the entrance.

Endangered monuments

There are literally hundreds of tombs on the Theban necropolis, only a sampling of which are open to the public. Some have been "lost", that is to say, they were opened and partly recorded by early Egyptologists in the 19th and early part of the 20th centuries, but have since become filled with sand, all signs of their presence obliterated. Locating them again, properly recording and documenting them is one of the chief tasks of Egyptologists today.

One of the most important archaeological projects being carried out is the production of the first detailed map of the necropolis since 1921. Known as the Theban Mapping Project it has made use of the most up-to-date equipment, and hot-air balloons for low-level photographs of the hidden valleys and mortuary temples. Only when the monuments have been properly identified can steps be taken for their protection. The project has also been instrumental in introducing fibre optic lighting in the tombs (safer and cooler than the old fluorescent lighting) and developing sophisticated methods of controlling temperature levels.

Map on page 204

BELOW: for a taste of Luxor during colonial days take a *calèche* ride along the Corniche.

Map on page 204

Luxor is today one of the most threatened archaeological sites in the world. The threat comes from three sources: contamination, desecration and abuse – environmental contamination from humidity and sub-soil water, plunder by grave robbers, and damage by tourists. The first is the most difficult to control and although efforts to curb the environmental contamination have been made, it seems to be a losing battle. As the British Egyptologist Michael Jones observed, "You cannot save a monument; all you can really do, in the long run, is to delay its rate of destruction."

The deterioration of the reliefs on ancient monuments is even visible to the naked eye. The atmosphere – more humid as a result of water stored in Lake Nasser – and air pollution from factories is adversely affecting Egypt's ancient treasures. But worse still is the higher than average watertable since the construction of the High Dam, which results in salt-laden moisture creeping up the temple walls, leaving the reliefs pimpled, festered and spoiled, after which they quite literally flake off.

Plunder of tombs is another serious problem. So long as there have been tombs, there have been robbers (*see Grave robbers and Curse, pages 51–55*), but the tragedy of modern-day plunder is that the antiquities are lost to the world of art and scholarship, as they usually make their way into private collections. The Egyptian government has clamped down on illicit digging and is working at many levels to curb or restore any damage, but with literally tens of thousands of monuments on both sides of the Nile, the task is a enormous. Meanwhile epigraphers are hard at work, accurately documenting whatever they can. The Theban Mapping Project is creating a detailed database on the Theban tombs, with plans and isometric drawings of each tomb and a system for monitoring deterioration. Its aim to to create a useful resource for professional archaeologists, but also to open up the fascinating subject of ancient Egypt to the ordinary public, including schoolchildren.

As well as working on the Theban necropolis, the organisation is embarking on another project to solve the problems caused by rising ground-water in the 30 or more mortuary temples along the edge of the valley floor. It is hoped that by working with the ministries of agriculture and irrigation, they can introduce new irrigation techniques that will halt further damage and allow restoration to take place.

Lightening the load

The damage caused by tourists is being attended to on many levels. In such places as the valleys of the Kings and Nobles tombs are opened on a rotating basis in order to spread the load and ease pressure on particularly popular tombs, tourists and tour leaders are expected to follow elementary ground rules (such as not touching the reliefs and paintings), and new access roads are being constructed.

One recurring suggestion is to keep tourists out of the most visited royal tombs altogether. The possibility of building concrete replicas of some of the most famous tombs has been considered. However, few people think it likely that visitors would be interested in seeing mere reproductions. ❑

BELOW: looking at the wares inside an alabaster workshop.
RIGHT: a mule with a decorative haircut.

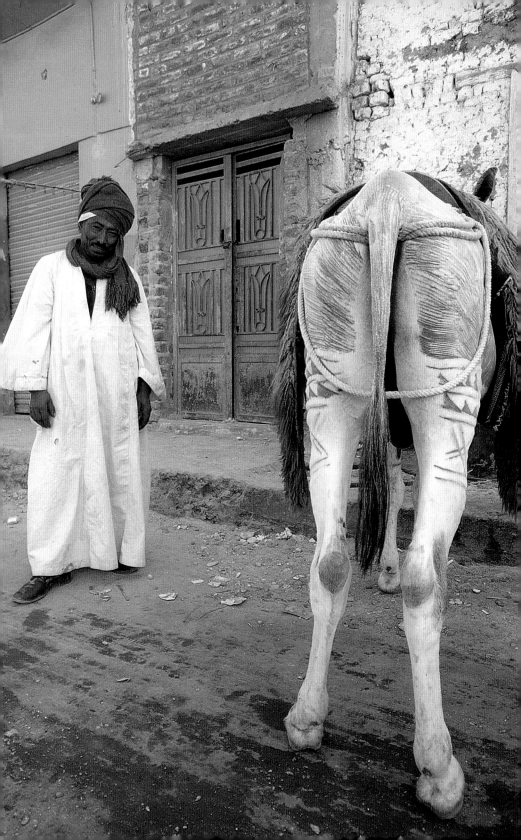

LUXOR TO ABYDOS

Map on page 235

Although little visited by tourists since the terrorist attacks of the 1990s, this region has a good deal to offer visitors, including a superb Ptolemaic temple and the ancient cult city of Osiris

Lush with crops and peppered with low, mud-built villages, the riverbanks north of Luxor are picturesque. Unfortunately, in recent years travelling in the region has been severely restricted because of security concerns. However, the route is covered by taxis, which travel in armed convoys, or can be completed on board one of the two cruise ships that ply the route under armed guard *(see box page 234)*.

There are two main reasons for making the trip – the city of Abydos, which was of major importance from the time of the first dynasties *(circa* 3100 BC) and the impressive Ptolemaic Temple of Hathor at Dendarah, which has a wealth of beautifully preserved reliefs and carvings.

To Dendarah

Leaving **Luxor ❶** *(see pages 203–228)* the River Nile sweeps to the northeast, flowing smoothly past verdant fields and the town of **Qift ❷** (ancient Coptos). With no ancient monuments, it is of no particular interest today but it crops up again and again in the literature on ancient Egypt as the area was sacred to the licentious god Min, a guardian of the Eastern Desert. The town was an important trading centre and the starting point of a caravan route from the Nile Valley to the Red Sea through the Wadi Hammamat. Today a tarmac road and a new railway connect this point of the Nile Valley to the Red Sea, following the route of ancient traders, who would have made their way from the port of Al-Qusayr on the coast, laden with goods from the Far East.

Just south of **Qena ❸**, the chief town of the province, situated about 20 km (12 miles) north of Qift, is the village of **Al-Ballas** on the west bank of the Nile, where the distinctive *ballas* pottery is made from the large clay deposits in the region. If you are lucky, you may see pots lined along the banks awaiting shipment. These are the kind of pots that you see women carrying on their heads as they go to draw water from the Nile. You may also catch sight of a cargo boat laden with *ballas* being shipped northwards. In ancient times Qena, like Qift, was linked by a trade route to the Red Sea, but today it is of no particular significance.

At this point the river takes a great curve to the southwest before continuing its flow north. Within the curve is the first port of call, **Dendarah ❹**, famed for its great **Temple of Hathor** (daily 7am–5pm; admission charge). Although just a kilometre or so from the bank of the Nile, the temple is hidden by copious palm trees, and lies on the edge of the fertile plain with desert behind. Sacred to the cow-goddess Hathor, the temple was begun by Ptolemy IX (116–107 BC) and

PRECEDING PAGES: drying dates near Luxor. **LEFT AND BELOW:** visitors and a local in Dendarah.

completed in the Roman era 250 years later. In dedicating a temple to Egypt's cow-goddess, the Ptolemaic kings were honouring one of Egypt's best loved deities. Usually depicted as a cow, Hathor was sometimes portrayed as a female figure with the head of a cow, and there are representations of her in most Egyptian temples.

An early Egyptian Earth Mother, depicted as a cow, or as a woman with cow's ears or horns, Hathor (pronouned Hat-Hor and meaning "House of Horus") was the goddess of beauty, love and music. The Greeks identified her with Aphrodite and she was also linked with Isis.

BELOW: detail, the Temple of Hathor.

The Temple of Hathor, like that of Horus at Edfu, is one of the best preserved and most lavishly decorated in Egypt, even though after it ceased to be a place of worship some of the chapels and chambers were used as homes by local people up until the early 20th century. The temple is surrounded by the rubble of its largely decaying outer walls. Unlike most temples, it is not approached by a pylon and peristyle court but via the pillared facade of the **hypostyle hall**, where 24 Hathor-headed columns support a roof divided into seven registers and decorated with remarkable astrological scenes depicting the six signs of the Egyptian zodiac (the crab, the twins, the bull, the ram, the fishes and the water carrier), stars and the phases of the moon. The original colours are remarkably well preserved.

Proceed through the smaller, inner temple, to the **Hall of the Company of Nine Gods**. A series of reliefs here link the traditions of Hathor of Dendarah with those of Horus of Edfu. Husband and wife, Horus and Hathor were deities of equal standing and at both sites the triad consisted of Hathor, Horus and their son. Twice a year, on the occasion of the birthday of each deity, the "Festival of the Good Union" was celebrated. Reliefs on the walls of the staircase leading to the roof of the Temple of Hathor – approached from the antechamber to the rear of the second hypostyle hall, and affording an excellent view of desert and floodplain – describe the event.

TRAVEL RESTRICTIONS

Militant Islamic fundamentalists have attacked government and tourist targets in Cairo and Upper Egypt since 1992. A massive government clamp-down resulted in the imprisonment of the leaders of the movements, but it has proved harder to fully control some of the more remote towns and villages of Upper Egypt, which have traditionally been a hotbed for Islamic extremism and long been troubled by religious tensions between Copts and Muslims.

Since 1997 and the appalling massacre of 58 foreigners and four Egyptians at Queen Hatshepsut's Temple in Thebes, an area that had previously been considered safe, police have become much more of a feature all over the country. There are regular checkpoints along the Nile highway, and there is a huge police force to protect visitors at tourist sites. Unfortunately, increased security means restrictions on travelling freely and journeys between towns in the Nile Valley are now only possible in armed convoys which leave 2 or 3 times a day – check departure times at the tourist offices. It is also possible to make a twice-weekly one-day cruise to the Temple of Hathor in Dendarah only with the *Lotus*, which leaves from the Novotel in Luxor, or the *Tiba*, from the Winter Palace Hotel.

The small chapel on the roof of the temple housed the sacred statue that would, at the start of the festival, be taken out of its shrine for the reunion. The vessel bearing the statue of Hathor would be carried upstream, while that of Horus would set off downstream, each in a splendid procession. Where the boats came together, they were encircled by a rope cast by other vessels, in a gesture of unity. Then the river craft would proceed to the appropriate temple to celebrate the reunion of husband and wife amidst joy, song and prayer. The mere mortals celebrated the union by copying the gods, or by getting drunk.

In the Ptolemaic period Hathor was identified with the Greek goddess Aphrodite and began to enjoy immense popularity as "Mistress of music, dance and joy". However some of the dignity of Hathor as the mother-goddess sacred to the Egyptians was lost when her temple became the "home of intoxication and place of enjoyment". Among the Roman emperors depicted in the temple are Augustus, Tiberius, Caligula, Claudius and Nero, who all played a role in the temple's construction.

In the precincts of the temple are two Roman era **"birth-houses"** containing scenes of the birth of Hor-sma-tawny, the son of Hathor and Horus. Nearby is a Christian **basilica**. It is one of the earliest Roman basilicas and may be the 4th-century Christian centre where 50,000 monks assembled to celebrate Easter, an event described by St Jerome as taking place somewhere in the neighbourhood of Dendarah.

Christian sites

The river now continues its great sweep from east to west, so that the eastern bank of the Nile is to the north, and the western to the south. The tiny village of **Faw**

Map on page 235

An anteroom off the Hall of the Company of Nine Gods has a ceiling depicting Nut, the lovely sky goddess, arching her body from fingertips to toes. She was said to swallow the sun in the evening and give birth to it each morning. According to one legend, she gave birth to Osiris, Isis, Seth, Nephthys and Horus.

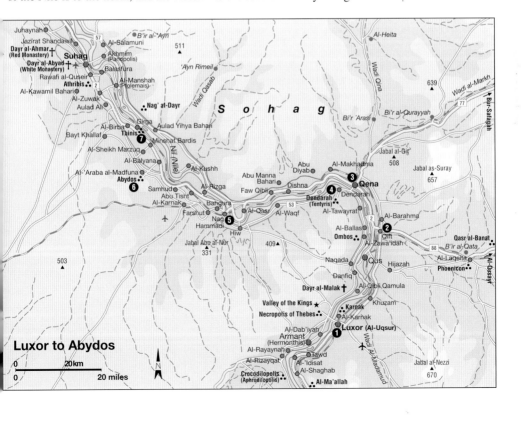

The Gnostics were
hounded into silence,
in the name of
orthodox
Christianity, from the
4th century onwards,
and their writings
were burned. The
Nag Hammadi
manuscripts are
thought to have been
copied from original
writings that may
date from the second
half of the 1st
century.

Qibli to the north, is the site of the basilica of St Pachomius. Born in Thebes in AD 292 to pagan parents, Pachomius converted to Christianity as a young man, devoted to the ascetic Palamon *(see below)*. He went on to establish nine monasteries along the Nile and he is considered to be the father of monasticism

As the Nile continues north, the rugged cliffs of **Jabal al-Tarif** become visible. They often appear murky against the skyline, especially when the sun is overhead, but look closely and you will see that they are of immense height. This was the range of hills where the Gnostic codices, or books – as famous and as important as the Dead Sea Scrolls – were discovered in 1947. Now the 12 codices, known as the Nag Hammadi Library, are housed in the Coptic Museum in Cairo *(see page 276)*.

Accounts of the discovery differ. According to one, a huge boulder fell off a slope revealing a jar that was found by peasant farmers. In another account, two brothers chanced upon the jars while they were digging for fertiliser. It may be that the codices themselves were deliberately hidden when the Byzantine church stamped out what they regarded as heretical Christian groups.

The 12 Hammadi codices were collected by Egyptians and translated into Coptic, the Egyptian language of the time. They vary widely in content, presenting a spectrum of heritages that range from Egyptian folklore, Hereticism, Greek philosophy and Persian mysticism to the Old and New Testaments.

Christian sites in this part of Upper Egypt become more numerous from this point on, although few can be seen as you sail along the river. Within a great loop of the Nile at al-Qasr the land is extremely fertile and picturesque. Look out for the **Monastery of St Palomon**, the bell-tower and latticed walls of which can be seen rising above the surrounding agricultural land. St Palomon,

BELOW: the desert
at Dendarah.

Map
on page
235

or Anba Balamun in Arabic, was one of the earliest anchorites in Upper Egypt and was said to have died from excessive fasting. A *mawlid* or annual celebration is still observed in his honour.

Nag Hammadi ❺ is a large and sprawling provincial town. Its population exploded in the 1960s when a large refinery and an aluminium factory were built here. A bridge crosses the Nile at this point, and cruise boats, when sailing this far north *(see box on Travel Restrictions, page 234)*, dock here, their passengers transferring to buses to visit the archaeological site of Abydos. Taxis can be hired by those who wish to venture even further north to see the many sites of Middle Egypt.

Abydos and the Osiris legend

Abydos ❻ (open daily, winter 7am–5pm, summer 7am–6pm; admission charge) lies on the west bank of the Nile 30 km (18 miles) from Nag Hammadi. Al-Balyana is its nearest riverside town, and a broad plain leads to the village of al-Araba al-Madfuna, which flanks the site.

Abydos was one of Egypt's most important cities. Not only was it associated with the kings of Ancient Egypt's founding dynasties, who came from nearby Thinis *(see page 240)*, but also with the great god Osiris. Ancient Egyptians aspired to make a pilgrimage to the revered city of Osiris at least once in a lifetime, just as today devout Muslims journey to Mecca, or Christians and Jews go on pilgrimages to Jerusalem. The ancients also aspired to be buried here. The temple was the cult centre of Osiris, Egypt's most beloved god whose legend is depicted in the wall reliefs of many Egyptian temples. Osiris might have been an actual king of Egypt who was so loved by his people that his memory lingered on long after his death, passing from generation to generation. The Greek historian Plutarch in the 1st century AD was the first to record the Osiris legend in a coherent account. He described Osiris as the creator of law and agriculture, who, with his wife Isis at his side, ruled the world with justice. His brother Seth, however, was jealous and conspired against him. At a banquet, he tricked Osiris into entering a chest which was then slammed closed, sealed and thrown into the Nile.

The broken-hearted Isis wandered far and wide in misery seeking the body of her loved husband. Accompanied on her sad mission by the goddess Nepthys, she eventually found the body entangled in a tamarisk bush in the marshes of the Delta. She carefully hid it, but the vicious Seth, out boar-hunting, came across the body and cut it into 14 pieces, scattering them in all directions. The dismayed Isis searched out the pieces of her husband's body and at each spot where a part was found a monument was erected. She sought the help of the jackal-god Anubis – the god of embalming and greeter of the dead in the underworld – to prepare the body for burial. While he carried out her orders, Isis wept then prayed. She transformed herself into a bird (symbol of the spirit) to revive Osiris, but only managed to stir him long enough to impregnate herself with his heir.

In due course she bore a son, Horus, whom she

Before the rise of Osiris, the original god of the Abydos region was Wepwawet, the "Opener of Ways". Depicted as a wolf-god, he guided the dead through the underworld.

BELOW: the Temple of Hathor.

Guardians share a simple meal below the temple walls at Abydos.

raised in the marshes of the Delta until he was strong enough to avenge his father's death by slaying Seth. Horus then set out to seek his father and raise him from the dead. The risen Osiris, however, could no longer reign in the kingdom on earth and now became king of the underworld, while Horus took over his terrestrial throne.

Interpreting the legend

This widely known and most loved of ancient legends has been subject to many interpretations. One of the functions of mythology is to explain certain natural, social or political ideas, and the mythical Osiris (who was associated with settled community living and hence involved in agriculture and the annual rebirth of the land) falling victim to Seth (who was associated with the desert) is thought to represent the constant battle against the encroaching sands.

Seth's act of tearing the body of Osiris to pieces and scattering its parts up and down the Nile Valley may be interpreted as the concept of sowing grain, following which, with the necessary incantations (like those performed by Isis and Nepthys), or rural festivals, the stalks of grain would be reborn as Osiris was reborn. Thus Horus, son of gods related to the rebirth of the land, triumphed over the desert (Seth) and became the prototype of the pharaohs.

The myth of Osiris had become so well known by the Middle Kingdom, (2134–1633 BC), that thousands of pilgrims from all walks of life annually came to Abydos to pay homage to their legendary ancestor. They would travel long distances to witness the ritualistic killing of Osiris by his brother Seth, followed by several days of mourning and lamentation in the manner of Isis. At a prescribed site a mock battle took place between Horus, son of Osiris and

BELOW: the Temple of Seti I.

Isis, and Seth his father's murderer. The death of Osiris was duly avenged, Horus became king and life would go on.

Map on page 235

The temples

Abydos reached its zenith during the New Kingdom (1567–1080 BC), when pharaohs left signs of their devotion in the great monuments they erected there. The most frequently visited of these are the temples of **Seti I** and Ramesses II. The former, begun by Seti I and completed by his father Ramesses II, is considered one of the most beautiful in Egypt. Seti encouraged an artistic and architectural revival in his reign and the temple is decorated with finely carved and coloured reliefs, in a good state of preservation.

Scenes on the eastern and northern walls of the Hypostyle Hall are particularly interesting in that they record the pharaoh's active participation in the planning of the temple. He is portrayed, in one scene, facing the goddess Seshat, the patron deity of records and archives, who is shown driving stakes into the earth to measure out the ground-plan. Behind her, Osiris watches over the activities being conducted on his behalf. Above is a scene of Seti, assisted by Horus, stretching out a measuring rope.

In each of the shrines of the temple seven scenes depict daily ceremonies that were performed by the priests. They include burning incense, perfuming and anointing the statue of the deity, adorning it with a crown and jewels, and then withdrawing, backwards, while brushing away all footprints from the shrine before finally closing the door.

The reliefs display a naturalism unusual in the conservative canons of Egyptian art. The many representations of Seti, for example, may appear carbon

Osiris was the Judge of the Dead, King of the Underworld and the God of resurrection. Represented as a mummified figure with the royal crook and flail, he rivalled Re in importance.

BELOW: an artist's impression.

Pillar relief in the Hall of Osiris, the Temple of Seti I, Abydos.

copies of one another, but, on close scrutiny, they are found to differ. As the king looks into the face of an honoured deity, his expression is one of reverence. Before a goddess, there is a look of loving trust. Facing one of the great gods, he bends slightly at the waist to indicate awe. Such emotional expression is rarely found in temples, as the pharaoh is generally depicted larger than life, standing proudly erect and exalted. In the Temple of Seti, even the gods have human emotions: Osiris looks benevolent and majestic; Isis is gracious and tender; Horus is competent and direct.

To the rear of the temple is a wall covered with a record of Egypt's ancient rulers, known as the **List of Kings**. Containing the cartouches of 76 pharaohs, it has formed the basis of much of our understanding of pharaonic chronology. There are, however, notable omissions from the list: Queen Hatshepsut and Kings Amenhotep (Akhenaten) and Tutankhamun. Originally, the **Temple of Ramesses II** (now in poor condition), northwest of the Temple of Seti I also contained a list of kings; segments of this are now in the British Museum in London.

By the Graeco-Roman period, Abydos had come to be regarded as a place of healing. Sufferers from all over Egypt and, indeed, all over the Graeco-Roman world, gathered in the corridors and halls of the temple of Seti to make humble pleas for health or fertility. Graffiti on the walls in hieratic (a late form of hieroglyphics), Greek, Phoenician and Aramaic attest to this.

Unfortunately, the Temple of Seti, like others throughout Egypt, is suffering from sub-soil water and air pollution. One of the most seriously threatened parts of the temple is a separate structure that lies behind the main temple, known as the **Osirion**. It is sunk into a depression and has variously been called a cenotaph and a mortuary temple. Most experts think it was built for Seti I, so that his body could rest here, in the company of Osiris, before being entombed in Thebes.

There is a long-standing tradition of the sanctity of the area around the Osirion, and when the 13th-Dynasty Pharaoh Neferhotep (*circa* 1786 BC) erected a boundary stele at Abydos, it stated that none should set foot in the sacred place. Up until the time of its restoration in the 1980s, the waters of the Osirion were regarded as advantageous to health. This recalls the hundreds of texts connecting Osiris with Abydos, with water and with rebirth, in which this most beloved figure of ancient Egyptian tradition "sleeps in the midst of water".

BELOW: excavations in progress at Abydos.

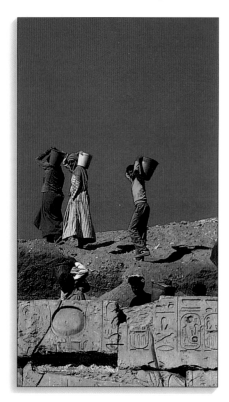

Vestiges of powerful magic still cling to the spot. Local women, who blithely mix elements of paganism with Islamic or Christian beliefs, can sometimes be seen circling the pool of the Osirion. Quite recently an English mystic deeply versed in Egyptian history and religion spent the last 25 years of her life living at Abydos, working daily in the temple and living in the nearby village of Qerba. To the local people she was known as Umm Seti ("mother of Seti").

Oldest cemetery

Slightly to the north of Abydos is the site of ancient **Thinis ❼**, the home town of Narmer (Menes), the first pharaoh, who is credited with the unification of the two lands of Upper and Lower Egypt around 3100 BC.

Map on page 235

Narmer and his successors ruled from Memphis, the apex of the Delta, but they never forgot their ancestral home. Among the barren hills west of Abydos they constructed impressive cenotaphs where people could make offerings.

Generation after generation left offerings in pottery vessels, particularly at the cenotaph of the First Dynasty Pharaoh Djer which was considered to be the actual tomb of Osiris. Today the site has acquired the name **Om al-Gaab**, or "mother of potsherds". It is not on the tourist trail, but for those with time to spare, this archaic cemetery, approached from a track leading westwards from the village of Qerba, is worth seeing.

The huge funerary structures are believed to be the cenotaphs of Ancient Egypt's earliest kings, who were buried in similar graves on the Saqqarah plateau. The huge outer walls of the tombs were decorated with recessed panelling, and surrounding them were two enclosure walls built of mud brick. The subterranean chambers, hewn deep into the bedrock, contained funerary equipment such as tools, weapons and stone and copper vessels, as well as jewellery. Surrounding many of the tombs were subsidiary graves for the retainers of the deceased pharaoh, who, as and when they died, were buried in the vicinity of their monarch in order to serve him in the afterlife as dutifully as they had served him on earth.

Before leaving Abydos it should be mentioned that, according to some of the mortuary texts, the "afterlife" lay in a gap in the mountains to the west of here. Indeed, the afterlife is depicted as a long mountainous valley with a river running through it; the banks are lined with wheatfields, fruit orchards and gardens of flowers. Here the deceased would enjoy hunting and fishing forever in the "Field of Reeds". ❏

BELOW: carving in the Temple of Seti I.

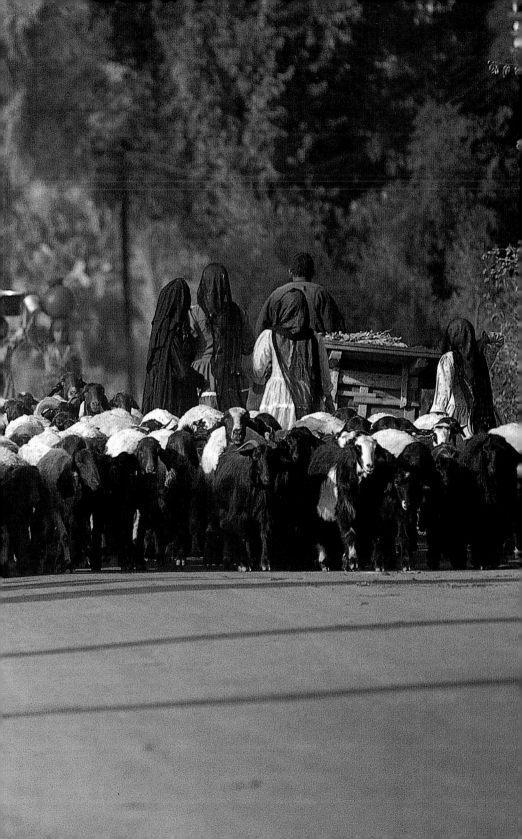

MIDDLE EGYPT

*The broad flood plains of Middle Egypt see few tourists, in spite of
the stunning Middle Kingdom tombs of Bani Hasan and the
important site of Tall al-'Amarnah, the power base of Akhenaten*

Map on page 246

The term "Middle Egypt" describes the area between Abydos and Memphis. It is a long stretch, where the river is wide and flows a smooth course through verdant fields, with good paved roads on both sides of the river. The road on the east bank runs through the desert while the west bank route passes picturesque canals, cultivated fields, towns and villages. Despite the heavy traffic, the latter route is the more interesting one, especially for observing the rural scene; farmers can be seen at work at much closer quarters than is possible on a river cruise.

In ancient times, this central area was a distinct political entity, one of three. It was the Middle Kingdom Pharaoh Senusert III (*circa* 1898 BC) who defined the first area, between Aswan and Abydos, as "the head" of Upper Egypt; the region from Abydos to Memphis as Upper Egypt (not Middle Egypt as it is called here) and the third region as the Delta.

Although the archaeological sites of Middle Egypt are less well known than those of Upper Egypt, the region has four areas of special historic importance: Tall al'-Amarnah, Al-Ashmunayn, Tunat al-Jabal and Bani Hasan. There are tourist facilities at each of these – regular barge services across the river and vehicles for transport to the sites – and the local officials, guards and guides are refreshingly informative. However, because of terrorist incidents in the 1990s, travel between Al-Minya and Luxor has been seriously restricted. There is a heavy police presence in the area and especially at tourist sites; travelling is often only possible in armed convoys *(see also page 234)*.

Visitors keen to see the best of the region should, if circumstances permit, arrange overnight accommodation in **Al-Minya ❶**, the principal town of the province, about 250 km (155 miles) south of Cairo, which marks the divide between Upper and Lower Egypt. A good springboard for visiting the sites south of the city, it has a choice of hotels ranging from the colonial-style Palace, where there is more charm and atmosphere than comfort, to the five-star Etap. The town itself has some lovely early 20th-century buildings, and a popular *souq* near the town centre. On the east bank is the impressive Zouriyyet al Mayyiteen, a very large Muslim and Christian cemetery with hundreds of mud domes

Rock chambers

Bani Hasan ❷ (daily 7am–5pm; admission charge), on the east bank of the Nile, 20km (12 miles) south of Al-Minya, opposite the modern town of Abu Qurkas, is named after an Arab tribe that settled in the area in the 9th century. The site is famous for its Middle Kingdom tombs, dating from around 2000 BC. At one

PRECEDING PAGES:
goat-herding in
Egypt's pastoral
heart.
LEFT: the Nile
at Al-Minya.
BELOW: rice fields.

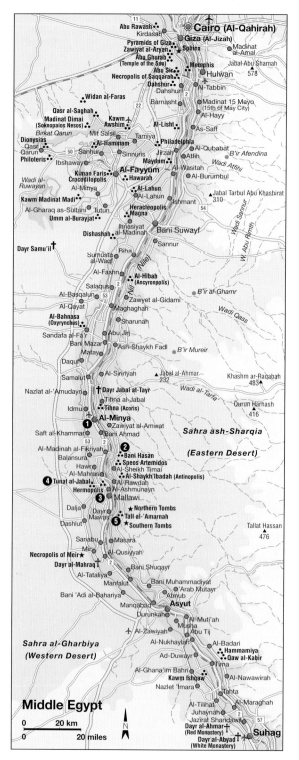

Middle Egypt

0   20 km

0   20 miles

time Bani Hasan was seldom visited, as it was not easily accessible. The reliefs on the tombs were in poor condition, owing to the site's occupation by Christian hermits during the persecutions of Decius and Diocletian in the 2nd and 3rd centuries AD, and most of the wall paintings were blackened with soot from open fires and dulled by time and neglect.

But all that has changed. Access to the site is now easy, and the paintings have been superbly restored, some of the colours appearing as fresh as on the day they were painted.

The tombs comprise a long series of rock-hewn chambers about 200 metres (655 ft) above the flood plain, extending for several kilometres along the face of the cliff. The most interesting group of 39 chambers, in the upper range, belong to noblemen who governed the province some 4,000 years ago. They have simple facades, some with elegant octagonal columns and others with 16-sided columns flanking the entrance doorways.

Inside, the main chambers have triple-vaulted ceilings, with two rows of rock-hewn pillars. The walls are adorned throughout with vivid scenes. The tomb belonging to the governor and commander-in-chief **Amenemhat** (tomb No. 4), for example, includes a scene (near the centre of the left-hand wall) of a caravan of Semites arriving in Egypt with their herds; they are characterised by hook noses and multicoloured robes.

This representation dates from the time when Abraham, the "father of many nations", is believed to have lived (about 1900 BC). It was a time when food was scarce in the land of Canaan and "Abraham went down into Egypt to sojourn there; for the famine was grievous in the land" (Genesis 12:10). Egypt, by then, was a long settled monarchy with Egyptian governors at the seaports on the Phoenician coast and, as is clear from this representation, willing to welcome strangers.

Another noteworthy scene painted in the same tomb, above the doorway leading into the inner shrine, shows Amenemhat hunting in the marshes. It shows he nobleman seated behind a hide made of reeds, from where he can observe hoopoes in a papyrus thicket. These, and other vivid scenes of men hunting, fishing and wrestling, and of women weaving, present a panorama of the everyday life of governors, courtiers and princes who lived in Upper Egypt during the Middle Kingdom.

Map on page 246

Beak-headed Thoth

Twenty kilometres (12 miles) south is the town of **Mallawi** with a small **museum** (Mon–Tues, Thur, Sat–Sun 9am–4pm, Fri 9am–noon; admission charge), housing a collection of finds from the nearby sites of Tunat al-Jabal and Hermopolis.

Hermopolis ❸, 8 km (5 miles) north of Mallawi, is known under its modern name of Al-Ashmunayn (at the time of writing the site was closed for restoration; it is advisable to confirm that it has reopened at the tourist office in Al-Minya before setting out). A good road from Mallawi runs across the fertile floodplain towards the site, which, even in its ruined state, can be clearly seen in a picturesque palm grove.

This was the site of the ancient Egyptian city of *Khnumi* where Thoth, the beak-headed god of wisdom, was worshipped. Represented as an ibis or a baboon, Thoth was also viewed as the god of science and medicine, since it was Thoth that cured Horus's scorpion sting. To keep a record of the judgement of the dead, Thoth invented hieroglpyphics and became the scribe in the Hall of Judgement.

Of the original pharaonic site, however, little remains apart from two gigantic statues of baboons, sacred animals of Thoth, which were erected in front of

Statue of a baboon at Hermopolis. Baboons were sacred to Thoth, the god of wisdom.

BELOW: the Temple of Thoth at Hermopolis.

the Temple of Thoth by Amenhotep III (1402–1364 BC). In the centre of the city is a low mound surmounted by red granite columns. Though originally thought to be an *agora* (market place), dating from Greek times, it is now known that it was a Christian basilica built out of bricks from an earlier temple erected by Ptolemy III (246–221 BC).

The Greeks identified Thoth with one of their own gods, Hermes, and under Greek rule the province experienced a revival. The annual Festival of Thoth was one of the most important in the land. It started at the beginning of the season of the inundation, when the flood waters began to rise, and Thoth, the "messenger of the gods", made announcements to the local priests.

Ibis worship

A few kilometres southwest of Hermopolis, just beyond the limits of the valley is the necropolis of **Tunat al-Jabal** ❹ (7am–5pm; admission charge), a unique archaeological site devoted to the mummified remains of the sacred ibis – also sacred to Thoth .This was the necropolis that the inhabitants of Hermopolis would visit. The ibis compound has been identified and near it is an extremely deep well fed by a waterwheel not unlike those that are still used for irrigation today. The ibis galleries themselves are long underground passages leading to the chambers where the mummified ibis and baboons were interred. Although most of the remains are now in the nearby museum in Mallawi *(see page 247)* there are plenty *in situ*.

There is only one tomb at Tunat al-Jabal, which may appear to be small and insignificant compared to the ones in Upper Egypt, but it is well worth seeing. It is the **tomb of Petosiris** (dating from around 300 BC), a family tomb in which

Copts account for about one-fifth of the population of Middle Egypt. At one time their peaceful cohabitation with the Muslim majority was held up as a model of Egyptian tolerance, but tensions have risen over recent years and antagonism is rife.

BELOW: children playing near Tunat-al-Jabal.

eight generations of high priests of Thoth at Hermopolis were buried. Although the facade is decorated with traditional Egyptian reliefs showing the deceased making offerings before the more important deities, the inside is covered in charming scenes displaying a particularly strong Greek influence in their workmanship. The scenes themselves are traditional – farming, hunting and fowling – but the farmers are portrayed with thick jowls, muscular legs and togas that are decidedly non-Egyptian. Not only do the men have curly hair, but the branches of the trees also curl, and so do the horns of the animals.

Behind the tomb spreads a large cemetery dating from late Ramesside times to the Roman period. It includes many house-tombs in which relatives of the dead could reside during festivals for the dead. The guardian will probably draw your attention to a small house-tomb which belongs to a girl called Isadora who drowned in the Nile in 120 BC. The walls of her tomb are covered with stucco and painted with architectural themes such as imitation woodwork and marble.

Map on page 246

Akhenaten's city

Tall al-'Amarnah ❺ (daily, winter 7am–4pm, summer 7am–5pm; admission charge), known today simply as Amarnah, lies on the east bank of the Nile a further 10 km (6 miles) south, opposite the modern town of Dayr Mawas (a ferry takes visitors over to the east bank). It was the site chosen by the Pharaoh Akhenaten (formerly Amenhotep IV) to found a city dedicated to the worship of a single god, the Aten (literally the sun's disc), rather than the whole pantheon of gods worshipped by his predecessors who had founded Thebes.

Akhenaten's introduction of the worship of one god is frequently regarded as

BELOW: a marriage ceremony in Asyut.

a form of monotheism, and in Akhenaten himself some scholars have seen metaphysical reasoning far ahead of his time. He has been variously described as a mystic and ascetic, and alternatively as a rebel and fanatic.

In fact, worship of the Aten was not so much a new realm of thought, since worship of the sun in one form or another was a constant thread throughout ancient Egyptian history. The novelty lay in the recognition of the unlimited power of the sun-god as the creator and preserver of all mankind. The celebrated hymn, which is inscribed in the tomb of one of his officials, has been ascribed to Akhenaten himself: "O living Aten... how manifold are thy works... thou sole god, like to whom there is no other. Thou didst create the earth after thy heart... even all men, herds and flocks, whatever is upon the earth, creatures that walk upon feet, which soar aloft flying with their wings..." (From a translation by Sir A. Gardiner in *Egypt of the Pharaohs*, Clarendon Press Oxford.)

When Akhenaten revolted against the priests of Amun-Re at Thebes, he chose to base his new capital on this expansive crescent-shaped plain over 4 km (2½ miles) long and about 800 metres (½ mile) across. The site had no history of cult activity, no earlier settlement nor any existing priesthood. Akhenaten called it *Akhet-Aten*, the "Horizon of Aten".

City planning

At first sight Tall al-'Amarnah appears to be devoid of ancient structures and it is difficult to visualise a bustling city here. The site is a far cry from the legendary "hundred-gated Thebes" and this is because the city was totally razed after Akhenaten died. Once the priests of Amun-Re had been reinstated and Luxor restored as capital, all evidence of the religion of the Aten and the rule of "the heretic" were obliterated. All that was left of Akhenaten's unique city were a few walls and columns little more than waist high.

Yet it is from these ruins and from ground-plans that archaeologists have been able to get their clearest picture of city-planning in ancient Egypt. Elsewhere the palaces and dwelling-places built of sun-dried brick perished. The city of *Akhet-Aten,* however, was constructed on a plain above the level of the flood and was occupied for such a brief time (it was never reinhabited) that it provides a unique opportunity to learn how an ancient city developed.

The site was designed with three main streets running parallel to the river. The central quarter, which spreads south from the modern village of at-Till to al-Hag Khandil, was the main residential area and also the site of the temple of the Aten. Some of the ruins of these can still be seen.

To the north and south were habitations for officials and priests. The side streets contained the houses of the middle classes and their servants; the working classes, especially those employed on the necropolis, lived in special compounds to the east of the plain. Their houses were built on parallel streets and were uniform in size, apart from one larger house to each compound which probably belonged to the community's supervisor.

Akhenaten took up residence at *Akhet-Aten* in the

eighth year of his reign, about 1367 BC. He set up boundary stelae on the cliffs on both sides of the Nile, recording an oath in the name of his "father", the Aten, that neither he, his wife (the beautiful Queen Nefertiti) nor children would pass the limits he was setting, and that the land would remain sacred to the Aten forever. This was not to be. Shortly after the 14th year of his reign, Queen Nefertiti, for unknown reasons, took up residence in her northern palace. Akhenaten appointed his half-brother Smenkhare as co-regent, and died shortly afterwards. The sacred city, which was still under construction, was destroyed.

Tomb scenes

Akhenaten's body has not been found, but his **tomb** is approached through a long narrow valley between the two mountain ranges to the east. Although not open to the public, it is worth mentioning because studies suggest that it was not a single tomb but a tomb complex; it may originally have been intended for the entire royal family. This would make it unique among royal tombs because kings were usually buried alone to ensure safety.

The tombs of the noblemen at Tall al-'Amarnah, however, can be visited, and it is from these that we get an insight into life during the short rule of Akhenaten. Although many were badly damaged, not all the reliefs were destroyed and the most important ones have been carefully restored.

The tombs were hewn out of the rock and are similar in plan to the tombs of the 18th Dynasty at Thebes, with a forecourt leading to a large columned hall. Among the northern group of tombs, one of the largest and best preserved belongs to a high priest of the Aten called **Meri-Re** (No. 4). In one of the reliefs Akhenaten can be seen at a palace window casting forth golden ornaments to the owner of the tomb. In another he is depicted driving from his palace in a chariot, preceded by guards and followed by the queen, the princesses and escorts, some in chariots and some on foot. Priests await their arrival at the temple, where, after the necessary prayers the royal couple emerge and are greeted by other priests. They then proceed to inspect the storehouses, barns and other chambers, some of which are enclosed in a garden.

Similar scenes are found in the tombs of **Pentu** (No. 5), the royal physician, **Ahmose** (No. 3), the fan bearer, and **Panehesi** (No. 6), chief servitor of the Aten. The scenes were decorated in the realism characteristic of what has become known as the "Amarnah period". Unlike traditional ancient Egyptian art, in which the pharaoh ruled as a god and was symbolically depicted as a giant at a temple entrance and in relief, Akhenaten was portrayed quite naturalistically. He is often shown as the same size as his people, as a mortal rather than as an aloof ruler, a family man who could delight in his daughters, eat a hearty meal and demonstrate tender affection.

Fragments of slabs carved in relief were found in many homes at Amarnah. They show figures of the royal family making offerings to the Aten, with a clear message: adore the one whom Akhenaten adores, and make offerings directly to the one to whom Akhenaten makes offerings. ❏

Map on page 246

Akhenaten's wife, Queen Nefertiti, was renowned for her great beauty. The claim is supported by a stunning bust of her, now in the Egyptian Museum in Berlin (see picture on page 59).

BELOW: tomb of Meri-Re at Tall al-'Amarnah.

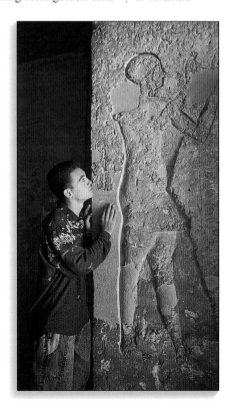

MEMPHIS, SAQQARAH AND GIZA

Map on page 256

This area close to modern Cairo was the power base of the Old Kingdom. Its capital was Memphis and its rulers were buried in the tombs and pyramids of Saqqarah and Giza

The Mediterranean Sea once reached at least to the foot of the Muqattam Hills that shelter modern Cairo to the east, and probably even as far south as ancient Memphis. In other words, the vast triangle of the Nile Delta that exists today was once a wide bay. This bay was gradually filled up by the ceaseless accumulation of alluvial deposits. According to classical writers the River Nile flowed through seven outlets in ancient times: today there are only two outlets; the Rosetta and Damietta branches of the river.

Memphis, the first capital of Upper and Lower Egypt was founded, according to legend, by King Menes, traditionally identified as the first king of the 1st Dynasty, who united Upper and Lower Egypt. The city stood at the apex of the Delta. For 1,000 years it held the title of capital, and even with the growth of other cities, it retained its importance as a religious and commercial centre right through to Graeco-Roman times. The necropolis of the ancient city was situated at nearby Saqqarah, though the pyramids of the Memphite kings were built along the desert edge over a distance of about 30 km (18 miles) from Abu Rawash to Dahshur *(see page 266).* However, the most spectacular was the Great Pyramid at Giza, which ranked among the Seven Wonders of the Ancient World.

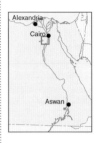

PRECEDING PAGES: at the Pyramids. **LEFT:** date palms near Memphis. **BELOW:** the Sphinx at night.

Many hotels and travel agents offer tours of Memphis, Saqqarah and Giza, but it is easy to arrange things independently. Though it would be difficult to complete a tour of the three sites on public transport, you can hire a taxi for the day fairly inexpensively – if you prefer, you could take a taxi just for the morning, to drive you to Memphis and Saqqarah and then drop you off at the Pyramids around lunchtime; from there you can later hire another taxi or catch a bus to take you back to town.

The first capital

Memphis ❶ is situated on the west bank of the Nile some 25 km (15 miles) south of Giza and almost opposite modern Cairo's suburb of Maadi. It was honoured by Egypt's most famous kings (some of whom built palaces there), as the place where they were crowned.The city was lauded by classical writers in glowing terms, and was regarded as a place of pilgrimage or a place of refuge. It was so great that any who sought control of Egypt knew that they first had to make themselves masters of Memphis.

Little remains of the ancient city today. Even the Temple of Ptah, one of the great gods of ancient Egypt, is in ruin and most of that ruin lies beneath and around the mound on which the modern village of

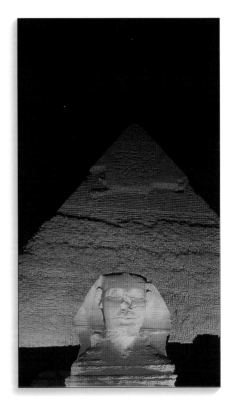

Mit Rahina stands. It is hard to imagine this derelict place as the former heart of one of the most important cities in ancient Egypt, as well as one of the most heavily populated.

Memphis is no more. It has suffered the ravages of war, fanaticism and time. Its monuments have been torn down, usurped, pillaged and used as quarry material. Whatever remained of the ancient city was buried beneath alluvial soil that started to build up in medieval times when the canals were neglected. Where once stood a mighty metropolis with a river port, factories and settlements, modern-day villagers cultivate date-palms in the enriched earth.

French scholar Gaston Maspero described Memphis well when he said it was, in ancient times, "what Cairo has long been for us moderns, the oriental city *par excellence*, the representation, the living symbol of Egypt."

Essential monuments

Because of the scanty remains, most visits to Memphis focus on the monuments in the **Museum Compound** (daily, winter 7.30am–4pm, summer 7.30am–5pm; admission charge), where the tourist buses park and where there is a cafeteria as well as shops selling imitation antiquities.

The main feature of the compound is a statue of Ramesses II in a covered enclosure. Regarded as the finest statue of this pharaoh ever carved, it lies in a horizontal position and can only be viewed properly from the gallery. Part of the crown and the lower legs are missing but the fine craftsmanship is apparent in the details of the king's mouth, with indentations at the corners, the muscular shoulders and the sturdy torso. The royal name, in an oblong cartouche, can be seen on the right shoulder, the breast and on the pharaoh's girdle.

In its position at the apex of the Delta Memphis was in an ideal location for local trade as well as foreign commerce, and coins and sculptures found in the ruins show that Carians, Lydians, Attic Greeks and Macedonians came in great numbers, as well as Semites, Syrians and Persians.

BELOW: the statue of Ramesses II, Memphis.

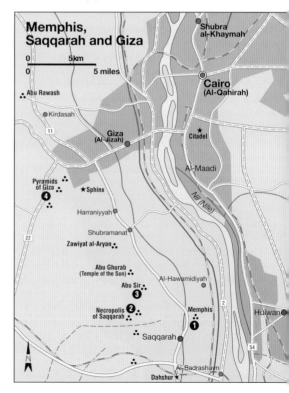

Memphis, Saqqarah and Giza

Map
on page
256

Ramesses II built extensively at Memphis. As he always erected his statues in pairs, it is not unreasonable to suppose that this limestone statue, as well as the red Aswan granite monolith from Memphis which today stands outside the railway station on Ramesses Square in downtown Cairo, and the fragments of statues in other qualities of granite, all had counterparts adorning entrances to the various monuments of Memphis.

There are two other objects of particular note in the museum compound – the **alabaster sphinx**, which is the largest statue ever found fashioned of this stone (it weighs some 80 tonnes and has been attributed to either Amenhotep I or Tuthmosis I), and the **Stele of Apries**, a huge round-topped stone slab erected by the 26th Dynasty pharaoh, which bears an important historical text and the figures of the gods Ptah and Sokar.

Despite its importance and continuous occupation for thousands of years, not more than 10 percent of the central city of Memphis has ever been excavated. The Survey of Memphis is an Egypt Exploration Society project which is attempting to draw together all existing material (including those relics which are now in museums worldwide), excavate the site systematically, and draw up a stratified map of ancient Memphis giving, where possible, ground plans of different structures at different stages of their history.

The word "Memphis" no longer exists in Egypt. It was a Greek derivation of *Men-nefer*, the name of the pyramid of Pepi I on the Saqqarah necropolis. The villagers of Mit Rahina, however, still call their village *Menf* or *Manf*. It is not known whether they adopted this name to please early archaeologists and travellers who talked about "Men-nefer", or whether the original built-up area gradually crept beyond the site of Pepi's pyramid towards Mit Rahina.

It was one of the names of Memphis, Hikaptah, "House of the ka [spirit] of Ptah" that gave Egypt its name. This became Agyptos in Greek and hence "Egypt" – just as, today, the Arabic word for Egypt (Misr) is also the word for Cairo.

BELOW: old and new transport, Saqqarah.

The Step Pyramid at Saqqarah, built by the ground-breaking architect Imhotep.

First pyramids

To the southwest of Memphis on a very arid plateau is **Saqqarah ❷** (open daily 8am–5pm; admission charge), the ancient city's necropolis and one of the most important sites in Egypt. Its name is derived from Sokar, an agricultural god believed to dwell in the earth; the annual Festival of Sokar took place at the "White Wall of Memphis". Herds of draught animals would be driven round the walls of the ancient city, as if going round a threshing floor, in a ritual to awaken the soil. Because Sokar lived in the earth, he also came to be regarded as one of the gods of the dead; hence the adoption of his name for the whole necropolis.

Dominating the horizon of Saqqarah is the **Step Pyramid ❹**, the central feature of a funerary complex built by Imhotep for Pharaoh Zoser, the first king of the Third Dynasty in 2686 BC. Zoser's reign marks the beginning of the Old Kingdom or "pyramid age", an era of great vision and invention.

Until this time no stone had ever been used for large-scale construction and there was no architectural tradition from which to draw. But Imhotep, a brilliant innovator, builder and "wise man", whose sayings were quoted for thousands of years, drew inspiration from contemporary buildings constructed of perishable materials: reeds, mud-brick and logs of wood. It is thanks to his genius that we can see today, sculpted in stone, how bundles of reeds were tied together with the heads fanning out to form the earliest capital; how logs were laid across parallel walls to form a roof; and how reed fences separated property. In short, the detail of Saqqarah mirrors the structures of the state capital of Memphis which, as already mentioned, have almost disappeared.

The Step Pyramid, which rises in six unequal tiers, originally had one single step. This was the superstructure over the burial chamber. But during the long reign of Zoser the structure underwent no fewer than five alterations: the ground plan was successively enlarged, and the height was increased in stages until, superimposed on top of one another, the six steps of the terraced structure emerged in their final form. Imhotep's Step Pyramid is the forerunner of the true pyramid, which reached its apogee in the three magnificent Fourth Dynasty pyramids at Giza *(see page 261)*. At the back of the Step Pyramid, don't miss seeing the *seidab,* a box with a life-size statue of Zoser staring towards the North star in the hope of immortality.

In visiting the Step Pyramid complex it is as well to remember that the pyramid is a symbolic structure. It was never meant to be used by man, as a temple would be. It was a funerary structure in which the pharaoh could re-enact, in his afterlife, all his experiences on earth. For this reason, the various courts, including the main **Heb-Sed Court** to the east of the pyramid, are not massive or cumbersome. They have simple, remarkably fine lines with perfect proportions, and it is difficult to believe that such sophisticated forms were created so long ago. Beyond the Heb-Sed court, for example, there are three engaged columns remarkably and realistically fashioned in the form of a papyrus plant, the triangular stem thickening just above the ground, and then tapering towards the fanning head of the plant.

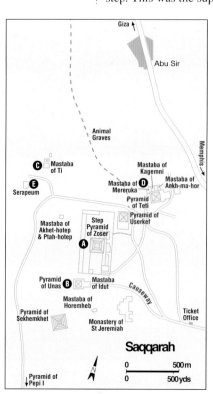

Giza

Abu Sir

Memphis

Animal Graves

❸ Mastaba of Ti

❺ Serapeum

Mastaba of Akhet-hotep & Ptah-hotep

Step Pyramid of Zoser
❹

Pyramid of Unas **❸** Mastaba of Idut

Pyramid of Sekhemkhet

Mastaba of Horemheb

Monastery of St Jeremiah

Mastaba of Kagemni

Mastaba of **❻** Mereruka

Mastaba of Ankh-ma-hor

Pyramid of Teti

Pyramid of Userkef

Causeway

Ticket Office

Saqqarah

0   500m

0   500 yds

N

Pyramid of Pepi I

The Pyramid Texts

Among the other structures on the Saqqarah plateau are several Fifth and Sixth-Dynasty pyramids which were built of poor quality local limestone and fell to ruin when the outer casings were removed. Although unimpressive from the outside, they are of great interest and historical importance because many are inscribed with mortuary literature known as the Pyramid Texts. (The Giza pyramids, incidentally, were not decorated at all.)

Long columns of inscribed hieroglyphics, the texts include hymns, prayers and rituals for the deceased pharaoh, as well as lists of offerings of food, drink and clothing for the afterlife. They are beautifully carved into the stone and filled with blue or green pigment. In the Fifth-Dynasty **Pyramid of Unas ❸**, for example, which was built about 2345 BC and situated outside the southwest corner of the Zoser pyramid complex, the texts cover all the available space in the tomb chamber, apart from the walls behind and beside the empty sarcophagus, which are themselves painted to represent the facade of a building.

The noblemen's tombs

It is from the noblemen's tombs dotted around the plateau, however, that we gain a real insight into everyday life in ancient Egypt, especially from a group of tombs that date from the age of the pyramid builders. These are decorated with painted reliefs of everyday life, including agricultural activities, animal husbandry, hunting, various trades and industries, as well as family life.

The **Mastaba of Ti ❸**, a court dignitary, is one of the best preserved. It includes representations of the shipbuilding industry (in the sacrificial chamber) which are particularly interesting, depicting every stage of the work from the un-

Maps:
Area 256
Site 258

BELOW: the funerary complex of Zoser, Saqqarah.

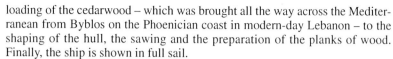

Statue of an Apis bull with a sun disc between its horns. If it is open, don't miss the labyrinthine Serapeum at Memphis, where mummified sacred bulls were buried.

BELOW: riding near the Pyramids, Giza.

loading of the cedarwood – which was brought all the way across the Mediterranean from Byblos on the Phoenician coast in modern-day Lebanon – to the shaping of the hull, the sawing and the preparation of the planks of wood. Finally, the ship is shown in full sail.

Also in the sacrificial chamber is a series of rural scenes, in one of which a grey cow gives birth with the help of a farmer, while, behind her, restive calves have their hind legs bound together or are tethered to pegs in the ground. Ti himself is charmingly depicted in the second corridor with his wife seated at his feet and being entertained by a flautist, two singers and two harpists.

The **Mastaba of Mereruka** is a family tomb, with chambers belonging to the nobleman himself, his wife and children, and it is decorated with the largest number of different activities to be found in any single tomb. They include scenes of industrial activities such as the manufacture of jewellery from gold that is first weighed in a balance and registered by a scribe; pottery-making by workers who comment to each other on the excellence of one another's work; and life-size statues of the deceased being hauled to the tomb on sledges. (These are to be found in the first chamber leading off the entrance chamber to the right.) In the latter scene, note how the men pour water on the earth just in front of the runners, to render the Nile clay slippery.

On the left-hand wall of the third chamber of this tomb is a representation of the estate headquarters. It shows clerks seated in a hall with lotus-bud columns, while village elders are forcibly dragged before them to give evidence on their apparently faulty tax returns. One man has been stripped, and his arms and feet are bound around a post where he is being beaten.

The standing statue of Mereruka, in the burial chamber, is one of the few Old Kingdom statues preserved intact. He is shown walking forward, out of his tomb and into the sacrificial chamber. The statue survived *in situ* because the tomb had become filled with sand by Graeco-Roman times when the road leading to the Serappeum *(see below)*, was constructed. Unaware of what lay beneath, the workers preserved it by building over the top. Further outstanding mastabas or tombs belonged to the priest **Ptah-Hotep** and his son **Akhtet-Hotep**. The reliefs are smaller than in Ti's mastaba, but it is interesting to see the various stages of completion. The chapel in the father's tomb has some exquisite reliefs of Ptah-Hotep in his function as a high priest of Maiot.

The tombs of the Apis bulls

The **Serapeum** , as it was called in Graeco-Roman times, is a vast sepulchre of rock-hewn galleries for the internment of the sacred Apis bull of Memphis. It is within walking distance of the huge tent on the necropolis where refreshments are served and from where camels and donkeys are available for hire if you do not wish to walk to the site.

The tombs are hewn out of solid rock, and the flanking chambers contain mighty granite sarcophagi of an average weight of 65 tonnes each, and measuring some 4 metres (13 ft) long, by over 3 metres (9 ft) high. Most of the lids are of solid granite.

When the discoverer of this sepulchre, the French archaeologist Mariette, first entered the galleries in 1851, he found that most of the sarcophagus lids had been pushed aside and the contents pillaged. Only one had been left intact because the robbers had been unsuccessful in their efforts to open it; Mariette succeeded where they had failed by using dynamite. Inside the sarcophagus he found a solid gold statue of a bull which is now in the Louvre in Paris.

The monuments that can be seen on the Saqqarah plateau today represent a mere fraction of what still lies beneath the sand. In fact, the whole plateau is literally riddled with sand-filled depressions, any one of which could be the top of a shaft leading to a tomb. Archaeological teams from many parts of the world are conducting excavations, restoring and clearing tombs, and the Supreme Council for Antiquities is planning to open up many others.

Maps:
Area 256
Site 258

The road to Giza

On the road from Saqqarah to Giza, look for more pyramids at **Abu Sir ❸**, including the **Pyramid of Neferirkare**, which at its intended 70 metres (230 ft) would have been higher than the Great Pyramid of Khufu (it was never finished), and the **Pyramid of Sahure**, around which the temple complexes have been relatively well preserved. A little further north is the Pyramid field of Zawiyat al-Aryan with the **Unfinished Pyramid** made of granite blocks, and a Layer Pyramid which was probably intended to be a step pyramid.

The pyramids of Giza

The great **Pyramids of Giza ❹** (open daily 7am–7.30pm for the plateau, 8.30am–4.30pm for inside the pyramids; separate admission charges for the

BELOW: aerial view of the Sphinx and the Pyramids.

Great Pyramid, the Solar Boat Museum, Khafre's Pyramid and Menkaure's Pyramid) stand on a rocky plateau on the west bank of the Nile 25 km (15 miles) north of Saqqara, almost directly opposite Cairo. The Pyramids Road from Cairo is a dual carriageway that takes you to the foot of the desert plateau where the Mena House Oberoi Hotel, escaping the fate of many other once-ancient hotels, has been upgraded and modernised

It is not unusual for modern travellers to observe the Pyramids for the first time and say, "I thought they would be bigger." It is only when one has been on the plateau for several hours, looking at them in relation to people and the sur-rounding desert, that one starts to appreciate their incredible size. They are the most famous, intensely measured, studied and debated monuments in the world, and also, probably, the least understood. The geometrical accuracy and techni-cal skill that went into their making is truly awe-inspiring.

The **Great Pyramid Ⓐ**, which was built in honour of the Fourth-Dynasty Pharaoh Khufu (Cheops) *circa* 2600 BC, is the sole survivor of the Seven Won-ders of the Ancient World. Originally 147 metres (480 ft) high and covering an area of 5 hectares (13 acres), the pyramid was constructed of some 2.3 million blocks of stone of an average weight of 2.5 tonnes (some weighed as much as 16 tonnes), which were brought into contact to tolerances as close as 0.05 mm (one 500th of an inch). The sides of the pyramid themselves were oriented al-most exactly true north, south, east and west, with the four corners again at perfect right angles. The maximum error in alignment has been calculated as be-ing a little over one-twelfth of a degree.

The outlines of the pyramids were once smooth and covered with a lime-stone facing that was fitted and polished, nowhere betraying an entrance. The

The classic pyramid complex comprises the pyramid for the pharaoh, a satellite pyramid, thought to be for his queen, and a mortuary temple connected to a valley temple by a causeway.

The entrance to a pyramid was normally on the north side.

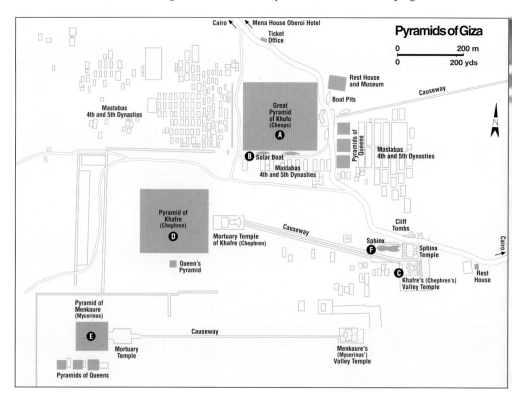

Pyramids of Giza

shape was inspired by the *ben-ben* stone, the sacred symbol of the sun-god at Heliopolis. Each pyramid was originally part of a funerary complex that comprised the pyramid itself, its mortuary temple, and the valley temple, which was situated at the edge of the cultivable land.

After the death of the reigning pharaoh, his mummified body would be brought by river to the valley temple, from there to be borne on the shoulders of white-robed priests to the mortuary temple where rituals and prayers were carried out before the internment of the body. The valley and mortuary temples were linked by a covered causeway.

Entering the pyramid is not for the claustrophobic, as the corridor is low and narrow, often with lots of tourists. The shaft leads left into the Queen's Chamber and right into the 47-mere (154-ft) long Great Gallery, which in turn leads up to the King's Chamber with its empty sarcophagus.

The Solar Boat

Behind the pyramid is an ancient boat, known as the **Solar Boat** **B** (daily, winter 9am–4pm; summer 9am–5pm; admission charge), housed in a special museum. Discovered in a pit covered in limestone blocks and mortar near the Great Pyramid in 1954, it is regarded as one of the most important finds of the 20th century. Its exact purpose is a matter of debate. It was either the funerary boat of Khufu, which carried the pharaoh's body to Giza prior to embalming, or it was a solar boat, intended to carry the dead pharaoh across the sky from east to west to be united with the solar god Re.

The boat was built of cedarwood imported from Lebanon and the entire structure had been dismantled and laid in the pit. Reconstructed, it proved to be

Maps:
Area 256
Site 262

A human figure provides a sense of scale at the foot of the Great Pyramid.

BELOW: leading the way inside the Great Pyramid.

43 metres (141 ft) long and 8 metres (26 ft) high. Although 4,500 years old it is still in excellent condition, with a massive curving hull which rises to elegant prow and stern posts. It had six pairs of long oars, two of which were larger than the others and used as rudders. The thick planks were "sewn" together by a system of ropes through holes that met in pairs on the inside. The expansion of the rope and wood in water ensured the boat would be watertight without the need for caulking.

Four other boat pits have been discovered. Three of these are empty but an unexcavated boat is known to lie under the ground beside the boat museum. In time, it, too, will be excavated, as there is evidence that the bedrock in which it lies is not hermetically sealed, and that the boat is, even now, deteriorating.

Pyramid of Chephren and the Sphinx

The **Valley Temple** ●, also known as the Granite Temple, is part of the funerary complex of Khafre (2558–2532 BC), Khufu's son. The **Pyramid of Khafre (Chephren)** ● appears taller than the Great Pyramid but is simply built on higher ground. The smaller **Pyramid of Menkaure (Mycerinus)** ●, illustrating that the pharaohs were getting weaker at that point, belonged to Khafre's successor. The pyramid was sheathed in Aswan granite.

At the entrance to the Valley Temple stands the **Sphinx** ●, a recumbent lion with a human face – that of Khafre. Fashioned out of the bedrock of the Giza plateau, it is 255 metres (840 ft) long and some 20 metres (65 ft) high at its head. Repeatedly covered in sand, the Sphinx has been the victim of rescue and conservation efforts since ancient times. Between its outstretched paws a red granite slab tells the story of the first attempt at conservation under the Pharaoh Tuthmosis IV of the 18th Dynasty. The text relates how the pharaoh was sleeping in its shadow one day, when the Sphinx appeared to him and instructed him to clear away the sand that was choking it. The Sphinx declared that if Thutmosis harkened to his words then he would be king and wear the crown of Upper and Lower Egypt – which, indeed, he did.

This inscription, which dates from *circa* 1400 BC, is the first record of any excavation on the Giza plateau, where wind-blown depressions are continually being filled with sand. The Sphinx itself was cleared of sand again in the Saitic period (600 BC), in the late-Ptolemaic (Greek) period, and again in Roman times. In the modern era Napoleon's team of *savants* cleared and measured the monument during the 1789 expedition to Egypt, and it has been successively cleared and restored by the Egyptian Antiquities Organisation. Unfortunately, despite all these efforts, the Sphinx is suffering badly from age, environmental pollution and sub-soil water seepage. In addition, current restoration measures include replacing earlier, poor quality repairs with "healthy stone".

In front of the Granite Temple and the Sphinx is the **Sphinx Theatre** where a *son et lumière* performance takes place every night, in a variety of languages (tel: 02-3857320 for more information or check www.sound-light.egypt.com/pyr.htm). There are no English-language performances on Sunday.

The Sphinx has suffered over the years. Its nose was used for target practice by Mameluk soldiers, and its beard is now in the British Museum.

BELOW: the funerary boat of Khufu.

Tourist development

In the late 1980s a plan was set in motion to upgrade the Giza plateau as a tourist site; to clear and restore the monuments, open up tombs for tourists to visit, and set up facilities such as cafeterias, restaurants and souvenir shops in such a manner as not to detract from the natural and archaeological environment. The plan was known as the "Pyramid Plateau Project" and stage one was quickly accomplished. Accumulated sand was removed from the Great Pyramid of Khufu, its inner corridors were cleared, and closed-circuit TV, microphones, and suitable lighting and ventilation were installed.

Stage two involved clearing and restoring tombs on the necropolis, allowing 15 tombs of nobility to receive their first visitors since they were discovered in the 19th century." Stage three concentrated on the third and smallest pyramid, belonging to the Pharaoh Menkaure. Weakened parts were strengthened, and it, too, has been provided with closed-circuit TV and suitable lighting.

Meanwhile, another project is also moving forward. Known as the Giza Mapping Project, it is an in-depth archaeological study of the plateau, its geology and topography. The aim of the project is to provide the first complete and detailed map of every feature of the plateau. It will enable, among other things, the identification of different qualities of stone used to build the pyramids with the bedrock from which they came. For example, while good quality limestone for its outer casing came from the Tura quarries on the eastern bank of the Nile, local limestone of mediocre quality was used for constructing the main body of the pyramids around a core of bedrock that was left intact. And where exactly this quantity of limestone – the volume of which must be equivalent to that used in the pyramid – came from, is one of the mysteries to which answers are sought.

Maps:
Area 256
Site 262

The Mena House Oberoi Hotel.

If you want to wake up with the Pyramids filling the view out of your window, then this is the place to stay – particularly in the Old Wing.

BELOW: the Sphinx.

More pyramids

Most tourists to Cairo visit the Step Pyramid at Saqqarah and the pyramid complexes in Giza, but there are many more of these intruiging buildings. In fact, between the beginning of the Pyramid Age in the 27th century BC and the end of the Middle Kingdom in the 18th century BC more than 80 pyramids were built along the Nile between Giza and the oasis of al-Fayyum.

A few kilometres south of Saqqarah is the impressive but rarely visited site of **Dahshur**, comprising five pyramids, which is essential viewing if you want to understand the history of pyramid building. On the east of the site are three Middle Kingdom pyramids, built in the 19th–18th centuries BC, at the time of a pyramid-building revival, including the **Black Pyramid** of Amenemhet III built in black mudbrick. More interesting, however, are the two Old-Kingdom pyramids, illustrating attempts at pyramid building by Snofru, the father of Khufu. The **Red Pyramid** was larger than Khafre's pyramid in Giza, but more intriguing is Snofru's **Bent Pyramid**, which starts at an angle of 52° and then changes to a gentler 43°, either because the architect realised that the initial angle was impossible to sustain or because such a steep pyramid would have put tremendous pressure upon the internal chambers.

The Bent Pyramid has the most intact casing of any Egyptian pyramid, and is unusual in having two entrances – one on the north side, like most pyramids, and the other on the west. On the south side of the Bent Pyramid is a smaller pyramid, possibly for Snofru's wife, Heterpheres, which still retains some of its original limestone casing at its base.

About 50 km (30 miles) south of Saqqarah is the spectacular **Pyramid of Maydum** (open daily 8am–7pm; admission charge), another step pyramid that was supposed to be transformed into a smooth pyramid but, due to a design flaw, the outer layers collapsed into rubble. The main structure originally rose to a height of 93 metres (305 ft). The surrounding tombs date from the 3rd or 4th Dynasty and include those of Prince Rahotep, the high priest of Heliopolis, and his wife Nafret, whose double sculpture in painted limestone is one of the most famous exhibits in the Egyptian Museum in Cairo *(see page 273).*

About 16 km (10 miles) southwest of the Pyramid of Maydum, at **Al-Hawarah**, is the crumbling **pyramid complex of Amenemhet II** (daily, 7am–5pm; admission charge), dating from the 18th century BC, towards the end of the Middle Kingdom. It has the remains of an intricate mortuary temple known as the Labyrinth, though its stone was extensively plundered during the Roman period and the remains are scant.

A few kilometres further south is the earlier 12th-Dynasty **Pyramid of Al-Lahun** (daily 7am–4pm; admission charge), the tomb of Senusert II (1897–1878 BC). Here, the pyramid's architects diverged from the usual method of pyramid building, empoying limestone pillars on a rock base as the framework for a mud-brick structure that was then encased in stone. Also in the Fayyum area are the even more dilapidated Pyramids of al-Lisht that belonged to the 20th-century BC pharaoh Amenemhet I and his son Senusert I (1971–1928 BC). ❏

BELOW: the countryside near Saqqarah.
RIGHT: visiting the Giza Pyramids.

CAIRO

With a history spanning five millennia and a population of 17 million people, Cairo is a diverse and fascinating metropolis and the hub of the Arab world

L arger than any other city in the Middle East or Africa, Cairo stretches along the east bank of the Nile for more than 35 km (20 miles), guarding the head of the Delta and marking the division between Upper and Lower Egypt. Across the river is Giza, technically a separate administrative district, but part of the same urban agglomeration. In the river between Cairo and Giza are two islands: Rawdah, formed out of bed-rock, which has been the site of human settlement since since ancient times, and Gazirah, formed alluvially within the past six centuries, where the suburb of Zamalik has grown up since 1870.

With a head-count of approximately 17 million – there are more Cairenes than there are Scandinavians, Greeks, Dutch, Austrians or Hungarians – Cairo, Giza and the islands constitute the most populous urban area in the world between America and India.

Beginnings

The city-site has been settled since Neolithic times. Memphis, the first political capital of Egypt, was founded on the west bank near the end of the 4th millennium BC and later expanded northward to occupy the entire site of modern Giza.

Some 25 km (15 miles) northeast of the Giza pyramids on the opposite side of the river, and thus directly north of Memphis, was the temple-city of On, the Old Kingdom's greatest religious complex, centre of the cult of the sun-god Re. Mentioned in Genesis by its ancient Egyptian name, On was called Heliopolis ("Sun-City") by the Greeks, but its ancient site has no connection with the modern residential suburb of Heliopolis (Misr al-Gadidah), situated some 5 km (3 miles) away.

At Giza the main road from Memphis to On crossed the river, using the island of Rawdah as a stepping stone. The small settlement at the landing place opposite Rawdah on the east bank was probably called Per-Hapi-n-On – "The Nile House of On" – and became known to Greek travellers as Babylon. It became more important during the first Persian occupation of Egypt, when a canal was opened from the Red Sea to the Nile.

When Egypt became a Roman province in 30 BC, one of the three legions controlling the whole country was garrisoned in the fortress at Babylon (now Old Cairo). It is probably the place where St Peter wrote his first Epistle. Under the Roman emperor Trajan (AD 98–117) the old Persian canal was reopened and extended through the centre of the fortress. Later repaired by the Emperor Arcadius (395–408), the fortress of Babylon stood largely complete until around the end of the 19th century, when British army engineers demolished half of it.

PRECEDING PAGES: downtown Cairo.
LEFT: city on the Nile.
BELOW: Maydan al-Tahrir.

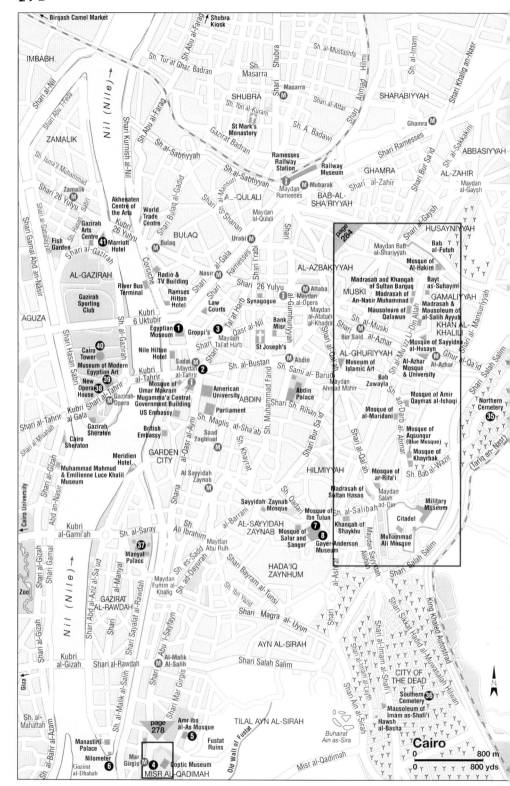

By the time of the Arab invasion in 641, Memphis had declined into a large own and Heliopolis had virtually disappeared; Alexandria had taken over the mantle of the most important city in Egypt. The Delta, however, the country's richest region, remained impassable in any direction except north or south along one of the branches of the Nile, which also provided the only route between Upper Egypt and the Mediterranean. Babylon (as the embryonic Cairo was still called at the time) controlled not only access to the Delta, but also access to Upper Egypt, and was thus a gateway to the entire country.

After a brief siege the fortress fell to the Arabs under their leader Amr ibn al-As, who then founded the city of Al-Fustat ("The Tent" or perhaps "The Earthworks"), where he settled his troops. For their spiritual needs he built the large congregational Mosque of Amr ibn al-As (today situated a couple of hundred metres north of the Roman fortress in Old Cairo, on the main road parallel to the Metro line, *see page 278*). Originally constructed in 641 or 642, this was the first mosque in Africa.

For 500 years Al-Fustat was the centre of a trade network that spread from Spain to China. Very little of the original city remains (the site is behind Old Cairo to the east but is closed to visitors), but many of the most beautiful and interesting items excavated from the ruins are in Cairo's Museum of Islamic Art on Shari' Bur Said.

Cairenes themselves do not call their city "Cairo". They call it "Misr", which means "metropolis", "capital", "that which is inhabited and civilised", but also means "Egypt". When Al-Fustat became the capital of the country under the Arabs, it was called "Misr-Fustat", and every succeeding settlement to be added to the agglomeration was simply absorbed into Misr. The Fatimids, who arrived from Tunisia in the 10th century, built the royal enclosure called "Al-Qahirah" north of the original city, and it was this new area which was then mis-pronounced by Italian merchants as "Gran Cairo", a name which caught on throughout Europe.

Downtown and the Egyptian Museum

Modern Cairo, today's city's centre, contains few major historical attractions, though it does have some fine colonial-style architecture. At its heart is the **Egyptian Museum** ❶ (9am–4.30pm; admission charge, plus extra charges for the Mummy Room and for photography), founded by the great French Egyptologist August Mariette (who is buried in a tomb in the museum's garden). The museum has a large collection of ancient Egyptian artefacts on display, but its basement is often referred to as the largest unexcavated area in Egypt. A new museum is planned near the Pyramids of Giza.

Displays on the ground floor are arranged chronologically, in a clockwise direction. Thus Pre-Dynastic and Old Kingdom exhibits are displayed to the left of the entrance,and Roman-period objects towards the right, ending with a replica of the Rosetta Stone (the real one is in the British Museum in London).

The Narmer Palette in the first room marks the beginning of Egyptian art and history, recording the unification of Upper and Lower Egypt by King Menes

Map on page 272

A wooden model of Maket Re in the Egyptian Museum.

BELOW: mummy masks of Yhuya and Yuya.

The Mummy Business

The Ancient Egyptians may have thought they were safe for eternity in their hidden stony tombs and sarcophagi, but very few mummies were allowed to remain in their original tombs. Some were hacked to pieces by early tomb robbers in search of jewels; others were ground to dust in Europe in medieval times and sold as aphrodisiacs or remedies against "abscesses, fractures, bruises, paralysis, migraine, epilepsy, haemoptysis, coughs, sore throats, high blood pressure, stomach insufficiencies, sickness, liver and spleen illnesses, internal ulcers and poisoning." Even though dealing in mummies was illegal, many wholesalers made a fortune in the trade. It was only heavy taxation that finally stopped the export business in the 17th century.

Mummification came about because of the ancient Egyptians' belief in life after death, for which they needed a body and soul. In a long procedure that took around 70 days in the case of a noble, the inner organs were removed and the corpse was dried with natron and then embalmed to turn the papyrus-like skin into leather. In order to maintain its physical presence the body was often filled with mud, saw-dust or sap and covered in hundreds of metres of sap-soaked bandages.

When mummification was at the peak of its popularity it was a massive industry, with embalmers working day and night shifts to wrap not only the "upper ten thousand" of society, but also holy bulls, ibis, crocodiles, pavians, cats, mice and scarabs.

A lot has been learned about the early Egyptians from mummification. X-rays of mummies have proved that illnesses such as rheumatism, arthritis, polio and even arteriosclerosis were well known in pharaonic days. Some mummies show death through heart attack or in pregnancy or childbirth (in one case a mummified foetus was discovered in the womb of its mummified mother).

In the 19th century surgeons and anatomists found a new source of income by unwrapping mummies in front of audiences. A British anatomist, T.J. Pettigrew, began by staging shows in his own house but soon moved to bigger venues. On 10 April 1834, a crowd of some 600 people gathered in his local town hall to witness the unwrapping of the "most interesting mummy ever discovered in Egypt". But the mummy proved to be a tough match. Neither hammer nor scissors nor knives succeeded in cutting through the thick protection. After three hours of cutting and sawing Mr Pettigrew gave up and announced that "the result of the operation would be published some other time."

At the end of the 19th century, America also tried to turn the mummy trade to gold. A paper manufacturer called August Stanwood had the apparently brilliant idea of making brown wrapping paper from the ancient bandages and shrouds. None of the American housewives ever knew that her vegetables and meat were wrapped in the remains of Egyptian mummies. However, a cholera epidemic traced back to Stanwood's paper mills marked the end of the trade. ❑

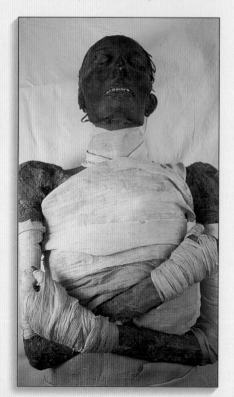

LEFT: the mummy of Tuthmosis II displayed in the Mummy Room in the Egyptian Museum.

(*circa* 3,000 BC). Among the Old Kingdom highlights are statues of the first kings and great scribes, and the double sculpture of Prince Rahotep and his wife Nafret. In the same room is the unusual wooden statue of the Shaykh al-Balad with rock crystal and alabaster eyes.

Another important collection dates from the Amarnah period of the rebel kingdom of Akehnaten *(see page 57)*. Carvings from Tall al-'Amarnah illustrate the revolution in religion, politics and art. The pharaoh Akhenaten is depicted in a much more naturalistic manner than artistic convention previously allowed; he plays freely with his wife Nefertiti and their children.

A staircase leads up to the museum's biggest crowd-puller, the treasures of Tutankhamun, the items discovered by Howard Carter in 1922 *(see page 218)*. Some 3,500 items were found by Carter, 1,700 of them on display here, including the pharaoh's jewellery and sarcophagus, games, clothes and furniture, many of them gold-plated and encrusted with jewels.

Other galleries upstairs are also worth seeing. In Room 27, for instance, are models found in an 11th-Dynasty tomb showing life as it was in 2000 BC. A few years ago the **Mummy Room** reopened after being closed for many years. Many of the mummies here, including those of Ahmose I, Amenhotep I, Tuthmosis I, II and III, Seti I and Ramesses II and III, were found in a cache near Deir al-Bahari, Thebes, in 1899 *(see page 220)*.

In the foyer at the head of the stairs near the entrance don't miss Case H, containing some of the museum's particular prizes, many of them made famous from postcards or photographs in books that give no idea of their diminutive size: an ivory statuette of Khufu from Abydos; a black bust of Queen Tiyi; the statuette of a Nubian girl with a single earring; the gilded statuette of Ptah, the

Map on page 272

The wooden statue of Shaykh al-Balad was discovered in Saqqarah by August Mariette, the founder of the museum's collection.

BELOW: the Egyptian Museum.

A statue of Muhammed Ali on Maydan al-Tahrir. Muhammed Ali is known as the father of modern Egypt.

BELOW: exterior of the esteemed American University.

god of Memphis; ivory pygmies that dance to the tug of a string; and the blue faïence hippopotamuses that have been reproduced all over the world.

Central Square

The museum faces the sprawling **Maydan al-Tahrir ❷** ("Liberation Square"). Originally called Maydan Ismailiyyah, the square once boasted a statue of the Magnificent Khedive in its centre. After the 1952 Revolution the square was renamed and the statue was hauled away, though its massive plinth was not dismantled for 25 years. Its site marks the approximate centre of modern Cairo, from which all distances in Egypt are measured. Most of the streets, squares and parks of this area appear in the master plan for the city, modelled on the Paris of that time, that Khedive Ismail's ministers developed between 1867 and 1873. The square has several of the city's most important landmarks: the **Mosque of Umar Makram**, used for the funerals of important Cairenes; the **Mugamma**, a Soviet-style building devoted to Egypt's notorious bureaucracy; the **Nile Hilton**, the city's first modern luxury hotel, and the **American University**, occupying a 19th-century palace, where many children of the country's elite receive an excellent education.

Much more intimate than Maydan al-Tahrir, and for many the true heart of downtown Cairo, is **Maydan Tal'at Harb ❸**, better known by its pre-revolution name of Maydan Suleyman Pasha. On the corner of this intersection stands the once legendary coffee house **Groppi**, a reminder of how elegant the area used to be. The facades are crumbling along the two streets that radiate from here, Shari' Qasr al-Nil and Shari' Tal'at Harb, but it is still a pleasure to look up at the buildings as you walk along. The Opera on **Maydan al-Opera** was burned down in 1971 (a new Opera House was later built on the island of Al-Gazirah) and made way for a much-needed car-park, and the Azbakiyyah Gardens have disappeared, but the downtown area is still full of charm. Some of the 500 rooms of the **Abdin Palace** (Sat–Thur 9am–4.30pm; admission charge) are open to the public.

THE AMERICAN UNIVERSITY IN CAIRO

Coptic Cairo

The fortress of Babylon, the mosque of Amr and the ruins of Al-Fustat are all situated in the quarter called **Misr al-Qadimah ❹**, a district known as Mar Girgis by Egyptians, and by Western visitors as **Old Cairo**, though it has no historical or topographical connection with Al-Qahirah and offers only the dimmest foretaste of the city's true splendour, which is its medieval architecture. The easiest way to reach Old Cairo is by Metro (the station is called Mar Girgis).

Useless for military purposes after the Arab conquest, the fortress of Babylon evolved into a Christian and Jewish enclave and many churches were built within its walls. The Metro stops by the modern Greek Orthodox Church of St George (Mar Girgis), built on the remains of one of Trajan's two great circular towers. Originally created to flank the canal built to link the Red Sea and the Nile in the 6th century BC, the towers now frame the entrance to the garden of the **Coptic Museum ❹** (daily 9am–4pm; admission charge). The museum contains many items from the surrounding churches, but its pride is a fine collection of ancient manuscripts, including the earliest known copy of the Book of Psalms and the Nag Hammadi codices, nearly 1,200 papyrus pages of Gnostic texts in Coptic, which were bound into books – the oldest leather-covered volumes known – and hidden in an Upper Egyptian cave in the 4th century *(see page 236)*. Also important are objects from the monastery of Apa Jeremiah at Saqqarah.

A portal in the south wall of the museum garden leads to the **Church of the Blessed Virgin Mary** ❸ (daily 7am–5pm; Mass on Fri 8–11am, Sun 7–10am; donations welcomed), known as "Al-Muallaqah" ("The Suspended"), built atop the bastions of another Roman gate. According to tradition, the church was built in the 7th century, but like the other churches in Old Cairo it has been repeatedly rebuilt, especially in recent times. Many items of furniture have been preserved, however, including a fine 11th-century marble *ambon* (pulpit) and a screen of ebony inlaid with ivory (12th- or 13th-century). The church also has a fine collection of icons.

A stairway near the museum's ticket office leads from the garden down to the stone-paved main street of the enclave. The **Church of St Sergius** ❹ (daily 8am–5pm) lies down the street to the right. Traditionally regarded as the oldest in Misr al-Qadimah, it is said to have been built in the 5th or 6th century over a cave where the Holy Family stayed during their sojourn in Egypt. The **Church of St Barbara** ❺ (daily 8am–5pm) is further down the main alleyway, then to the left. Though continuously rebuilt, it has a fine inlaid medieval iconostasis, one of the few surviving medieval icons of St Barbara, and an extraordinarily beautiful 13th-century icon of the Virgin with Child Enthroned.

Maps:
City 272
Area 278

The best way to get to the Coptic quarter of Old Cairo is by Metro.

BELOW: the Convent of St George.

Some ancient Egyptian symbols were incorporated into Coptic iconography. The Coptic cross above, for example, is clearly derived from the ankh, *the ancient Egyptian symbol for life.*

BELOW: a Copt pays homage in the chain room of the Convent of St George.

A few steps away is the **Ben Ezra Synagogue** (daily 8am–5pm), used as a church in the 8th and 9th centuries, closed under the fanatic Caliph Al-Hakim (996–1021), then sold to the Sephardic community. From the 11th century onward, it served as a *geniza*, a repository for discarded documents, which were discovered when it was rebuilt in the 19th century and have since provided a wealth of information. The spring next to the synagogue is supposedly where Mary collected water to wash Jesus, and also where the pharaoh's daughter found the baby Moses in the bulrushes.

The shortest route back to the main road outside the fortress returns past the Church of St Sergius, then curves round to the **Convent of St George** (daily during services) where modern believers wrap themselves in chains in remembrance of the persecution of St George. The convent incorporates a remarkable room with wooden doors 7 metres (23 ft) high, thought to have originally formed part of a Fatimid (12th-century) house.

About 200 metres/yds north is the first mosque to be built in Africa, the **Mosque of Amr ibn al-As** (daily 8am–5pm), built in AD 641–642 by the Muslim conqueror of Egypt *(see page 273)*. It has been rebuilt several times, but the latest remodelling, finished in 1983, tried to recreate its original appearance.

The island of Rawdah

Across a narrow branch of the Nile from Old Cairo onto the island of Rawdah is the earliest Muslim structure still extant in the city: the Rawdah **Nilometer** (daily 9am–4pm; admission charge), built in 861 by the governor of Egypt on the order of the Abbasid caliph. The building's conical dome is not part of the original nilometer, but a replica of the Ottoman-style dome that covered it in the 17th

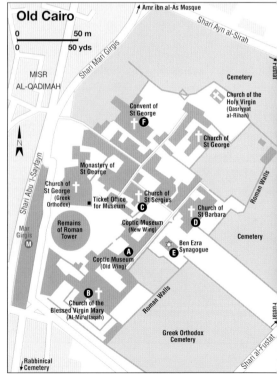

Old Cairo

0 — 50 m
0 — 50 yds

Amr ibn al-As Mosque

Shari Ayn al-Sirah

Shari Mari Girgis

MISR AL-QADIMAH

Cemetery

Church of the Holy Virgin (Qasriyyat al-Rihan)

Convent of St George **F**

Church of St George

Monastery of St George

Church of St George (Greek Orthodox)

Ticket Office for Museum

Church of St Sergius **C**

Church of St Barbara **D**

Coptic Museum (New Wing)

Ben Ezra Synagogue **E**

Cemetery

Remains of Roman Tower

Mar Girgis **M**

Coptic Museum (Old Wing) **A**

Roman Walls

Church of the Blessed Virgin Mary (Al-Mu'allaqah) **B**

Roman Walls

Greek Orthodox Cemetery

Rabbinical Cemetery

Fustat

Fustat

Shari al-Fustat

Shari Abu 'l-Sayfayn

and 18th centuries. In the middle of a square, stone-lined shaft is the Nilometer itself, an octagonal column divided into cubits, which stands on a millstone at the bottom of the shaft. A stairway around the walls of the shaft leads past inlets at three levels: the level of the uppermost inlet is indicated by recesses outlined with what a Gothic architect would have recognised as "tiers-point" arches, but they were built three centuries before the earliest European example. Nilometers measured the height of the annual flood and thus the richness of the harvest, which would determine the level of taxes for that year.

The so-called **Manastirli Palace**, next to the Nilometer, is the *salamlik* or reception kiosk of a palace complex built in the 1830s by the founder of a distinguished Cairene Turkish family. Restored in 1990, it offers a romantic view of the Nile and it is intended to become a museum dedicated to the much-loved singer Umm Kalthoum, displaying her memorabilia, photographs and an audio library of her performances.

Vanished quarter

Like all the rulers of Misr, the invading Abbasids of the 8th and 9th centuries built a new quarter to the city. Called "Al-Askar", it was occupied by a succession of governors, the most famous of whom was Ahmed ibn Tulun, who declared his independence from the Baghdad caliphate in 872 by having the caliph's dedicatory inscription removed from the Nilometer. The autonomous state he established – the first in Egypt since 30 BC – soon became an empire.

He founded a regal new city north of both Al-Askar and Al-Fustat, naming it "Al-Qatai" (The Wards), because of its division into separate districts defined by class and type of inhabitants. Al-Qatai covered around 260 hectares

Maps:
City 272
Area 278

BELOW:
the Nilometer.

The interior of the Gayer-Anderson Museum. Each room is elaborately furnished in a different orientalist style. Visit the Chinese Room, the Turkish Room or the Persian Room.

(640 acres) and contained palaces, government buildings, markets and even a hippodrome. At its centre was the congregational **Mosque of Ibn Tulun ❼** (daily 8am–6pm; admission charge), designed to contain an army for Friday prayers. Erected between 876 and 879, it is one of the great masterpieces of Muslim architecture and all that remains to testify to the magnificence of the Al-Qatai quarter. Echoing the architecture of Baghdad, it consists of a square enclosed by a massive flat-roofed arcade of baked brick, which is covered with fine plaster and surmounted by anthropomorphic cresting. In the centre of the mosque is a massive courtyard of nearly 2 hectares (4 acres) with an ablution fountain in the middle.

The arcading consists of elegant Syrian-style pointed arches, less elaborate than the arches of the Nilometer. The arcade is five rows deep on the eastern or Mecca-facing side, where several *mihrabs*, ornamental recesses, indicate the direction of prayer.

Also on this side is a wooden *minbar* – a structure like a staircase, which serves some of the same function that a pulpit fulfils in a church – the oldest (1296) still in use in Cairo and one of the finest. Carved stucco decoration is used throughout with wonderful inventiveness and a band of sycamore wood carved with Koranic verses runs around the building's whole interior circumference – more than 2 km (1 mile). The minaret was built in 1296 as a replacement for Ahmed ibn Tulun's original, which was modelled in turn on the minaret of the Great Mosque at Samarra near Baghdad.

Built against one end of the mosque are the two old houses that compose the **Gayer-Anderson Museum ❽** (daily 8am–4pm, closed Fri noon–1pm; admission charge), also known as Bayt al-Kritlujya. The British major John

Gayer-Anderson restored two beautiful 16th- and 17th-century houses, and filled them with his collection of Islamic *objets d'art* and paintings. Across the road from the museum is Khan Misr Touloun, an excellent handicrafts emporium with fair prices.

Maps:
City 272
Area 284

To the Citadel

Shari' Salibah, running east of the Mosque of Ibn Tulun, is lined with monuments, most of them restored after earthquake damage in the 1990s, including the Khanqah of Shaykhu and Sabil-kuttab of Qaytbay. The street leads to Maydan Salah ad-Din, above which towers the **Citadel ❾** (daily 9am–4pm; admission charge), easily identifiable from the outline of the Ottoman-style Mosque of Muhammed Ali, completed nearly 1,000 years later than the Ibn Tulun.

Both a fortress and a royal city, the Citadel continued the tradition among Cairo's rulers of building enclosures for themselves and their retainers. It was begun by Salah ad-Din ibn Ayyub (1171–93), the founder of the Ayyubid dynasty, the "Saladin" of the medieval Western chroniclers and Sir Walter Scott's novel *The Talisman*. The original walls and towers were erected between 1176 and 1183. Between 1200 and 1218 Salah ad-Din's round towers were encased in massive new constructions and square keeps were planted around the perimeter. His nephew Al-Kamil (1218–38) became the first sultan to live in the Citadel, which remained the seat of government for the next 650 years.

After the Bahri Mameluks overthrew the Ayyubids in 1250, their first great sultan, Baybars al-Bunduqdari (1260–77), divided the fortress into two enclosures linked by an inner gate, the **Bab al-Qullah.** During the various reigns of the Bahri Mameluk Sultan An-Nasir Muhammed (1294–95, 1299–1309, 1310–41), most of the buildings in the Southern Enclosure were torn down and replaced by much grander structures, such as the **Mosque of an-Nasir Muhammed ❿**, finished in 1335. Standing next to the Bab al-Qullah, it is one of the finest arcaded mosques in Cairo, as well as the only Mameluk building in the Citadel to survive. Its inner court is a virtual museum of reused pharaonic and Roman-period columns, while its two minarets show Persian influence in their upper pavilions, which are covered with green tiles. The marble that adorned its walls was stripped off by the Ottoman conquerors in 1517 and shipped to Istanbul.

The other three of the four mosques in the Citadel date from between 1517 and 1914, when Egypt was an Ottoman province. One Ottoman landmark is the massive tower facing the Muqattam, the **Burg al-Muqattam.** Another is the fortified gateway called the **Bab al-Azab,** which has been well restored.

Under the rule of Muhammed Ali Pasha (1805–48) the outer walls of the Citadel were rebuilt to suit the needs of a modern army and the decaying medieval buildings in the interior were replaced by new palaces, barracks, military schools, armament factories, and his own colossal **Mosque of Muhammed Ali ⓫**. Alien to the architectural style and spirit of the rest of the city, this mosque was built between 1830 and 1848 and imitates the great religious structures of Istanbul,

TIP

Most monuments in the Islamic part of Cairo are open from 9am–7pm daily. Some lesser visited monuments may open later or not at all, but a guardian can always be found nearby. Many mosques and museums close for the Friday prayers from noon–2pm.

BELOW: Mosque of Muhammed Ali.

The Mosque of Muhammed Ali is also known as the Alabaster Mosque because of the extensive use of alabaster from Beni Suef in Middle Egypt.

BELOW: Tomb and Madrasah of Sultan Hasan.

though the decoration is a hybrid of European, pharaonic and Islamic motifs. Its size, setting and ease of access, however, have made it a popular tourist site; and the Pasha himself is buried here under a marble cenotaph. The clock tower in the outer court was given to him in 1846 by Louis Philippe, in belated exchange for the obelisk set up in the Place de la Concorde in Paris in 1833.

South of the mosque are the remains of Muhammed Ali's **Gawharah ("Bijou") Palace**, completed in 1814, the seat of the viceregal court and the centre of government from then until 1874, when the Khedive Ismail, Muhammed Ali's grandson, moved his family and administration to the vast new Abdin Palace. A museum for decades, the Gawharah was gutted by fire in 1972. The administrative wing has not been rebuilt, but a refurbished audience hall and private apartments display furniture and curios that belonged to the Ali dynasty.

The **National Police Museum**, near the Mosque of an-Nasir Muhammed, has a terrace that was built over the site of a Mameluk palace, commissioned by Muhammed Ali. It was originally intended as an artillery platform from which to bombard the city and thus offers a spectacular panorama of medieval Cairo's minarets and domes. On a rare clear day it is possible to see as far as the pyramids of Giza and Saqqarah.

Dominating the Northern Enclosure is Muhammed Ali's **Harim Palace**, constructed in 1827 and now housing the **Egyptian Military Museum**. Especially attractive is the Summer Room, built around a cooling complex of marble fountains, basins and channels. Beyond the Harim Palace is a small **carriage museum**, containing eight carriages used by Muhammed Ali's family. At the far end of the Northern Enclosure is the **Mosque of Sulayman Pasha**, erected in 1528 to serve the Janissary regiment quartered in the Northern Enclosure.

The Red Way

The glory of Cairo is its medieval architecture, plainly visible below the Citadel. Northwest is the 10th-century royal enclave of Al-Qahirah, built by the Fatimid dynasty. Between the Citadel and Al-Qahirah lies the district developed as an aristocratic quarter in the 14th century by the relatives and retainers of the prolific Sultan an-Nasir Muhammed. It is named **Darb al-Ahmar** (The Red Way), after its major thoroughfare. On Maydan Salah ad-Din immediately below the Citadel, opposite the Bab al-Azab, soar the walls of the **Tomb and Madrasah of Sultan Hasan** ⑫ (daily winter 8am–5pm; summer 8am–6pm; admission charge), the seventh son of An-Nasir Muhammed

The noblest and most outstanding example of Bahri Mameluk architecture, this mosque was begun in 1356 and not finished until seven years later. Sultan Hasan disappeared in 1361, presumably murdered, and therefore never saw it completed. In contrast with the congregational mosque of Ibn Tulun, it combines four residential colleges (*madrasahs*) with a mausoleum. From the towering main entrance, with its canopy of stalactites, a bent passageway leads to the cruciform central court. Here four great arched recesses, or *iwans*, create sheltered spaces for instruction in each of the four schools of Islamic jurisprudence, the Hanafi, the Shafii, the Maliki and the Hanbali. Multistoreyed living quarters for teachers and students are built into the corners of the court. From the domed tomb chamber behind it six ground-level windows offer a splendid and unobstructed view up to the Citadel.

Across the street is the **ar-Rifa'i Mosque** ⑬ (daily 8am–5pm; admission charge), begun in 1869, six centuries later than the Sultan Hasan mosque, and completed in 1912. Because it was planned as a complement to its Mameluk

A nippy vehicle in Cairo's horrendously busy traffic.

BELOW: baking traditional bead.

Maps:
City 272
Area 284

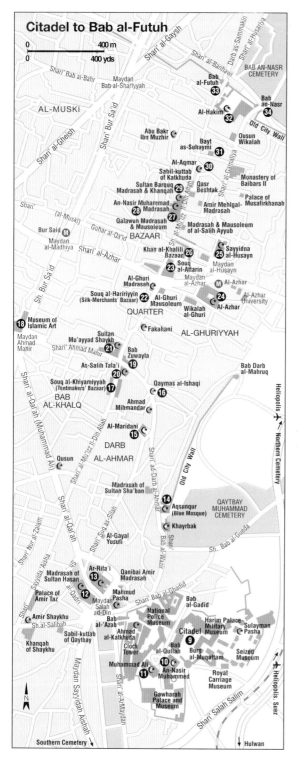

Citadel to Bab al-Futuh

neighbour in scale, fabric and architectural style, tourists frequently mistake it for an ancient monument. In it are interred the Khedive Ismail, his mother, two of his daughters, three of his wives, four sons including Sultan Husayn Kamil and King Fu'ad, Fu'ad's son King Farouk, whose body was moved here from the Southern Cemetery, and Muhammed Reza Pahlevi, the last Shah of Iran, whose first wife was Farouk's sister. The roofed and carpeted interior is magnificently adorned with Mameluk-inspired motifs.

Running north

The Darb al-Ahmar runs from the Citadel to Bab Zuwayla, the southern gate of Al-Qahirah, and is lined with medieval buildings. Visitors are sometimes taken to see the mosque of the amir **Aqsunqur** ⓮ (1347), also known as the "Blue Mosque" which contains the tomb of Kuchuk, the brother of Sultan Hasan, murdered in 1341 at the age of six. Over 300 years later (1652) it was half-heartedly renovated by an Ottoman officer, who had the walls partially covered with Damascene tiles.

More notable is the nearby **Mosque of Al-Maridani** ⓯, built in 1339 by a son-in-law of An-Nasir Muhammed. Demarcated by a superb 14th-century wooden *mashrabiyyah*, its sanctuary contains a fine marble dado and a *mihrab* decorated with coloured marble, mother-of-pearl and blue faïence.

Between these two mosques are the *mashrabiyyah* casements of an 18th-century townhouse called Bayt ar-Razzaz, constructed around a 15th-century core. As the Darb al-Ahmar curves westward towards Bab Zuwayla, the exquisite **Mosque of Qaymas al-Ishaqi** ⓰ (1481) appears on the right; it is notable for its carved stucco windows and vari-coloured marble panelling.

Just outside Bab Zuwayla is the 14th-century **Souq al-Khiyamiyyah** ⓱ (Tentmakers' Bazaar), where you will see tentmakers sitting cross-legged on raised platforms in tiny shops on either side of the street, stitching away at the bright appliqué from which temporary pavilions are made. A continuation of the Darb al-Ahmar, which here changes its name to **Shari' Ahmad Mahir**, heads past Bab Zuwayla west towards the **Museum of Islamic Art** ⓱ (daily 9am–4pm, closed Fri 11am–2pm; admission charge), containing over 75,000 objects, many of them inscribed with the names of Cairo's princes, kings and caliphs.

Inside Al-Qahirah

Massive **Bab Zuwayla** ⓳, finished in 1092, marks the southern boundary of Al-Qahirah, the walled royal enclosure founded by the Fatimids in 969. Enclosing about 2 sq km (1 sq mile), sections of its stone walls still stand, pierced by Bab Zuwayla in the south and two other fortified gates in the north, **Bab al-Futuh** (1087) and **Bab an-Nasr** (1087). Except for the objects preserved in the Museum of Islamic Art, the Fatimids' considerable material wealth – including 120,000 manuscripts, the greatest library of the medieval world – was dispersed when they were overthrown by Salah ad-Din, who opened up their enclosure to ordinary citizens.

Inheriting the commercial role of Al-Fustat, Al-Qahirah became an international entrepôt specialising in Eastern luxuries. *Wikalahs* – warehouses with residential accommodation – sprang up throughout the city and many are still in use today. Three important mosques from the Fatimid golden age survive within the Fatimids' royal enclosure; and a fourth – the **Mosque of As-Salih Tala'i** ⓴ (daily 9am–5pm; admission charge), dating from 1160 – stands outside Bab Zuwayla.

Running in a straight line between Bab Zuwayla and Bab al-Futuh, thus bisecting Al-Qahirah, is a street that has various names in short stretches, but is conveniently known as the **Qasabah** or High Street. It has been a vital artery

Maps:
City 272
Area 284

The Museum of Islamic Art contains many items from the Fatimid era (969–1171), a golden age for Cairo in terms of art and architecture.

BELOW:
Bab Zuwayla.

since medieval times, as it continues beyond both Bab al-Futuh and Bab Zuwayla and links the entire city. The modern street called **Shari' al-Azhar**, which was built through the district in 1927, crosses the Qasabah at right angles and divides Al-Qahirah into northern and southern zones.

Just inside Bab Zuwayla is the **Mosque of Sultan Mu'ayyad Shaykh** , built to fulfil a vow in 1412. To serve this last great courtyard mosque, the Burji Mameluk sultan erected two minarets on top of the adjacent Fatimid gate and built an adjoining bath complex of palatial scale. The interior is decorated in marble and stucco, ebony, mother-of-pearl and blue faïence; the doors came from the Mosque of Sultan Hasan.

Large sections of the Qasabah comprise bazaars and therefore have names derived from the particular trades or occupations conducted there. From Bab Zuwayla northwards the street offers all manner of household goods: brass bedsteads, tarbooshes (felt hats with tassels), feather dusters, and cheap shoes. Just before Shari al-Azhar is the area called the **Ghuriyyah**, named after Qansuh al-Ghuri, one of the last Mameluk sultans. In 1504 he built the mausoleum and *madrasah* that stand on opposite sides of the Qasabah here, with the **Souq al-Haririyyin** (Silk-Merchants' Bazaar) occupying the basement vaults of both buildings and the space between them. Al-Ghuri also built a superb *hammam* (bath), now restored, a *wikalah* (warehouse), the ground-floor rooms of which now display traditional crafts, and a palace, the remains of which are still visible behind the mausoleum. The latter now serves as a cultural centre, which is a venue for spectacular performances of the Whirling Dervishes, a Sufi sect. Wearing multi-coloured robes, the dervishes twirl and twist until they reach a state of mystical ecstasy in which they are free of physical bonds.

TIP

The Whirling Dervishes perform at the al-Ghuri Mausoleum at 9pm on Wednesdays and Saturdays. However, to be sure of a seat plan to arrive no later than 7.30pm. The mausoleum is on the corner of Al-Muizz and Al-Azhar streets.

BELOW:
a perfume shop off Souq al-Attarin.

Part of the **Souq al-Attarin** ㉓ (Herbalists' Bazaar) extends north of Shari' al-Azhar, which cuts through Al-Qahirah at this point and can only be crossed by using the iron bridge or the tunnel. Slashing across the Qasabah, the street brings heavy traffic past the main entrance of the **Mosque of Al-Azhar** ㉔ (The Resplendent"), founded in 970, the most famous seat of learning in the Muslim world. Now a university, its centre is the original congregational mosque built by the Fatimids, a courtyard surrounded by keel-arched arcading.

Khan al-Khalili

Opposite the university on the other side of Shari al-Azhar, in the northern zone of Al-Qahirah, is the popular shrine of **Sayyidna al-Husayn** ㉕, grandson of the Prophet, who was murdered in AD 680 (closed to non-Muslims). Between here and the Qasabah is the city's most famous tourist market, the labyrinthine **Khan al-Khalili bazaar** ㉖, which takes its name from the ruins of a 14th-century *khan* or *wikalah*. Most people enjoy browsing through its welter of wares, though better quality and more variety are offered elsewhere in the city.

The stretch of the Qasabah running alongside Khan al-Khalili is the **Souq as-Sagha** (Goldsmiths' Bazaar). Gold and silver are sold by weight, as are brass and copperware in the neighbouring **Souq an-Nahhasin** (Coppersmiths' Bazaar), which has occupied the same place since the 14th century.

Between the palaces

Northwards the Qasabah widens out into the **Bayn al-Qasrayn**. The name means "Between the Two Palaces" and refers to two Fatimid palaces that once stood on this site. Dominating the area is a splendid monumental ensemble

Maps:
City 272
Area 284

The minarets of the Mosque of Al-Azhar, one of the oldest universities in the world.

BELOW: in the Khan al-Khalili bazaar.

The newly renovated Darb al-Asfar, just off the Qasabah, forms part of the Bayt as-Suhaymi restoration project, the aim of which is to document, restore and conserve historic Cairene architecture.

BELOW: coffee shop in the old city.

built by a succession of Mameluk sultans. The largest element is the Qalawun complex erected in 1284 for the Bahri Mameluk sultan Qalawun, who founded a dynasty that lasted almost a century. It includes a *madrasah*, a mausoleum, a mosque and the remains of a *maristan* (charitable hospital); clinic still operates on the site.

Qalawun is buried in the majestic **Qalawun Mausoleum ㉗**. His son An-Nasir Muhammed – who reigned longer than any other Mameluk – chose to be buried with him rather than in the next-door **Madrasah of An-Nasir Muhammed ㉘** (1326), which was intended to be his mausoleum. The Gothic-looking doorway was taken from a crusader church at Acre; the Spanish-looking stucco-work on the minaret was carved by Andalusian craftsmen, refugees from Christian persecution. The third important building in the ensemble is the **Madrasah and Khanqah of Barquq ㉙**, the first of the Circassian Mameluk sultans. Barquq's son Farag built another and far grander mausoleum in the Northern Cemetery (where Barquq is actually buried).

Almost directly across the street is the **Qasr Beshtak**, the five-storey palace built by Amir Beshtak, a son-in-law of an-Nasir, in 1339. The remains of a water-raising device that supplied running water to every floor are still in evidence. At a corner a few metres further on stands the charming little 18th-century *sabil-kuttab* (fountain-school) of **Abd ar-Rahman Katkhuda**.

The Qasabah proceeds to the left here, leading past the badly restored Fatimid **Mosque of Al-Aqmar ㉚**, "the Moonlit" (1125), which sits below street-level a few metres/yds further along. At No. 19 in the totally renovated Darb al-Asfar, the first large lane to the right beyond Al-Aqmar, is **Bayt as-Suhaymi ㉛**, a charming 17th-century townhouse, open to the public.

Another hundred metres/yds up the Qasabah stands the great congregational **Mosque of Al-Hakim** ❷ (1010), the second Fatimid caliph, rebuilt in the early 1980s by a Shi'ite sect from western India who claim descent from the Fatimids. The Al-Hakim mosque stands against a surviving section of the **North Wall** that connects the round-towered **Bab al-Futuh** ❸ ("Gate of Conquest") with the square-towered **Bab an-Nasr** ❹ ("Gate of Victory"). The wall and both towers are well worth exploring and the views southwards take in countless domes and minarets. Northwards is the **Bab an-Nasr cemetery**, in continuous use since Fatimid times.

Burial grounds

Cairo's key burial places – and part of the living city because more than a million people live in and around the tombs – are the Northern and Southern Cemeteries. Principal monuments in the **Northern Cemetery** ❺, northeast of the Citadel, include the **Khanqah of Farag ibn Barquq** (1410), one of the most impressive buildings in Cairo. Two other huge complexes, built by Sultan Inal (1456) and Amir Qurqumas al-Kabir (1507), are part of long-term restoration projects.

A hundred metres/yds south of the Khanqah of Farag ibn Barquq is the complex of **Sultan Ashraf Barsbay** (1432) and further down the same road is the **Mosque of Qaytbay** (1472), an architectural jewel that is depicted on the Egyptian one-pound note. With this building, the most exquisite of the Circassian Mameluk monuments, the art of stone carving in Cairo reached its pinnacle.

In the larger and older **Southern Cemetery** ❻, to the south of the Citadel, is the **Mausoleum of Imam as-Shafi'i**, the founder of the Shafi'ite school of Islamic law, whose tomb was built by order of Salah ad-Din in 1180. Salah

Maps:
City 272
Area 284

BELOW:
the cemeteries
are inhabited
by the living as
well as the dead.

Map on page 272

ad-Din's carved cenotaph for the saint still stands in the tomb chamber. Nearby is the **Hawsh al-Basha**, built by Muhammed Ali in 1820 as a family tomb, though he himself is buried at the Citadel. Many Bahri Mameluk princes are buried here.

Island retreats

Congestion and air pollution make touring modern Cairo either on foot or by car increasingly unpleasant. The islands, however, offer great escapes from the dirt and bustle. On Rawdah, for example, is the **Manyal Palace complex ❽** (daily 9am–5pm; admission charge), which can be visited in combination with Old Cairo and the Nilometer mentioned previously. Built by Prince Muhammed Ali, the younger brother of Khedive Abbas II Hilmi, first cousin of King Farouk and Heir Apparent until 1952, it contains a huge *salamlik* (reception palace), the two-storey *haramlik* that was the prince's residence, a model throne room, a museum with superb examples of furniture, calligraphy, glass, silver, textiles, costumes and porcelain and a hunting museum (to the right of the main entrance).

On the island of **Gazirah** the most important structure is the Japanese-built **New Opera House ❽** at the Gazirah Exhibition Grounds. Opened in 1988, it offers three stages, as well as exhibition halls and practice rooms, and has hosted troupes from all over the world. Also within the Exhibition Grounds are the **Museum of Modern Egyptian Art ❽** (Tues–Sun 10am–1pm, 5–9pm, Fri 10am–noon; admission charge) and the **Nile Hall**, devoted to contemporary art. In the Planetarium building next to the New Opera House is the **Museum of Egyptian Civilisation** (closed for restoration) and, upstairs, the **Gazirah Museum** (also closed for restoration), displaying a miscellaneous collection of paintings and *objets d'art*, some of which were confiscated from the Muhammed Ali family.

BELOW: the tea terrace of the Marriott Hotel.
RIGHT: al-Fishawi, a famous Cairene coffee house near the Khan al-Khalili Bazaar.

The 187-metre (614-ft) **Cairo Tower ❹** (daily winter 9am–midnight; summer 9am–1am) offers magnificent views from its viewing platform and restaurant. Nearby are the Gazirah Sporting Club (members only), which was laid out by the British Army on land given by Khedive Tewfiq. The **Gazirah Palace**, built by Khedive Ismail between 1863 and 1868, form part of the **Cairo Marriott Hotel ❹**, which contains much of the furniture that the Khedive brought back from the Paris Exposition of 1867. Next door, another small palace contains the **Gazirah Arts Centre** (open daily 9am–1pm except Fri), with a unique collection of Islamic ceramics.

The residential area of **Zamalik** occupies the northern half of Gazirah; it is here that many of the embassies are located. The suburbs on the Giza side of the Nile – Mohandiseen, Aguza, Al-Duqqi – look pretty much like the new suburbs of any city.

On the west bank of the Nile, on Shari al-Gizah, the **Muhammed Mahmud and Emilienne Luce Khalil Museum** (Tues–Sun 10am–5.30pm, closed Mon; admission charge) houses the **Khalil Collection**. This bequest to the nation contains primarily French 19th-century painting – Ingrès, Delacroix, Daumier, Corot, Courbet, Renoir, Sisley, Pissarro, Degas, Manet and Monet. The house, confiscated from the Muhammed Ali family, is worth visiting in its own right. ❑

THE DELTA

Criss-crossed by streams and canals, the fertile lands of the Delta are heavily populated. The coast, however, has a rather melancholy air, with the exception of Alexandria, the capital of the Ptolemies

Map on page 296

After the noise of Cairo, the River Nile is ready for the peace of the sea. In its hurry to get there it splits, first in two, then into the myriad canals and streams of the Delta. But in this densely populated region of Egypt, so named by the Greeks for its similarity on the map to their triangular letter D, the river has yet to endure its most intensive use by man.

Around 160 km (100 miles) wide at its Mediterranean base and about the same length, the flat, rich Nile Delta contains more than half of Egypt's agricultural land and much of its industry. More than 16 million Egyptians live in its thousands of villages, cultivating extensive mango and citrus orchards, cotton, wheat and vegetables for the stomachs of the insatiable capital. Roads, railways, bridges and canals crisscross the land. To the east and west the once impenetrable desert is giving way to mammoth land reclamation projects.

Unsurprisingly, the people of the Delta are known chiefly for their industriousness, in contrast to the laid-back image of the Upper Egyptians. Yet despite a proximity to Cairo and Alexandria and a relatively prosperous economic base, patches of the Delta do not display much of this prosperity, as can be seen from the vintage taxis that chug along its byways.

The Delta was once part of the sea. Millennia of Nile alluvia washing down from Ethiopia created first swamps, then exceptionally fertile farmland. During the annual flood, river water turned the Delta into a vast lake. Consequently the Ancient Egyptian inhabitants built their towns on hills and hummocks which appeared like islands when the inundation was at its height.

PRECEDING PAGES: boats on Lake Manzilah. **LEFT:** village bread oven. **BELOW:** a pigeon house.

A watery past

Early in Egyptian history the Delta was a relatively wild region and its people were distinct from their cousins in Upper Egypt. Some 5,000 years ago the first pharaohs joined Egypt's marshy north to the south in a united kingdom, symbolised in their headdress known as the double crown, whichcombined the red crown of Lower Egypt and the white, conical crown of Upper Egypt. In the course of time the Delta became much tamer, and by late antiquity its cities – Tanis, Sais, Naucratis, Bubastis – had largely overtaken Memphis, Thebes and other southern cities in importance.

But sadly for us, whereas Upper Egypt enjoyed an accessible supply of sturdy building stone, the Delta had to make do with mudbrick. As a result, little of the glory of its past has endured. Although many of the most precious individual objects in the Egyptian Museum were found in the Delta, its ancient sites are for the most part mounds of mud and shards intelligible only to the most patient of excavators. The greatest of

them, Tanis in the Eastern Delta, is nothing but a desolate heap of dirt littered with chunks of masonry.

Because of their lack of standing structures, the Delta sites have until recently received little attention from archaeologists. But with the intensification of agriculture that followed the building of the High Dam at Aswan, waterlogging has become a serious worry to Egypt's Antiquities Organisation, which now actively promotes excavation in the Delta to save what they can before its too late.

Environmental concerns

The Delta environment is perhaps the most fragile and threatened of any in the Nile basin. Overuse of irrigation has caused serious drainage problems, pushing salts to the surface and reducing the fertility of the soil – which is no longer replenished by the Nile's flood-borne silt. Pollution from untreated waste and agricultural chemicals has sharply reduced the fish catch, particularly in the nothern lakes where fishing was once a major source of livelihood. Attempts to control some hazards have exacerbated others: government use of weedkiller on the water hyacinth, an attractive blue-flowered plant that clogs canals, was found to be decimating aquatic fauna.

Worst of all, the Mediterranean Sea is swelling with the melting of polar ice caps caused by global warming, and threatens to drown the low-lying Delta. Where the Nile flows into the sea at Damietta (Dumyat) and Rosetta (Rashid), gigantic concrete dykes have been built to prevent shore erosion. Already lighthouses built onshore have been swamped. In the resort of Ras al-Barr, just north of Damietta, a whole row of beach houses has been swallowed up and high tides now lap in the living rooms of the next row.

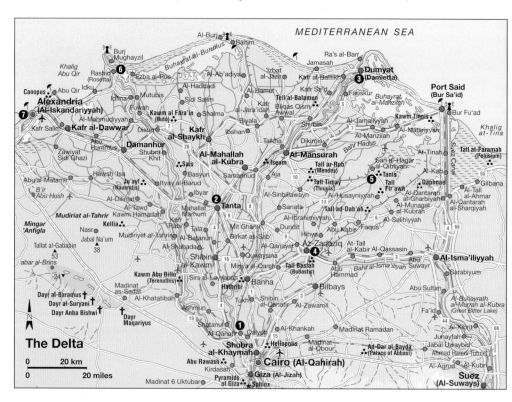

The Delta

0   20 km

0   20 miles

A Delta tour

The Delta begins in Cairo itself, where the first of its canals branches eastwards, heading ultimately to the Suez Canal at Al-Ismailiyyah along the route of the ancient seaway built by the Persians in the 6th century BC. But the great city's industrial suburbs do not end until the river itself divides. This spot is marked by the multiple arches and sluices of the barrages at **Qanatir ❶**, built in the 19th century to control the annual flood. Here extensive parks, now somewhat scruffy, are a favourite destination for summer outings.

Northwards the plain broadens continuously, dotted with tiny hamlets and the remnants of the huge estates that were divided up by the revolutionary government of the 1950s. Sadly, a loss of local pride seems to have accompanied the decline of the landed gentry that once built stylish villas and parks here. Provincial towns like Shibin al-Kawm, Damanhur, Kafr al-Shaykh, Banha and Al-Mansurah are overgrown and have little to offer.

The largest city of the Delta is **Tanta ❷**, a ramshackle place that marks the halfway point between Cairo and Alexandria. Every October its half-million inhabitants are swollen to four times their number during the Islamic saint's day of Ahmed al-Bedawi, a 13th-century mystic who founded Egypt's biggest Sufi brotherhood. This ancient, perhaps even pre-Islamic, *mawlid*, the biggest of the Egyptian calendar, is celebrated with the enthusiastic use of megaphones, strobe lights and riot police. By day pilgrims flood to the grandiose tomb and mosque of the saint, which is ringed by the kind of commercial enterprises that usually surround an important tomb or pilgrimage centre – from circumcision booths to stalls selling nougat, dates, whistles and party hats. By night increasingly rowdy revellers throng the streets.

Other towns hold smaller festivals for their local saints, but these days Delta cities are better known for their industries. **Talkha** is dominated by its mammoth fertiliser plant, **Kafr al Dawwar** and **Al-Mahallah al-Kubra** are centres of the cotton industry. **Dumyat ❸** (Damietta), an ancient seaport near the mouth of the river that bears its name, rivalled Alexandria in the Middle Ages. In modern times, it has grown prosperous as a centre for the production of lurid rococo-style furniture.

Ancient sites of the Delta

The town of **Zaqaziq ❹**, heavily polluted by the fumes from a soap factory, is the nearest town to the ancient site of **Bubastis** (daily 9am–4pm; admission charge), a thriving cult centre for the cat goddess Bastet. Some 157 km (97 miles) northeast of Zaqaziq is one of the oldest known sites in Egypt, the town of **Tanis ❺**, thought to have been the capital of the 21st Dynasty, In 1939 the French archaeologist Pierre Montet discovered the tombs of Osorkon II and Psusennes II filled with the so-called treasure of Tanis, now on display in the Egyptian Museum in Cairo. There are further remains of a large Ramessid temple devoted to Amun. Nearby is Tall ad-Dabah where discoveries have led archaeologists to believe that this was Avaris, the vanished Hyksos capital. In 1991 in a Hyksos palace, archaeologists discovered beautiful

Map on page 296

TIP

If you want to visit the barrages at Qanatir, on Friday special boats, packed with weekending Cairenes, leave from the Maspero dock opposite the television building in Cairo.

BELOW: an effective means of transport in the mud lanes of the Delta.

It was in Tanis that Indiana Jones discovered the Ark of the Covenant in the 1981 movie Raiders of the Lost Ark.

Minoan-style frescoes. One layer revealed the bodies of non-Egyptians, mainly of children under the age of two, which probably indicates that the Israelites stayed here during their sojourn in Egypt and the killing of the male newborns by the pharaoh.

Alone among its sister towns, **Rosetta ❻**, where the famous stone that provided the key to deciphering hieroglyphics was found *(see page 303)*, *was a* notable city in the Middle Ages. It still has charm; its neat, narrow lanes lined with brick houses characteristic of the Delta, run down to a waterfront crammed with fishing vessels and boatyards. Eight kilometres (5 miles) downstream, the Rosetta branch of the Nile, much reduced by man's exploitation, slides quietly into the sea. To the west, the Damietta branch does the same, entering the Mediterranean at Ras al-Barr. In between, the windswept coast is largely barren.

Along the Delta shore lies a series of wide, marshy lakes: **Maryut**, **Idku**, **Burullus** and **Manzilah**. Accessible only by elegant pointed punts, these wetlands have long been the hideout for fugitives from justice. They also provide refuge for the migrating waterfowl of Europe.

The Bride of the Sea

Although it is not strictly of the Nile – the river is linked to it by canal – no description of Egypt would be complete without mentioning its second city, **Alexandria ❼** (al-Iskandariyyah), easily reached by train from Cairo's main railway station on Maydan al-Ramesses. To Egyptians this great and ancient port is known as the "Arousat al-Bahr" or the Bride of the Sea. The name may seem corny, but Alexandria's intimate relationship with the Mediterranean makes it strangely appropriate – it has always been Egypt's conduit to the

BELOW: Pompey's Pillar, Alexandria.

Mediterranean world. The city of over 6 million inhabitants is slender, but it stretches along the shore from east to west for over 48 km (30 miles), and almost anywhere in the city one is never far from the sound of surf or the smell of fresh fish. In summer millions of festive Egyptians descend upon its streets and its beaches, while in winter occasional sea storms bombard the buildings, rusting away the wrought iron balconies on the Corniche. The sea lends a sense of freedom to Alexandria, which is refreshing after the claustrophobic confinement of the the Nile Valley.

A wealth of history

Alexandria was named after its illustrious founder, Alexander the Great, who marked the city's boundaries around the small fishing village of Rhakotis in 331 BC, but he never saw his great city as he left for Siwa shortly afterwards and died a few years later in 325 BC. Ever since, emperors, monarchs, archaeologists and admirers of the great general have searched for his lost tomb, believed by some to lie beneath the city.

Under Alexander's successors, the Ptolemies, the city grew into the most illustrious centre of Hellenistic culture in the Mediterranean. The Ptolemies embellished their capital with fine buildings, including the Pharos (lighthouse) which was considered to be one of the Seven Wonders of the Ancient World. The city's famous Library and Mouseion carried the baton of Greek science and literature until the fall of the Roman Empire. It was here that Eratosthenes declared that the Earth was round, the Old Testament was translated, Euclid developed geometry, and medical science made more advances than in the ensuing thousand years. The last and probably most famous Ptolemy was

Maps:
Area 296
City 300

Montazah Park lighthouse. In ancient times the city's Pharos was one of the Seven Wonders of the Ancient World.

BELOW: the Cap d'Or bar, Alexandria.

Cleopatra VII (69–30 BC), the lover of first Julius Caesar and later Mark Antony.

Alexandria's wealth and glory slowly disappeared after the Arabs conquered Egypt in AD 641. The city regained some of its fame, wealth and splendour during the 19th century when Muhammed Ali decided to make Egypt a maritime power and needed a suitable harbour. The Mahmudiyyah Canal linked the city to the Nile, and a large modern harbour was created; the city also became the centre of Egypt's prosperous trade in cotton. As European merchants settled in town it became the cosmopolitan city of many pleasures that is described by Lawrence Durrell in his novel *Alexandria Quartet*.

In retaliation for the Orabi revolt against foreign influence in 1882, British warships bombed the city. Although this did not deter the foreign nationals in the city, when President Nasser nationalised foreign businesses after the Suez Crisis in 1956 most foreigners decided it was time to leave town. Since then Alexandria has become more Egyptianised every year, but a faded cosmopolitan air lingers on, and it remains one of Egypt's more outward looking cities.

Illusion or disillusion?

In spite of so much history, no other city reveals so little of its past. At first sight modern-day Alexandria offers little more than illusion and disillusion. Its streets and buildings seem tired and dilapidated to the first-time visitor, nothing like the magical city that the name Alexandria conjures up. Where are Cleopatra's Palace, the legendary Pharos or even the elegant city where the glamorous Justine conducted passionate affairs in Durrell's *Alexandria's Quartet*? Or where are the sleazy brothels in which the city's most famous poet, Cavafy, sought to relieve his loneliness? The answer is quite simple: in Alexandria the past is always underneath your feet.

The Graeco-Roman museum

As most of Alexandria's history is hidden the best place to start exploring the city is at the **Graeco-Roman Museum Ⓐ** (daily 9am–4pm, Fri 9–11.30am, 1.30–4pm; admission charge). It contains Egypt's largest collection of Graeco-Roman artefacts (*circa* 331 BC–AD 300) from sites in and around Alexandria. Most exhibits are arranged chronologically, starting with a magnificent 2nd-century AD black-granite Apis bull and a Roman bust of the main god of Alexandria, Serapis, a hybrid of Dionysos and Osiris, which was an attempt by the Ptolemies to unite the Egyptian and Greek cults. Other highlights include a head of Alexander the Great, imposing busts of Roman emperors and life-like encaustic paintings, portraits painted onto mummy cases. Particularly pleasing are the elegant terracotta *tanagra* figurines (4th–2nd century BC), placed in tombs of women and children to celebrate their youth and beauty. The garden is strewn with more sculptures and sarcophagi.

Head of Serapis, a composite of the Greek god Dionysus and the Egyptian Osiris, in the Graeco-Roman Museum, Alexandria.

BELOW: cutting it fine in a barber's shop.

EXCAVATING THE HARBOUR

Alexandria has been continuously inhabited since antiquity, with each civilisation building on top of the previous one. Today, every construction site is studied by archaeologists before building can commence, and new fractions of the ancient city, statues and pottery are continually being revealed. Holes have been known to open up suddenly in a road, uncovering catacombs or other treasures. But it is offshore that the most exciting finds have been uncovered. Two separate teams have recently been at work beneath the Eastern Harbour, raising thousands of fragments from Cleopatra's Palace and the Pharos, including large statues, obelisks and some 20 sphinxes. In many cases, inscriptions have been eroded, but under the barnacles covering one obelisk they found the title of the New Kingdom pharaoh Seti I (1291–1278 BC).

Conserving the discoveries has been a priority. Each piece is immersed in water containing the same level of salt as seawater. The salt content of the water is then gradually reduced until the blocks are left standing in fresh water and the salts absorbed by the stone have been leeched away. It is hoped that eventually visitors will be able to see some of the remains in situ; plans for an underwater museum are currently underway.

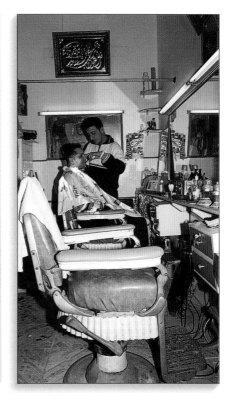

Downtown Alexandria

Alexandria's modern centre still more or less follows the plan of the Ptolemaic city – the two main streets, Canopic and Soma Street, are now **Shari' Tariq al-Hurriyyah** and **Shari' al-Nabi Danyal**. Some believe the tomb of Alexander lies underneath the **Nabi Danyal Mosque** , on Shari' al-Nabi Danyal, which also houses the tombs of Danyal al Maridi and Lukman the Wise. In Shari' Sharm al-Shaykh, a small side street off Shari' al-Nabi Danyal, the former flat of the Greek poet Constantine Cavafy (1863–1933) has become the **Cavafy Museum** (Tues–Sun 10am–3pm,; admission charge), a place of pilgrimage for fans from all over the world. Just off the shopping street Shari' al-Hurriyyah, near the Pastroudis patisserie (a favourite hang-out for Durrell and Cavafy), is **Kom al-Dikkah** ("Pile of Rubble"; daily 9am–4pm; admission charge), with an elegant 2nd-century Roman Odeon, the only surviving theatre of the Graeco-Roman city; it has marble seating and a beautiful mosaic floor.

On the seafront is the slightly faded but once glamorous **Cecil Hotel** . Its rooms look out over the site of the Ptolemies' palaces and of the Caesareum, Cleopatra's monument to Mark Antony. Recent excavations in the Eastern Harbour have revealed fragments of a royal palace, believed to be Cleopatra's, as well as sections of the Pharos lighthouse *(see box, page 301)*. Near the Cecil Hotel is the large Maydan al-Tahrir, the centre of the European quarter during colonial times, when it was known as Frank Square. It has an equestrian statue of Muhammed Ali and several grand colonial-style buildings.

A splendid modern **Alexandrian Library** is a recent addition on the eastern end of the Corniche. Dominating the other end of the bay is the 15th-century **Fort of Qaytbay** (open daily 9am–4pm, Fri 9–11.30am and 1.30–4pm; admission charge), which stands on the site of the 125-metre (400-ft) high Pharos built in 279 BC by Sostratus for Ptolemy II but destroyed by several earthquakes.

Temples and catacombs

In the southwest of central Alexandria is one of the city's best-known landmarks, **Pompey's Pillar** (daily 9am–4pm; admission charge), a 27-metre (89-ft) high pink granite column, built in around AD 295. Crusaders thought it supported a statue of Pompey, but it is more likely to have been one of Diocletian. This was the area of Rhakotis, where Alexander first marked out the city; nearby are the scant remains – two sphinxes and a few statues – of the **Serapeum**, which was destroyed by Christians in the 4th century. With its splendid Serapis temple and the Second Alexandrian Library containing Cleopatra's private collection of some 200,000 manuscripts, the Serapeum was for 400 years the most important intellectual and religious centre in the Mediterranean.

A donkey falling through the ground led to the discovery of Egypt's largest Roman burial site, the 2nd-century **Catacombs of Kom al-Shuqqafah** (open daily 9am–4pm; admission charge). The rooms of this eerie catacombs are decorated in the distinctive Alexandrian blend of Egyptian, Greek and Roman motifs exemplified in the Egyptian gods Anubis and Sobek dressed as Roman legionnaires. ❏

BELOW: Alexandria is a port of call for sailors from all over the world.

The Rosetta Stone

Pierre Bouchard, a Frenchman working for Napoleon, was strengthening a fort at Rosetta when he turned up a stone about the size of a gravestone. Its implications were obvious even to an army engineer. He announced his discovery in the armed forces newspaper which Napoleon's printing presses were producing in Cairo: "a stone of very fine granite, black, with a close grain, and very hard... with three distinct inscriptions separated in three parallel bands."

Two of the bands were in the meaningless scripts to be seen on monuments all along the Nile. No one had been able to understand the hieroglyphs since the 4th century AD, and the few words which had passed into the Coptic language were no help.

The exciting part of Bouchard's discovery was the last of the parallel bands, which was in readable Greek. The stone identified itself as a proclamation by Ptolemy V in 196 BC and said that the other languages were Egyptian. One was the classic form of hieroglyphs, the other a more manageable demotic script derived from it. The stone was hurried to Cairo where Napoleon had casts made.

Napoleon later sneaked back to France, and in due course his army surrendered to the British. One of the terms of surrender was that Britain would take everything the *savants* had collected in Egypt. The French scholars were appalled and threatened to dump the whole lot. Happily the British were willing to negotiate – but not over the Rosetta Stone. On this point the British army officers were being strenuously lobbied by two civilians, one of them being William Hamilton, on whose advice Lord Elgin had carted off large chunks of the Parthenon in Athens, the still controversial "Elgin Marbles". Like the Marbles, the stone was taken to London's British Museum.

The decipherment of the Rosetta Stone became something of a race, albeit at a snail's pace. A Swede named Akerblad spotted that royal names in the Greek part had fairly obvious equivalents in the demotic. He also recognised three words: "his", "Greek"

and "temple". In England the pioneering work was done by Thomas Young, who went on to become the *Encyclopaedia Britannica*'s authority on some 400 languages.

He made quick work of the demotic signs, establishing that the "rope-loops" now called cartouches were the names of kings. Recognising that all three versions had letters which spelt out p-t-o-l-e-m-y meant that hieroglyphs must have been a kind of alphabet and had a grammar.

Young forwarded his findings to a professor Jean-François Champollion in France, who was still labouring under the conventional idea that hieroglyphic symbols represented whole ideas when Young put him on the right track, a debt he never acknowledged.

Nonetheless full credit is due to Champollion for the conclusive decipherment. Unluckily he died in 1832 at the age of 42 before the publication of his historic grammar, after which, instead of being mere decoration on walls and papyri, hieroglyphs sprang to life as the deeds, words and thoughts of people who had been muted for 1,500 years. ❑

RIGHT: the Rosetta Stone, the key to deciphering hieroglyphics.

INSIGHT GUIDES

TRAVEL TIPS

New Insight Maps

Maps in Insight Guides are tailored to complement the text. But when you're on the road you sometimes need the big picture that only a large-scale map can provide. This new range of durable Insight Fleximaps has been designed to meet just that need.

Detailed, clear cartography
makes the comprehensive route and city maps easy to follow, highlights all the major tourist sites and provides valuable motoring information plus a full index.

Informative and easy to use
with additional text and photographs covering a destination's top 10 essential sites, plus useful addresses, facts about the destination and handy tips on getting around

Laminated finish
allows you to mark your route on the map using a non-permanent marker pen, and wipe it off. It makes the maps more durable and easier to fold than traditional maps.

The first titles
cover many popular destinations. They include Algarve, Amsterdam, Bangkok, California, Cyprus, Dominican Republic, Florence, Hong Kong, Ireland, London, Mallorca, Paris, Prague, Rome, San Francisco, Sydney, Thailand, Tuscany, USA Southwest, Venice, and Vienna.

☒ INSIGHT GUIDES
The world's largest collection of visual travel guides

CONTENTS

Getting Acquainted

The Place

Area: 1,002,000 sq. km (626,000 sq. miles).
Capital: Cairo.
Longest River: The Nile.
Population: 65 million, (estimated 1996)
Language: Arabic (official), English and French are widely understood by educated people.
Religion:
Muslim (mostly Sunni): 90 percent, Coptic Christian and other: 10 percent.
Time Zone: GMT plus 2 hours.
Currency: Egyptian pound of 100 piastres.
Weights and measures: metric.
Electricity: Power supply in Egypt is 220 volts.
International Dialling Code: 20.

Egypt links the northeastern corner of Africa and the southwestern edge of Asia. Its longest distance north–south is 1,025 km (640 miles) and widest distance east–west is 1,240 km (775 miles).

Temperatures

Average Year-round Temperatures

	winter	summer
Alexandria		
Celsius	21/11	30/21
Farenheit	70/34	86/70
Cairo		
Celsius	21/11	36/20
Farenheit	70/52	97/68
Luxor		
Celsius	26/6	42/22
Farenheit	79/43	108/72
Aswan		
Celsius	26/9	42/25
Fareneheit	79/48	108/77

The **deserts** of Egypt comprise over 90 percent of the land surface. They are part of an arid region that stretches from the Atlantic coast in the west to Central Asia in the east. Though sparsely populated (they are inhabited by less than 1 percent of the population), they contain six inhabited depressions known as oases.

The **Eastern** or **Arabian Desert** is east of the Nile Valley and extends to the Red Sea. It is far higher than the **Western Desert**, rising to a series of ranges, parallel to the sea, called the Red Sea Mountains. It covers approximately 223,000 sq. km (86,101 sq. miles), or 21 percent of the land mass of Egypt.

The Arabian Desert has two distinct areas, the northern Al Ma'aza Plateau, which is composed primarily of limestone, and the southern Al 'Ababda Plateau. Water is very scarce in these areas.

The Western or Libyan Desert is much larger than the Arabian Desert, covering 681,000 sq. km (332,434 sq. miles) and comprises two-thirds of Egypt. It is separated from the North African or Great Sahara by highlands and is composed primarily of Nubian sandstone and limestone.

South of the Qattarah depression there is a band of north–south sand dunes that continue as far south as the Kharga Depression. The Western Desert is the most arid region of Egypt.

The **Red Sea** is 2,359 metres (7,785 ft) deep, 1,932 km (1,207 miles) long from north to south and 306 km (191 miles) from east to west. Cutting through the Gulf of Aqaba from the Dead Sea and continuing south through the Red Sea and on into East Africa is the **Great Rift Valley**, the juncture of the African and Arabian Tectonic plates. The Red Sea is highly saline with small tides and exquisite coral shelves and reefs.

Climate

Summers are hot and dry in Upper Egypt, humid in the Delta and along the Mediterranean Coast. In recent years the humidity has spread to Cairo and the city swelters in August. Winters are mild with some rain, but usually there are bright, sunny days and cold nights.

Women in Society

Before the famous Egyptian feminist Hoda Shaarawi deliberately removed her veil in 1922, veils – which had no religious significance – were worn in public by all respectable middle-class and upper-class women, Muslim, Jewish, or Christian. By 1935, however, veils were a comparative rarity in Egypt, though they continued to be worn in neighbouring countries like Syria and Jordan for 30 more years and have remained obligatory in the Arabian Peninsula to this day.

Nowadays in Egypt, veils are worn by Bedu women, who are the inheritors of the urban fashions of a century ago, or by younger middle-class urban women demonstrating deep Muslim piety. Feminine modesty alone – not necessarily identified with any religion – is shown by wearing a covering over the head. With younger women this is often a fashion statement, but the main reason for wearing it is that it discourages male advances.

From the 1930s onwards, Egyptian women began to enter into businesses and professions. Thus by 1965, thanks in part to social changes effected in the course of the July Revolution, Egypt could boast a far higher proportion of women working as doctors, dentists, lawyers, professors or high officials than might have been found in the US or in any European country outside of Scandinavia. Egyptian women still do not have equality with Egyptian men, however, either in law or by custom; and no matter how much they may rule the roost in the home, Egyptian public places are still mainly male preserves.

Spring and autumn are short, and during the 50 days (*khamseen*) between the end of March and mid-May, dust storms can occur sporadically.

The Economy

Since 1979 there has been a massive influx of foreign aid into Egypt. As a result infrastructure has improved: there are new roads linking all areas of the country, villages up and down the Nile and in the deserts have been now got electricity, new schools, hospitals, and other services have sprung up by the dozen, telephone systems continue to undergo renovation and expansion, and investment has been encouraged in the private sector. The change in Egypt has been dramatic.

For the tourist there are dozens of new hotels and restaurants opening up. Monuments are being restored and their environments spruced up. Tour guides are now licensed and retail shops are full of high-quality products. Most of Sinai and the Red Sea coastline are being developed into tourist resorts aimed at the foreign market as well as local holidaymakers.

The Egyptian pound has been floated, with an exchange value fixed daily, and has shown itself to be remarkably stable. For Egyptians, however, life is expensive. Rents are high, food, though abundant, is costly, and salaries lag behind the cost of living.

Until the Gulf War, remittances from Egyptians working abroad were amongst Egypt's largest foreign currency earners, but now tourism and revenues from the Suez Canal generate more.

In recent years, both foreign and local businesses have invested heavily in Egypt, and the country is now considered an emerging market by the IMF.

The Government

Egypt is officially known as the Arab Republic of Egypt (ARE). Its capital city is Cairo and other major cities include Alexandria, Giza, Port Said, Asyut, Suez, Al-Minya, and Aswan. It is a republic with an elected president, who is commander in chief of the Army, and leader of the National Defence Council. The prime minister and cabinet are appointed by the president.

There is one legislative body: the National Assembly, composed of elected representatives from all districts of the country, 50 percent of whom must be from the working class or farmers. Copts and women are elected according to a quota. The Shura Council is an advisory body with 140 elected members and another 70 appointed members.

Culture & Customs

Whether Muslim or Copt, the Egyptians as a whole tend to be religious, and piety is important in their daily lives. So is commitment to the extended family. Each family member is responsible for the integrity of the family and for the behaviour of other members. Certainly, one result of these concerns is that the city of Cairo is safer than any western metropolis.

Yet when westerners visit Egypt they are often apprehensive. Their views of Egyptians and Arabs, fomented by exaggerated media stories, often bear no relation to reality at all. Travellers normally receive friendly, hospitable treatment and take homepositive impressions about the warmth and goodwill of the Egyptian people.

Religion

ISLAM

Islam is the official religion of Egypt, but there is a large Coptic community and other Christian sects represented in the country. There is still a small Jewish community. The founder of Islam is Muhammed, a merchant who in about AD 609 was chosen as God's prophet.

Islam has five major principles, known as "pillars", which form the foundation of the religion. The first principle is the belief that there is only one God and that Muhammed is the messenger of God. The second is ritual prayers, performed five times every day. Almsgiving is the third principle and Muslims often donate a percentage of their earnings to religious foundations.

The fourth pillar is fasting during the holy month of Ramadan. The fifth pillar is pilgrimage to Mecca, *haj*, which all Muslims hope to perform at least once. The pilgrimage is performed during the month of Dhu'l-Higga, which begins 70 days after the end of the Ramadan fast. Non-Muslims should not enter mosques while prayers are in progress, and may be asked, in mosques listed as antiquities, to pay entry fees. Muslims may enter any mosque free of charge.

COPTIC ORTHODOX

The Copts, a large minority in Egypt, are a Christian sect which separated from the Byzantine and Latin churches in AD 451 over a disagreement in religious doctrine. Copts founded the world's first monasteries, and the monastic tradition is an important part of the Coptic faith. Visitors may attend any Coptic service.

Listed below is a selection of Christian services. Hours should be checked against the foreign language weekend newspapers.

CATHOLIC CHURCHES

Church of the Annunciation
36 Muhammed Sabri Abu Alam, near Maydan Talaat Harb
Tel: 393-8429
Armenian Rite. Holy Liturgy Sunday 8.15am (in Coptic with Arabic readings); 9.30am, 10.30am and 6.30pm.
Our Lady of Peace
(Melkite, Greek Catholic), 4 Maydan al Sheikh Yusef, 96 Qasr el Aini
Byzantine Rite in Arabic. Holy Liturgy Sunday at 8.30am, 10.30am, and 6pm.
Holy Family Catholic Church
55 Road 15, Maadi

Tel: 358-2004
Latin Rite. Daily Mass in French
or English Mon-Thur–6.15am, Fri
9am. Family Mass 5.30pm
Saturday in English, 6.30pm in
French. Sunday Mass 9.30am
in French, 6pm in English.
St Joseph's Church
(Italian and Egyptian Franciscan
Friars), 2 Bank Misr at corner of
Muhammed Farid Street
Tel: 393-6677
Latin Rite. Holy Mass daily in
French at 7.30am and 6.30pm,
Sunday 7.30am. 8.30am and
6.30pm in French; 10am in Arabic;
12pm in Italian; 4.30pm in English.
St Joseph's Roman Catholic Church
4 Ahmed Sabri, Zamalik
Tel: 735-8902
Latin Rite. Holy Mass Sunday
8.30am in Arabic; 11am and
7pm in French; 6pm in English.
Weekdays 6pm in French. Friday
6pm in English.

ORTHODOX CHURCHES

Armenian Orthodox
Cathedral of St Gregory the
Illuminator, 179 Ramesses near
Coptic Hospital
Armenian Rite in Armenian. Holy
Liturgy Sunday 9–11am.
Abu Serga Church
Old Cairo
Coptic Rite in Coptic and Arabic.
Holy Liturgy Sunday 8am–noon.
St Mark's Cathedral
222 Ramesses, Abbassiyah
Coptic Rite in Coptic and Arabic.
Holy Liturgy Sunday 6–8am.
Church of the Virgin Mary
6 Muhammed Marashli
Zamalik
Tel: 735-5153
Coptic Rite in Coptic and Arabic.
Holy Liturgy Sunday 7.30–9.30am
and 9.30–11am.

PROTESTANT CHURCHES

All Saints' Cathedral
5 Michel Lutfallah
Zamalik, behind the Marriott Hotel
Tel: 736-8391
Episcopal/Anglican.

Services in English: Sunday
8.30am, 10.30am and 7.30pm.
Mon–Thur 9am, Fri 9.30am, 6pm.
Christian Science Society
3 Midan Mustafa Kamil
Tel: 392-9032/525-3782
Service and Sunday School, Sunday
7.30pm. Testimony Meeting
Wednesday 7.30pm. Reading Room
with Bible references and Christian
Science literature open Wednesday
and Sunday 6–7.20pm and Friday
11am–2pm.
**Church of God Cairo Christian
Fellowship**
St Andrew's Church, corner of
Galaa and 26 July
Sunday service 6pm in English.
**Church of Jesus Christ of Latter-
Day Saints** (Mormon)
21 Road 17, Maadi
Tel: 358-8746
Weekly sacrament service Friday at
9.30am.
Maadi Community Church
(The Church of St John the Baptist)
Corner of Port Said and Road 17,
Maadi
Tel: 359-2755
Interdenominational. Services in
English Friday 8.30am and 11am,
with nursery; Sunday 7pm.
Saint Andrew's United Church
38, 26 July and Ramesses Street
Tel: 358-6295
Protestant. Service in English Friday
and Sunday 9.30am.

Planning the Trip

What to Bring

Almost everything is available in Cairo, but may be cheaper at home.
Special medication should be
brought with you. A small supply of
plasters, antibiotic ointments and
anti-diarrhoea tablets may well come
in handy. If you have a favourite sun
lotion, make-up, toothpaste, or
shampoo that you cannot possibly
live without, bring some with you.

What to Wear

Be modest, be sensible, and travel
light. Egypt is a conservative country.
It is an affront to your hosts to
appear in a mosque or even on the
street in clothing that is considered
immodest. Women should keep
shoulders and upper arms covered.
Neither men nor women should wear
shorts except at holiday resorts or
on the tennis court. No topless or
nude bathing is permitted.
    On the practical side, leave your
synthetics at home as they will prove
too hot in the summer and not warm

Disabled Facilities

Few hotels or cruise boats and
no public buildings, restaurants,
theatres or historical sites
provide any facilities for the
infirm or disabled. Major airlines,
however, provide services both
entering and leaving the country
that match worldwide standards.
    Dr. Sami Bishara of ETAMS
tours, 13 Shari' Qasr an-Nil,
Cairo (02-345-0761) specialises
in making travel arrangements
for individual disabled travellers
or groups.

Porter Service

For a rental of 2LE, baggage trolleys are available at Cairo International Airport. There are also porters with larger trolleys to service individuals and groups.

enough in the winter. Cotton is suitable for all of the seasons; wool for winter and many summer nights.

Loose and flowing garments are extremely practical in a hot climate. Hats are vital to protect against heat stroke, as are sunglasses, to defend the eyes against the glare.

Bring stout, comfortable shoes. You will be doing a lot of walking and neither Cairo's streets nor Luxor's temple floors are friendly to feet.

Entry Regulations

VISAS & PASSPORTS

All travellers entering Egypt must have the appropriate travel documents: a passport with at least 6 months to run and a valid visa. Lost or stolen passports must be reported to the police immediately. New passports can be issued in a matter of hours at the consular office of your embassy in Egypt but procedures will require a copy of your police report verifying loss. Tourist visas valid for one month are also routinely issued at Cairo International Airport and other international airports, and the Port of Alexandria, but may also be acquired in advance of your visit at any Egyptian Consulate.

See page 312 for embassy and consulate addresses.

Extension of Stay

Visas can be renewed at the Mugama'a (Cairo's central administrative building on Maydan al-Tahrir), usually after a long wait. Visas are usually considered valid for 15 days after the expiry date, but if not renewed then a letter of apology from your embassy must be presented to the Mugama'a or you will have to pay a small fine.

Customs

A visitor is permitted to enter the country with 250 grammes of tobacco, 200 cigarettes or 50 cigars, one litre of alcohol and personal effects. Animals must have a veterinary certificate certifying good health and a valid rabies certificate.

Duty-free purchases of liquor (3 bottles per person) may be made within a month of arrival twice a year at ports of entry or at the tax-free shops in Cairo and Luxor.

Persons travelling with expensive electronic equipment may be required to list these items in their passports so that authorities can ensure that they will be exported upon departure.

On Departure

Although the traveller is free to buy and export reasonable quantities of Egyptian goods for personal use, the export of large quantities of items requires an export licence. Egyptian-made items over 20 years old are not permitted to leave the country, nor are foreign-made items deemed to have "historic value". Export of carpets is restricted. Travellers may be requested to show bank receipts as proof of payment for valuable

Type of Visa

Single entry visas obtained upon arrival are good for one entry into Egypt for a period of up to one month. If you require a longer stay than this, obtain your single entry visa from an Egyptian embassy or consulate before departure. It will be valid for three months.

Multiple entry visas should be requested from the Egyptian embassy or consulate before departure (valid for three months) if you plan to exit and re-enter Egypt during your visit.

Student visas for people studying in Egypt are valid for one year and are not issued until verification of registration at an Egyptian university.

Business visas are issued to those with business affiliations in Egypt.

items. Excess pounds may be changed back at the airport on showing valid bank receipts.

Animal Quarantine

It is not wise to bring a pet to Egypt on holiday. Rabies is a problem in the country and very few hotels have facilities for animals.

Health

Evidence of yellow fever and cholera immunisation may be required from persons who have been in an infected area up to six days prior to arrival. No other inoculations are officially required, but it is always good to be up to date with polio, tetanus and cholera.

Money

Airport Exchange
Banks are available at the airport for currency exchange. Egyptian money, with both Arabic and English numerals, consists of these denominations:
Pound notes: 100, 20, 10, 5, 1.
Piaster notes: 50, 25.
Coins: 50, 25, 20, 10, 5 piasters.

Credit cards are used in most major hotels, but not always in

Tourist Residence visas are issued for extended visits. Holders are not permitted to work in Egypt and must be prepared to present evidence of having exchanged $180 a month for up to six months at a time. This type of visa is only issued in Egypt at the Passport Department of the Mugama'a, Maydan al-Tahrir. Persons holding a Tourist Residence visa must apply for a re-entry visa whenever they plan to leave the country.

Visas may be renewed up to 15 days beyond their expiry. If not renewed during that time a fine is imposed and a letter of apology from your embassy must be taken to the Mugama'a.

shops. Bring some traveller's cheques. More and more cities now have ATM machines which allow you to withdraw cash using Visa, MasterCard and so on.

Public Holidays

There are six official government holidays a year when banks, government offices, many businesses, and schools are closed. In addition there are Islamic and Coptic holidays spread throughout the year.

New Year's Day. Public holiday.

Coptic Christmas, January 7. Copts observe the birth of Christ on the same date as all other Orthodox churches except the Armenian. Prior to the feast they abstain from animal flesh and animal products for 43 days.

Feast of Breaking the Fast, Id al-Fitr, celebrates the end of Ramadan, the month of fasting. During daylight hours, Muslims will have abstained from food, drink, sex and violence for some 30 days. Business hours are shortened during Ramadan and social life, centring on the meal eaten after sunset, called *iftar*, becomes nocturnal and intense. The Id al-Fitr is a happy celebration with new clothes, gifts, and plenty of good food. Festivities usually last for three days.

Feast of the Sacrifice, 'Id al-Adha, begins approximately 70 days after the end of Ramadan and commemorates Abraham's sacrifice of a sheep in place of his son, Isaac. It is traditional to kill a sheep and share the meat with the extended family, neighbours and the poor. Festivities last for four days.

Coptic Easter ends the Coptic Lenten season. Usually celebrated one week after Western Easter, Coptic businesses are closed.

Sham an-Nissim, "sniffing the breeze", is a holiday celebrated the Monday after Coptic Easter. Dating from Pharaonic times, it is celebrated by all Egyptians regardless of their religious affiliation. The entire population goes to the countryside or to some urban green space for a day-long outing, with picnic baskets filled

with hard boiled eggs and pickled fish. Businesses are closed.

Liberation of Sinai Day, April 25. Public holiday.

Labour Day, May 1. Public holiday.

Islamic New Year, Ras al-Sana al-Higriya. Public holiday.

Anniversary of the 1952 Revolution, July 23. Businesses are closed.

Prophet's Birthday, Mawlid al-Nabi, is celebrated in honour of the Prophet Muhammed. A parade complete with drums and banners is held in the historic zone of Cairo. Public holiday.

Armed Forces Day, October 6. Public holiday.

Calendars

The business and secular community in Egypt operates under the Western (Gregorian) calendar. But other calendars have official status in Egypt. The Islamic (Hegira) calendar is used to fix religious observances, and is based on a lunar cycle of 12 months of 29 or 30 days. The Muslim year is thus 11 days shorter than the year in the Gregorian calendar and months move forward accordingly.

In the Gregorian calendar, for example, April is in the spring, but in the Muslim calendar all months move through all seasons in a 33-year cycle.

The Coptic calendar is the Julian calendar, which was replaced in the West by the Gregorian calendar between 1582 and 1752, but the months carry their current Egyptian names. The Coptic year consists of 12 months of 30 days and one month of 5 days. Every four years a sixth day is added to the shorter month. An adaptation of the Coptic calendar is often used for planting and harvesting crops. It is used by the authorities of the Coptic Orthodox Church.

Muslim Calendar	Coptic Calendar
Muharram	Toot (begins Sept 11 or 12)
Safar	Baaba
Rabi' il-awal	Hatour
Rabi' it-tani	Kiyaak
Gamada-l-uula	Tuuba (mid-Jan)
Gamada-l-ukhra	Amshir
Ragab	Baramhat
Sha'aban	Barmuda
Ramadan	Bashans
Shawal	Bauna
Dhu'l	Abiib
Dhu'l	Misra
	Nasi (5–6 days)

Getting There

BY AIR

Egypt is served by international airports at Alexandria, Cairo, Luxor, Hurghada and Sharm al Shaykh.

Return tickets must be confirmed before departure. Check with a travel agent in your hotel or contact the airline office in Cairo. Most major airlines have offices at the Cairo International Airport and in and around Maydan al-Tahrir in downtown Cairo.

Cairo International Airport is now a first-class facility. Despite the fact that it is located to the north of the city, most airlines from Europe approach the air field from the south. In daylight passengers have a magnificent view of Cairo, the Nile, and the Giza Pyramids.

Alexandria airport is served by Olympic Airlines and Egyptair. **Luxor** Airport now has direct flights from most European cities via Air France, Lufthansa and several charter companies. **Hurghada** Airport is also serviced by Lufthansa while **Sharm el Shaykh** Airport receives charter flights from all over Europe. Other airports in Egypt are Asyut, Aswan, Abu Simbel, Al Arish, St Catherine's, Al-Khargah Oasis, Siwa Oasis.

Domestic Airlines

Egypt has two national carriers for internal flights, Egyptair and Air Sinai. Egyptair flies daily from Cairo to Alexandria, Luxor, Aswan, Abu Simbel, Sharm al-Shaykh and Hurghada and twice a week to Al-Khargah Oasis. Air Sinai flies from Cairo to Hurghada, Sharm al-Sheikh, St Catherine's Monastery, Al Tor, and to Tel Aviv, Israel.

Cairo Terminals

Terminal 1: Egyptair domestic and international flights.
Terminal 2: International Airlines.
Terminal 3: Saudia Arabia Airline.
Terminal 4: International cargo. English language information,
Tel: 245-0260

Egyptair Offices
www.egyptair.com.eg
Alexandria: 19 Midan Zaghlul
Tel: 482-5701
9 Talaat Harb Street
Tel: 393-2836
Cairo: 6 Adli Street
Tel: 390-0999
Zamalik Club Force, 26th-of-July St
Tel: 305-1431
Nile Hilton Hotel
Tel: 579-3049
Cairo Sheraton
Tel: 748-8630
Heliopolis: 22 Ibrahim al Lakani
Tel: 290-8453
Luxor: Winter Palace Arcade
Tel: 095-380-580
Aswan: Corniche
Tel: 097-315-000
Hurghada: Tourism Center near the National Hotel
Tel: 065-447-503
Sharm al-Sheikh: Mövenpick Hotel, Naama Bay
Tel: 069-661-056

Private Airlines
In November 1997 the Egyptian Government gave permission for private airlines to begin operations and announced that they would build more domestic airports. One of the first of the new, independent operators was **Orascom Air**, which operates regular flights from Al Gouna to Luxor and Cairo. Orascom Cairo office, tel: 02-301-5632.

BY SEA

Alexandria and Port Said on the Mediterranean Sea, and Suez and Nuweiba on the Red Sea are ports of entry. There are no longer any direct ferries from Europe to Egypt.

BY LAND

From Israel
Private vehicles are not permitted to enter Egypt from Israel; however travellers may use public transport and enter Egypt via Rafah on the northern coast of Sinai or from Eilat on the Red Sea. Buses run regularly from Tel Aviv and Jerusalem to the border at Rafah. Passengers disembark from the Israeli vehicle, go through customs, and take an Egyptian bus or taxi. There are no facilities for issuing visas at the border. You will be subject to pay the Israeli departure tax and the Egyptian entry tax. In Eilat, Israeli buses are permitted to enter Egypt and travel as far as Sharm al-Shaykh at the southern tip of Sinai.

From Sudan
A ferry leaves Aswan every Monday at 2pm and arrives the following morning in Wadi Halfa. Tickets are available in 1st or 2nd class from the Nile Navigation Company in Aswan, tel: 097-303-348 – closed on Thursdays and Fridays. You must show the visa for Sudan when buying the ticket. All arrangements to enter Sudan, including visas, must be made in Cairo. Be aware that it can take the Sudanese embassy up to a month to issue a visa (3 Ibrahim Street, Garden City, tel: 794-5043). You must have a transit or tourist visa to enter Sudan. If you plan to pass through the Sudan you must have a visa for your next destination.

From Libya
The border with Libya is open and buses and taxis make regular runs between Cairo and Alexandria and Benghazi or Tripoli. However, there are some travel restrictions for Westerners. Consult your or the nearest Libyan embassy for details.

Motoring to Egypt
All private vehicles entering Egypt must have a triptyque or *carnet de passage en douane* from an automobile club in the country of registration or pay customs duty which can be as high as 250 percent. Emergency triptyques are available at the port of entry via the Automobile and Touring Club of Egypt. This permits a car to enter Egypt for three months with one extension. The extension is available from the Automobile and Touring Club of Egypt, Qasr al-Nil, Cairo. All persons travelling in the vehicle must have a valid passport. Drivers must have an International Driver's Licence. (*See Getting Around, Private Transport, page 316* for details on driving in Egypt.)

Useful Addresses

Tourism websites
http://pharos.bu.edu/Egypt/Homel
http://interoz.com/Egypt
http://www.egypttoday.com
www.touregypt.net
www.tourism.egnet.net

Egyptian Tourism & Information Centres
Athens: 10 Amerikis St
Tel: 360-6906
New York: 630 Fifth Ave
Tel: 332-2570
San Francisco: suite 215, 83 Wilshire Boulevard, Wilshire San Vincente Plaza, Beverly Hills
Tel: 280 4666
London: 3rd floor, Egyptian House, 170 Picadilly, W1
Tel: 020-7493-5282
Rome: 19, Via Bissolati
Tel: 482-7985
Paris: 90, Ave de Champs-Elysées
Tel: 45-62-94-42
Frankfurt: Kaiserstrasse 64, Bürohaus A
Tel: 23-98-76

Egyptian Consulates Abroad
Canada: 454 Laurier Ave. East, Ottawa; 1, place Ste Marie, Montreal
France: 58, avenue Foch, Paris
Germany: Waldstrasse 15, Berlin; Eysseneckstrasse 34, Frankfurt
UK: 2 Lowndes Street, London SW1
Tel: 0891-887777
www.egypt-embassy.org.uk
USA: 3521 International Court NW, Washington DC 20008;
1990 Post Oak Blvd., suite 2180, Houston TX 77056; 500 N Michigan Ave., suite 1900, Chicago IL60611

Practical Tips

RADIO

European Radio Cairo broadcasts on 557 AM and 95 FM, from 7am–midnight. This popular music station plays a variety of European classical, pop and jazz. News is broadcast in English at 7.30am, 2.30pm, and 8pm; in French at 8am, 2pm and 9pm; in Greek at 3pm; in Armenian at 4pm; in German at 6pm.

BBC World Service broadcasts to Egypt on 639 kHz and 1323 kHz. The higher metre band provides better reception between sunrise and sunset. There are also shortwave alternatives. News is on the hour.

The **VOA** (Voice of America) broadcasts on a variety of wavelengths from 3–10am daily, on 1290khz.

TELEVISION

The arrival of satellite TV, and more recently cable TV have revolutionised viewing in Egypt. Most hotels, even the more down-market ones, offer satellite TV and satellite dishes now top many of Cairo's apartment blocks. Local TV is rarely exciting.

Channel 1: on the air from 3.30pm–midnight (local time), and found on 1 and 5 on the dial, is mainly in Arabic.

Channel 2: broadcasting from 3pm–midnight daily, and also from 10am–noon on Fridays and Sundays, has many foreign language programmes.

Channel 3: is a Cairo-only station broadcasting, in Arabic, from 5–9pm.

CNN: arrived in Egypt in 1991. It broadcasts to subscribers 24 hours a day with an uncensored programme.

See the *Egyptian Gazette* for daily television schedules. These vary during Ramadan and in the summer.

NEWSPAPERS

In Cairo all major English, French, German and Italian daily newspapers are available at larger hotels and at newsstands in Zamalik and Maadi usually a day late. The two most important local dailies are *Al-Ahram* and *Al-Akhbar*. *Al-Ahram*, "The Pyramids", was established in 1875, making it the oldest newspaper in Egypt. Published daily, it also has a UK edition, a weekly English-language edition, *Al-Ahram Weekly* and a weekly French-language edition, *Al-Ahram Hébdo*. Other English-language weeklies include the *Middle East Times* (online at: metimes.com), the *Cairo Times* (online at: www.cairotimes.com) and the *Arab Times*. *Al Akhbar al Yaum*, "The News", established in 1952 offers a weekly edition in Arabic.

The Egyptian Gazette, established in 1880, is the oldest foreign language daily newspaper still in operation in Egypt.

In French there are *Le Progrès Egyptien* and *Le Journal d'Egypte*; in Greek, *Phos*; and in Armenian, *Arev*.

Informal newsletters serve to keep foreign residents in Egypt in touch: the *British Community Association News* for the British community; *Helioscope*, serving the residents of Heliopolis; the *Maadi Messenger* for foreigners in Maadi, and *Papyrus* for the German community.

English-language magazines include *Arab Press Review*, a biweekly political magazine, *Business Monthly*, featuring business news, *Cairo's*, a monthly what's on, *Egypt Today* and *Insight*, monthly general interest magazines, and the *E Croc* (www.ecroc.com), a monthly free listings magazine for Cairo.

Banks: 8.30am–1.30pm daily, closed Friday, Saturday and most holidays.

Businesses: Business hours throughout the week are flexible. Few businesses function before 8am; many are open until 5pm, but some close during the afternoon and then re-open at 5pm. Clinics are customarily open from 5–8pm.

Government offices: 8am–2pm daily, closed Friday, Saturday, most holidays.

Shops: Shops keep hours according to demand. In central Cairo, many shops, including those owned by Muslims and Jews, are closed on Sunday.

Khan al-Khalili bazaar: open 10am–7 or 8pm daily and most shops close Sunday.

Most 5-star hotels offer a direct dial service. The Central Telephone and Telegraph offices (8 Shari Adli, on Maydan al-Tahrir, 26 Shari Ramesses) are open 24 hours a day, as are many branch exchanges. Others are open from 7am–10pm daily. Telex and fax services are also available from the above, and fax facilities in particular are available at business centres dotted around the city.

Orange card phones are increasingly common; buy cards from telephone offices.

Calls booked at telephone offices must be paid for in advance, with a three minute minimum. Between 8pm and 8am the cost of phone calls is greatly reduced.

If your have an AT&T calling card it is possible to charge a call from Egypt to the United States to a US account. You may place a call with a New York operator by dialing 356-0200 or 510-0200. You must supply both the American number and the number of your AT&T account.

Internet facilities are available through both commercial offices and educational institutions.

Telephone Codes

Alexandria	03
Aswan	097
Asyut	088
Cairo	02
Fayyum	084
Hurghada	065
Ismailia	064
Luxor	095
Port Said	066
Suez	062

For general enquiries tel: 140.

Emergencies

SECURITY AND CRIME

Like many other countries, such as Italy and the USA, Egypt has been troubled in recent years by right-wing extremists and radical Islamic terrorists. Like the US in the late 1960s, Germany in the 1970s, the UK and France throughout the 1970s, 80s and early 90s, it has also suffered from terrorist violence. In 1997 two attacks specifically targeting tourists – one outside the Egyptian Museum in Cairo and another at Hatshepsut's Temple, Luxor – significantly raised the overall death toll. These attacks appear to have been the work of a breakaway group from the main terrorist organisation. A heavy military response from the government designed to protect tourists and deter further terrorist activities cannot guarantee security and this further clamp-down may exacerbate the situation. However, even during the violence of 1991–2 tourists were statistically safer in Egypt than in many American cities and Egyptian drivers presented a greater threat than terrorists.

Visitors from abroad should nevertheless be warned that there may be restrictions on travel into or through Middle Egypt, the zone along the Nile in Upper Egypt between Al-Minya and Luxor. This region is beautiful, but poverty-stricken, and historically given to violence, much of it directed against officialdom or formal authority. Travel between towns in Middle and Upper Egypt is only allowed in armed convoys which leave 2 or 3 times a day.

Elsewhere, common caution is advised. Social restrictions on women in Egypt can make foreign women seem particularly enticing to young Egyptian men, who may have heard lurid stories about sexual encounters (a situation not helped by the insensitive dress of some tourists). Care should be taken. Also, as Egypt's economic reforms have created great hardship, the number of petty thefts have increased although you are still more likely to have a lost wallet returned intact than in many countries.

If you do experience serious difficulties, you should report immediately to the nearest tourist police post or police station.

HOSPITALS

There are good hospitals in Cairo and Alexandria. However they require a cash deposit to cover the cost of treatment and patients cannot use foreign medical insurance plans. Some hospitals are listed below:

Anglo-American Hospital Zohoreya next to the Cairo Tower, Zamalik. Tel: 736-8630

As Salam International Hospital Corniche al-Nil, Maadi. Tel: 363-8050/363-4196/363-8424.

Cairo Medical Centre Shari' Higaz, Heliopolis Tel: 258-1206

PHARMACIES

Pharmacies are usually open from 10am to 10pm and are staffed by competent professionals. Both

Postal and Courier Services

The Central Post Office at Maydan al Ataba in Cairo is open 24 hours a day except Friday and occasional holidays. All other post offices are open from 8.30am–3pm daily, except Fridays. Mailboxes found on street corners and in front of post offices are red for regular Egyptian mail, blue for overseas airmail letters and green for Cairo and express mail within Cairo. Allow seven days for air mail to Europe, 14 days to America. Mail sent from hotels seems to be quicker.

Express Mail Agencies

The major post offices, marked with the EMS sign, offer an Express Mail Service (EMS), which is more expensive but much faster (tel: 390-5874). In addition to this there are various international courier services:

DHL
El-Mona Tavas, 16 Lebanon Street, Mohandisseen
Tel: 302-9801
34 Abdel Khalek Sarwat
Tel: 393-8988
35 Ismail Ramzi, Heliopolis
Tel: 246-0324

Federal Express
1081 Corniche al-Nil, Garden City
Tel: 354-0520

TNT
International Express
33 Dokki Street, Dokki
Tel: 760-9695

Aramex
14 Yehia Ibrahim
Mohandisseen
Tel: 332-2225

Overseas Courier International
Darih Saad Street, Downtown
Tel: 356-0141
Mail can be received at American Express offices, and you don't need to be a cardholder to use the mail pick-up service. Letters can also be sent poste restante to most Egyptian cities or to 15, Shari' Qasr al-Nil, Cairo, A.R.Egypt. Remember to bring along your passport when you pick up your mail. Some embassies may offer a mail holding service for their nationals.

Embassies in Egypt

Australia
World Trade Center
11th floor, 1191 Corniche al-Nil
Bulak
Tel: 575-0444.
Canada
3rd floor, 4 Shari' Kobra
Garden City
Tel: 354-3110.
Germany
8 Shari' Hassan Sabri
Zamalik
Tel: 341-0015.
Ireland
7th floor, 3 Shari' Abu el-Feda
Zamalik
Tel: 340-8264.
UK
7 Ahmed Ragheb
Garden City
Tel: 354-0850
USA
5 Shari' Latin America
Garden City
Tel: 355-7371
www.usis.egnet.net

locally made and imported
medication is subsidised by the
government and is inexpensive.
Some medication requiring
prescriptions abroad is sold over
the counter in Egypt. Pharmacists
can usually recommend treatment
for minor ailments.
　24-hour pharmacies in Cairo
include:

Ali and Ali
37 Seliman Abaza Street
Mohandisseen
Tel: 719-3417
and
33 Qasr al-Aini
Tel: 565-3880

Central Cairo
Isaaf Pharmacy
(corner of 26th-of-July Street and
Ramesses Street)
Tel: 574-3369

Maadi
El-Rhama
35 R276 New Maadi
Tel: 519-3430

Esam Pharmacy
101 Road 9
Tel: 358-4126

Zamalik
Zamalik Pharmacy
3 Shagaret el Dorr
Zamalik
Tel: 735-2406

LEFT LUGGAGE

At the airport luggage is claimed via
airline offices. .

Photography

Egypt is a photographer's
paradise. The best film speeds for
daylight outdoors are low (100 and
under), but fast film (400, 1000) is
necessary for interiors, high-
powered lenses and night shots.
Photography is forbidden in
security zones, often curiously
defined, and a variety of rules
pertain to Pharaonic monuments.
Signs are usually posted in
restricted areas. In other areas
photography is permitted for a fee.
Fees for still cameras run as high
as LE50, for video cameras up to
LE200. There are no restrictions
on photography anywhere in Cairo.
　Scholars and professional
photographers working on projects
may apply for a special permit from
the Supreme Council for Antiquities.
The procedure may well take some
time, and passes are not given out
freely.
　Photographing individual people
requires a bit of consideration. The
Egyptian people are constantly
having cameras pushed in their
faces, so be courteous and ask
first. If a person does not want you
to take his or her photo, do not take
it. If he or she wants to be paid,
pay. If you don't want to pay, don't
take the picture. You will find plenty
of good shots elsewhere.

Getting Around

From the Airport

All airports in Egypt have a taxi
service to city centres, operated on
a flat fee basis (ask your airline). In
Cairo transport includes limousine,
taxi, and bus. Curbside limousine
service is offered by Misr
Limousine (Tel: 285-6124).
　Official Cairo taxis are predomi-
nantly black and white and
Alexandria taxis are black and
orange. There are also larger
Peugeot taxis in a variety of colours,
but they all have an emblem and
number painted on the driver's
door. Fees are the same as the
limousine service.
　The Airport Bus Service operates
from Terminal 1. The bus leaves
when full and stops at Maydan al-
Tahrir in downtown Cairo, in
Muhandesseen, and along Pyramids
Road in Giza.

Public Transport

BY RAIL

The Egyptian State Railway is a government-owned system founded in
1851 which services the entire Nile
Valley down to Aswan, the Red Sea
cities of Suez and Port Said, the
Delta and Northern Coast cities of
Alexandria (two stops) and Marsa
Mutrah. There are at least half a
dozen through trains a day on major
routes. Fares are inexpensive, but
unless one is travelling with a tour,
tickets must be purchased at the
main stations (in Cairo at
Ramesses Station at Maydan
Ramesses).
　The privately-owned Wagon-Lits
train company runs three fast turbo-
trains a day from Cairo to

Alexandria (2 hours). Booking should be done in advance at Ramesses Station, Cairo or at Alexandria station. Wagon-Lits also operate trains and sleepers between Cairo and Luxor (10 hours) and Aswan (15 hours). Tel: 02-574 9474. Bring passports for everyone travelling.

BY BUS

Air-conditioned buses link most parts of Egypt to Cairo and Alexandria. Seats may be reserved up to two days in advance. There is also a fleet of cheaper non-air-conditioned buses. Although bus times may change without any notice, departures are so frequent that schedule changes are not a problem at all.

Tickets for air-conditioned buses should always be booked in advance.

The fastest buses to Alexandria (3 hours) are operated by the Superjet and Golden Rocket companies. The principal carrier to Aswan and Luxor is the Upper Egyptian Bus Company. Two buses a day complete the run to Aswan, departing early morning and arriving in the evening.

Air-conditioned Superjets to Luxor and Aswan are not advisable as the services involve overnight travel with loud and rarely interesting end-to-end videos.

The East Delta Co covers the Canal zone and most of the Delta; the four main operators are at the time of writing being moved to the new Turgoman Garage, 600 metres/yds west of Ramesses Station in Bulaq, in preference to the terminals being spread out in different corners of the city.

By Bus Around Cairo
The large red-and-white and blue-and-white buses are usually so over-crowded they assault one's sense of private space. They also provide ample opportunity for petty theft and unwelcome sexual encounters. But here are a few interesting routes for the adventurous tourist:

Orientation

The Nile flows through the country from south to north. Upper Egypt is therefore the south, Lower Egypt the Delta. Upstream is south, downstream north. Many good maps are available.

● Number 400 and 949 from the airport to downtown.
● Number 186, 815 in Maydan Tahrir to the Khan al-Khalili.
● Number 179, 194 in Maydan Tahrir to the Citadel.
● Numbers 900, 30, 108 in Maydan al-Tahrir to the pyramids.
More comfortable are the smaller orange-and-white minibuses which do not permit standing. Here are a few major routes (from Maydan al-Tahrir):
● Number 27 to Ramesses station, Abbassiyah and the Airport.
● Number 183 to the Pyramids.

METRO & TRAM

Both Alexandria and Cairo have tram or metro systems that run through at least part of the city. Trains run every few minutes from early morning (5.30am) to midnight and fares are inexpensive.

By Tram Around Alexandria
Tram lines in Alexandria run only between Ramleh Station (called "Terminus") near the Cecil Hotel and destinations to the east of the city.
● Tram 1 (Bacos line), Ramleh Station to Sidi Bishr.
● Tram 2 (El Nasr line), Ramleh Station to Sidi Bishr.
● Tram 3, Ramleh Station to Sidi Gaber.
● Tram 4, Circular route: Sidi Gaber, Ramleh Station, Sidi Gaber.
● Tram 5, Ramleh Station to San Stefano via Bacos.
● Tram 6, Ramleh Station to Sidi Bishr via Glym.

By Metro Around Cairo
In Cairo the metro system is identified by circular signs with a big red

M. The metro is clean and efficient, and an easy way to get around. Note that every train has a special carriage for women and if you are a woman travelling on your own you may prefer to use it. The system runs north–south from Heliopolis to Helwan through the heart of the city. Another line was opened from the northern suburb of Shubra el-Kheima to Bulag al-Dakrour and other lines are currently under construction. Additional routes, east and west, are currently under construction. Useful stations:
Mubarak Station Ramesses Square with access to the main train station and bus stations to Upper Egypt and the Oases.
Urabi Station Sh Gala'a. *Al Ahram* newspaper.
Nasser Station Maydan Tawfiqiyyah.

Travel Agents

Abercrombie & Kent
18 Youssef el buindi,
El Boustan Centre, 10th floor
Tel: 393-6255
E-mail: tourism@abercrombiekent.com.eg
American Express
Nile Hilton, Maydan al-Tahrir
Tel: 578-0444
Also at 15, Shari' Qasr al-Nil
E-mail: aets@ritsec2.com.eg
Eastmar
13 Qasr el Nil
Tel: 574-5024
E-mail: eastmar@es.egnet.net
Erneco Travel
2 Talaat Harb Sheik, Cairo
Tel: 574-9360
Gezira Travel
28 Sharia Shaparet el-Dorr
Zamalik
Tel: 736-0585
Email: geziral@geziragrp.com.eg
Misr Travel
1 Talaat Harb Shaykh
Cairo
Tel: 393-0010
E-mail: misrtrav@link.com.eg
Thomas Cook
4 Champollion
Tel: 574-3776
E-mail: tcintlsales@attmail.com

Sadat Station Maydan Tahrir with 10 entrances and access to Egyptian Antiquities Museum, the American University in Cairo, Nile Hilton, all major airline offices, and the Mugama'a (central administrative building).

Mar Girgis at Old Cairo with access to the Coptic Museum, Coptic churches, and Roman fortress.

Saad Zaghlul Station The National Assembly. Zaghlul monument.

By Tram Around Heliopolis
Cairo also has tram systems and Heliopolis is served by six tram lines.

The major three lines are as follows:

Abd el Aziz Fahmi line (green) from Midan Abd el Monim Riad (behind the Egyptian Museum) via Ramesses to Roxi, Merryland, Mahkama, Heliopolis Hospital to the Shams Club;

Nuzha line (red) runs Midan Abd el Monim Riad, Ramesses, Roxi, Heliopolis Sporting Club, Salah al Din, and Maydan al Higaz to Nuzha;

Mirghani line (yellow) Midan Abd el Monim Riad, Ramesses, Roxi, Shari' el Merghani, Saba Emarat, Midan Triomphe, Military College.

By Taxi

For one of the experiences of your life, take an Egyptian taxi. Taxi drivers seem to need to fill every empty space on the road (and sometimes the pavement). All taxis have orange licence plates and are identified by a number on the driver's door. Drivers are required to have their licence and identity numbers displayed on the dashboard. Sharing a taxi is not unusual. In Cairo and Alexandria taxis ply the streets at all hours of the day or night and can be flagged down. There are also taxi ranks at all the major hotels and public squares.

Official or metered prices are unrealistic and meters are seldom used. The fare should be agreed beforehand. The majority of taxi drivers are honest, but some try to cheat unwary foreigners, espe-cially between five-star hotels and such destinations as the pyramids or Khan al-Khalili. Do not hesitate to ask for assistance from the tourist police. At your destination, pay the fare in exact change and walk away. No tip is expected.

Taxi drivers are friendly, many speak English, some are college graduates moonlighting to supplement their incomes, and most are very eager to be hired by the day. The fee is negotiable, something in the region of £30–40 (150–200le) per day. Such an arrangement is ideal for shopping or for seeing several scattered monuments.

Taxis in Luxor and Aswan are equally easy to find (they line up outside all the hotels), but for the distance travelled they work out more expensive than those in Cairo.

BY SERVICE TAXI

Collective service taxis are a faster alternative to the bus, and will get you just about everywhere in Egypt. The fare is about the same as for the bus, and on the main routes there are several departures daily. These taxis, often estate Peugeots – hence their pet name of "Beejoo" – seat six or seven and leave as soon as they are full. Drivers are renowned for their speed, since the sooner they arrive the sooner they can load up again. The service station is usually beside the bus or train station.

Private Transport

CAR RENTAL

Driving in Egypt is very demanding (*see Driving Conditions below*). The best alternative is to hire a driver and a car together, thus freeing yourself to enjoy the changing scenery.

Car rental agencies exist at most major hotels. Foreigners must have an International Driver's Licence and be at least 25 years of age to rent a car in Egypt. Some agencies offer four-wheel drive vehicles, with or without driver, for desert travel. You will need your passport, driver's licence, and a prepayment. Credit cards are accepted.

Rental Agencies
Avis
16 Maamal al-Sukkar
Garden City
Tel: 354-7400
Bita
34A Abu Babel al-Seolik
Heliopolis
Tel: 454-2620
Budget
9 al-Maqrizi
Zamalik
Tel: 735-0070/735-9474
Europacar
39 Shari' Lebanon
Mohandisseen
Tel: 347-4712
Also for four-wheel drive vehicles with or without experienced desert drivers. Branch office in Sharm al Shaykh.

Limousines
Limousines are available for those who want to travel in style:
Bita Limousine Service
Gazirah Sheraton
Tel: 736-1333/736-1555
Marriott Hotel
Tel: 735-8888
Rawas Limousines
Gazirah Sheraton
Tel 736-1333
Ramesses Hilton
Tel: 575-4999
Mlsr Travel Tower
Abbaseya square
13th floor
Tel: 285-6721

DRIVING CONDITIONS

The roads that go from Cairo to Upper Egypt are the longest, most congested, and most dangerous in Egypt. Most traffic moving south from Cairo must travel a route along the western shore of the Nile.

It is not advisable to drive at night; vehicles stop dead on the road and turn out their lights; unlit donkey carts move at a snail's pace and are usually not seen until it is too late; and long distance taxis and overloaded trucks travel too fast, often without lights, and are driven by drivers who use "stimulants".

There are petrol stations throughout the country, with those operated by Mobil, Esso, and Shell offering full service with mini-markets on the premises. Fuel, inexpensive and sold by the litre, is available in 90 octane (*tisa'iin*) which is super, or 80 (*tamaniin*), regular. Super is the better fuel for most purposes.

Road signs are similar to those used throughout Europe. Driving is on the right-hand side of the road. Speed limits are posted on major highways and are enforced by radar.

Nile Cruises

A cruise on the Nile still is one of the best ways both to visit the temples and ancient sites and sample the peaceful life along the river. Hundreds of ships now cruise along the Nile following more or less the same itinerary but offering a wide choice of accommodation, suitable for every budget. Most people book cruises before they leave for Egypt, which is advisable as it is usually cheaper to buy them as part of a package. Most boats travel between Luxor and Aswan in 3-4 days, or sometimes for 6 days to include Abydos and Dendarah. Today, boats hardly ever sail the whole way from Cairo to Aswan.

Differences in price usually reflect the standard of service, the numbers and the size of the cabin and the quality of the food. More expensive boats tend to have fewer and larger cabins and will make the effort to prepare good food. All boats provide guides to accompany passengers to the sites and some have small libraries on Egyptian history and culture.

But there is no doubt that cruising is no longer as romantic as it used to be. There are often delays at Esna due to the large number of boats passing through

the lock, forcing some companies to bus their passengers to a sister boat on the other side of the lock. For the same reason not all boats dock in the centre of Aswan or Luxor; cheaper boats are often moored further along the river bank, or will be wedged between other boats and therefore without any Nile views from the inside. Your travel agent should know if you will have a Nile view.

To get a real feel of what cruising used to be like before the traffic jams on the Nile, a cruise on Lake Nasser is recommended. Two companies now offer the 3–4 day cruise, visiting the Nubian monuments on the shores of Lake Nasser. Watch Abu Simbel at dawn before breakfast (and the crowds) or take an apéritif at one of the rarely visited Nubian temples. The beautifully decorated MS *Eugenie* and *Qasr Ibrim* are run by Belle Epoque Travel in Cairo, tel: 02-703-7935, and the larger MS *Prince Abbas* is operated by the Nile Exploration Corporation, tel:02-332-3384 and Nubian Sea, tel: 02-361-3680. Some more upmarket tour operators in Europe and the US offer the cruise in their brochures.

There are scores of Nile cruise-companies offering packages to suit every pocket and taste. Most offer 4-, 5- and 7-day tours between Luxor and Aswan. Trips are as comfortable and often cheaper if they are arranged outside Egypt.

Here are some of the boats and operators:

Felucca Trips

In Aswan or Luxor a *felucca* trip is a great way to get a feel for the Nile, either for an afternoon or morning, or, security concerns in the region permitting, for a 2–4-day cruise between the two towns. On a longer cruise, you normally sleep on board and your captain cooks for you. If the wind is unreliable, you are advised to sail from Aswan to Luxor, so at least the current will carry you downstream.

Distances from Cairo

Distances between Cairo and other cities

North to Alexandria
225 km/140 miles (Delta road)
221 km/138 miles (desert road)
to Damietta
191km/119 miles
to the Barrages
25km/15 miles

South to Al-Minya
236km/151 miles
to Asyut 359km/224 miles
to Luxor 664km/415 miles
to Esna 719km/449 miles
to Edfu 775km/484 miles
to Kom Ombo 835km/521 miles
to Aswan 880km/550 miles

★★★★★
Alexander the Great
Jolley Travel and Tour Company
8 Talaat Harb
Tel: 579-4649
E-mail: atg@jolleys.com
This cruise ship was featured in the American series *The Love Boat*.
Anni, Aton, Hotp, and Tut
Sheraton Management Corporation
48B Shari' Giza
Dokki
Tel: 305-5600
Isis and Osiris
Flash Nile Cruises
Tel: 419-3451
The first modern day cruise boats on the Nile, these sister ships offer 4- and 5-day cruises.
Neptune
Trans Egypt Travel Company
37 Qasr al-Nil
Tel: 392-4313
Aida I, Aida II
Aida Boats
8 Halim Square, Ezbebiya
Tel: 590-4666
Seven-, 10-, and 11-day cruises.
Nile Admiral, Nile Emperor, Nile Legend, Nile President, Nile Princess, Nile Ritz, Nile Symphony
Presidential Nile Cruises
13 Marashli Street
Zamalik
Tel: 735-0517
4-, 7-, and 10-day cruises.

Nile Queen, Nile Sphinx
Sphinx Tours
2 Behler Passage
Qasr al-Nil
Tel: 392-0704
Oberoi Shehrayar, Oberoi Shehrazad, Oberoi Philae Nile
Oberoi Corporation Ltd
Mena House Hotel,
Ahram
Tel: 383-3222
Ra
Eastmar Travel
23B Ismael Muhamed
Zamalik
Tel: 735-3087
Sunboat IV
Abercrombie & Kent
18 Youssef el buindi
El Boustan Centre, 10th floor
Tel: 393-6255

★★★★
Atlas, Nile Star
Eastmar Travel
23B Ismail Muhamed
Zamalik
Tel: 735-3087
E-mail: eastmar@eis.egnet.net
Accor
8 Abdel-Khaled Saruat Street
Tel: 578-2061
Horus
International Company for Hotels
and Nile Cruises
23B Ismail Muhammed
Zamalik
Tel: 735-0675/6
LTI Anabella, Pasha, Sudan
Seti First Travel
16 Shari', Ismail Muhamed
Tel: 736-9820-22

★★★
Abu Simbel, Nile Delta
Hapi Travel and Tourism Company
17 Qasr al-Nil
Tel: 393-3611/93, 393-3562
7- and 14-day cruises
Karnak, Pyramids, Queen Nefertiti, Akhenaten
Pyramids Nile Cruise Company
Hotel Les 3 Pyramides
229 al-Amam,
Tel: 583-5557
Nile Ark
Belle Epoque Cruises,
7 Okba Street, Dokki
Tel: 761-5307

Where to Stay

In 3-, 4- and 5-star hotels payment for non-Egyptians and non-resident foreigners must be made in foreign currency, by credit card, or in Egyptian currency with a bank exchange receipt. Motels do not exist in Egypt. Booking a hotel as part of a package reduces the rates considerably.

Abu Simbel

★★★★
Nefertari Abu Simbel
Abu Simbel
Tel: 400-508 Fax: 400-510
For those who want to spend longer on the site than the one or two hours usually allowed for an excursion, an overnight stay is the answer. About 400metres/yds from the temple, set in a garden, The Nefertari offers smallish air-conditioned rooms and a swimming pool. In winter it is advisable to book in advance.

★★★
Nobaleh Ramesses
Abu Simbel
Tel: 400-294 Fax: 400-381
Although located further away, about 1.5km (1 mile), from the site, this hotel has larger, more comfortable rooms,equipped with air-conditioning and a fridge.

Alexandria

★★★★★
El-Salamlik Palace Hotel
El-Montazah Palace
Tel: 547-7999 Fax: 547-3585
E-mail: salamek@sangiovanni.com
The recently renovated Salamlik (guest house) of the Montazah palace provides peaceful rooms in great surroundings.

Helnan Palestine Hotel
Montazah palace grounds
Tel: 547-3500 Fax: 547-3378
E-mail: reshp@helnan.com
An Alexandrian institution, very popular with ex-pat residents and local families, who come on weeekends to enjoy the peaceful bay and to swim in a slightly cleaner sea. Rooms are worn, but the view makes it worthwhile.
Sheraton Montazah
Corniche Muntazah
Tel: 548-0550 Fax: 540-1331
The most upmarket of Alex's hotels, with a pool and private beach across the road. A long drive from the centre, near Montazah.

★★★★
Paradise Inn Metropole
52 Shari' Saad Zaghlul
Tel: 482-1465
Recently renovated period hotel with lots of atmosphere, mouldings and antiques in the reception, now also comfortable beds and all mod cons. Much cheaper than the Cecil. Highly recommended.
Sofitel Alexandria Cecil Hotel
16 Midan Saad Zaghlul
Tel: 483-7173 Fax: 483-6401
The Cecil is haunted by the ghosts of Noel Coward, Somerset Maugham and others, including Lawrence Durrell who immortalised it in *The Alexandria Quartet*. The glamour has long gone, but the charm of the place, and views over the bay still pull the romantics. The coffee shop is a popular rendezvous for a cup of tea.

★★★
Agami Palace
El-Bittash Beach
Agami
Tel: 433-0230
Spacious but basic rooms with balconies overlooking the beach and swimming pool.

★★
Ailema
21 Shari' Amin Fikry, Downtown Tel: 482-7011
Old-style, adequate rooms in a quiet, downtown backwater, overlooking Ramlah Square.

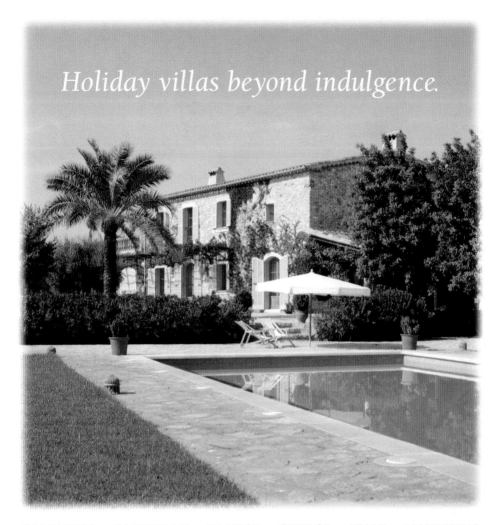

Holiday villas beyond indulgence.

BALEARICS ~ CARIBBEAN ~ FRANCE ~ GREECE ~ ITALY ~ MAURITIUS
MOROCCO ~ PORTUGAL ~ SCOTLAND ~ SPAIN

If you enjoy the really good things in life, we offer the highest quality holiday villas with the utmost privacy, style and true luxury. You'll find each with maid service and most have swimming pools.

For 18 years, we've gone to great lengths to select the very best villas at all of our locations around the world.

Contact us for a brochure on the destination of your choice and experience what most only dream of.

 INTERNATIONAL
CHAPTERS

Toll Free: 1 866 493 8340
International Chapters, 47-51 St. John's Wood High Street, London NW8 7NJ. Telephone: +44(0)20 7722 0722
email: info@villa-rentals.com www.villa-rentals.com

Live it up!

Ride through the past in a trishaw and be welcomed into the future by lions.

For the time of your life, live it up in Singapore!
Explore historic back lanes and shop in malls of the future. Take part in a traditional tea ceremony at a quaint Peranakan house, then tee off for a birdie at one of our challenging golf courses.

Spice things up with some hot Pepper Crab and unwind in a world-class spa. Join a Feng Shui Tour to harness positive energy and later channel it into a night on the town. Come to Singapore and catch the buzz and excitement of Asia's most vibrant city.

Singapore NEW ASIA

www.newasia-singapore.com

For more information, mail to: Singapore Tourism Board, Tourism Court, 1 Orchard Spring Lane, Singapore 247729 or Fax to (65) 736 9423.

Name: _____ Address: _____

Email: _____

Seastar
24 Shari' Amin Fikry
Tel: 480-5343
Modernised spacious rooms,
great value.

★
Piccadilly
11 Shari' al-Hurriya, Downtown
Tel: 493-2839
The lobby of this hotel oozes faded
grandeur with slightly tatty Art Deco
furniture and old oil paintings. The
rooms are spacious, light and
clean. Good budget choice.

Unclassified
Acropole,
27 rue Chambre de Commerce
Tel: 480-5980
No stars, but the rooms in this
atmospheric, clean, Greek-owned
pension enjoy the same views
as the much more expensive
Cecil Hotel.

Aswan

★★★★★
Aswan Oberoi
Elephantine Island
Tel: 314-667
Luxurious spa-hotel with a good
swimming pool, set in a garden on
the tip of Elephantine island.
Isis Island
Tel: 317-400
Huge luxurious resort hotel, owned
by the Mubarak family, set on its
own island upriver from Aswan. The
rooms are set in a large landscaped
garden with swimming pool.
Complimentary boats sail regularly
into Aswan town.
Sofitel Old Cataract
Shari' Abtal et Tahrir
Tel: 316-002
For old-style, Agatha Christie
nostalgia and the smell of polished
wood there is nowhere quite like
the Old Cataract in Aswan. Rooms
are cosy and tastefully furnished.
North-wing, Nile-side rooms
overlook the temple on Elephantine
Island. Breakfast is served in the
splendid Moorish room, once the
ball room, and the Belvedere
terrace is still the place to watch
the sunset.

★★★★
Basma
Shari' el-Fanadek
Tel: 310-901/2/3
One of the more recent arrivals in
town, a full-blown resort hotel with
all the modern conveniences you
would expect, including a huge
swimming pool. Most rooms
overlook the river.

Price Guides

Price ranges for double rooms
with bath are:

★	$10–20
★★	$20–30
★★★	$30–100
★★★★	$50–180
★★★★★	$100–400

★★★
Amoun Hotel
Amoun Island
Tel: 313-800
A favourite hotel, now run by Club
Med, with peaceful rooms
overlooking the river and the desert
with the Aga Khan mausoleum. A
great place to relax for a few days,
with good food.
Cleopatra
Shari' Sad Zaghloul
Tel: 324-001
Very clean rooms with phone and
private bathroom, near the *suq*,
with a small pool on the roof.

★★
Abu Simbel
Corniche an-Nil, Downtown
Tel: 302-888
Slightly tatty-looking hotel, but with
spacious and clean rooms, with
little balconies overlooking the Nile.
The hotel can get rather noisy in the
evenings, as locals come to the
hotel to have a beer.
Happi Hotel
Shari' Abtaal at-Tahrir, just off
Corniche
Tel: 314-115
Pleasant and clean air-conditioned
rooms, some overlooking the Nile,
some overlooking the *souq* area.
Clients get a reduction to use the
swimming pool of the nearby
Cleopatra hotel.

Philae
Corniche an-Nil
Tel: 312-089
The rooms in this hotel are clean
and recently modernised, but
choose a room on the front with
Nile views – back rooms are less
pleasant and pretty airless.
Ramesses
Shari' Abtal et-Tahrir
Tel: 324-000
Modern hotel with well-kept rooms
all with phone and private
bathroom, offering very good value.

★
New Abu Simbel
northern end of the Corniche in the
Atlas area
Tel: 312-143
Modern carpeted rooms with private
bathrooms, some with balconies
overlooking the Nile, and a pleasant
garden terrace where cool beers
are served.

Asyut

★★★★
Badr Touristic Hotel
Shari' et-Thallaga
Tel: 329-811
So-called best hotel in town,
though both the modern
architecture and tasteless décor
can be depressing.

★★★
Assiutel
146 Shari' en-Nil
Tel: 312-121
Comfortable rooms and all
amenities.

Cairo

★★★★★
Cairo Marriott
Shari' Saray al Gazirah 33
Zamalik.
Tel: 735-8888
E-mail: marriott@link.com.eg
The Marriott Hotel has built this
facility around the former palace
of the Khedive Ismail, built to
commemorate the opening of the
Suez Canal in 1869. Antique
furniture graces the halls and public
rooms. The Eugénie's Lounge, an

elegant cocktail bar in the former rooms of the Empress Eugénie, and the Garden Promenade, the open air café in the Khedive Ismail's garden make this a good place to recover from Cairo's hustle and bustle. There are several other restaurants and the popular Harry's Pub.

Conrad International
1191 Corniche al-Nil, Bulaq
Tel: 850-8000
Fax: 580-8080
The ideal business hotel in Cairo, located beside the World trade Centre, and certainly one of the most luxurious in town. If offers fantastic views over the Nile and excellent service.

El-Gazirah Sheraton
Shari' Madis Quaset al-Fhawrg
Gazirah
Tel: 736-1333
South of the Cairo Opera House, on the southern tip of the island, the Gazirah Sheraton has excellent Nile views. In summer there are several outdoor riverside restaurants. The later Oriental show at the nightclub usually has one of Cairo's best belly dancers, while the Kebabgy al-Gazirah restaurant offers excellent Middle Eastern food. Has an excellent view of the Nile.

Four Seasons
35 Shari' al Giza, Giza
Tel: 573-1212 Fax: 568-1616
Cairo's newest five star hotel, the Four Seasons, lives up to its name, and is one of the city's most sumptuous hotels. The large, airy and elegant rooms command glorious views over the Pyramids, Cairo's Zoo and the Nile. The staff are attentive and the service is excellent. Spa, Wellness Centre with wide range of well-being treatments, sauna, sophisticated exercise room and outdoor swimming pool.

Mena House Oberoi
end of Shari' al-Haram
Pyramids Road
Giza
Tel: 383-3222 Fax: 383-7777
E-mail: obmhobc@oberoi.com.eg
An historic landmark refurbished by the Oberoi chain, the Mena House is the only hotel in Egypt that has a golf course. The rooms in the 19th-century khedival hunting lodge are particularly recommended, as they are tastefully decorated with antiques, But most rooms are in the less-characterful modern garden wing. The elegant Moghul Room is the best Indian restaurant in town, with live music. Outlets include: the Greenery Coffeeshop, a buffet in the garden; Khan al Khalili, a coffeeshop featuring international and Middle-Eastern entrées; the Mogul Room offering Indian food and one of the best restaurants in Egypt; the Rubayyat, the main dining room with continental and Middle-Eastern meals and live entertainment. There are also a large number of different bars and nightclubs. Even if you are not staying in the Mena House Oberoi, lunch by the pool is strongly recommended after a visit to the Giza Pyramids.

Price Guides

Price ranges for double rooms with bath are:

★	$10–20
★★	$20–30
★★★	$30–100
★★★★	$50–180
★★★★★	$100–400

Le Meridien Heliopolis
51 Shari' Oruba
Heliopolis.
Tel: 290-5055 Fax: 290-8533
One of Cairo's best hotels, a short ride from the airport, offers luxurious accommodation and a selection of excellent restaurants, including the Pool restaurant and Marco Polo, where Italian dishes have a delicate touch of the Orient.

Nile Hilton
Corniche
Maydan Tahrir
Tel: 578-0444/578-0666
E-mail: rhilton@internetegypt.com
This was one of the first international hotels in Cairo, the Hilton, located on the Nile in the city centre, has an authentic ancient Egyptian statue in the lobby. Abu Ali's Café serves *sheesha*, green tea, and light snacks on the terrace and is a popular meeting place in downtown Cairo. Jackie's is one of the best discos in town, and when it closes the casino continues. The Safari Bar on the first floor offers cosy armchairs, a nostalgic atmosphere and good cocktails, while the Taverne du Champs de Mars, a genuine Art Nouveau Pub shipped in pieces from Brussels, is a more casual place for drinks and snacks.

Swissotel Cairo as-Salam Hotel
Shari' Abd al-Hamid Badawi
Heliopolis
Tel: 297-4000 Fax: 297-6037
Email: Swisscai@link
Peaceful and elegant hotel set in a garden with swimming pool, offering large and airy rooms with all mod cons. Perfect for those who want to see some of the Art Deco architecture in Heliopolis.

★★★★
Atlas Zamalik
20, Shari' ad-Duwal al-Arabiya
Muhandesseen
Tel: 346-5782
Modern hotel in this upcoming part of town with a swimming pool on the roof and one of the most popular discotheques in town. All business facilities.

Golden Tulip Flamenco Hotel
2 Shari' Al-Gezirah al-Wusta
Tel: 735-0815
E-mail: flamenco@nite.com
Modern hotel in a quiet, tree-lined street in the residential part of Zamalik, with some rooms overlooking the Nile and even the Pyramids on a clear day. The Florencia restaurant serves excellent paellas.

★★★
Cosmopolitan
1, Shari' Ibn Tahlab
Downtown
Tel: 392-3845 Fax: 393-3531
A grand Art Nouveau building offering spacious, comfortable rooms with all modcons. Surprisingly quiet.

Horus House
21, Shari' Ismail Muhamed
Zamalik
Tel: 340-3977
A home away from home, the Horus

is often booked up by returning guests. The restaurant offers a good-value lunch, popular with older residents. Book well in advance.

Odeon Palace
6 Shari' Abdel Hamid, Qasr an-Nil
Tel: 577-6637
Perfectly located budget option in downtown Cairo, with modern clean and airy rooms. The rooftop terrace is a popular meeting place at night serving cold Stella beers.

President
22, Shari' Dr. Taha Hussein
Zamalik
Tel: 735-0652 Fax: 736-1752
More like a four-star hotel, this efficient, friendly hotel with a good business centre is a well kept secret in a quiet Zamalik street. The Cellar Bar, always crowded, serves good *mezze*.

Umm Kulthoum
5, Shari' Abu al Feda, Zamalik
Tel: 735-5317
The villa of the late Umm Kulthoum, one of Egypt's greatest singers, had to make way for a not very attractive tower block. However her memory lives on, as a hotel in her name was recently opened in the tower, which should appease her many fans. The lobby is filled with her memorabilia and the only music on offer is her passionate love songs. The clean, comfortable rooms overlook the Nile.

Saqqara Country Club & Hotel
Zawit Abu Moslam, Saqqarah Road
Tel: 381-1415 Fax: 381-0571
This is more a club than a hotel with many outdoor sporting facilities, including excellent riding stables, but the rooms are charming and comfortable, far from the noisy city centre.

Saqqara Palm Club
Saqqarah Road, Badrashein
Tel: 013-221-187 Fax: 220-791
A small resort type-hotel near the Saqqara Step pyramid, in the middle of the Egyptian countryside. The rooms are set in gorgeous lush gardens in the middle with a large lagoon-style swimming pool. This is the perfect escape from the traffic jams, and a good base from which to explore nearby Memphis, Saqqarah and Giza.

Victoria
66 Shari' al-Gumhuriya, Midan Ramesses
Tel: 589-2290
Another old-style hotel between Midan Opera and Ramesses Station, with faded spacious rooms furnished with dark brown furniture. Young Egyptian couples use the shaded garden to discuss their married future over a cold drink.

Windsor
19, Shari' Alfi Bey, Downtown
Tel: 591-5277
Email: wdoss@link.com
For nostalgic souls, this is a place to sniff a Cairo that is no more. Faded but clean rooms and friendly service. The bar, with its old waiters, sunken sofas and heavy air, is an institution.

★★
Ambassador
31 26th-of-July Street, Downtown
Tel: 578-3225
Moderate hotel in an apartment block in downtown Cairo. The large, comfortable rooms on the higher floors command great views over the minarets of central Cairo. All rooms have air-conditioning, minibar and satellite TV.

An-Nil Zamalik
21 Shari' Maahad as-Swisri, Zamalik
Tel: 735-1846
Quiet hotel in the heart of Zamalik. The modern rooms are comfortable and equipped with bathroom, phone, satellite TV and air conditioning. Some of the rooms have a balcony on the Nile, the others overlook Zamalik square.

El Hussein,
Maydan al-Hussein
Al Azhar
Tel: 591-8664/591-8089
A noisy affair during religious festivals, this hotel is the place to stay if you want to get lost in Cairo's old city. Clean, basic rooms.

Lotus
7th floor
12 Shari' Talaat Harb
Tel: 575-0627
Good value and as central as it gets. Airy, clean rooms with balconies and air-conditioning.

Tulip
3 Maydan Talaat Harb
Tel: 392-3884
Opposite Groppi's patisserie, this long-established budget hotel is still going strong, offering large clean rooms to young travellers, with private or shared bathrooms. Some overlook the elegant square which can be noisy at night – the ones at the back are quieter.

★
Garden City House
23, Shari' Kamal ad-Din Saleh
Garden City
Tel: 794-4969
Pleasant, dusty pension, popular with scholars and archaeologists, with large clean rooms. Half board is compulsory but meal times provide a good opportunity to meet some interesting people.

Mayfair
9, Shari' Aziz Osman
Zamalik
Tel: 735-7315
Tranquil hotel with tidy rooms overlooking a tree-lined street. Pleasant terrace for an afternoon drink.

Pension Roma
169 Shari' Muhamad Farid
Downtown
Tel: 391-1088
This is a popular hotel with travellers. All rooms have shiny wooden floors and old-style furniture. Book ahead.

Unclassified
Berlin Hotel
2 Shari' Shawarby, Downtown
Tel: 395-7502
Berlinhotelcairo@hotmail.com
Large double or triple rooms as well as dormitories in a quieter back street of downtown Cairo. The Art Deco rooms still retain many period features including the furniture and bathrooms, but modernity has arrived in the form of internet access and a good sauna.

Magic Hotel
10 Shari' al-Bustan, Downtown
Tel: 579-5918
magichotel@hotmail.com
The Magic is an increasingly popular option for budget travellers,

with clean and comfortable rooms as well as a communal satellite TV lounge and Internet access.

New Palace
17 Shari' Suleyman al-Halibi, Downtown
Tel: 575-1322
newpalacehotel@hotmail.com
Large airy rooms in the heart of Cairo with very friendly young staff. The rooftop bar is a popular meeting place in downtown Cairo and the atmosphere is always lively.

Pension Oxford
32, Shari' Talaat Harb
Downtown
Tel: 392-2659
One of the cheapest and oldest of the backpacker haunts with more or less clean dormitory beds, and belly-dancers and Italian hairdressers amongst the residents. The Oxford has a lot of history, but is now even more run down than it ever was.

Ismailia House
1 Maydan Tahrir, 8th floor
Tel: 356-3122
Recent arrival and already very popular with backpackers on account of its clean white rooms, many communal bathrooms and most of all its view.

Luxor

East Bank
★★★★★
Movenpick Jolie Ville Luxor
Crocodile Island, 6km (4 miles) out of town
Tel: 374-855
E-mail: mpluxor@Intouch.com
The best hotel in town, Swiss-managed, with excellent service, good food, relaxed atmosphere and simple, comfortable rooms set in a splendid garden, most overlooking a beautiful stretch of the Nile.

Sheraton Hotel & Resort
Shari' Khaled Ibn Walid
Tel: 374-544
Faded luxury hotel which nevertheless offers spacious rooms overlooking the Nile or bungalows in a shaded garden. The Italian restaurant in the garden with pond inhabited by pelicans and flamingos is a popular choice in Luxor.

Sofitel Winter Palace
Shari' Corniche en-Nil
Tel: 380-422
Old-style hotel, recently refurbished to some of its former splendour. The rooms in the old building have more character than the new garden wing, but service everywhere can be slow at times.

Sonesta St George
Shari' Corniche an-Nil
Tel: 282-575
One of the newer luxury options in Luxor, perhaps built in a disputable style, but offering good value for money, as well as good views over the Nile and all modern conveniences.

Price Guides

Price ranges for double rooms with bath are:

★	$10–20
★★	$20–30
★★★	$30–100
★★★★	$50–180
★★★★★	$100–400

★★★★
Akhtetaton Village (Club Med)
Shari' Khaled Ibn Walid
Tel: 380-850
Comfortable rooms set in a garden on the Nile, usual Club Med amenities, with sport facilities and very good food.

Mercure Luxor Hotel
10, Shari' Maabad Luxor
Tel: 580-944
The old-Etap hotel offers adequate and clean rooms though little atmosphere. Half the rooms overlook the river and west bank mountains. The hotel's terrace is a popular place to come for a sunset drink.

★★★
Emilio Hotel
Shari' Yousef Hassan
Tel: 373-570
This is a very good mid-range hotel with comfortable rooms that are equipped with all mod cons. There is a rooftop pool and sundeck. Book in advance in winter, popular with tour groups.

Philippe
Shari' Labib Habashy
Tel: 372-284
Excellent three-star hotel offering spotless air-con rooms, TV, fridge and some balconies. The pleasant roof terrace has a small pool and bar. Recommended, but book ahead, especially in winter.

★★
Horus
Shari' al-Maabad
opposite Luxor Temple
Tel: 372-165
Rooms overlook either the temple or the lively souq. Central, well-kept, with recently renovated bathrooms.

Mina Palace
Shari' Corniche en-Nil
Tel: 372-074
Good value and friendly, on the Corniche, recently refurbished air-con rooms and private bathrooms. Some corner rooms have balconies overlooking the Nile and Luxor Temple.

West Bank
Unclassified
Amoun al-Gazira
Geziret al-Bairat (near the ferry landing, left at the Mobil petrol station)
Tel: 310-912
Pleasant family-run hotel in a standard modern building overlooking the Theban hills and fertile countryside. The rooms are simply furnished, but spotless and comfortable, some with private bathroom. From the roof terrace you can watch the stars. A gorgeous sunset, breakfast and tea are served in a pretty shaded garden.

Habu Hotel
opposite Medinat Habu
Nag Lolah, West Bank
Tel: 372-477
Very basic rooms but popular for the price, the village atmosphere and a spectacular view over Madinet Habu temple from the large upper terrace.

Mersam Hotel
also known as Shaykh Ali's Hotel, opposite the Tombs of the Nobles, West Bank
Tel: 372-403

In 1881 the Abdul Rassoul family discovered the Deir el Bahari cache of royal mummies, now on show in the Cairo Museum. The late Shaykh Ali's son now runs this simple hotel. The tranquil garden has views over green fields.

Nur al-Quma
(on the corner opposite the ticket office, no phone yet)
This new addition to the West Bank hotels is run by an Egyptian and his French friend. There are only a few rooms, looking out over ancient Thebes and the sugarcane fields, elegantly but simply decorated with local palm-frond furniture and colourful fabrics. Breakfast is served in the café-restaurant in the quiet shaded garden.

Pharaoh's
near the ticket office on the West Bank
Tel: 374-924
This is the only mid-range hotel on this side of the Nile with clean rooms, some with private bathrooms and a pleasant garden bar/restaurant.

Al-Minya

★★★★
Mercure Nefertiti/Aton
Shari' Corniche en-Nil
Tel: 341-515
Most upmarket hotel in the area with comfortable rooms, some facing the Nile, and a swimming pool in the garden. Functioning restaurant and bar.

★★
El-Shatee (Beach Hotel)
31 Shari' al-Gumhuriya
Tel: 362-307
Pleasant and clean rooms with fan or air-conditioning.

Lotus
1, Shari' Port Said
Tel: 364-500
Clean rooms with fans and a good bar-restaurant frequented by beer-drinking locals.

Where to Eat

Cairo and Alexandria have a good selection of restaurants, but smaller towns have a rather limited choice. Set menus and buffets in hotels offer an international cuisine with the occasional Egyptian dish, but Egyptian food is definitely worth trying out. Apart from the regular fare, 5-star hotels often fly in European chefs for week-long ethnic extravaganzas. Hotel restaurants will only be mentioned here if they are really notable. In recent years prices have risen steeply in Egyptian restaurants, and a good meal can cost almost as much as in London or New York although the more basic restaurants are still a bargain. Cheaper restaurants often don't serve alcohol, while more upmarket places may only serve the much more expensive imported wines. Local Stella beer is good, and is often preferred to Stella Export and the new Stella Premium.

Drinking Notes

The traditional **hot and cold drinks** served in coffeehouses are delicious and thought to be health-giving, including yansun (anis), helba (fenugreek) and kankadeh (hibiscus). The usual idea of American coffee is instant Nescafé. If you want decaffeinated coffee then you will have to bring your own.

Fresh juices such as orange, mango, strawberry, pomegranate, lime or whatever, depending on the season, are available in juice bars everywhere *except* in major hotels.

Internationally formulated drinks made and bottled locally under licence include a range of Schweppes and Canada Dry mixers, Coca-Cola, Seven-Up, Sport, and Pepsi-Cola.

Middle Eastern Food

Egyptians, like other Arabs, enjoy eating *mezze* whilst chatting around a table with family and friends. *Mezze* are hors d'oeuvres, salads and dips, served as a starter with drinks or as a meal. Dishes keep on arriving, hot or cold, an endless variety, and are eaten with the fingers or scooped up in pieces of flat bread. For newcomers, there follows a list of the most common dishes:
tahinah (a sesame paste mixed with water, oil and lemon juice) served as a dip or a sauce
baba ghanough is tahinah mixed with garlic and roasted eggplant
hummus is a paste of chick peas, garlic, *tahinah* and lemon topped with parsley, and sometimes served topped with tiny bits of fried lamb
ful mesdames is a stew of fava beans, Egypt's national dish, served with egg, meat, yoghurt or white cheese
tamiya are deep-fried fava-bean balls
kibda is fried chopped calf's or lamb's liver
torshi are pickled vegetables
salata baladi is chopped lettuce, tomato and cucumber with lots of parsley and lemon
waraa eynab are stuffed vine leaves
kofta is minced meat
kibbeh is a fried ball of cracked wheat stuffed with ground beef.

The local **beer** is Stella, a lager that comes in two varieties: Stella Export and ordinary Stella, which is less sweet and therefore usually preferred. Other beers are brewed in Egypt. The adventurous may encounter a mild home-brew called buza, which is recorded to have been made in the Third Dynasty.

Long established vineyard Gianaclis in the Delta produces red, white and rosé wines that are drinkable. The other local wine – red and white – Obelisque is made in al-Boura from a good-quality Italian grape concentrate. Egyptians were making **wine** even earlier. Reds include Omar Khayyam, Pharaohs, and Château Gianaclis; there is one rosé, called Rubi d'Egypte. Among the whites – Gianaclis Village, Cru des Ptolemées, Castel Nestor, Nefertiti, and Reine Cléopatre – Gianaclis Village (ask for Qaryah) is the driest and is preferred with fish or seafood. Reine Cléopatre (ask for Kliobatra), sweeter and fruitier, is a suitable accompaniment to turkey or veal. Caution is advised when dining out, however, since Egyptian wine has only recently recovered from several years of faulty manufacture and quality is still apt to vary from bottle to bottle. If there is a risk of spoiling an evening, the worst should be sent back immediately. Mediocre French or Italian wine is available in the major hotels, at prices roughly 10 times their maximum value on the western market.

Imported spirits are available, although they are fairly expensive. Local spirits are quite popular among Egyptians. They include several kinds of brandy and various versions of **zibeeb** or **araq**, the Arab World's heady and dangerous version of ouzo, but beware!

Alexandria

EGYPTIAN/LEVANTINE

Tikka Grill
Al-Kashafa el-Baharia Club
no.26 on the Corniche
Tel. 480-5114
Excellent fish kebabs and meat dishes. Good views over the bay.
Hassan Bleik
opposite 18 Shari' Saad Zaghloul
Tel: 484-0880
Old fashioned and cheap Lebanese restaurant with a large menu of delicacies including stuffed pigeon and chicken with almonds. Lunchtime only.
Mohamed Ahmed
17 Shari' Shakour
Tel: 483-3576
By far the best *ful* and *tamia* in town, known as the Great Pyramid of Alexandria. No alcohol.

SEAFOOD

Adoura
33 Shari' Bayram al-Tonsi
Tel: 480-0405
Popular cheap outdoor restaurant in a quiet back street with an excellent range of fresh fish, but no alcohol. They even have a sister branch in Brooklyn, New York these days.
Fish Market
Al-Kashafa al-Baharia Club
no.26 on the Corniche
Tel: 480-5114
More upmarket fish restaurant with a huge display of fresh fish cooked the way you want it. Good service, excellent salad bar and a perfect view of the harbour.
Samakmak
92 Shari' Ahmed Orabi,
Muhandesseen
Tel: 347-8232
One of the best fish restaurants in town, serving a selection of the freshest fish or seafood. You choose from the display and then discuss how you want it cooked. All dishes are served with superb mezze and Oriental rice or bread. Finish the meal like the locals do, by smoking a digestive sweet sheesha (waterpipe).
Sea Gull
al-Maks, on the road to Agami
Tel: 445-5575
Famous fish restaurant in a mock medieval castle with a playground for children. Lobster and shrimps are a speciality.
Zephyrion
41 Shari' Khalid ibn Walid, Abu Qir
Tel: 560-1319
The only reason to venture to Abu Qir is to go to this great fish restaurant, perched over the Mediterranean and run since 1929 by Greeks. Very busy at weekends with Alexandrian families.

COFFEEHOUSES/BARS

Athinelos
21 Maydan Sad Zaghlul
Tel: 482-0421
This is an old-fashioned patisserie, nightclub and pleasant restaurant. Levantine and Mediterranean fare.

Cap d'Or
4 Shari' Adib
off Shari' Saad Zaghlul
Tel: 483-5177
Wonderful art nouveau bar serving the best squid stew in town and good fried fish. Difficult to find, but it attracts a loyal crowd of lcoals and ex-pats who come to chat over a beer and vintage French pop.
Pastroudis
39, Shari' al-Hurriya
Tel: 492-9609
Another famous patisserie with a large terrace overlooking the excavations at Kom al-Dikka. The dark red plush restaurant is perfect for that illicit rendez-vous or for some typical Alexandrian fare.If you are in Alexandria, this is a must.
Spitfire Bar
7 Shari' al-Bursa al-Qadima
Tel: 480-6503
Smoky and fun rock-and-roll bar with walls decorated with interesting memorabilia. Attracts a mixed crowd of local die-hards, ex-pats and a few American sailors if the fleet is in town.
Trianon
Maydan Sad Zaghlul
Tel: 482-0986
Wood-panelled elegant restaurant with Mediterranean-Levantine food and occasionally live music. The next-door patisserie a large, good value breakfast.

GREEK/EUROPEAN

Elite
43 Shari' Safia Zaghlul
Tel: 482-3592
Endless menu of Greek and Egyptian dishes and windows with a view on the world. Cheap.
Mamma Mia
Sheraton Hotel
Muntazah
Tel: 548-0550
This is a good Italian restaurant specialising in fresh pastas and pizzas, served in a kitsch Italian décor.
Santa Lucia
40, Shari' Safia Zaghlul
Tel: 482-0332
Not as glamorous as it used to be,

but the staff tries hard to keep up standards and the food is still far better than in many places in Alexandria.

Aswan

Aswan Moon
Corniche an-Nil
Tel: 326-108
Floating restaurant on the Nile which attracts many *fellucciyas*. Beer, fresh fruit juices and standard Egyptian fare in a relaxing atmosphere.

Al-Misri Tour Restaurant
Shari' al-Matar, off Shari' al-Suq.
Not easy to find but everyone knows the restaurant as it serves the best *kofta* and kebab in town. The décor is Islamic kitsch and there is a family room for couples at the back.

La Trattori
Isis hotel, Corniche an-Nil
Tel: 315-500
Standard Italian restaurant, but still a good option when you get tired of too much kebab.

Darna
New Cataract Hotel,
Shari' Abtal al Tahrir
Tel: 316-002
Hotel restaurant in a mock Egyptian house serving a large buffet of mainly Egyptian specialities.

Nubian Restaurant
Essa island south of Elephantine, free shuttle boat from the dock opposite the Egypt Air office
The Nubian Restaurant offers a three-course set menu with a folklore show of regional music and dance. The food is tasty and usually includes grilled meats and Nubian spicy stews, but you will probably be surrounded by tour groups.

Old Cataract Terrace
Old Cataract Hotel
Tel: 316-001
English tea is served on the terrace from 4pm onwards, following an old tradition of watching the sun set on the West Bank. However, as this is has become a very popular way to end the day for all visitors to Aswan, the terrace is closed to non-residents when the hotel is full.

Cairo

EGYPTIAN/LEVANTINE

Abou Shakra
69 Shari' Qasr al-Aini
Tel: 364-8811
Known as 'the King of the Kebab' this is one of the best places to eat kebab, and prices are very reasonable.

Alfi Bey
3 Shari' al-Alfy
Downtown
Tel: 577-1888
Cheap 1940s restaurant with wonderful décor, antiquated waiters and traditional Levantine fare. No alcohol.

Andrea's Chicken and Fish Restaurant
(on the left bank of the Maryutiya Canal heading towards Kerdassa, Giza)
Tel: 383-1133
Some of the best *mezze* in town and certainly the best grilled chicken. Mostly outdoors under the trellices, with simple wooden and bamboo furniture. Recommended.

Arabesque
6 Shari' Qasr an-Nil
Downtown
Tel: 574-7898
Even though this restaurant with adjacent art gallery serves some of the best French food in town, it is worth trying the Egyptian dishes like *meloukhia* or grilled pigeon with rice. Whatever your main course, leave space for their Umm Ali dessert.

Casino des Pigeons
On the Nile south of Abbas Bridge, Giza.
Specialities are pigeon, cooked in many ways, and *mezze*.

Egyptian Pancake House
Between Shari' al-Azhar and Maydan al-Husayn.
Delicious and cheap *fateers*, a cross between a pizza and a pancake that can be sweet or savoury. No alcohol.

Felfella
15, Shari' Hoda Shaarawi
Tel: 392-2833
The original Felfella restaurant, which now has several branches

Street Food

Streetfood in Egypt is often delicious but take care if your stomach is unacclimatised. *Koshari*, a mixture of rice, macaroni, fried onions, lentils and chickpeas, topped with a spicy tomato sauce, is popular, as are *ful* and *tamia*. A wide variety of sandwiches are available, filled with *pasturma* (a local dried meat), white cheese, chopped liver, kidneys and *tameya*. Roast corn, chicken soup and baked sweet potatoes are popular snacks in winter.

in Cairo and other Egyptian cities. Started as a cheap vegetarian restaurant, it still serves plenty of cheap vegetable dishes and *mezze* beside the traditional *kofta, kebab* and stuffed pigeon. The Cafeteria around the corner serves good *ful* and *tamia* sandwiches.

Al-Omdah
6 Shari' al-Gazair (next door to the Atlas Hotel).
Tel: 345-2387
One of the best places to eat a superior version of *kushari,* the national dish of rice, macaroni, lentils, fried onions and a spicy tomato sauce.

SEAFOOD

Flying Fish
166 Shari' an-Nil, Agouza
Tel: 749 3234
Aquariums filled with fish, stained glass windows with mermaids and candlelight make for a relaxed ambience, in which an extensive menu of fish dishes is served, from Egyptian fish kebab to British-style fish fingers. Excellent.

FRENCH

Champollion
Meridien Le Caire Hotel
Corniche al-Nil, Garden City
Tel: 362 1717

Cairo's finest French cuisine served in plush surroundings, overlooking the Nile, with a few specialities for the weight conscious.

Justine
Four Corners
4 Shari' Hassan Sabri, Zamalik
Tel: 736-2961
Creative French cuisine and a cosy luxurious atmosphere in the most upmarket of the Four Corners restaurants.

ITALIAN/MEDITERRANEAN

La Piazza
Four Corners, 4 Shari' Hassan Sabri, Zamalik
Tel: 736-2961
Good and easy-going Italian restaurant with fresh pasta and superb desserts like profiteroles and chocolate tiramisu.

INTERNATIONAL

Cue Club
28 Road 7 (parallel to Road 9), Maadi
Tel: 378-3300
Decorated as a Bedouin café with palm fronds and low sofas, you imagine yourself more in Sinai than in Maadi. The Tex Mex food served is excellent and the service is friendly and efficient. This can make for a nice change after one kebab too many

Estoril
12 Shari' Talaat Harb
Downtown
Tel: 574-3102
Tucked away in a passage, the Estoril has been going for many years and has a loyal clientele of Cairene actors and intellectuals as well as expats.

Le Steak
Le Pacha 1901 boat
Shari' Saray el-Gezirah
Zamalik
Tel: 735-6730
Excellent mezze served with an apéritif and those with a larger appetite can tuck into a tender steak with several sauces or grilled seabass.

Le Tabasco
8 Amman Square, Muhandesseen
Tel: 336-5583
One of the trendiest bar-restaurants serving modern Mediterranean dishes accompanied by swinging music. After 10pm the music and air-con are turned on full, and in come Cairo's young and beautiful.

ASIAN

Buo Khao
9 Road 151, Maadi
Tel: 350-0126
Genuine and well-prepared Thai food served in the typical blue and white china.

Peking
14 Shari' Saraya el-Ezbekiya
Downtown
Tel: 591-2381
Well-prepared Chinese food served in a pleasant décor. The strange house speciality is Irish coffee served with much drama and accompanied by taped bird-song.

Taj Mahal
5 Shari' Lebanon
Muhandesseen
Tel: 302-5669
Some of the best Indian food in town is served in a stark black and white room. Vegetarians will be particularly happy with the wide selection of vegetable curries.

CAFÉS/BARS

Absolut
10 Amman Square, Muhandesseen
Tel: 336-5583
Trendy bar taking the overflow of the next door restaurant Le Tabasco, run by the same owner.

Cairo Jazz Club
197, 26th-of-July Street, Aguza, opposite the Balloon Theatre
Tel: 345-9939
Cairo's only live jazz venue doesn't only play jazz. Also on offer is reggae, rock and sometimes even classical music, as well as a good table of mezze and simple pastas.

Al Fishawi
Khan al Khalili, just off Maydan al Husayn
Since 1773 they have apparently never closed, and you can see why, This great exotic café in the heart of the souq is a great place, at any time of the day or night, to hang out, have a cup of mint tea or smoke a sheesha (waterpipe). As it is close to the mosque of al Husayn no alcohol is served. It's a great place to watch the entire world go by, or at least half of Cairo.

Deals
2 Shari' al-Maahad al-Swissri
Zamalik
Tel: 736-0502
Tiny bar decorated with vintage film posters is popular with 20- and 30-something expats attracted by the casual atmosphere and good prices. Good mezze.

Groppi
MaydanTalaat Harb
Downtown
Tel: 574-3244
Only vaguely reminiscent of its former grandeur, the tearoom now serves increasingly stale pastries, but the old waiters are still smiling.

Harry's Pub
Cairo Marriott Hotel
Zamalik
Tel: 735-8888
Popular English pub.

Marriott Garden
Cairo Marriott Hotel, Shari' Saray al Gezirah, Zamalik
Tel: 735-8888
The garden of this old palace is an oasis in the city. You can eat, drink, meet people or watch the continuous flow of well-heeled Egyptians and Arabs. Ice creams are served as well as some good sandwiches, pizzas and excellent grilled Egyptian specialities.

Naguib Mahfouz Coffee Shop & Khan el-Khalili Restaurant
5, al-Badestan alley in Khan al Khalili
Tel: 590-3788
The only "upmarket" place in the souq. Less character, more hygienic precautions (equally, the only decent toilets). The coffee shop serves traditional Egyptian hot drinks, fresh juices, water pipes and sweets in an Oriental décor. The restaurant serves mezze and Egyptian cuisine.

Simmonds Coffee Shop
112, 26th-of-July Street
Zamalik
Meeting place for locals, Ethiopian students and foreign correspondents. Good cappuccinos and fresh juices.

Luxor

Brasserie 1886
Winter Palace Hotel
Corniche en-Nil
Tel: 380-422
This smart new restaurant is elegant, though the food is not always up to standard and service can be slow.
Kushari Sayyida Nefisa
Shari' Mustapha Kamel, near the suq. The best *kushari* in town.
La Mamma
Sheraton hotel
Shari' Khaled Ibn Walid
Tel: 374-544
Italian restaurant in a quiet garden with pelicans and ducks, and live accordion music in the evening.
Møvenpick restaurants
Crocodile Island
Tel: 374-855
The pleasant terrace restaurant serves fresh pasta, salads and grills as well as excellent Møvenpick ice-creams. Two indoor restaurants serve a good buffet or expensive French à la carte.
Tutankhamun
At the public ferry landing on the West Bank. Simple but clean serving good food – the chef trained at a five-star restaurant. Worth crossing the Nile for

Culture

Art Galleries

Alef
14 Shari' Mohamed Anis
Zamalik
Tel: 735-3690
Daily 10.30am–2pm and 5–8pm, closed on Sunday
Furniture, lighting and textiles by young artisans, often inspired by pharaonic and Islamic motifs.
Arabesque
6, Shari' Qasr an-Nil
Downtown
Tel: 574-8677
Open daily noon–4pm and 7pm–midnight. Smart art gallery with works by Egyptian painters
Atelier du Caire
2, Shari' Karim ad-Dawla
Downtown
Tel: 574-6730
Open daily 10am–1pm and 6–10pm, closed Friday. Egyptian and foreign artists.
Cairo-Berlin Art Gallery
17, Shari' Youssef al-Guindi
Bab al-Louq
Tel: 393-1764
Open Mon–Sat noon–3pm and 5–8pm. Contemporary art from Germany and Egypt.
Centre of Arts, Akhnaton Halls
1 Shari' Maahad as-Swissri
Zamalik
Tel: 735-8211
Often stages very interesting exhibitions.
Hanager Arts Centre
Opera House Grounds, Gazirah
Tel: 735-6861
Open daily 9am–9pm.
Mashrabia
8 Shari' Champollion
Downtown
Tel: 578-4494
Open Sat–Thurs 11am–8pm.
Contemporary Egyptian artists.

Sony Gallery
Adham Center for Television Journalism, American University
Tahrir Square
Tel: 357-5422-4
Open Sun–Thurs 9am–noon.
Photo exhibitions.
Town House Gallery
Shari' Husseyn Pasha, off

Cultural Centres

Cultural centres tend to be very active in Cairo, putting on concerts, lectures, film, theatre and exhibitions. For non-Arabic speakers they may be good places to soak up some Western culture. For programmes check with the daily English-language *Egyptian Gazette*, or the *Al-Ahram* Weekly.
American Cultural Center,
U.S. Embassy
5, Latin America Street
Garden City
Tel: 795-3529
American Research Center in Egypt
2, Midan Simon Bolivar
2nd floor, Garden City
Tel: 794-8237
Excellent library for researchers, lectures, films.
British Council
192, Shari' en-Nil, Agouza
Tel: 347-6118
Centre Français de Culture
1, Shari' Madrasset al-Huquq
al-Faransiya, Mounira
Tel: 795-3725
Egyptian Center for International Cooperation
11, Shari' Shagaret ad-Dorr
Zamalik
Tel: 736-5410
Goethe Institut
5, Shari' Abd al-Salam Arif
Downtown
Tel: 575-9877
Good films and concerts.
Netherlands Institute,
1 Shari' Mahmoud Azmi
Zamalik
Tel: 332-2522
Very interesting lectures every Thursday evening on Egyptian history or archaeology (Sept–June).

Cavafy Museum

Shari' Sharm ash-Shaykh
Alexandria
Housed in this flat for 25 years,
this small museum pays tribute to
Constantine Cavafy (1863–1933),
one of Alexandria's major poets.
Daily 9am–2pm, and on Tue and
Thurs 6–8pm. Closed Mon.

Hahmaud Bassiouri, Downtown
Tel: 575-5901
Open Sat–Wed 10am–2pm, 6–9pm,
Fridays 6–9pm.
The best gallery in town for
contemporary art.

Music

Arabic Music Troupe
(Shirket al Musiqa al Arabia)
Al Galaa Building, Shari' Galaa
This all male choir performs songs
for mixed voices, solo and group.
Cairo Conservatoire, City of Art
Pyramids Road
Tel: 385-1475
Egypt's leading music school has in-
struction in composition, musicolo-
gy, percussion, piano, singing,
string, and wind, and offers
concerts at the Sayed Darwish
Concert Hall.
Cairo Symphony Orchestra
Performs at the Cairo Opera House
every Friday at 8.30pm from Sep-
tember to mid-June.
**Umm Kalthum Classical Arabic
Music Troupe**
Tel: 560-2473
Performs classical Arabic music
from September–May at the Sayed
Darwish Theatre.

Opera

Cairo Opera Company
From 1869 to 1971 Cairo was
regularly visited by foreign opera
troupes, which performed in the
old Opera House. A local
company has performed in
Arabic since 1961, and features
fine individual singers.
Performances are at the Cairo
Opera House.

Ballet & Dance

BALLET

Egyptian ballet dancers are trained
at the National Ballet Institute in
the City of Art complex on the
Pyramids Road. The Institute was
founded with Russian help in 1960
and staffed with Russian experts.
In 1966 the Institute's first
graduating class premiered with *The
Fountain of Bakhchiserai* in the old
Cairo Opera House. The Cairo Ballet
currently includes Russian and
Italian dancers and performs in the
new Opera House.

TRADITIONAL DANCE TROUPES

Folk dance is popular in Egypt and
there are over 150 troupes. The
most prominent are the National
Troupe and Reda Troupe which perform in Cairo and Alexandria.
**Al-Tannoura Egyptian Heritage
Dance Troupe** performs every
Wednesday and Saturday evening
from 9pm (9.30pm in winter) at the
Mausoleum of Al-Ghouri, near the
pedestrian bridge on Shari' al-Azhar.
Islamic Cairo. They perform
a whirling ceremony, a form of
ecstatic mystical dance, though
here it is a cultural performance.

Venues

Balloon Theatre
(Om Kalthum Theatre)
26 July and Shari' Nil
Agouza
Tel: 347-1718.
Various performances, mostly in
Arabic, fill this vast theatre from
October to May. A favourite venue
for folklore troupes.
Cairo Opera House
(The Egyptian Education and Culture
Centre). Gazirah
Tel: 737-0601
In 1971 the Cairo Opera House, an
elegant wooden structure with
perfect acoustics built to celebrate
the opening of the Suez Canal in
1869, burned to the ground along
with the scenery, costumes, and

props of 100 years. Included in the
loss were the costumes for the first
performance of *Aida*. A new opera
house has since opened at the
Gazirah Exhibition Grounds. Built
with the cooperation of the
Japanese, the new facility has three
theatres (the largest has about
1,000 seats), an art gallery,
conference rooms, and a library.
Gumhuria Theatre
12 Shari' Gumhuria
Cairo
Tel: 391-07707
Used as temporary quarters for the
performing arts in Egypt until the
Cairo Opera House was built, the
Gumhuria Theatre is still a venue
for performing arts.

Sound & Light Shows

The Pyramids
Every evening two performances
of a one-hour sound and light
show are held on the Giza
Plateau in front of the Sphinx.
English language shows are held
every night apart from Sundays.
For more information on all the
shows and timetables, tel: 02-
386-3469/385-2880 or check
the website: www.sound-
light.egypt.com. Information is
also given in the monthly
magazine *Egypt Today*.
Photography is permitted but no
video cameras are allowed.
Luxor
The Karnak sound and light show
is one of the best in Egypt. It is
held three or four times a night,
with a daily English language
performance. It lasts around 90
minutes. To get to Karnak in the
evening, hire a taxi, the driver will
wait for you.
The Temple of Isis
This rescued temple, rebuilt on
Aqilqiyyah Island near Aswan,
also has a light and sound show
outlining its history. English
language shows are held every
evening except Sunday and
Thursday. For further details
contact the Tourist Office in
Aswan or use the phone numbers
or website mentioned above.

Theatre

Theatre season in Cairo is September–May. There is a summer season in Alexandria. Curtain is at 9.30pm, 10.30pm during Ramadan. Theatres are dark on Tuesday or Wednesday. Except at the American University or the Brtitish Council, all performances are in Arabic.

Sayed Darwish Concert Hall
Gamal al Din al Afghani, Giza
Tel: 560-2973
There are two Sayed Darwish Concert Halls, one in Cairo and another in Alexandria in the old Alexandria Opera House. This one is used by the ballet, opera company, student performers of the conservatory and the Academy of Arts. It is a showcase for performers of traditional Arabic music and composers working to develop new music with classical themes. There are Classical Arabic Music concerts every Thursday at 9.30pm.

Cairo International Conference Centre (CICC)
Tel: 263-4632/4631/4637
Fax: 263-4640
On Shari' an-Nasr, next to the Monument of the Unknown Soldier and the Sadat Memorial in the northeastern suburb of Madinat Nasr. Set in landscaped grounds, it was presented to Egypt in 1991 as a gift from the Chinese people.

The American University in Cairo Theatre Company
Tel: 357-5436
Performs in Wallace Theatre and Howard Theatre on the AUC campus.

Talia Theatre
Maydan Attaba
Tel: 593-7948
This large company performs modern Arabic plays and western plays in translation in two halls, the Zaki Tolaimat and the Salah Abdel Sabour (Pocket Theatre).

Cairo Puppet Theatre
Azbakkiyah Gardens
Tel: 591-0954.
Dialogue is in Arabic, but the gestures and meanings are not too difficult to follow. Thursday to Saturday at 6.30pm, Friday and Sunday at 11am.

Modern Theatre
Al Salam Theatre
101 Qasr al Alini
Tel: 795-2484, 794-3016.
The hardworking cast performs contemporary Arabic plays in three nightly shows beginning at 5.30pm.

Hilton Ramesses Theatre
Hilton Ramesses Annex
Tel: 574-7435
Regular performances of good Egyptian plays.

Miami Theatre
Shari' Talaat Harb
Tel: 574-5651
Good political satire in Arabic.

Cinemas

Many cinemas are old with poor acoustics. Some new venues have opened in recent years, mostly featuring western films.

Commercial cinemas change their programmes every Monday. Films are listed in the daily *Egyptian Gazette* or in *Al Ahram* weekly.

Cairo Sheraton Cinema
Shari' el-Galaa, Giza
Tel: 7600-6081

Hyatt al-Salam Hotel
65 Shari' Abdel-Hamid Badawi
Heliopolis
Tel: 293-1072
Mainly foreign films

Karim I & II
15, Shari' Emad ed-Din, Downtown
Tel: 592-4830

Ramesses Hilton Cinema
Shari' Corniche en-Nil, Downtown
Tel: 574-7435

Tahrir
112 Shari' Tahrir, Dokki
Tel: 335-4726

Casinos

Gambling is only available for foreigners, and only in 5-star hotels. Most casinos are in Cairo, but there is one at the Hilton International, Luxor. They offer the usual games such as roulette, black jack, *chemin de fer* and slot machines until the early hours. (Note: in Cairo casino is used to describe a teahouse.)

Shopping

Amber

Pale yellow, honey, brown, red, white, and almost-black amber can be found in shops in the Khan al Khalili in the form of beads, necklaces, pipe parts and cane handles. The most famous shop is Mohammed R. El Kady.

Antiquities & Antiques

Pharaonic and Islamic antiquities can only be exported though a few shops. Each sale should be accompanied by a letter of authenticity and permission to export the item. Street vendors selling antiquities are selling fakes, worth purchasing for their own merit, but not as authentic articles. In fact, the best buys in Cairo are European antiques. There are many little antique shops in Cairo around 26th-of-July Street, Shari' Huda Shaarawi in Zamalik, and in Maadi. In Alexandria the Attarin district around the street of the same name is popular with antique-hunters.

Appliqué

The Tentmakers' Bazaar (Souq al Khiyamiyyah), the only covered bazaar left in Cairo, is the place to buy appliqué tenting. This wonderful craft, probably traceable to ancient Egypt, when appliqué banners billowed from the tops of temple gates, comes in Pharaonic and Islamic designs in the form of pillow cases, tablecloths, and wall hangings.

Senouhi on the 5th floor, 54 Shari' Abd el-Khaled Sarwat, Downtown, tel: 391-0955. Good selection of appliqué work and

Jewellery

From modern pharaonic cartouches to antique Turkish, Art Deco and Art Nouveau, jewellery is one of the best buys in Egypt. Gold is sold up to 21 carat for traditional jewellery, and 18 carat for modern jewellery of chains and charms. One of the best places to shop is the Souq al Sagha in the Khan al Khalili. Here you will find traditional designs coveted by the farmers' wives in the form of necklaces, earrings and bracelets. Special shops sell 21 carat handtooled or stamped Nubian designs. Shops that sell gold plate are identified by a large gilded camel in the window. Modern designs are found in jewellery stores throughout the city. Many

are found on Abdel Khalek Sarwat west of Opera Square in Cairo.

In Luxor the jewellery bazaar is just behind Luxor Temple to the north of the Luxor Hotel. In Aswan look for jewellery shops in the suq.

Although gold is the preferred metal today, silver traditionally dominated the market. Designs tend to be large and heavy, and are therefore too costly to be made in gold.

If you are interested in Bedu ware, ask, for these wonderful items are often hidden away in giant sacks under the counter. Silver items are sold in all shopping areas and suqs in Egypt but predominate in the Khan al Khalili in Cairo.

Baskets

Every region has its own distinct type of basket. it is best to buy them in the village souqs. In Aswan, the flat Nubian baskets are still available. The oases crafts shops have an abundance of baskets.

Brass & Copper

The Souq al-Nahhasiin in the Qasabah near Khan al Khalili is the best place in Egypt to buy brass and copper, both antique and modern.

Clothing

The world's finest cotton is Egypt's major export product, but it can be hard to find good quality cotton inside the country. Imported

Exporting

If your items cannot be easily carried it is best to let the merchant handle the export. Items over LE200 may require export licences.

hand-woven carpets from the Wissa Wasef school in Haraniyya.

designer wear and casual wear are now available in the cities. On Safari (branches in the major tourist resorts) sell good, locally-produced cotton holiday wear. The **World Trade Center** on 1191 Corniche en-Nil in Bulaq, Cairo is the largest and shopping mall in Egypt, where most chains are represented.

For lounging around there is nothing like an Egyptian *gallabiyya*. A good place to buy them as well as cotton fabrics is **Ouf** in the alley beside the Madrasah of Barsbay off Shari' al-Muizz, Islamic Cairo. Most popular are red and white striped *gallabiyyas* from the north coast; the most difficult to find are green and orange diamond patterns from Sinai.

Designs or can be made to order in a day. Bedu dresses are handmade. Those from Northern Sinai are cross-stitched in reds, oranges and yellows, or blues and pinks. They can be bargained for in villages on the way to Al Arish, or in Khan al Khalili, or at Kirdassah, or bought in the more upmarket shops like Nomad in the Cairo Mariott.

Crafts

Khom Misr Tulun, opposite the Ibn Tulun Mosque (tel: 365-2227) and Marketing Link on 27 Shari' Yahia

Ibrahim, 1st floor apt. 8, Zamalik (tel: 736-5123) sell and promote high-quality Egyptian crafts at fixed prices. Nagada & Shari' Dar al-Shefa, 3rd floor, Garden City (tel: 736-4500) sells stunning, handwoven cotton fabrics.

Furniture & Woodwork

Mashrabiyyar, traditional screens of turned wood, covered the windows of Cairene houses and shielded the sanctuaries of mosques.

Alif, 14 Shari' Mohamed Anis, Zamalik (tel: 735-3690), is a good place to look for furniture. Even better is the shop of interior designer **Zaki Sherif** on Taha Husayn, 27 Shari', Zamalik (tel: 736-5250). Zaki, who has styled some of the country's hippest bars and hotels, sells old furniture as well as his own designs, inspired by his pharaonic and Ottoman predecessors.

Leather

Everything from large and small pieces of luggage to clothing is found in many designs. Leathers include buffalo, crocodile, serpent, lizard, cow, moose and goat.

Musical Instruments

Middle Eastern instruments of all qualities are made in Cairo on Shari Muhammed Ali near the Citadel.

Muski Glass

Recycled glass products come in six main colours: blue; brown; turquoise; green; aqua; and purple. The glass is hand-blown into pitchers, beakers, cups, vases, dishes, ornaments and amulets. Imperfections and bubbles make this inexpensive glass fragile.

Papyrus

The cultivation of papyrus has been revived by the Dr Raghab Papyrus Institute. Shops all over Egypt now sell hand-painted papyrus sheets. Designs are stunning and many duplicate ancient wall paintings.

Perfume

Perfume shops with their beautifully decorated bottles are easy to spot. Egypt grows and exports jasmine, geranium, rose, violet, camomile, and orange for the major perfumiers in France, from whom essence is then re-imported.

Weaving

Kirdassah, on the western fringes of greater Cairo, has a large market where weaving is sold. Harraniyyah, on the Saqqarah road, is famous for its tapestries, woven by villagers using naturally dyed wools. Bedu rugs vary in design between tribes.

Bookshops

Cairo is the publishing capital of the Middle East and there are hundreds of bookshops. English language books can be found in all major hotels. For rare books try The Orientalist, 15 Qasr en-Nil Street, tel: 575-3418.

Some bookstores that offer foreign language publications are:
Ahram
Outlets at: 165 Muhammed Farid; Cairo Sheraton; Cairo International Airport; Meridien Hotel; Semiramis Inter Continental Hotel; Nile Hilton Hotel; Ramesses Hilton Hotel Annex.
American University in Cairo Bookshop
Hill House, 113 Shari' Qasr al Aini
Tel: 357-5377
Excellent collection of English language books on Egypt.
Livres de France
36 Shari' Qasr en-Nil, Downtown
Tel: 393-5512
French and English books.
Lehnert and Landrock Bookshop
44 Sherif. Tel: 393-5329
German and English books, maps, and old postcards.
Reader's Corner
33 Shari' Abdul Khalek Sarwat
Tel: 392-8801
General English.
Zamalik Bookshop
19 Shagaret el Dorr, Zamalik
Tel: 736-9197

Sport

Participant

FISHING

The Nile, Lake Nasser and the lakes along the northern coast support commercial fishing.

For information about international tournaments contact:
The Shooting Club
Shari an Nadi as Sayd
Dokki.
Tel: 337-3337/3337-4678.

GLIDING

For a spectacular view of the pyramids and portions of the city of Cairo, gliding excursions are available on a hit and miss basis on Thursday and Friday at the Imbaba Airfield to the west of Cairo. The Egyptian Gliding Institute and the Egyptian Aviation Society offer motorgliders and lessons.

GOLF

There are two nine-hole courses in Cairo, at the Gazirah Club in Zamalik and at the Mena House Oberoi in Giza (with the pyramids as a backdrop). Equipment can be rented, but the courses are extremely busy.

RIDING

There is little to compare with a dawn or dusk gallop through the desert. The Bedu at the Giza Pyramids have been catering for eager riders for generations and there are several good stables in the area. Horses and camels are on offer. Lessons are available. Overnight trips to Saqqarah can be arranged. Stables include MG, KM, SA, AA (tel: 850-531), M6 (tel: 385-1241) and FF stables.

ROWING

There are 10 rowing clubs in Cairo, and almost all are located on the west bank of the Nile from Giza to Imbaba. Competitions start in November and run through April. They are held every Friday on the Nile. Schedules can be obtained from any rowing club and lessons are available at some clubs.

For information see the
Egyptian Rowing Club
11 Shari' al Nil
Giza, near the Cairo Sheraton
Tel: 373-1639.

YACHTING

Docking facilities exist at major ports in Egypt and along the Nile at major cities. Yachts may enter the country through the various ports if they have the proper documents. The Egyptian Tourist Information Centres throughout the world have a booklet for yacht enthusiasts entitled *Egypt for Yachtsmen* giving entry information and maps. See Useful Addresses for listing.

Spectator

HORSES

There are several spectator equine sports. Horse racing takes place on Saturday and Sunday, mid-October through May, at the Heliopolis Hippodrome Course in Heliopolis, Cairo, and at the Smouha Race course in Alexandria. Races begin at 1.30pm.

Arab horses are known through-out the world for their beauty, stamina and intelligence. Originally bred on the Arabian Peninsula, stud farms for Arab horses now exist worldwide. Characteristics include a compact body with a straight back, a small head, wide eyes, wide

Football

Professional football has been known to cause traffic jams, slow down service in restaurants, and empty the streets. It is the national pastime of Egypt. Three leagues compete at 3pm each Friday and Sunday afternoon from September to May at various stadiums throughout Egypt. Among the top teams in Egypt are Ahly, Zamalik, and the Arab Contractors.

nostrils, a wide forehead, small ears and a wide jawbone.

There are many stud farms in Egypt, but only four major ones. The biggest, with 300 horses, is the government-owned Egyptian Agricultural Organisation (EAO), El Zahraa Station, Shari' Ahmad Esmat. Tel: 243-1733. This farm has only pure-bred bloodlines and is the home of the most famous Arabian stallion of this century, Nazeer. Every important stud farm in the world has some of his offspring.

Riding a horse in the desert near the Pyramids can be a great experience if you avoid the touts on the plateau. Rent a good horse from a reputable stable in Nezlat as-Semaan, tel: 385 0531, or from the Saqqara Country Club on the Saqqara Rd (tel: 384-6115) which provides excellent riding facilities and temporary memberships.

Language

Pronunciation

Vowels
c = cayn, as explained right
' = glottal stop
a = a as in cat
aa = a as in standard English castle or bath
e = e as in very
i = i as in if, stiff
ii = ee as in between
o = o as in boss
u = u as in put
uu = o as in fool

Consonants
(all emphatic consonants have been omitted):
All consonants are pronounced individually and as they normally are in English with these exceptions:
kh = ch as in Scottish loch.
sh = sh as in shut.
gh = Arabic ghayn, usually described as resembling a (guttural) Parisian r.
q = Arabic qaf, frequently pronounced in Cairo as a k or a glottal stop.

Vocabulary

airport matár
boat mérkeb
bridge kubri
car arabiyya, sayára
embassy sefára
hospital mustáshfa
hotel fúnduq
post office bosta
restaurant matáam
square maydan/midáan
street shaaria
right yemiin
left shemáal
and/or wa/walla
yes/no aywa/laa'

Sounds

Many sounds in spoken Arabic have not been represented by the transliteration used in this book. A particularly characteristic Arabic sound, however, is represented in the following list: cayn, represented as c. All Arabic-speakers, native and otherwise, delight in producing the appropriate noise, described as a guttural hum or a voiced emphatic "h", which occurs in such common names as cAbbas, cAbdallah, Ismæil, and cAli. Non-Arabic-speakers generally find pronouncing c impossible without instruction and practice; and if it seems too difficult, it may be ignored. One will merely be marked as a non-Arabic-speaking foreigner.

Most Cairenes speak English to some degree, though real ability to use languages other than Arabic is confined to the educated. A few words of colloquial Egyptian Arabic are therefore useful.

The words and phrases listed below are not transliterated strictly, but spelt more or less phonetically. Take care over long and short vowel sounds, which may alter the meaning of a word substantially.

please/thank you minfadlak/shukran
big/little kibiir/sughayyar
good/bad kwáyyis/mish kwáyyis
possible mumkin
impossible mish mumkin
here/there hena/henáak
hot/cold sukn/baarid
many/few kitiir/olayyel
up/down fo' (foq)/taht
more/enough kamáan/kefáya
breakfast iftar
dinner asha
today innahárda
tomorrow bokra
yesterday embáareh
morning is-sobh
noon id-dohr
afternoon bcad id-dohr
at night belayl

next week *il esbuul-iggáy*
next time *il mara-iggáya*
last time *il-mara illi fáatit*
after a while *b-ad shwayya*
I/you *ana/enta*
he/she *huwwa/hiyya*
they/we *humma/ehna*

Common Expressions

Hello, welcome *ahlan wa sahlan*
Good morning *sabáh-il-kheyr*
Response *sabaah in-nur*
Good evening *masaa-il-kheyr*
Response *masaa-in-nur*
Goodnight *tisbah* (m)/*tisbahi* (f)
ala kheyr
Goodbye *m-as-saláama*
What is your name?
(to a male) *íssmak ey?*
What is your name? (to a female)
íssmik ey?
How are you?
(to a male) *izzáyak*
How are you?
(to a female) *izzáyik*
I am fine
kwayiss (M), *kwayíssa* (F)
Thank God *il-hamdo li-lah* (standard
reply). Often heard is "*insha'Allah*",
which means "God willing".
Thank you *shukran*
Please *min fadlak* (m)/*min fadlik* (f)
You are welcome *afwan*
Sorry *aasif* (m)/*asifa* (f)
My name is *ismi...*
I don't understand *ana mish fahim*
(m)/*fahma* (f)
Where is...? *feen....?*
Left/right/straight ahead
shimaal/yameen/ala tuul
Nothing *walla haaga*
Not yet *lissa*
Never mind *maalesh*
Leave me alone *sibni li wahdi*
Go away *imshee*
I don't want *mish ayyiz* (m)/*ayyiza* (f)
How much is this? *bi-kam da?*
It's very expensive *da ghali awi*
That's OK *mashi*
How much is the bill? *bi-kam il-
hisab?*

Numerals

1 *wáhid*
2 *itnéyn*
3 *taláatah*
4 *arb-á*

5 *khamsa*
6 *sitta*
7 *séb-a*
8 *tamánya*
9 *tíssah*
10 *áshara*
11 *hedásher*
12 *itnásher*
13 *talatásher*
14 *arbatasher*
15 *khamastásher*
16 *sitásher*
17 *sabatásher*
18 *tamantásher*
19 *tiss-atásher*
20 *ashríin*
30 *talatíin*
40 *arba-íin*
50 *khamsíin*
60 *sittíin*
70 *saba-íin*
80 *tamaníin*
90 *tissa-íin*
100 *miiya, miit*

Money

money *filúus*
50 piastres
khamsíin 'ersh (qersh)
75 piastres *khamsa wa saba-íin
'ersh (qersh)*
change/no change
fakka/mafiish fakka
this/that *di/da*
how much? *bekáam?*
all/half *kull/nus*

Days/Months

Sunday *yowm al had*
Monday *yowm al-itnéyn*
Tuesday *yowm it-taláat*
Wednesday *yowm al-árba*
Thursday *yowm al-khamíis*
Friday *yowm ig-góm-a*
Saturday *yowm is-sabt*
January *yanáyer*
February *febráyer*
March *máris*
April *abreel*
May *mayuu*
June *yuunyuu*
July *yiilyuu*
August *aghustus*
September *sibtímbir*
October *októbir*
November *nofímbir*
December *disímbir*

Further Reading

General

Ammoun, Denise *Crafts of Egypt.*
Cairo, 1991.
Biegman, Nicolas *Egypt: Moulids,
Saints, Sufis.* The Hague/London,
1990.
Bloom, Jonathan and Sheila Blair
Islamic Arts. London, 1997.
Buonaventura, Wendy *Serpent of
the Nile: Women and Dance in the
Arab World.* London, 1989.
Danielson, Virginia, *The Voice of
Egypt: Umm Kulthum, Arabic Song
and Egyptian Society in the
Twentieth Century.* Chicago, 1997.
Herodotus *The Histories.* London,
1996.
Hoath, Richard *Natural Selections:
a Year of Egypt's Wildlife.* Cairo,
1992.
Mitchell, Timothy *Colonising Egypt,*
Cairo, 1988.
Moorehead, Alan *The White Nile*
London, 1973.
The Blue Nile. London, 1984.
Roden, Claudia *A New Book of
Middle Eastern Food.* London,
1986.*The Book of Jewish Food.*
London, 1997.
Rodenbeck, Max *Egypt from the Air.*
London, 1991.
Sattin, Anthony *Lifting the Veil.*
London, 1988.

Cairo

Behrens-Abouseif, Doris *Islamic
Architecture in Cairo.* Cairo, 1996.
Cooper, Artemis *Cairo in the War,
1939-45.* London, 1989.
Lane, Edward William *Manners and
Customs of the Modern Egyptians.*
London, 1833–5.
Parker, Richard *Islamic Monuments
in Cairo: A Practical Guide,* 1999,
Raafat, Samir *Maadi 1904–1962:
Society and History in a Cairo
Suburb.* Cairo, 1994.
Rodenbeck, Max *Cairo.* New
York/London, 1998
Stewart, Desmond *Great Cairo,*

Mother of the World. Cairo,1996
Williams, Caroline *Islamic Monuments in Cairo: a Practical Guide.* Cairo, 1993.

Alexandria

Bowman, Alan K. *Egypt After the Pharaohs: 332BC–AD642 from Alexander to the Arab Conquest.* London, 1986.
Ellis, Walter *Ptolemy of Egypt.* London, 1993.
Forster, E.M. *Alexandria, a History and Guide.* London, 1986.
Grant, Michael *Cleopatra: a Biography.* London 1992.
Haag, Michael *Alexandria, City of Durrell, Forster and Cavafy.* London, 1998.
Pinchin, Jane Lagudis *Alexandria Still: Forster, Durrell and Cavafy.* Cairo, 1989.
Whitehorne, John *Cleopatras.* London, 1994.

Ancient Egypt

Andreu, G *Egypt in the Age of the Pyramids.* London, 1997.
Baines, John and Jaromir Malek *Atlas of Ancient Egypt.* Oxford, 1980.
Bauval, Robert and Adrian Gilbert *The Orion Mystery.* London, 1994.
Clayton, Peter *The Rediscovery of Ancient Egypt.* London, 1990.
Clayton, Peter *Chronicle of the Pharaohs.* London, 1994.
Edwards, IES *The Pyramids of Egypt.* London, 1991
Lichtheim, Miriam *Ancient Egyptian Literature.* California, 1975–80.
Reeves, Nicholas and Richard Wilkinson *The Complete Valley of the Kings.* London/Cairo 1996.

Travellers

Duff Gordon, Lucy *Letters from Egypt, 1862–69.* London, 1986.
Edwards, Amelia *A Thousand Miles Up the Nile.* London, 1982.
Flaubert, Gustave *Flaubert in Egypt.* London, 1983.
Frank, Katherine *Lucie Duff Gordon, a Passage to Egypt.* London, 1994.
Ghosh, Amitav *In an Antique Land.* London, 1992.

Manley, Deborah *A Traveller's Amthology.* London, 1991.
de Nerval, Gerard *A Journey to the Orient,* London 1973
Nightingale, Florence *Letters from Egypt* – edited by Anthony Sattin. London, 1999.
Pick, Christopher *Egypt, an Anthology.* London, 1991.
Pye-Smith, Charlie *The Other Nile.* London, 1986.
Sattin, Anthony *The Pharaoh's Shadow, Travels in Modern and Ancient Egypt,* London 2000.
Steward, Stanley *Old Serpent Nile: A Journey to the Source,* London 1992.

Fiction

Abdullah, Yahya *Taher The Mountain of Green Tea and Other Stories.* Cairo, 1991.
Aciman, André *Out of Egypt: A Memoir.* London, 1998.
Christie, Agatha *Death on the Nile.* London, 1995.
Durrell, Lawrence *The Alexandria Quartet.* London, 1968.
Ghali, Waguih *Beer in the Snooker Club.* London, 1987.
al-Ghitani, Gamal *Zayni Barakat.* London, 1988.
Lively, Penelope *Moon Tiger* London, 1989.
Mahfouz, Naguib *The Cairo Trilogy, Miramar* and many others. Cairo/London.
el Saadawi, Nawal *Woman at Point Zero.* London, 1983.
Soueeif, Ahdaf *In the Eye of the Sun.* London, 1999.

Other Insight Guides

Other books in the **Insight Guides** series which highlight destinations in this region include *Egypt, Cairo, Jordan, Israel, Jerusalem, Syria and Lebanon* and, slightly further afield, *Oman and the UAE.* Each contains the same standard of insightful text and lavish photography as the present book.

Egypt is also covered in two companion series, Insight Pocket Guides and Insight Compact Guides. *Insight Pocket Guide: The Nile* offers a selection of tailor-made itineraries,

plus a large-size pullout map.

Insight Compact Guide: Egypt is essentially a mini-encyclopedia packed with facts and comprehensively cross-referenced to make it ideal for on-the-spot use.

ART & PHOTO CREDITS

AKG London 58, 63, 64, 65
Apa 74
The Art Archive 60, 82, 85
Bettmann/Corbis 31, 71, 77
Marcus Brooke 54, 190, 232, 304
Christie's Colour Library 72, 76
Thomas Cook Ltd front flap bottom,
34, 39, 40, 44
Corbis 28, 32
Gianni Dagli Orti/Corbis 55
J. D. Dallet 159, 160, 164T, 164,
169
Andrew Eames 37, 38, 84, 179,
196, 197, 236, 257
Tor Eigeland 6/7, 12/13, 44, 45,
69, 107, 128, 133, 142/143,
166/167, 178, 180, 182/183, 194,
200/201, 202, 211L/R, 233, 244,
254, 261, 292/293
Mary Evans Picture Library 47, 73,
80, 218
Guild Home Video 21, 134/135
Robert Harding Picture Library
16/17, 50, 90
D & J Heaton 36, 66
Israel Government Press Office 126
Axel Krause/Apa back cover left,
centre & top, front flap top, back flap
top & bottom, spine centre, 2/3,
4/5, 162, 174, 176T, 176, 190T,
191, 198, 203, 210T, 212, 213T,
213, 215T, 216, 220, 221, 234,
237, 245, 247T, 247, 248, 249,
255, 256, 263, 265T, 265, 271,
273T, 274, 275, 276T, 276, 277T,
287, 289, 296, 299T, 250, 251,
282T, 285T, 285, 297, 298, 301T

Lyle Lawson 23, 148/149,
268/269, 282
Mansell Collection 70
Richard Nowitz spine bottom, 8/9,
14, 18, 20, 41, 48/49, 52, 53, 56,
68, 132, 150/151, 152/153,
156/157, 162, 163, 170, 184, 195,
205, 209, 215, 216T, 219, 222,
227, 228, 242/243, 260, 270, 280,
283
Christine Osborne 145R, 168,
252/253
Eddy Posthuma de Boer back cover
bottom, 10/11, 158, 177, 187, 192,
206, 229, 267, 286, 294, 295, 302
Sarah Louise Ramsay/Apa 1, 3B,
4B, 5B, 165, 171, 173T, 173, 175T,
175, 178T, 180T, 181, 185, 188,
193T, 193, 194T, 198T, 207T, 208T,
208, 209T, 214, 217T, 217, 223,
224T, 224, 225, 226T, 235T, 258T,
259, 260T, 263T, 266, 273, 275T,
278T, 278, 280T, 283T, 287T, 288T,
288, 291, 299, 301, 303
Topham Picturepoint 33, 35, 59, 67,
75, 87, 91, 112, 114R , 116, 119,
120, 121, 122, 123, 127, 130, 131,
136, 137, 138, 139, (141R), 161
Cassandra Vivian 147
Wallace Collection 88/89
Marcus Wilson-Smith 19, 114L,
145L, 189, 277, 279, 281

Map Production Stephen Ramsay
© 2002 Apa Publications GmbH & Co.
Verlag KG (Singapore branch)

Cartographic Editor **Zoë Goodwin**
Production **Linton Donaldson**
Cover Design
Klaus Geisler, Tanvir Virdee
Picture Research **Hilary Genin**

✵ INSIGHT GUIDES

The world's largest collection of visual travel guides

A range of guides and maps to meet every travel need

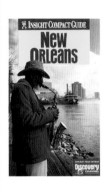

Insight Guides

This classic series gives you the complete picture of a destination through expert, well written and informative text and stunning photography. Each book is an ideal background information and travel planner, serves as an on-the-spot companion – and is a superb visual souvenir of a trip. Nearly 200 titles.

Insight Pocket Guides

focus on the best choices for places to see and things to do, picked by our local correspondents. They are ideal for visitors new to a destination. To help readers follow the routes easily, the books contain full-size pull-out maps. 120 titles.

Insight Maps

are designed to complement the guides. They provide full mapping of major cities, regions and countries, and their laminated finish makes them easy to fold and gives them durability. 60 titles.

Insight Compact Guides

are convenient, comprehensive reference books, modestly priced. The text, photo-graphs and maps are all carefully cross-referenced, making the books ideal for on-the-spot use when in a destination. 120 titles.

Different travellers have different needs. Since 1970, Insight Guides has been meeting these needs with a range of practical and stimulating guidebooks and maps

" I was first drawn to the
Insight Guides by the
excellent "Nepal" volume.
I can think of no book
which so effectively
captures the essence of
a country. Out of these
pages leaped the Nepal
I know – the captivating
charm of a people and
their culture. I've since
discovered and enjoyed
the entire Insight Guide
series. Each volume deals
with a country in the
same sensitive depth,
which is nowhere more
evident than in the
superb photography. "

Sir Edmund Hillary

✵ INSIGHT GUIDES

The world's largest collection of visual travel guides

Insight Guides – the Classic Series
that puts you in the picture

Alaska	China	Hungary	Munich	South Africa
Alsace	Cologne			South America
Amazon Wildlife	Continental Europe	Iceland	Namibia	South Tyrol
American Southwest	Corsica	India	Native America	Southeast Asia
Amsterdam	Costa Rica	India's Western	Nepal	Wildlife
Argentina	Crete	Himalaya	Netherlands	Spain
Asia, East	Cuba	India, South	New England	Spain, Northern
Asia, South	Cyprus	Indian Wildlife	New Orleans	Spain, Southern
Asia, Southeast	Czech & Slovak	Indonesia	New York City	Sri Lanka
Athens	Republics	Ireland	New York State	Sweden
Atlanta		Israel	New Zealand	Switzerland
Australia	Delhi, Jaipur & Agra	Istanbul	Nile	Sydney
Austria	Denmark	Italy	Normandy	Syria & Lebanon
	Dominican Republic	Italy, Northern	Norway	
Bahamas	Dresden	Italy, Southern		Taiwan
Bali	Dublin		Old South	Tenerife
Baltic States	Düsseldorf	Jamaica	Oman & The UAE	Texas
Bangkok		Japan	Oxford	Thailand
Barbados	East African Wildlife	Java		Tokyo
Barcelona	Eastern Europe	Jerusalem	Pacific Northwest	Trinidad & Tobago
Bay of Naples	Ecuador	Jordan	Pakistan	Tunisia
Beijing	Edinburgh		Paris	Turkey
Belgium	Egypt	Kathmandu	Peru	Turkish Coast
Belize	England	Kenya	Philadelphia	Tuscany
Berlin		Korea	Philippines	
Bermuda	Finland		Poland	Umbria
Boston	Florence	Laos & Cambodia	Portugal	USA: On The Road
Brazil	Florida	Lisbon	Prague	USA: Western States
Brittany	France	Loire Valley	Provence	US National Parks: East
Brussels	France, Southwest	London	Puerto Rico	US National Parks: West
Budapest	Frankfurt	Los Angeles		
Buenos Aires	French Riviera		Rajasthan	Vancouver
Burgundy		Madeira	Rhine	Venezuela
Burma (Myanmar)	Gambia & Senegal	Madrid	Rio de Janeiro	Venice
	Germany	Malaysia	Rockies	Vienna
Cairo	Glasgow	Mallorca & Ibiza	Rome	Vietnam
Calcutta	Gran Canaria	Malta	Russia	
California	Great Britain	Mauritius, Réunion		Wales
California, Northern	Greece	& Seychelles	St Petersburg	Washington DC
California, Southern	Greek Islands	Melbourne	San Francisco	Waterways of Europe
Canada	Guatemala, Belize &	Mexico City	Sardinia	Wild West
Caribbean	Yucatán	Mexico	Scandinavia	
Catalonia		Miami	Scotland	Yemen
Channel Islands	Hamburg	Montreal	Seattle	
Chicago	Hawaii	Morocco	Sicily	
Chile	Hong Kong	Moscow	Singapore	

Complementing the above titles are 120 easy-to-carry Insight Compact Guides, 120 Insight Pocket
Guides with full-size pull-out maps and more than 100 laminated easy-fold Insight Maps ✵